BETWEEN BAB]

D1648224

ANDRÉ CORTEN
RUTH MARSHALL-FRATANI
editors

Between Babel and Pentecost

*Transnational Pentecostalism in
Africa and Latin America*

INDIANA UNIVERSITY PRESS
BLOOMINGTON AND INDIANAPOLIS

This book is a publication of

Indiana University Press
601 North Morton Street
Bloomington, IN 47404-3797 USA

http://iupress.indiana.edu

Telephone orders 800-842-6796
Fax orders 812-855-7931
Orders by e-mail iuporder@indiana.edu

Manufactured in Malaysia

Library of Congress Cataloging-in-Publication Data

Between Babel and Pentecost : transnational Pentecostalism in Africa and
Latin America : edited by André Corten and Ruth Marshall-Fratani.
    p. cm.
Includes bibliographical references and index.
ISBN 0-253-33730-5 (alk. paper) — ISBN 0-253-21378-9 (pbk. : alk.paper)
1. Pentecostalism—Latin America. 2. Pentecostal churches—Latin
America. 3. Latin America—Church history. 4. Pentecostalism—Africa,
Sub-Saharan. 5. Pentecostal churches—Africa, Sub-Saharan. 6. Africa,
Sub-Saharan—Church history. I. Corten, André. II. Marshall-Fratani, Ruth.

BR1644.5.L29 B48 2001
289.9'4'096—dc21
                                                    99-058781

1 2 3 4 5 06 05 04 02 01

CONTENTS

v

Part II. THE CARIBBEAN AND LATIN AMERICA

THE CO-AUTHORS

Diane J. Austin-Broos holds the Radcliffe-Brown Chair of Anthropology at the University of Sydney. Her most recent book is *Jamaica Genesis: Religion and the Politics of Moral Order* (University of Chicago Press, 1997). Among her previous books is *Urban Life in Kingston, Jamaica*.

Jean-Pierre Bastian is Professor of the Sociology of Religion, and Director of the Centre de Sociologie des Religions at the Université des Sciences Humaines, Strasbourg. Among his books are *Le protestantisme en Amérique latine. Une approche socio-historique* (Geneva: Labor et Fides, 1994); *La mutación religiosa de América Latina. Para una sociología del cambio social en la modernidad periférica* (México: Fondo de Cultura Económica, 1997) and *Donner une âme à l'Europe. Les Eglises entre l'Europe et la nation:* edited in collaboration with J.-F. Collange (Geneva: Labor et Fides, 1998).

Waldo César is a journalist and sociologist at the Institute of Social Sciences, Federal University of Rio de Janeiro. He has been a member of the Institute for the Study of Religion (Rio de Janeiro) and a student of the Graduate Course of the Ecumenical Institute (World Council of Churches). He has been the coordinator and author of articles on religion for two encyclopaedias; author of articles on the Pentecostal movement published in *Religião e Sociedade*, and coordinator, with the theologian Richard Shaull, of the interdisciplinary work on Brazil: *Pentecostalism and the Future of Christian Churches: Promises, Limitations, Challenges* (1949).

André Corten is tenured Professor of Political Science and Discourse Analysis at the Université du Québec à Montréal. He has been Professor and Visiting Fellow in several universities including those of São Paulo, Santiago de Chile, Santo Domingo, Oran (Algeria), Paris VIII, Essex, Cambridge and Columbia. In 1998 he was guest researcher at the Centre d'Études Africaines de la Maison des Sciences de l'Homme in Paris. His many books, have generally focused on the formation of new political categories in Third World societies. His *Pentecostalism in Brazil* is published in London.

Elisabeth Dorier-Apprill is Senior Lecturer at the Institut de Géographie, University of Aix-en-Provence. She has undertaken research in Brazzaville since 1985 for ORSTOM, notably on the links between urban modernity and the growth of religious movements in a context of geopolitical tension. She has published extensively on this subject in relation to Brazzaville.

André Droogers studied Human Geography and Cultural Anthropology at the University of Utrecht, obtaining his PhD in Anthropology, and worked as a researcher and lecturer in Zaire and Brazil (five years in each country). Since 1989, he has been Professor of the Cultural Anthropology of Religion at the Vrije Universiteit, Amsterdam, and founded the Centre for the Study of Pentecostalism and Charismatic Movements at the Vrije Universiteit.

Harri Englund is a Research Fellow at the Nordic Africa Institute, Uppsala, Sweden. He has conducted fieldwork in Malawi, among Mozambican refugees and their local hosts, and in a township of Lilongwe.

Paul Freston, currently lecturer in Sociology at the Federal University of São Carlos, Brazil, has researched and published extensively on the sociology of Brazilian and Latin American Protestantism. He has taught at the Methodist University of São Paulo and done post-doctoral studies at St Antony's College, Oxford. His current research interests are in a comparative study of Evangelicals and politics in the Third World, and in questions of Evangelicalism and globalisation.

Paul Gifford is a lecturer at the School of Oriental and African Studies, University of London, whose published works include *Christianity and Politics in Doe's Liberia* (Cambridge University Press, 1993) and *African Christianity: its Public Role* (London: Hurst/Bloomington: University of Indiana Press, 1998).

Laënnec Hurbon is a sociologist and Research Director at the CNRS, Paris, and his particular field of study is religion, culture and politics in the Caribbean. His publications include *Les mystères du vaudou* (Paris: Gallimard, 1993) and *Le barbare imaginaire* (Paris: Ed. du Cerf, 1998).

Pierre-Joseph Laurent teaches anthropology at the Université Catholique de Louvain-la Neuve in Belgium. He has spent more than ten years in Southern (Mozambique) and West Africa (Benin, Burkina Faso, Ivory Coast, Guinea-Bissau, Mali, Mauritania, Niger, Senegal).

Ruth Marshall-Fratani is a Research Fellow at the School of Oriental and African Studies, University of London, working on a British Academy funded project entitled "The Role of Print and Electronic Media in the Constitution of New Religious Publics in Yorubaland". Her D Phil thesis in Politics at Oxford University examines the rise of Pentecostalism in Lagos, Nigeria, and she has published several articles on the subject, in: *Journal of Religion in Africa; Review of African Political Economy*; P. Gifford, ed., *New Dimensions in African Christianity* (Nairobi: AACC, 1992); T. Ranger and F. Vaughn, eds, *Legitimacy and the State in Twentieth Century Africa* (Oxford, Macmillan, 1993); P. Gifford, ed., *The Christian Churches and the Democratisation of Africa* (Leiden: Brill, 1995).

Cédric Mayrargue is research and teaching assistant at the Institut d'Etudes Politiques de Bordeaux (Université Montesquieu-Bordeaux IV). A doctoral student in politics at the Centre d'Etude d'Afrique Noire (CEAN) at Bordeaux, he is completing his thesis on the relationship between the religious field and the construction of democracy in Bénin. He has also completed research on the development of new Christian churches and their implication in politics. He has published several articles in collective volumes on voodun, new Christian movements, and politics in Bénin.

Ari Pedro Oro, a Brazilian, obtained his PhD in social anthropology at the University of Paris, and is Professor at the Federal University of Rio Grande do Sul, in Porto Alegre, Brazil, and a researcher at the National Research Council (CNP) in the field of the anthropology of religion. He has published books and articles on popular religions.

Pablo Seman, an Argentine, obtained his PhD in social anthropology at the Federal University of Rio Grande do Sul, Porto Alegre, Brazil, and has researched into Argentine Pentecostalism.

Rijk van Dijk, an anthropologist, is a Researcher at the African Studies Centre, Leiden University, the Netherlands. He has researched extensively on Pentecostalism in Accra and the Ghanaian Pentecostal diaspora in The Hague. He has published articles on Pentecostalism in Malawi and Ghana, and a book, *Young Malawian Puritans* (Utrecht: ISOR Press, 1993).

INTRODUCTION

André Corten
Ruth Marshall-Fratani

Over the past two decades, Latin American and African societies have experienced the phenomenal growth of Pentecostal movements. This form of Christianity, only marginally present in many Latin American and African countries at the middle of this century, now represents more than a hundred million faithful across these two continents, and continues to grow at an astonishing rate. Despite the enormous differences which separate these continents and the individual societies within them, the observer is struck by the similarity of pentecostal manifestations across these diverse cultures. A *'bricolage'* of extremely heterogeneous elements, contemporary Pentecostalism provides a most striking example of the paradox of difference and uniformity, of flow and closure, that seems to be at the heart of processes of transnationalism and globalisation. Presenting itself as a kind of New Reformation of the twentieth century, particularly in the developing world, Pentecostalism projects a new vision of the world, responding in particular to processes and promises of 'modernity' and 'modernisation'. The 1980s and '90s have seen the development of an increasingly complex web of transnational Pentecostal networks, where flows of people, money, ideas and images circulate with growing speed and intensity, defying all attempts to pin them down to any particular source or destination. Modes of identification have become transnationalised, and converts place the representation of a global movement with a historical mission to accomplish at the heart of their new faith. Could this 'movement' be expressing a new form of Protestant ethic, or to use current theoretical language, a new *'imaginaire'*?[1] What relationship might this new 'ethic' have with the 'spirit of globalisation'? 'Spirit' might be just the word to evokes the evanescent, ambiguous and inconsistent nature of globalisation, both as an analytical construct and in terms of the processes it seems to imply. As Geschiere observes, 'The

[1] In Anglophone literature, the term *'imaginaire'* is often translated as 'imaginary'. We prefer to keep it in its original French form. See Jean-François Bayart's Introduction to his edited volume *La réinvention du capitalisme* (Paris: Fayard, 1994) for a discussion of the ways in which the notion of 'ethic' can signify in the context of globalisation. See also J.-F. Bayart, *L'illusion identitaire*, Paris: Fayard, 1996, especially 'Conclusion. L' invention paradoxal de la modernité', pp. 231-48, for a critical discussion of the significance and utility of the term *'imaginaire'*.

1

main merit of the term "globalisation" might be that it continues to defy all attempts to tie it to an empirical core', a remark which also applies equally to the terms 'modernity' and 'identity'.[2] The generality of these terms and their tendency towards abstraction has the effect of performing a sort of vanishing trick with the object of research. And yet they are not simply empty signifiers, but rather bring us up against a series of questions at once practical and analytical. How do local processes of identification, which imply fix and closure, find their articulation in a global context marked by an open-ended and unbounded flux of people, objects, money, ideas and images? How can we make the link among our case studies of Pentecostalism in Brazil, Malawi, Nigeria or Jamaica and relate them to the idea of a transnational Pentecostal identity, reconciling local appropriations, with their rich and unique historical and cultural particularities, with the overarching representation of similitude that the idea of a transnational identity implies?

We must make the distinction between the diffuse, polycentric nature of networks and flows that make up the transnational Pentecostal reality and the representation of this transnational community constructed and appropriated by believers. In the tension between the representation of this global community of the faithful sharing a historical mission, brothers in Christ and soldiers together in the global war against Satan, and the multitude of its local variations, we find an echo of the apparent paradox of flow and closure, of homogeneity and heterogeneity that seems to be at the heart of the globalisation problematic. As many recent studies note, the homogenising tendencies associated with the globalisation of capital, particularly processes of commodification, accumulation and consumption which were the focus of the early literature on globalisation,[3] appear to give rise to, or at least are associated with, a new emphasis on cultural difference, with the hardening of existing cultural contrasts and affirmation of new oppositions.[4] Meyer and Geschiere show in their collection on globalisation and identity that 'people's awareness of being involved in open-ended global flows seems to trigger a search for fixed orientation

[2] Peter Geschiere, 'Witchcraft and Spirit Cults in Africa and East Asia' in *Development and Change*, vol. 29, no. 4, 1998, p. 816.

[3] See, for example, Marshall MacLuhan, *Understanding Media: The Extensions of Man* London: Routledge; MacLuhan and Powers, *The Global Village*, Oxford University Press, 1989; C. Hamelink, *Cultural Autonomy in Global Communications*, New York: Longman, 1983; and work by world systems theorists such as Immanuel Wallerstein. For a stimulating treatment of global 'consumer ideology', see Paul Vieille, 'Du Transnational au Politique-Monde' in 'Fin du National?', a special issue of *Peuples Méditerranéens*, no.35-36, 1986.

[4] See M. Featherstone, S. Lash and R. Robertson (eds), *Global Modernities*, London: Sage, 1995; M. Featherstone (ed.), *Global Culture: Nationalism, Globalization and Modernity*, London: Sage, 1991; Arjun Appadurai, *Modernity at Large: Cultural Dimensions of Globalization*, Minneapolis: University of Minnesota Press, 1997; Jean-François Bayart, *L'illusion identitaire*; Daniel Miller (ed.), *Worlds Apart: Modernity through the Prism of the Local*, London: Routledge, 1995.

points and action frames, as well as determined efforts to affirm old and construct new boundaries'.[5] The challenge for research, they point out, is to recognise the precariousness of locality, both as the central basis for constructing the object of research, and as a new and often troubling experience for people being studied.

Globalisation opens up new worlds as processes of migration and mass mediation accompany new forms of wealth and accumulation, opening wide vistas of possible lives, inciting desire and fantasy, but also anxiety, frustration, downward mobility and insecurity. With the crisis in the old mechanisms of identification, as nation-states seem, to be losing their monopoly over the moral resources of community formation,[6] new forms of transnational 'fix' emerge from this flux, escaping or defying their control. In the developing world, the failed promises of the nation-state concerning modernisation have resulted in the de-legitimisation of their 'mega-rhetoric of development' and have opened the field to the work of the imagination of everyday individuals, fuelled by images, ideas and resources from elsewhere, to re-script their lives, both individually and collectively, finding new ways to appropriate and inscribe themselves within global modernity.[7] These processes of identification are above all relational – it would be mistaken to understand the local in terms of closure or fix, and the global as embodying openness and flux. Rather, as the studies which follow will make clear, the dynamics of transnational Pentecostal flows and their representation as a global community simultaneously allow for an opening up of possibilities which go beyond local cultural repertoires, often rendering other modes of identification, such as national or ethnic, much less salient and involving the creation of broad, inclusive communities, as well as creating a new vector for the fixing of identity in an exclusive, rigid, almost Manichean vision of the world and the self, which can have the effect of hardening local differences, or creating new ones.

The force of contemporary Pentecostalism and the reason for its remarkable growth seems to lie partly in this capacity to embody the openendedness of a global network of flows, a composite of heterogeneous elements flexible and indeterminate enough in meaning to allow their setting to work in a multitude of contexts, yet offering at the same time a stable collection of narrative formulae and well-organised structures which provide a solid anchorage for individuals at large in the frightening sea of possibilities and frustrations. More precisely, Pentecostal doctrine and practice seem to offer that opening on to the world that globalisation promises, involving a radical transformation of the self and a new collective identity that seems to deliver 'the goods' in a context where

---

[5] Peter Geschiere and Birgit Meyer, 'Globalization and Identity: Dialetics of Flow and Closure – Introduction' in *Development and Change*, vol. 29, no. 4, 1998, p. 602.

[6] Appadurai, *Modernity at Large*, p. 39.

[7] *Ibid.* p. 10.

most people's participation in the global marketplace of wealth and goods, dreams and desires is reduced to 'window shopping'.[8] As Van Dijk notes in his chapter, Pentecostalism constitutes not only a discourse within modernity, but also a discourse *about* modernity, insofar as it elaborates a series of reflections on the present, adopting and adapting modernity's techniques, discourses, and practices into a new *imaginaire*.[9] This process will be elucidated in its empirical reality and variations in the following chapters; in this introduction, we will simply outline some of the central characteristics which make up this transnational Pentecostal *imaginaire*, characteristics which appear to be common to the new wave of Pentecostalisms found throughout the world, albeit articulated in various different ways.

This entity that we call transnational Pentecostalism is thus not only an analytical abstraction created by sociologists of religion in order to group together under a handy term people whose practices and adherence to a set of doctrines bear a close family resemblance. If anything, the use of the term Pentecostalism is perhaps itself misleading, since it is very often ignored or even rejected by believers. In any case, there is very little agreement among researchers about terminology, a situation which reveals not only the artificial nature of the appellations but also the multiplicity and diversity of religious practice which invariably slips through the spaces between even the best made categories. The observer may be tempted to locate the grounding for the new Pentecostal *imaginaire* in doctrinal novelty; indeed, some imply that the most recent wave of Pentecostal growth implies the creation of a 'new religion', which, it is argued, is 'neither evangelical, Pentecostal, nor even Protestant'.[10] Yet this somewhat polemical position contrasts with our observation that Pentecostalism, from its inception at the beginning of this century, has not distinguished itself doctrinally from historical Christianity by a marked departure from theological orthodoxy. Of course, as we discuss below, and as the chapters in this volume will show, the 'new wave' of Pentecostalism over the past two decades has brought with it new characteristics and doctrinal positions. However, these do not replace the doctrinal tenets of early Pentecostalism but are superimposed upon them.

In relation to historical Protestantism and even Catholicism, Pentecostalism does not offer a substantially new interpretation of the Bible. One of its central tenets is the baptism by the Holy Spirit, the sign of which is

---

[8] Geschiere and Meyer, *Globalization and Identity*, p. 605.

[9] See also Birgit Meyer, ' "Make a Complete Break with the Past": Memory and Post-Colonial Modernity and Ghanaian Pentecostalist Discourse', *Journal of Religion in Africa* vol. 28, no. 3, 1998.

[10] Ricardo Gondim, President of the Latin American Theological Fraternity, Brazil Sector, cited by Mariano, 'Neopentecostais. Os pentecostais estao mundando', PhD thesis, São Paulo, 1995, p. 63.

speaking in tongues, or glossolalia, expressed in this verse from the story of the Pentecost in the Acts of the Apostles: 'And they were all filled with the Holy Ghost, and began to speak with other tongues, as the Spirit gave them utterance' (Acts 2:4). Despite the fact that a few verses later, speaking in tongues is expressed as 'every man heard them speak in his own language' (Acts 2:6), Pentecostals generally understand glossolalia in a more psychological sense, as a kind of trance or ecstatic state in which individuals give voice in incomprehensible sounds. This expresses the desire to reach a fusional relationship with God, in which the individual's praise and prayers may reach Him unmediated even by language.[11] This emphasis on emotion is characteristic of a religious form which, as Cox points out, is more experiential than fundamentalist.[12] Especially in its contemporary forms, Pentecostalism tends to have a surprisingly open and flexible approach to Biblical interpretation. Certain fundamental doctrines aside (in particular a strict and ascetic understanding of personal ethics and bodily practices), the almost complete absence of any overarching structure or authority according to which orthodoxy may be determined and policed, or any institutionalised mode of legitimating leadership, as well as the emphasis on individual Biblical study, means that, in practice, the sacred text is more or less 'up for grabs'. If the formula of baptism by Holy Spirit and the bestowing of the 'gifts of the Spirit' are not universally accepted by the historical Churches, and if speaking in tongues is sometimes regarded with suspicion, the spirit of the 'wind of Pentecost' is nevertheless claimed by the majority of Christian denominations. Thus Pentecostalism has no clearly defined doctrinal specificity, and certainly does not imply the birth of a 'new religion'.

The 'doctrine of prosperity' or 'dominion theology' which is expounded by the new wave of contemporary Pentecostalism does not put into question basic Christian or Pentecostal dogma, but rather appears as a series of lateral interpretations which imply innovation at the level of practice and the relationship of believers to the world which surrounds them rather than any deep theological revision. From 'speaking in tongues' and the retreat from 'the world' which characterised early Pentecostalism, the 'new wave', a growing force in African and Latin American Pentecostalism from the early 1980s, has shifted the emphasis to the miracles of prosperity and 'divine healing' (understood in the broadest sense of alleviating the causes of suffering, be they physical, financial, spiritual or social) and 'global spiritual warfare'. It is with this shift that we see the enormous growth of transnational networks, the privileging of transnational

[11] See Webb Keane, 'Calvin in the Tropics: Objects and Subjects at the Religious Frontier' in Patricia Spyer (ed.), *Border Fetishisms: Material Objects in Unstable Spaces*, New York: Routledge, 1998.

[12] Harvey Cox, *Fire from Heaven: The Rise of Pentecostal Spirituality and the Reshaping of Religion in the Twenty-First Century*, Reading, MA: Addison-Wesley, 1995.

connections and experiences in the operation and symbolism of local organisations, and the embracing by converts of the representation of a transnational Pentecostal community. It is by a closer examination of the implications of this shift for doctrine, practice and organisation that we may begin to sketch out the ways in which Pentecostalism is articulated within, and responds to, the context of globalised 'late modernity'.

Before looking more closely at the characteristics which make up the new Pentecostal *imaginaire*, it is important to note that if these networks have become reified in the minds of believers, via the circulation of the representation of a global community of brethren waging global spiritual warfare, this does not mean that these diffuse and open-ended networks have some fixed centre, be it geographical, economic or even symbolic. Early studies of Pentecostalism's expansion into the Southern Hemisphere often interpreted it as a bridgehead of 'American imperialism', the alarming proliferation of churches being understood in terms of the millions of dollars spent 'buying' converts. Today, as the flows of money have reversed, and churches from the South outweigh their Northern neighbours in numbers and overall financial importance, one hears similar voices rail against what is seen as an immense mechanism for extorting money from the poorest of populations for the benefit of these increasingly powerful global organisations: a religious version of the relentless quest by multinationals for new markets and the hegemony of consumer culture. Such positions, although not without their grains of truth, fail to recognise two essential points. Firstly, they forget that all these converts are at the same time self-conscious agents, armed with a practical understanding of the society they live in and a certain amount of information about the world beyond it. If global flows create new inequalities, anxieties and frustrations, they also open up access to information and new possibilities. It seems impossible to maintain that these millions are not much more than unthinking dupes, bought over or swindled out of their pittance by scheming global powers. At the same time, as the critics of 'MacWorld' often forget, cultural flows are not uni-directional, and global circulation of the objects of material culture, be they Big Macs or Pentecostal tracts, in no way predicts their significance in a given context. In the case of Pentecostalism it is becoming clear that the influence of evangelism, media production and doctrinal innovation from Pentecostals in the developing world has definitively broken any American hegemony which may have previously held sway.

The emphasis on miracles of health and prosperity which are at the heart of the new wave implies a new relationship between the experience of conversion and the conception of salvation. Conversion, or 'getting born-again', is still conceived in terms of radical transformation of the self through rupture with a sinful past. An intensely private and emotional experience, it is a moment of great personal freedom and empowerment, where the possibility of 'all things becoming new' opens itself up for the first time to the individual. Yet the question follows of how to realise the project of transformation that this 'event' announces. Getting born-again is an event of rupture, with the self as it was, but also with the world as it is. Retreat from the world and sectarian behaviour was the typical mode of realising this rupture in an ongoing way, and salvation was deferred until the near arrival of the millennium. However, believers no longer retreat among themselves in order to maintain the purity of their beliefs and their moral rigour, far from the temptations and corruption of the 'world of sin'. Salvation is now resolutely this-worldly, and the evidence of new life has become as much material as spiritual. Moral rigour and strict personal ethics have not been superseded, yet the notion of transformation has been broadened to include the possibility of material change in everyday life.

Thus the original 'miracle' of conversion finds its new signs in the 'miracles' of divine healing. The notion of 'healing' embraces the physical, material and psychological well-being of converts. It is attained through a complex of actions on the part of converts, informed by globally circulating discourses and images accessed through processes of mass mediation and the movement of individuals, and a series of heterogeneous techniques for channelling divine power. Moral rigour is combined with the notion of investment in the faith – of time and effort (i.e. studying the Bible, praying, evangelising, fasting, participating in church work) and especially money (i.e. paying tithes, offering 'seed' money'). Biblical verses mixed with popular self-help discourses exhort converts to identify the sources of their frustration and suffering and embark on a process of continual self-overcoming. The image of salvation at the heart of this process increasingly means upward mobility and personal success. A combination of techniques such as the laying on of hands, prayers, fasting, counselling and deliverance from demonic possession is used to assist the convert in his quest for transformation. The idiom of divine healing allows for the enunciation by each convert of an image of his own personal suffering and fundamental malaise, and yet at the same time operates as a 'narrative machine' which appears to function in all sorts of social milieu and all sorts of countries, transforming the profane into the sacred. The new forms of wealth, new objects of consumption and signs of success that emerge in the context of globalisation are typically the subjects of much suspicion and anxiety. In the new Pentecostal *imaginare*, they are no longer 'at large', but rather fixed in a complex of discourses and practices that transform their threatening, potentially destructive force into signs of salvation.

Getting born-again is an event of rupture, but *being* born-again is an ongoing existential project, not a state acquired once and for all. If the realisation of the project of transformation that rupture announces does not occur as a rupture with or retreat from 'the world', then it must bring this rupture *into* the world, elevating the private experience of transformation to the level of the public, by the elaboration of a project of transforming the world itself. Hence the creation of a 'narrative imperative' to testify and publicise personal transformation. Giving public evidence of suffering, dreams, miracles of healing and prosperity not only confers social legitimacy and meaning on these highly individual experiences, but constitutes the central mode of passage between the sacred and profane. This imperative gives rise to a sort of common language, which comprises the often standardised narrative forms such as testimony, preaching, visions or prophecy, but also includes certain rituals, such as deliverance (exorcism), as well as dress-styles, bodily gestures, forms of speech and the display of objects of conspicuous consumption. In this regard, money is incontestably the most significant object in the creation of a common language, seen both as the mode of organising churches and as the means of entering into contact with God. It is the symbolic object which links *par excellence* the struggle within the public space and individual communication with the sacred.[13]

If money is global modernity's most central sign, then processes of mass mediation are perhaps its most important technique and form of expression.[14] Opening on to the world via the narrative imperative of public testimony and evangelism involves the greatest possible use of modern techniques of mass mediation. In African and Latin American societies, where media have often been monopolised by the state or powerful financial interests, where the majority of the population suffer from extreme poverty and semi-literacy, and where popular culture is far from being defined in terms of mediated images, the overwhelming amount of print, radio, tape, video and television production by Pentecostals is nothing short of miraculous. In many countries, Pentecostal organisations have succeeded in buying their own televisions stations or, when state control makes this impossible, buying airtime from stations whose empty coffers make it impossible to refuse. In Brazil the Universal Church of the Kingdom of God owns the third largest television station in the country, and in Nigeria there are dozens of televangelist programmes available each week on any given station. In Nigeria and Ghana, a new industry has grown up around Pentecostal video film productions: extremely popular dramas which stage the trials and tribulations of converts, gory satanic machinations, and the eventual triumph or downfall of the protagonists. Booklets, tracts and magazines have grown in popularity with the increased use of electronic media, signalling the cardinal importance

---

[13] See Birgit Meyer, 'Commodities and the Power of Prayer: Pentecostalist Attitudes Towards Consumption in Contemporary Ghana', *Development and Change*, vol. 29, no. 4, 1998.

[14] See Appadurai, *Modernity at Large*.

of processes of mass mediation not only to the transnationalisation of Pentecostalism – as these productions cross national boundaries, are translated, pirated, reworked – but also in the flourishing of rich local Pentecostal cultures. We can identify in both production and consumption of these globally circulating images and discourses the new social role that Appadurai accords the imagination: the work of the imagination 'is neither purely emancipatory nor entirely disciplined, but is a space of contestation in which individuals and groups seek to annex the global into their own practices of the modern'. With precedents in great revolutions and messianic movements of the past, the work of the imagination is, however, 'no longer a matter of specially endowed charismatic individuals injecting the imagination where it does not belong. Ordinary people have begun to deploy their imaginations in the practice of their everyday lives.'[15]

The transformation of the world at the individual level means the appropriation of its objects, signs and discourses and their integration into a new imaginary of salvation and transformation. In its collective form, it is expressed in the idiom of a public 'war against Satan'. In practical terms, this involves a project of rooting out the multitude of evil spiritual forces behind individual misfortunes, eliminating them through rituals of deliverance, and embarking on a project of global conversion. If salvation is to be in the world, it cannot be collectively achieved until all the world is saved. This idiom thus links individual experiences of suffering and desire to the collective project of an advancing front on the global battlefield of spiritual warfare. The current obsession with 'occult powers' as being the source of misfortune as well as embodying immoral and destructive forces is not unique to Pentecostalism. From a dramatic increase in witchcraft anxiety in 'modern' urban sectors in Africa to obsessions in the West about child abuse at the hands of Satanists, these apparently very different manifestations seem to stem from a common 'moral perplexity' and a need, among other things, to redefine the relationship between intimate spaces and vast open-ended networks.[16] As Jean Comaroff points out, rather than evidence of the tenacity of 'tradition' or signs of backwardness, this obsession with the occult seems to be a response to modernity's enchantment and contradictions: 'its inescapable enticements, its self-consuming passions, its discriminatory tactics, and its devastating social costs'.[17]

---

[15] *Ibid.* p. 5.

[16] Jean Comaroff, 'Consuming Passions: Child Abuse, Fetishism and 'The New World Order' ' in *Culture*, forthcoming, cited in Geschiere, 'Witchcraft'. See also Comaroff and Comaroff, *Modernity and its Malcontents: Ritual and Power in Postcolonial Africa* (University of Chicago Press, 1993); Birgit Meyer, 'Modernity and Enchantment: The Image of the Devil in Popular African Christianity' in P. van der Veer (ed.), *Conversion to Modernities: The Globalization of Christianity* (New York: Routledge, 1996).

[17] Comaroff and Comaroff, *Modernity and its Malcontents*, p. xxix.

Pentecostal discourse on the occult reveals a Manichean division of the world between the saved and satanic. And yet this does not necessarily imply the closing down of interpretative options or the fixing of identity. The idiom of occult powers is overloaded with notoriously ambivalent meanings; a constantly changing *bricolage* of extremely heterogeneous elements, it is perhaps the characteristic of contemporary Pentecostalism which best expresses its ability to forge a rapprochement between global and local, between new notions of selfhood and the public space. The search for moral certainties and the attempt by Pentecostal leaders to attain interpretative control over definitions of evil and affliction collide with this polysemic mixture where individual imagination and fantasies combine with a series of standardised formulas to produce an ever-shifting field of significations. It is perhaps not surprising that among all the Pentecostal discourses which circulate globally (i.e. Bible study, prayer, professional and financial success, children, marital relations, dress, diet, lifestyles), those concentrating on the occult are the least standardised and the most inventive, expressing all the messy exuberance of meaning that the idiom incites and, with it, the rich diversity of so many Pentecostalisms.

One example of the ambivalence inherent in the Pentecostal discourse on the occult is expressed through the symbolic role of money. Money is one of the symbolic objects which enables the passage from the profane to the sacred, yet the sacred is understood not simply in terms of the figure of Christ and the Holy Spirit, but of supernatural powers more generally. The satisfaction of worldly desires – wealth, social mobility, health – is the weapon the devil uses to lure souls from the straight and narrow path: desires which lead to anti-social and immoral behaviour such as jealousy, hatred, greed, and exploitation. Yet salvation is likewise expressed via the realisation of these very desires. The ambivalence and excess of meaning that the sacred embodies has the effect of creating a new form of uncertainty at the heart of the Pentecostal identity; insofar as no standardised formula exists for identifying the source of supernatural power, the convert cannot be sure of being totally free from satanic influence. Hence the need to exorcise personal experiences of satanic affliction through public rituals of deliverance, and to interpret such experiences not only in terms of individual moral failure, but as part of a global struggle between forces of good and evil.

The battle between the forces of darkness and the Holy Spirit thus expresses a fundamental ambivalence in terms of the boundaries implied by the stark distinction between good and evil, between the saved and the lost. The notion of a fixed identity, whether conceived in local or transnational terms, sits uneasily with idea of global spiritual warfare in which the boundaries are ever shifting, fronts advancing and retreating. The ambivalence of such definitions of evil and affliction also means an enormous flexibility for the creation of local forms of closure and opposition.

Exclusive or inclusive notions of Pentecostal identity are thus mobilised much more in response to context than according to any predetermined dogmatic and institutionalised position. This situation, coupled with the perpetual translation of the individual struggle for salvation into a struggle for the public space, allows for the expression of extremely diverse forms of local political mobilisation, and relations with the nation-state which range from complicity to direct opposition.

The relationship between individual communication with the sacred and the battle for the public space finds its expression in the representation of a transnational community. The transnational expresses both the fabrication by each individual of new attitudes towards everyday scenarios, which are often simply gestures of survival in a profoundly commodified and uncertain world, and at the same time the global circulation of collective representations, narrative formulae and smoothly functioning organisations. In the Pentecostal formulation, the sacred takes on the allure of an amalgam of extremely diverse elements, some particular and local, others standardised, both often trivial. This bizarre mixture, this *bricolage*, clashes with reigning conceptions of religion. The transnationalisation of Pentecostalism refers to a new 'ethic', but one which has little in common with Weber's 'Protestant ethic'. This new *imaginaire* provides an illustration of the work of the individual imagination as a social force, expressing the link between the search for self-affirmation and the constitution of a body of globally recognised forms, images and ideas.

It is by way of this capacity to give birth to new forms of behaviour, which both reproduce in many aspects the image of a 'homogenised consumer identity' associated with globalisation[18] and at the same time give expression to an imagination in which individuals find the inspiration for the radical transformation of their lives, that we can speak of one 'Pentecostalism' across the different countries of Africa and Latin America. The experience of getting born-again reproduces itself in an almost identical form across the world. At the same time it is an intensely personal phenomenon which takes on its social signification in communities of an unimaginable diversity. The aim in this volume is to discover the plural nature of these common forms through a study of selected African and Latin American countries. The differences between these two continents are enormous, from every point of view. Of course, this does not mean that Coca-cola is not drunk or alleluias sung everywhere. Each society gives its own signification to Coca-cola, just as each society, each group invests Pentecostalism with its own meanings. Yet in this case, we are not speaking about a product, but a composite, a patchwork whose very hybridity gives it its transnational form. These new forms which arise from everywhere and nowhere refuse any categorisation fixed by an elite,

[18] See Daniel Miller, *Material Culture and Mass Consumption*, Oxford: Blackwell, 1987.

be it political, cultural or intellectual. This hybridity is evident in the ways in which researchers have treated the subject, and we hope to reproduce this not simply through the multiplication of case studies from different parts of these continents, but also through the inclusion of authors from various disciplines.

There already exists an abundant literature on Latin America,[19] a large part of which has been produced by Latin American scholars. In that continent, one finds a multiplicity of denominations, some extremely large with important transnational connections, others much smaller and more localised. In Africa, too, one can observe next to the large denominations the dizzying growth of all sorts of small independent churches. Pentecostalism in Africa has only recently been treated as a separate religious phenomenon, even if it has existed on the continent since the colonial period. The studies done so far have been largely undertaken by a young generation of researchers, few of them African. Not all are anthropologists from the ex-colonial powers, especially those contributing to this volume. In any case, their approach to the subject is clearly different from that of the Latin Americanists.

The title of the volume draws its inspiration from the title of the first paper. The story of the tower of Babel can be read as the mythical creation of difference. In constructing the tower, the Babylonians believed they could reach God. The jealous Old Testament God punishes them for their audacity by creating diversity of language and confusion among peoples. Pentecost intervenes in the Biblical narrative as a reversal of this event. God descends upon each individual in the form of the Holy Spirit, and suddenly each begins to speak in a tongue unknown to him, yet comprehensible to others present. The intermediate space between these two narratives is perhaps an allegory for the transnational problematic. Babel, which represents the collective longing to reach God, resulting in the creation of difference and confusion among individuals, and Pentecost, when individual fusion with God is reached together with a collective understanding and coherence: both of these moments find their expression in the move between individual and collective, sacred and profane, particular and general, that we have outlined above. In the light of the opposition of these two stories, Waldo César explores the idea that 'the Pentecostal experience may be the basis for a new theology, and new paradigm of salvation'. In linking theological and sociological approaches, this text presents a most original view of the transnational character of Pentecostalism. Taking his inspiration from the perspective opened up by Ricoeur and de Certeau, the author introduces a sociological analysis in developing the hypothesis of a transcendental vision of the daily reality of transnationalisation.

---

[19] See André Corten, 'The Growth of Literature on Afro-American, Latin America and African Pentecostalism', *Journal of Contemporary Religion*, vol. 12, no. 3, pp. 311-34, 1997.

The everyday reality of Pentecostalism is taken up in other texts. Ruth Marshall-Fratani, Rijk Van Dijk and Laennec Hurbon analyse Pentecostalism as a way of reinventing daily life through the redefinition of the new socio-temporal frameworks introduced, at least in part, by globalised relations of exchange and communication. The conversion experience is the obvious starting point for the redefinition of the self, and yet an analysis of the process of the reinvention of daily life must go beyond the discourse which the convert produces about him/herself and his conversion experience. In these three chapters, we find three different ways of approaching the everyday construction of the Pentecostal subject. For Ruth Marshall-Fratani, it is as 'delocalised subjects' that individual Nigerian converts reimagine their lives, a process which involves the converts' participation in a transnational network of images, personalities, discourses and ideas. Her analysis of the construction of new transnational identities, borrowed in part from Appadurai, makes the link between everyday practices and the work of individual imaginations in their redefinition and the political consequences implied by such a process at the collective level. She shows that the reinvention of everyday life also expresses a new political imaginary.

Rijk van Dijk approaches the theme of everyday life through Michel Foucault's concept of 'technologies of the self'. Examining in particular the work of Ghanaian Pentecostal pastors in the diaspora, the author shows that the 'break with the past' characteristic of conversion does not necessarily imply a straightforward trajectory in which the individual is liberated from an imagined collective history and moves to a monolithic form of 'modern' individuality. Rather, the Pentecostalism offers the convert a plurality of 'technologies of the self'. Laennec Hurbon introduces the idea of an 'intermediate life space' offered by Pentecostalism in the Caribbean. This space appears a site of mediation between converts' past lives and the modern world, in which evil is not only associated with the values attached to the past, but also certain aspects of the modern, globalised world. In his analysis, he focuses on the place accorded by Pentecostalism to the body, and 'possession by the Holy Spirit'. In his discussion of the relationship between the convert's body, the image and the written Word we can see certain similarities with the Foucauldian approach taken by van Dijk. Although Hurbon's analysis does not make reference to Foucault's approach to subjectification, the converts' rejection of 'idols' (here the *lwas* of the voodoo cult) involves 'the work of the self on the self' (*le travail de soi sur soi*) in which bodily, linguistic and symbolic practices are combined in the process of Pentecostal subjectification.

Underlying the theme of the everyday construction of local subjects in terms of a transnational community is the question of the relative significance of the 'local' and 'global' and their mutual interpenetration. André

Droogers examines this analytical dilemma through a general discussion of the relative merits of constructivist and culturalist approaches, taking up the problematic of the paradoxical similitude and diversity of Pentecostalism that faces the researcher when he attempts to account for its global expansion. He proposes that rather than looking for the reasons for Pentecostalism's success in external factors, which might be equally applicable to other religions, analysis should begin by a treatment of the specific characteristics of Pentecostalism which appear to be central to its success everywhere. In a discussion which takes into account much of the literature on the relationship between religion and globalisation, he demonstrates the complex nature of the relationship between these 'internal' characteristics and processes of globalisation.

In a similar vein, Paul Gifford examines the extent to which the theological components of Pentecostalism have a local or global dimension. Gifford shows in his study of Pentecostalism in Africa that while in both the doctrine of prosperity and Christian Zionism the North America influence is obvious, deliverance theology, on the other hand, has a greater link with the African Pentecostal tradition. For Gifford, each component implies a different balance between local and global. In his analysis he emphasises the specificity of Africa as a marginalised continent. In this regard, Gifford opposes the thesis of Peter Beyer in his work on religion and transnationalism (a study which ignores Africa). Gifford argues that Beyer's vision, which describes religious networks functioning according to the same logic as banks, law, health, sport, technology and science, or higher education does not apply to the African context, since these networks simply pass over the continent, and are not implicated deeply within it. At the same time, Gifford takes issue with Beyer's argument that the dynamic growth of Christianity in Africa is due, along with the growth of Islamic fundamentalism, to a reaction to globalisation, expressed through the revitalisation of traditional religion. As Gifford shows, many new forms of Christianity, in particular Pentecostalism, although they may reinforce or reinvent old forms of belief, also serve as a mode of entering into the global order and expressing a desire for 'modernity'.

The theme of conversion to Pentecostalism as a form of conversion to modernity runs through most of the contributions. Rijk Van Dijk's study, by focusing on the 'rupture with the past' that appears to be at the heart of modernity's specific space-time conceptualisation, explores how this rupture, central to the Pentecostal conversion experience, entails a conversion to a modernity which is by no means defined in terms of classical sociological criteria such as individualisation or disenchantment. What nearly all of the studies in this collection show, echoing the approach of the collection by Peter Van der Veer which directly takes up this theme,[20] is that conversion to Pentecostalism is a conversion to various

---

[20] P. van der Veer (ed.), *Conversion to Modernities*.

modernities, in which the relationship between the past and present is ambivalent. The category 'modernity' should be thought of not so much as an analytical concept, but rather as the articulation by converts of the nebulous, multi-form and often contradictory representations of their desires and fears. However one defines it, what these chapters show is a situation that belies that the old sociological accounts of modernity in terms of individualisation and secularisation. In their study of Argentina, Oro and Semán show how the presence of the Universal Church of the Kingdom of God (UCKG) in Argentina exemplifies a 'desecularising-modernising' tendency, providing an example of a non-exclusive relationship between modernity and religion.

André Corten likewise links the new conditions of everyday life introduced by transnationalism and the revitalisation of religion by introducing the idea of 'new religious needs' which arise in the context of transnationalisation. In Corten's analysis, these needs are manifested in the form of an externalised emotion, the search for the sacred, expressed in the figuration of frightening powers, and fantasies of radical transformation. They are given form in the articulation of an extremely diverse popular culture outside the control of an elite; a culture which expresses the new conditions of everyday life introduced by transnationalisation, and in which processes of identification break with the national context.

While 'modernity' and 'transnationalism' are by no means interchangeable, it is true that, as Van der Veer points out, 'Christian conversion, is a "technology of the self", to use Foucault's notion, which, under modern conditions, produces a new subjecthood that is deeply emeshed in economic globalization and the emergence of a system of nation-states.'[21] Both Hurbon and Marshall-Fratani examine the ways in which the everyday construction of Pentecostal subjects is involved in larger-scale political processes and relations with the nation-state. Transnational communities in general pose new challenges to the nation-state, and Pentecostalism is no exception. Access to 'resources of extraversion' are particularly important in African societies, and have typically been monopolised by the nation-state. Via their transnational networks Pentecostals have such access and put it at the centre of their public identity, placing themselves in a new position of strength *vis-à-vis* the state, and enabling them to present themselves as offering an 'alternative' route to modernity.

As we have argued above, such an 'alternative route' does not necessarily imply homogenisation, nor does the challenge posed by Pentecostalism to modes of community formation and political subjectification associated with the nation-state take the same form everywhere. Diane Austin-Broos in her study of Jamaica argues that the growth of transnational relations in the context of a weak state is by no means a phenomenon of

[21] *Ibid.*, p. 19.

homogenisation. At first glance, the Pentecostalism which unites 25 per cent of all Jamaicans appears to be a purely American importation. And yet the perpetual movement which is part of leaders' international career strategies, visits from foreign pastors, participation in transnational associations, these all demonstrate that the links created are not evidence of the hegemony of an American model but rather the result of the difficulty in gaining access to state power and resources locally. In Jamaica, following the Zionist revival and Rastafarianism, Pentecostalism appears as the expression of an alternative imagined community confronting a weak nation-state. Using an approach distinct from that of Austin-Broos, Jean-Pierre Bastian also argues that transnationalisation, expressed in the construction of trans-local identities, does not imply the importation of a homogenising model. Rather, the construction of identity may be analysed in terms of market logic. Based on in-depth fieldwork, Bastian argues Pentecostal transnational identity is distinguished by it multilateral and hybrid character which implies the juxtapostion of diverse elements, from the most archaic to the most modern, and by the networking of practices and beliefs in a 'market situation'. He shows clearly how the rise of transnational Pentecostalism has resulted in a complete deregulation of religious practice, all the more remarkable given the fact that until recently, Costa Rica has been a predominantly Catholic country.

It is interesting to compare this situation of religious deregulation with that described in Elizabeth Dorier-Apprill's paper on Congo-Brazzaville. Until 1991, the one-party state regulated all religious activity through a strictly enforced 'anti-sect' law. In the ten years following the lifting of the ban, Pentecostalism has grown dramatically in a context of severe ethno-regional tensions. The author presents a comparative analysis of three Pentecostal networks, with the aim of evaluating their transnational affiliations and ability to transcend these ethno-regional cleavages. She shows that the success of these new churches depends to a large extent on their ability to respond to the transnational aspirations of certain social categories – in particular the educated – and project an alternative vision against the violence of the current political crisis. This case shows that while Pentecostalism may have become resolutely transnational in its operation, its structure and material and symbolic base, certain states may still wield considerable regulatory powers which can determine its local success and impact. Dorier-Apprill's study also provides evidence for the claim that Pentecostalism may foster new forms of difference and exclusion, but at the same time may be involved in undermining others.

Other chapters take up this important aspect of transnationalisation: the fact that it not only implies the crossing of borders, but puts into question existing modes establishing difference – national, social, and cultural. Thus in the case of Benin, Mayrargue shows how churches from Ghana and Nigeria transgress national borders, and may recreate community ties within ethnic groups located within different national territories. Other churches with a more pan-ethnic membership help to foster transnational modes of identification. Yet in the same context, the 'foreign' origins of churches may give rise to local conflicts and schisms. Oro and Semán's study of Argentina examines the ways in which Pentecostalism changes in crossing national borders. The 'neo-Pentecostalism' of Brazil, with its emphasis on the struggle against evil spirits and demons from the Afro-Brazilian tradition, is obliged to undergo a process of adaptation to the Argentinian context, where this religious tradition is much less present. Using the case of members of the Universal Church of the Kingdom of God (UCKG), the authors present a detailed analysis of the transformation in the consciousness of the believer of their malaise and their 'bodily grammar' when they cross the border between Brazil and Argentina.

The itineraries of Pentecostal implantation follow a resolutely transnational logic where churches and missions perpetually cross not only national, but also continental borders. However, such implantation is not even or homogeneous. Dominant poles for the 'production' of Pentecostalism exist both in Africa and Latin America. Brazil stands out in the latter context, as the studies by Corten, Freston, and Oro and Semán show. The relatively recent rise of Pentecostalism in the Francophone African countries, such as Congo-Brazzaville, Burkina Faso and Benin, where Protestantism has been historically dominated by Catholicism, contrast in this sense with countries like Nigeria and Ghana, where the Pentecostal movement now dominates the local Christian landscape.

At the same time, as we have stressed, the forms Pentecostalism takes owe a great deal to the particular social, economic, political and historical context in which it grows. In Englund's study of Malawi, which focuses on Pentecostals in poor urban neighbourhoods in search of transnational ties with missionaries, their relatively limited access to resources, be they mediated images and ideas or material wealth, contrasts sharply with the Nigerian and Ghanaian cases, where the urban Pentecostal population comprises a much higher percentage of relatively wealthy, educated, and upwardly mobile individuals. While the conversion to Pentecostalism is very often associated with ideas of 'progress' and 'modernisation', as we noted above, such notions are by no means always evaluated positively. As Hurbon argues, Pentecostalism allows for a certain critical equivocation on the nature of socio-economic relations that global modernity appears to foster, especially in urban centres. Englund's study, by focusing on the blockages produced by individual social relationships, shows that the 'quest for missionaries' reveals a complex and ambivalent position on the promises and threats of transnationalism. In the Nigerian case, on the other hand, it is most often in the rural hinterland that this ambivalence towards the new forms of wealth and commodities associated with 'modernity' finds its most marked expression in Pentecostal discourse.

Pierre-Joseph Laurent's study of the Assemblies of God in Burkina Faso demonstrates that differences in attitudes and practices exist within a given country when one moves from a rural to an urban context. Despite the fact that members of this Pentecostal church are locally known as 'the Americans', the ways in which new Pentecostal identity is articulated depend much more on the local context than on the strictures of an imported doctrine with 'homogenising' tendencies. In the rural areas, as Laurent has shown in his previous work, Pentecostalism allows the youth to distance themselves from the constraints of village social relationships, in particular kinship obligations. Yet, rather than leading to a rejection of local socio-economic relations, conversion opens up a space of negotiation in which the convert's participation in kinship relationships may be modified. Pentecostalism is thus implicated in a process of rural 'modernisation', where 'modernisation' is seen as a mode of liberation for the youth, and whose transnational aspect is less evident than in the urban centres. In the cities, on the other hand, Pentecostalism places the emphasis on healing and the restructuring of social relationships which have broken down in a context of urban crisis, where 'modernity' is judged with more ambivalence. In this urban context, Pentecostalism's transnational character is more salient. Cédric Mayrargue shows how a recently urbanised population in Benin confronted with severe economic difficulties and growing social anomie finds in Pentecostalism the symbolic resources with which to confront this situation. Motivated by individuals as well as transnational flows, Pentecostalism brings to the forefront processes of the reconstruction of identity already at work in Beninese society.

Despite many of the formal similarities in Pentecostal practice, organisation and doctrine across the two continents, the topography of the religious field in Africa is very different from that of Latin America, not only because of the importance of African religions (which exist in Latin America as well), but also because of the complex relationship among the colonial powers, traditional missionary based churches, both Protestant and Catholic, and African Independent Christianity. The explosion of Pentecostalism has provoked an enormous upheaval in the African religious field, and has acquired a great visibility in very little time. Although often more apparent in urban centres, Pentecostalism is equally present in rural areas. In the urban population, still a relative minority in Africa, Pentecostalism has its greatest success among the relatively educated members. Its urban clientele in Africa is thus quite different from that of Latin American cities, where it attracts, on the contrary, the poorest of the poor, or at most, the members of the lower middle class.

One of the more obvious differences between Pentecostalism in Africa and Latin America is that in Africa, unlike Latin America, its challenge to the nation-state does not take the form of participation in the classical political institutions, such as political parties. This may in part be related to the nature of African nation-states, which have maintained, until recently at least, their monopolies over discourses on development and the resources of community formation in very different ways than their Latin-American counterparts. As Corten's study shows, in Latin America Pentecostalism participates in a process of political delegitimation, all the more profound in the context of fragmentation of the political system in the post-populist period. Corten shows how logico-linguistic mechanisms set to work in the expression of new religious needs are in contradiction with the order upon which political legitimacy is founded. However, despite this conflict, this expression does not develop a political alternative. Thus we observe a process of political delegitimation, all the more profound since the end of the populist era the fragmentation of the political system.

It may also be related to the fact that in Latin America the sheer size and reach of a church such as the enormous Brazilian-based Universal Church of the Kingdom of God (UCKG) constitute an extremely powerful base for political mobilisation. This is true not only in Brazil, as César points out, where the UCKG is directly involved in party politics, but also more indirectly through the constitution of its own transnational community, as Oro and Semán show for Argentina, and Freston in his study of its implantation in Portugal and Great Britain. In Africa, the polycentric character of Pentecostal churches is very marked. There do exist churches such as the Assemblies of God, which have been present in some countries for more than half a century. However, the Assemblies of God does not function as one institution linked transnationally, but rather as a series of discrete and independent national institutions which develop transnational linkages very much in function of their local contexts. At the same time, the Assemblies of God in Africa still tends to belong, in most cases, to the conservative 'older wave' of Pentecostalism, very different in its doctrinal emphasis, social base and financial weight from the Brazilian giant. Even the largest Nigerian churches, which have branches in as many as twenty countries, cannot compare.

After twenty years of existence the UCKG now counts three to four million faithful and has churches in more than fifty countries. This church is without doubt the emblem of the 'third wave' of Latin American Pentecostalism. Oro and Semán as well as Paul Freston focus their chapters on this important church. Freston provides the most well informed account to date of the international expansion of the UCKG. In particular, he examines the transformations involved in its expansion into Portugal and England. In the case of Portugal, a highly Catholic country, the church develops in a hostile environment. Even the mainline Protestant churches strongly criticise its 'magico-sacramental' methods; nevertheless, Portugal has become the first country outside Brazil where it has developed a real national viability. In England, the UCKG tried to burst on to the Pentecostal scene with a splash when it attempted to purchase Brixton Academy, a famous music venue, and since then has gained popularity among the black population, largely consiting of first and second-generation immigrants. The question remains as to whether this will allow the church to attract members of the white English population, or whether the UCKG is destined to remain a 'black church'. Given the highly transnational and transcultural nature of the UCKG, and its ability to adapt doctrine and practice to local contexts, as shown also in Oro and Semán's study of Argentina, one can imagine that this distinction may be overcome.

This ensemble of studies reveals above all the extreme diversity of Pentecostalism, especially in its social composition. In Latin America, Pentecostalism remains for the most part a religion of the poor, even if the latest wave has involved greater numbers of the middle class. In African cities, it presents itself as new mode of identification among the relatively educated, one which places the emphasis on its modern and transcultural characteristics and which involves an attempt to colonise the public space. In rural areas in Africa, it is seen as a means by which the youth may create opportunities for upward mobility and a reconstruction of social relations and obligations. Between these two continents, these differences give rise to dissimilar modes of constituting, via Pentecostalism, a new form of popular transnational culture. The variety in the expression of the relationship with the sacred and the practices and symbols mobilised in the reconstruction of the individual reflect simultaneously the extreme diversity of history, culture and social groups among the countries presented, and the desire for an opening on to the world that Pentecostalism seems to provoke or express everywhere it is found.

BIBLIOGRAPHY

Appadurai, Arjun, *Modernity at Large: Cultural Dimensions of Globalization*, Minneapolis: University of Minnesota Press, 1997.
Bayart, Jean-François, *L'illusion identitaire*, Paris: Fayard, 1996.
———, *La Réinvention du capitalisme*, Paris: Fayard, 1997.
Jean Comaroff, 'Consuming Passions: Child Abuse, Fetishism and "The New World Order" ' in *Culture*, forthcoming.
——— and Comaroff, *Modernity and its Malcontents: Ritual and Power in Postcolonial Africa*, University of Chicago Press, 1993.

Corten, André, 'The Growth of Literature on Afro-American, Latin America and African Pentecostalism', *Journal of Contemporary Religion*,vol.12, no.3, 1997 pp.311-34.

Cox, Harvey, *Fire from Heaven: The Rise of Pentecostal Spirituality and the Reshaping of Religion in the Twenty-First Century*, Reading, MA: Addison-Wesley, 1995.

Geschiere, Peter, 'Witchcraft and Spirit Cults in Africa and East Asia', *Development and Change*, vol. 29, no. 4, 1998.

———— and Birgit Meyer, 'Globalization and Identity: Dialetics of Flow and Closure – Introduction', *Development and Change*, vol. 29, no. 4, 1998.

Featherstone, M., S Lash, and R. Robertson (eds), *Global Modernities*, London: Sage, 1995.

Featherstone, M. (ed.), *Global Culture: Nationalism, Globalization and Modernity*, London: Sage, 1991.

Hamelink, C., *Cultural Autonomy in Global Communications*, New York: Longman, 1983.

Keane, Webb, 'Calvin in the Tropics: Objects and Subjects at the Religious Frontier', in Patricia Spyer (ed.), *Border Fetishisms: Material Objects in Unstable Spaces*, New York: Routledge, 1998.

MacLuhan, Marshall, *Understanding Media: The Extensions of Man*, London: Routledge, 1964.

———— and Powers, *The Global Village*, Oxford University Press, 1989.

Meyer, Birgit, ' "Make a Complete Break with the Past": Memory and Post-Colonial Modernity and Ghanaian Pentecostalist Discourse', *Journal of Religion in Africa*, vol. 28, no. 3, 1998.

————, 'Commodities and the Power of Prayer: Pentecostalist Attitudes Towards Consumption in Contemporary Ghana', *Development and Change*, vol. 29, no. 4, 1998.

————, 'Modernity and Enchantment: The Image of the Devil in Popular African Christianity' in P. van der Veer (ed.), *Conversion to Modernities: The Globalization of Christianity*, New York: Routledge, 1996.

Miller, Daniel, *Material Culture and Mass Consumption*, Oxford: Blackwell, 1987.

———— (ed.), *Worlds Apart: Modernity through the Prism of the Local*, London: Routledge, 1995.

Vieille, Paul, 'Du transnational au politique-monde', *Peuples Méditerranéens*, no.35-6, 1986.

Part I. GENERAL

FROM BABEL TO PENTECOST
A SOCIAL-HISTORICAL-THEOLOGICAL STUDY OF
THE GROWTH OF PENTECOSTALISM

Waldo César

Therefore its name was called Babel, because there the Lord confused the language of all the earth. (Gen.11:9)

And they were all filled with the Holy Spirit and began to speak in other tongues, as the Spirit gave them utterance. (Acts 1:4)

The extraordinary growth of the Pentecostal movement throughout the world since its origins in the early twentieth centuries is best understood in its entirety if the transcendental dimension, expressed through doctrine and the religious experience it produces, is taken into account in historical and sociological research. In the surprising narrative of the day of Pentecost, in chapter 2 of the Acts of the Apostles, one finds the roots of a new type of church and Christian life.

Nowadays the phenomenon of Pentecost is repeated everywhere: multitudes of worshippers are flocking to the various versions of present-day Pentecostalism, proclaiming the rediscovery of that singular event. In this way they also cultivate the enthusiasm and energy of the early Christians - experiences which in general have been lost by the established Protestant churches and by the Catholic church. The movement is complex, combining a biblical symbolic content with modern forms of communication and global expansion. Elements of the religious revivals of the distant past are mixed with new and more dramatic problems and human experiences - elements which Max Weber identified as a *theodicéia*. Pentecostalism is now surprising not only historians and sociologists, but also ecclesiastical institutions, their clergy and theologians. The latter are confronted with a contradictory religious phenomenon, which does not fit the historical doctrinal categories of the established churches. For their part, social scientists have intensified their research and are attempting to find methodological procedures to understand the dynamics of a movement which is mobilising society. The simplicity of the Pentecostal message and the limited scholarship of its leaders have by no means hindered its astonishing growth over the latter part of the twentieth century, especially among the poorer sections of the population. On the contrary, its message, grounded in a transcendental view of everyday life, offers new hope to those facing hardship and difficulties in their present situation. Converts to Pentecostalism, full of enthusiasm and hope, become a contagious source of confidence and happiness. The impact of the Pentecostal movement has influenced other Christian denominations. The continued vitality and prosperity of many Protestant and Catholic churches are due to the charismatic inheritance which originated in Pentecostalism. These manifestations have revitalised church services and masses, combining traditional forms of worship with spontaneous verbal and bodily participation. Charismatic worshippers - who do not necessarily break away from their original confession - have promoted ways of blending a traditional style with a more active religious life. As in the life of the early church and present day Pentecostalism, charismatic believers are open to the work of the Holy Spirit, the power of prayer and miracles. This new expression of spirituality, for many a sign of an authentic conversion, penetrates both institutional and personal domains. In this way it introduces new possibilities for renovation in the heart of the many churches where it appears.

In this study, I will bring together different sources and forms of inquiry: historical, sociological, and biblical-theological. In this way I hope to offer a new perspective on much of the research that has been carried out in these separate disciplines. This paper has its origins in an interdisciplinary study which was carried out in Brazil in 1995-6, and which gave rise to a first attempt to understand the relationship between Pentecostalism and transnationalisation.[1] After a brief historical overview, some sociological issues are raised which may be indicative of 'signs of transcendence in the sphere of human existence'.[2] Given this juxtaposition of the theological and sociological, the study goes on to compare two biblical events – the building of the tower of Babel (in the book of Genesis) and the appearance of the Holy Spirit on the day of Pentecost (in the Acts of the Apostles). Texts that can provide meaning to present-day human events in the context of biblical revelation. In this sense they can be understood as signs which, from a hermeneutic perspective, produce an 'historical effect'.[3] Hence what is told about Babel and Pentecost

---

[1] Research sponsored by the Overseas Ministries Study Center - Research Enablement Program (New Haven) – with support of researchers from the Instituto de Estudos da Religião of Rio de Janeiro, was published in 1999 (by Editora Vozes of Petrópolis, Brazil) under the title of *Pentecostalism and the Future of the Christian Churches – Promises, Limitations and Challenges*, in two parts: *Daily Life and Transcendency in Pentecostalism* (by Waldo César) and *The Reconstruction of Life in the Power of the Spirit* (by Richard Shaull, an American theologian). Although the research was carried out in Brazil and refers predominantly to Brazilian sources, the arguments presented in this chapter are intended to have a general applicability to the institutional and doctrinal aspects of the Pentecostal movement.

[2] I use here an expression by Peter Berger, *A Rumour of Angels: Modern Society and the Rediscovery of the Supernatural, London:* Allen Love, 1970.

[3] Words by H.G. Gadamer, *Verdad y Método* (Truth and Method), Madrid: Cristianidad,

in these narratives has a meaning which surpasses those events and which transcends the human condition. In this way, these narratives are related to *kerygma* – in the triple sense of teaching, preaching and confession of the 'good news'.[4] This study is certainly ambitious and perhaps controversial in its nature, constituting a challenge in the search for relationships that go beyond the realms of 'our natural reality'.[5]

The gathering speed of a religious phenomenon

Pentecostalism locates its doctrinal originality in the events of the day of Pentecost in Jerusalem. In the house 'where they were staying' Jesus's disciples, men 'together with the women', were 'up to the upper room. [...] And suddenly there came a sound from heaven as of a rushing mighty wind, and it filled all the house where they were sitting. And there appeared unto them cloven tongues of fire, and it sat upon each of them. And they were filled with the Holy Ghost and began to speak with other tongues, as the Spirit gave them utterance.'[6]

This unexpected beginning – news of which spread throughout the populated world of the times – reoccurred in an equally extraordinary way nineteen centuries later, during Easter, in a house on Azuza Street in Los Angeles, California. Through the experience of similar events – the baptism by the Holy Spirit, speaking in tongues and the *charismata* (distribution of spiritual gifts) – those gathered in the house on Azuza Street renewed the promise to be Christ's witnessness, as He tells his disciples in Acts, 'unto the uttermost parts of the earth'.[7] In the same decade the movement spread to Asia, Africa, Europe and Latin America.

However the narrative in Acts is interpreted, the missionary zeal it created had spread Christianity to the entire Mediterranean world before the close of the first century. The historic and symbolic efficacy of Pentecost has been reproduced in the twentieth century, not merely as an unprecedented spiritual and emotional experience, but in its evangelical zeal. As in the distant past, the event in Los Angeles provoked wonder and perplexity, as well as considerable ridicule,[8] no doubt because of its origins in this small Baptist congregation of Afro-Americans. The historical

---

1977; J. Severino Croatto, *Uma hermenêutica da liberdade,* São Paulo: Edições Paulinas, 1981, p. 12.

[4] The various meanings of the term *kerygma* - confession, teaching, preaching - can be applied to the above-mentioned narratives, especially with regard to divine judgement by the prophets and the apostles' testimonies.

[5] Peter Berger, op. cit.

[6] Acts of the Apostles, 1: 13-14 and 2:2. The biblical texts are from the *Jerusalem Bible.* For the English version I have used the *Revised Standard Version.*

[7] Acts 1:8.

[8] See Acts 2: 12-13.

Protestant churches, after their initial concern, considered the event as a type of sectarian fanaticism, which would not have any major influence on their well-structured organisations and well-defined and restrictive doctrines. Nevertheless, the astonishing spread of this movement not only recalls the growth of the early church, but shows just to what extent the existing churches underestimated this new form of Protestantism.

The case of Brazil illustrates the evolution and development of that first moment; a trajectory which may well be found in other countries. Founded by converts from the Los Angeles experience in the north and south of the country in 1910-11, Pentecostalism caused no major concern to the denominations established during the nineteenth century by European immigrants and North American missionaries. For them it was a case of 'sectarian invasion'. However, from 1930 onwards, when almost 10 per cent of Brazilian Protestants had converted to Pentecostalism, a heated debate took place, provoked by the proselytising carried out by the new churches. The Protestant reaction later intensified with the explosion of the charismatic movement within their own churches.[9] In the 1990s, however, many Protestant and Catholic churches recognised that the Pentecostal movement occupies an important place within Brazilian Christianity. In 1993, the Assemblies of God in Brazil (with 7-8 million members) converted more than half a million new members (their target was to reach 50 million souls, a third of the country's present country's population, by the year 2000). Another older branch of Pentecostalism, the Christian Congregation of Brazil, baptised more than 2 million converts during the forty-four year period from 1952 to 1996, an average of around 50,000 new members per year. In 1996 alone, more than 100,000 persons were baptised, an average of over 2,000 each Sunday.[10] The Igreja Universal do Reino de Deus (the Universal Church of the Kingdom of God or UCKG) is building a church - the 'Cathedral of Faith' – in a suburb of Rio de Janeiro, which will seat 10,000 worshippers. In global terms, in the Third World alone, Pentecostals must amount to over 150 million individuals. The UCKG provides an example of a growing trend in the global expansion of Pentecostalism, insofar as this church, founded in Brazil merely twenty years ago, and today established in over fifty countries, demonstrates the inversion of traditional missionary activity, from the Third World to the developed countries of Europe and North America.

The global expansion of the Pentecostal movement can be compared to other contemporary process of acceleration, most of them recent or

[9] The charismatic movement also grew in the United States in 1967, among Catholic professors (laymen) of the University of Duquesne, Pittsburgh, who declared that they had received the 'baptism of the Holy Ghost'. The movement reached Brazil that same year.

[10] *Ultimato*, Viçosa, Brazil, March 1995 and Nov./Dec. 1998. See also André Corten, *Os pobres e o Espírito Santo* (The Poor and the Holy Spirit), Petrópolis: Vozes, 1966, pp. 12 and 67 ff.

reactivated in the context of globalisation and its by-products (consumerism, regionalisation, global economy, world culture, etc.). The complex world of international relationships, dependant on systems and subsystems of mass-production by large transnational corporations, has substantially reduced the sovereignty of Third World states. Although religious organisations are not beyond the influence of the dominant economic and ideological powers, their diversity and growing numbers may perform an 'integrative function in the social system', by reducing the complexity of the context in which modern social structures operate.[11] In a world of crises and growing uncertainty, both personal and collective, local and global, we cannot ignore the power of a movement which encourages a radical faith, hope and mutual responsibility, proposing new life-styles and enabling the elaboration, especially among the poor and downtrodden, of modes of survival which recover moral and ethical values in the midst of indifference and the chaos of modern society. In this sense, Pentecostalism, together with the charismatic movement, attains a trans-denominational and transnational dimension comparable to the unprecedented growth which took place in the time of the early church.

From the transcendental to everyday life: between symbolism and reality

The link between the contemporary Pentecostal movement and the event of Pentecost in the New Testament is both 'real' – Pentecostal churches attempt to reproduce literally the events described in the Bible – and symbolic – the event becomes a sign of power as well as institutional and personal freedom. The personal decision in favour of Pentecostalism appears to have a much more radical meaning than conversion to other religious groups. Converts not only break away from a previous religion and the 'world', but also consecrate the majority of their non-working lives to participation in church services and activities. The convert also takes up the new responsibilities implied by his conversion; for example, becoming a missionary, evangelising members of his family and colleagues at work, taking a significant part in the benevolent activities of the church, paying monthly tithes and voting for candidates in political elections according to his pastors' recommendations.

What is symbolic and what is real in this juxtaposition of past and present, and in the reconstruction of lives? How does the image of the sacred operate in the personal transformation of the newly-converted, through which daily life becomes a battleground for physical and spiritual survival?

[11] In the chapter 'Complex society and religion' of his *Sociologia da religião*, São Paulo: Edições Paulinas, 1990, Enzo Pace (sociologist, Faculty of Political Science, Padua, Italy) analyses the systemic theory of Niklas Luhmann on the concept of a complex society and the role of religion.

Despite Pentecostalism's renowned 'plurality of meanings',[12] there exists nonetheless a common point of departure: the transcendental dimension which gives new meaning to life and transforms its uncertainties into happiness and thanksgiving. The Pentecostal fervour – symbolised by the baptism in the Holy Spirit, in the gift of speaking in tongues, and the occurrence of miracles – is concretely manifested in converts' daily struggles. The 'miracle' which conversion announces makes its appearance in the form of a new standard of living and a new relationship with the community and society which go far beyond the formalities of traditional religious allegiance. This new lifestyle, the fruit of the conversion experience (*metanoein* – change in the inner self which results in a change in conduct[13]), imposes itself as a natural, straightforward and ineluctable outcome, despite the complex intermingling of the sacred and profane. The symbolic plays a fundamental role in this process. It functions as a language which blends what is immanent in the world with the transcendental; the 'experience of the sacred' reveals itself in concrete situations in everyday life. These situations, expressed in the people's common language, thus acquire a 'double meaning'. In the words of Paul Ricoeur, the symbolic 'establishes the common denominator of all the ways of giving meaning to reality'.[14] The transcendental and the real intermingle, breaking down the theological and cultural barriers between the sacred and the profane. This intermingling of the transcendental and the quotidian in Pentecostalism has the immediate effect of giving plausibility[15] to the hostile world in which the poor live.

The word, space and time of Pentecostalism

In order to understand more clearly this relationship between the transcendental and daily life which grounds Pentecostalism wherever it is found, and to help account for its remarkable growth, I will examine three of the Pentecostal experience's vital components: the *spoken word* (*parole*) – as the dominant mode of religious expression; *space* – the recovery of lost territory in the life of a person and society; and *time* – the overcoming of conventional limits in the human timeframe, in which daily life is mixed with millennial expectations of transformation. To a greater

---

[12] Christian Lalive d'Épinay, 'Religião, espiritualidade e sociedade' (Religion, Spirituality and Society), *Cadernos de ISER*, 6, March 1966.

[13] See *Vocabulário de teologia biblica* (A Glossary of Biblical Theology), Petrópolis: Vozes, 1984, article 'Penitência/conversão'.

[14] Paul Ricoeur, *Freud: una interpretación de la cultura*, Mexico: Siglo XXI, 1973, pp. 13 ff.

[15] Peter Berger explores the meaning of plausibility as an element of the sociology of knowledge, arguing that people's ideas about reality depend on what they consider worthy of faith and of the 'social support which those ideas receive'. Berger, *A Rumour of Angels*.

or lesser extent, these dimensions – word, space and time – can be associated with biblical-theological concepts of the announcement of the good news (*kerygma*), its spreading to the entire inhabited world (*oikoumene*) and the redemption of the present time by the promise of the second coming of Christ (*eschaton*). These three aspects are frequently interwined in Pentecostal activity, and demonstrate Pentecostalism's novelty; these apparently esoteric elements find their full expression in a religious phenomenon which directly confronts the polarisation between immanent and transcendent, thereby revealing new meanings at the heart of human experience.[16]

They started to speak in tongues. The spoken word is the motor which drives this new spirituality, and oral performance is the most important aspect of the religious service. Despite a high degree of improvisation, the service unfolds through various sounds, transmitted by powerful loudspeakers, which flood the church, as if following a programme prepared in advance: prayers, alleluias, songs, appeals, testimonies, more alleluias, offerings, confessions, casting out of demons, even more alleluias, biblical readings, sales of booklets and pamphlets, distribution of symbolic objects, miracles, and above all, speaking in 'strange tongues'. Speaking in tongues represents a powerful gift of the Holy Spirit – to 'say the unsayable: to want to say something other than what is spoken, that is the function of the symbolic'.[17] The leaders (there are always more than one person leading the services) and the members alternate in the ecstatic and urgent use of speech. What does it matter if the vocabulary is limited and frequently incorrect? What is important is the invasion of reality by the magic of speech, which simultaneously allows one to 'comprehend the world which has been created' and to 'foresee the possibilities of a creations which have not yet come to be'.[18] The diversity of words, music and gestures, both individual and collective, does not follow any predetermined order. The sermon can also be improvised and changed on the spot 'according to the guidance of the Holy Spirit'. This powerful network of internal communication links members together in their most profound needs as well as in their most elemental and immediate hopes. The word moves hearts (emotion) and pockets (offerings). The flood of sounds, above all speaking in tongues (*glossolalia*), does not limit itself to an inner process, but goes beyond the self in an expres-

---

[16] An expression used by Peter Beyer when referring to religion as 'a type of communication based on the immanent/transcendent polarity', among others, like 'life/death, good/evil, yin/yang, liberation/suffering'. (See *Religion and Globalization*, London: Sage, 1994, p. 6.)

[17] Paul Ricoeur, op. cit., p. 14.

[18] Leandro Konder, 'O paradoxo da linguagem' (The Paradox of Language), *O Globo* newspaper, Rio de Janeiro, 29 March 1998.

sion which is 'originally political. Through the spoken word, they express their solidarity with their own roots, with the poor and downtrodden of their country.'[19]

That is how it probably happened on the day of Pentecost. The recently formed Christian community lived through the interregnum between Jesus's physical presence and the promise of receiving 'power when the Holy Spirit has come upon you'.[20] The sign of that transcendental power manifests itself through the explosion of words – a radical act of communication of the 'mighty works of God' to all the people and all languages.[21] The events in Acts may be compared to the biblical narrative of the tower of Babel – both unfold under the sign of the Word. But, paradoxically, the unity to which Babel aspired, when 'the whole earth had one language and the same words',[22] was scattered by Yahweh ('Come, let us go down, and there confuse their language, that they may not understand one another's speech'). During Pentecost the various tribes which were gathered in Jerusalem – 'Parthians and Medes and Elamites and residents of Mesopotamia, Judea and Cappadocia, Pontus and Asia, Phrygia and Pamphylia, Egypt and the parts of Libya belonging to Cyrene, and visitors from Rome, both Jews and proselytes, Cretans and Arabians'[23] – were 'amazed and perplexed' to hear in their own tongues the telling of 'the mighty works of God.'[24] From the geographical scattering there blooms an unexpected unity, which depends not on a common historical language, but the power of a supernatural communication.

As is the case with all symbols and myth, the significance of Babel and Pentecost extends beyond the stories and images expressed in the biblical narratives. They gesture towards another, hidden reality which exists beyond the contingent moment when the texts were produced and thus, 'in a new cultural and historic context', overcomes the '*horizon* of the original narrative'.[25] At Babel, there were many different voices speaking one sole tongue; at Pentecost the many tongues make up *one* speech, with one sole meaning being understood by all. At that historical moment, a beginning is announced and the message of human salvation proclaimed ('So those who received his word were baptized, and there were added that day about three thousand souls'[26]).

Why did God condemn the intense effort of men seeking the apparent advantage of cultivating a single language? Babel represented the domi-

[19] Walter J. Hollenweger, 'The Pentecostal Elites and the Pentecostal Poor – a Missed Dialogue?', p. 205.
[20] Acts 1:8.
[21] Acts 2:11.
[22] Genesis 11:1 and 7.
[23] Acts 2:9-11.
[24] Acts 2:11.
[25] J. Severino Croatto, op. cit., p. 23.
[26] Acts 2:41.

nation of one culture over others, limiting the freedom to give a name to things according to the understanding and experience of each society ('Out of the ground the Lord God formed every beast of the field and every bird of the air, and brought them to the man to see what he would call them'[27]). Yahweh himself possessed many names (El, Elah, Elohim, El'Shaddai, Peniel, Adonai, etc.), according to his creatures' perception of his infinite powers. One name, one sole language, would reduce reality, the diversity of creation and the acts of God ('A tongue is destiny, a form not only of speaking but of being'[28]).

But this gigantic human effort, defying heaven and earth, is not limited to a question of language. The tower of Babel was a religious monument constructed in steps (a stepped tower or *ziggurat*) which already existed in Babylon (for which Babel became the Hebrew name), where cults worshipped the stars. These monuments were symbols of idolatry and human pride, foreign to the faith held by Israel. Besides its function as a bridge between heaven and earth, the tower included a special part reserved for 'sacred weddings' (*hierogamy*) and occasional meetings between the king and God Himself. Babel aspired to global religious domination (a tower 'whose apex pierced the skies') and simultaneously to political and social control ('Let us build a city').[29] Humans attempted to discover, through their own knowledge, the hidden God.[30] Their union by means of a sole language and a city was to symbolise the overcoming of their human limitations and their ascension into the divine realm.[31] God scatters them and confounds their language.[32]

---

[27] Genesis 2:19.

[28] A concept of Johann Gottfried Herder (1744-1803), poet, translator, literary critic, philosopher and theologian, quoted by Octavio Paz, 'Hablar y decir, leer y contemplar' (Speak and say, read and contemplate), *Vuelta* magazine, Mexico, March 1982. Paz also quotes Cassirer: 'El hombre no solamente piensa al mundo a través del lenguaje; su visión del mundo está ya determinado por su lenguaje' (Man does not merely think of the world by means of his language; his vision of the world is already determined by his language).

[29] *Vocabulário de teologia bíblica*, op. cit., article 'Babel/Babilônia' and *Como ler a Bíblia* (How to Read the Bible), several authors, chap. 'Por que a confusão das linguas em Babel?' (Why the Confusion of Languages in Babel?) by Franz J. Stendebach, S. Paulo: Edições Paulinas, 1983, pp. 26-32. Cities - urban life - perhaps even provoked a certain form of rejection, as the first builder, according to Genesis (4:17), was Cain who was damned as the murderer of his brother Abel.

[30] In his dialectic analysis of the tragic view in the *Pensées* of Pascal and in Racine's plays, Lucien Goldmann establishes an opposition between an intellectual, practical and loving structure, and spirituality and mysticism. In the chapter 'The Christian Religion' he states: 'En realité, le christianisme est vrai parce qu'il nous demande de croire en un Dieu paradoxal et contradictoire, qui correspond parfaitement à tout ce que nous savons de la condition et des aspirations de l'homme: en un Dieu devenu homme, un Dieu crucifié, un Dieu médiateur.' (*Le Dieu Caché*, Paris: Gallimard, 1975, p. 341)

[31] Paul Tillich *Systematic Theology*, London: SCM Press, 1978.

[32] In Hebrew *lashôn* means both 'language' and 'tongue' (Andrée Chouraqui, in *No princípio Gênesis*, Rio: Imago, 1995, p. 117). The author, in his famous translation, uses the word

The interpretation of Babel as a movement from below to above, from man to God, confirms the Pentecost as a divine action, in reverse movement from above to below, from God to man. At Babel, the immanent drove human actions, and God was conceived in terms of the human world. At Pentecost tongues and languages come from the Holy Spirit and perform the role of reconciliation between men. The crucial moment of Pentecost comes as a noise from heaven, 'like the rush of a mighty wind' and 'the tongues as of fire, distributed and resting on each one of them' at the initiative of the Holy Spirit.[33] The contemporary emphasis on glossolalia, proclaimed as a gift of the Holy Spirit, is a sign of a genuine personal transformation. As in the biblical story, 'a mighty wind' blows through churches, touching all those present and producing effects which are more than a simple moment of personal ecstasy. What matters in 'speaking in tongues', as Octavio Paz explains, is not so much the meaning of its components, or its symbolic import, but rather its evocation of a 'signification beyond meaning [*un sens au dela du sens*]'.[34] According to the testimony of those touched by this indescribable experience, it is the Holy Spirit descending upon them – 'like a wind, you know? .... You speak but do not understand. Not even those who are with you can understand you .... And after I leave the church feeling like another person.'[35] In contrast to the rationality of Babel, the religious ecstasy of Pentecost moves hearts, placing emotion above knowledge. What is important is the passion and its 'broad sociological, historical, transcendental implications'.[36]

Returning to our biblical stories, we can see that whereas the tower of Babel created confusion and the dispersion of nations, Pentecost announces the possibility of a new unity among people. This unity, which transcends

---

'tongue', because 'the French language establishes a language by the internal organ, the "tongue" ': 'Now the whole earth had one language and few words.' (Genesis 11:1). One should recall that the narratives contained in Genesis were prepared by at least four writers, only in the early part of the first millennium BC, when the Jewish people established themselves in Canaan and David was anointed king. According to Jewish theology, Good and Evil came from Yahweh and thus all what happened was attributed to him (see Isaiah 45: 7).

[33] Acts 2: 2-3. The term Holy Spirit was used by rabbis 'to indicate the presence of God on earth. A method of distinguishing the God we experience or know as separate from the absolutely transcendental divinity which is beyond our reach. In Christianity, the Holy Spirit was to become the third "person" of the Trinity.' See Karen Armstrong, *A History of God - Four Millennia in the Search by Judaism, Christianity and Islam*, London: Heinemann, 1993.

[34] Octavio Paz, op. cit.

[35] Selections from an interview with a member of the Assembly of God church, Rio de Janeiro, 1995.

[36] Paulo Leminski in the chapter 'Poesia: a paixão" (Poetry: a passion) in *Os sentidos da paixão* (The Senses of Passion), São Paulo: Funarte / Companhia das Letras, 1989, pp. 283-6.

linguistic differences and gives communal value to the individual emotional experience, transforms Pentecostalism into the greatest expression of religious communication. 'The symbolic and sacramental aspect of language gives a meaning to man's cultural and spiritual efforts. The history of human culture and man's struggle for spirituality (we can substitute "spirituality" with "humanity" for those who are allergic to traces of a religious past) would have been inconceivable without language as a symbolic transmitter of values.'[37] The Pentecostal process of transnationalisation starts with 'speaking in tongues' – the word – the culminating moment in the experience of the early church. The gospel extends throughout the Mediterranean world, breaks through religious, cultural and social frontiers (Jewish and gentile, for example) and reveals the new faith as anything but a mere Jewish sect. The movement breaches the walls of the largest cities, even Rome, the capital of the empire; today, Pentecostalism breaks down rigid traditional ecclesiastic structures and joins the secular, modern world, reaching out in all languages to all peoples and nations.

Go into to all the world. Space is the second dimension in the Pentecostal experience. While on the one hand Pentecostalism preaches the rejection of the outside world, on the other hand the world is transformed into the most intense battleground. In the battle against Satan it is necessary to invade his territory, to spread the testimony of conversion to the very heart of unbelief and sin. The missionary concept of the Pentecostal churches has that centrifugal force – from the evangelisation of family members, to companions at work, the unknown passerby, new neighbourhoods, cities and countries. Their national – and worldwide – growth, contrary to the experience of the majority of the historic churches, occurs through action that involves all the components of the movement: the institution, their own communication media, pastors, workers, and a great number of converts. The fact that theological or academic training is limited is no obstacle, and may even be a point in their favour, encouraging their adaption to local cultures (and languages) and their response to the objective and subjective needs of the population to whom they are sent.

If in the original Pentecostal experience the spreading of the Good News started from 'one place', from a centre, there are now many centres and places scattered around the world. The astonishing institutional independence of the Pentecostal movement sends new missionaries to

---

[37] Henrik Skolimowski, 'Poder, mito e realidade' (Power, Myth and Reality), *Humanidades*, V, 16, edited by the Universidade de Brasilia, 1988, p. 108. The author elaborates on the theme under the subtitle *A linguagem como poder* (Language as Power). Another author, the philosopher John Searle, when speaking of '*linguagem como ação*' (language as action), affirms that language is a certain type of reality, in his relation with the world and his concept 'as a form of human behaviour.' (Interview with *Folha de S. Paulo, Mais!* supplement, São Paulo, 5 July 1998).

locations totally unknown to them from a geographical or linguistic point of view. It does not matter; everything is *closer* today than in the times of the early church; and, in any case, they possess a tongue which transcends any national language. We could even say that the geographical space of Christianity has grown spectacularly in present times as a result of the rediscovery of the personal responsibility of the evangelical command: 'Go into all the world and preach the gospel to the whole creation.'[38]

This untiring modern missionary zeal contrasts, once again, with the paralysing phenomenon of Babel and its spatial concentration. Here we have a fundamental difference between space and location.[39] While in Genesis we are told of the reduction of the world to one tongue and one place, in the book of Acts 'the house where they were' opens on to new spaces, be they friendly or hostile. The event is repeated in Los Angeles and continues to express itself in the global advance of Pentecostalism. In the vertical aspect of the event in Acts we find a predominantly God-humanity-God relationship, as opposed to the horizontal aspect of Babel, where the emphasis on human power and knowledge indicates another narrative, which emphasises the horizontal relations among men. Although both places lead to dispersion, the tower produced confusion and the house (the temple) understanding.

In many ways, the conquest of physical space in the Pentecostal realm starts with the size of their monumental churches, where one or two thousand people can easily gather with a regularity which is now uncommon in traditional Protestant churches. The internal space allows an intense movement of people, as if in an indoor parade. This internal parade, however, is not limited by the church walls, but continues outside. The flow of humanity between the church and the street expresses, metaphorically, a new link between the sacred and the profane, a bridge between clergy and public, and projects outwardly the sign of solidarity between those who are within and those who have not yet entered. But the conquest of space for Christ does not end there. Beyond the street lies the neighbourhood, the city, the world – targeted by all Pentecostal evangelism and social outreach, aided, more recently, by its entry into the political scene (already present in Brazil, Evangelical political parties were recently established in EI Salvador and Nicaragua[40]). The territorial expansion has another

---

[38] Mark 16:15.

[39] Richard Sennett, *Flesh and Stone: The Body and the City in Western Civilization*, London: Faber & Faber, 1994, creatively explores the historic development of cities and the relationship between space, location and time and the human body.

[40] There are countless examples of close ties between the Pentecostal churches and military regimes in Latin America. In 1974 the dictator Pinochet, accompanied by high authorities of his government, were present by invitation at the inauguration of the imposing cathedral of the Pentecostal Methodist Church in Santiago, Chile; their appearance was repeated over several years. In Guatemala, Protestant fundamentalists endorsed the rise of a general (Rios Montt) to the presidency of that country. In Nicaragua, on the initiative of young

component, expressed by churches like the UCKG in its attempt at universality: the battle against demons. Their presence in daily life, which may even lead to deliverance sessions involving church members themselves, extends across the globe. According to the UCKG, the kingdom of Satan is simultaneously local, regional and universal, and believers must obey the divine command to fight against him, wherever he may be.[41]

Religious experience, Joachim Wach once said, is multiple and manifests itself in many forms.[42] In this sense it is also an experience which brings together different spaces in life. It does not stop at the level of the individual. Durkheim had already pointed out the apparent contradiction between 'individual personality' and 'social solidarity'.[43] These two dimensions, united in the Pentecostal conversion, become a compelling force of taking 'the gospel to the whole creation'.

One day is as a thousand years. In Babel, the calendar belongs to men. To overcome the limitations of *chronos*, they build a tower to reach the Eternal. According to the book of Genesis, it is not the first time that humanity had displeased its Creator. The fall in the Garden of Eden and the flood were examples of radical action when 'Yahweh saw that the wickedness of man was great in the earth'.[44] Babel reveals a more daring and elaborate attitude, in which the technology of the early biblical days becomes the expression of the knowledge and power of man to overcome space and time and go beyond the established limits. In the same way that the mechanical clocks placed in the towers of mediaeval churches were interpreted as a measurement of the rhythm of God,[45] the immense

---

Baptists, some Pentecostal churches supported the revolution of the Sandinistas. A study of the 'political variations of Pentecostalism in Latin America' has not yet been done in any great depth. See Francisco Cartaxo Rolim, *Pentecostalismo – Brasil e América Latina,* Petrópolis: Editora Vozes, 1995, pp. 66ff and 160ff.

[41] In a certain way, curiously enough, the Pentecostal emphasis on the struggle against the devil is much in line with the vision of Martin Luther, who referred to him countless times and at whom, on one occasion, he threw an inkwell. In the New Testament the *diabolos*, responsible for an infinity of sicknesses, is mentioned about 85 times, as opposed to the Old Testament, where mention is made merely three or four times.

[42] Francisco Cartaxo Rolim (ed.), *A religião numa sociedade em transformação* (Religion in a Society in Transformation), Petrópolis: Editora Vozes, 1997, p. 79. Wach also referred to the religious phenomenon as a radical experience of ultimate and essential reality, in the same line of thought as R. Otto (see *Sociology of Religion and Theology*, Madrid: Instituto Fé y Solidaridad/Editorial Cuadernos para el Diálogo, 1975, p. 42.).

[43] Otto, op. cit., p. 26.

[44] Genesis 6: 5.

[45] An interesting article by Henrik Skolimowski, 'Poder, mito e realidade', op. cit., p. 104, mentions this example when analysing the occidental concept of material progress as compared to alternatives of power in the sphere of moral authority.

ziggurats were to penetrate the secrets of creation, previously hidden in the flavour of the fruit of the tree of knowledge of Good and Evil.

At Pentecost time is something else: *kairos*, 'the fullness of time', according to its meaning in the New Testament; a moment of a 'historical-universal vision .... selected to be the centre of history'. It is a 'matter of vision' and not an 'object of analysis and calculation such as could be given in psychological or sociological terms'.[46] The experience of *chronos* is quantitative, and that of *kairos* qualitative. The great event at Pentecost creates an expectancy of an end to history, culminating with the second coming of Christ and his reign over the earth for a thousand years. Perhaps the apostle Peter, an active participant in the events described in the book of Acts, tried to soften the meaning of that early millennial expectancy. To those who asked 'where is the promise of his coming?', he proclaimed that 'with the Lord one day is as a thousand years and a thousand years as one day'.[47]

The age-old polemics about the coming of the millennium lose their meaning when confronted with the insertion of infinite time into the routine stories produced in Pentecostal daily life. In the Pentecostal movements of today, Peter's warning has taken on an uncontrollable symbolic power. The expectations of the millennium have been transferred to daily life through a literal interpretation of his answer: if a thousand years is 'as one day', why wait? Why not reinvest those promises in the things of daily life, including especially the power over the devil? The post-millennial optimism is transferred to daily living. But the *qualitative* aspect of *quantitative* time does not exclude the historical duality of Good and Evil. On the contrary, the Pentecostal articulation of the concept of Evil, as a personalised expression of the adversary of God on earth, is taken to an extreme.

In this conception, it is no longer a matter of waiting for the day when Satan will be bound ('He laid hold of the dragon, that old serpent, which is the Devil, Satan, and bound him a thousand years'[48]), because he may be bound every day, especially during the Friday exorcisms. The devil of daily life is more real than the Satan of the millennium, and must be eliminated each time he is encountered. The incorporation of this concept into the conversion process has both stimulated the transnationalisation of the contemporary Pentecostal movement and given rise to an eschatological view of abbreviating time and conquering all the space in the world. The blending of everyday time and millennial time reveals in many ways the very ethos of Pentecostalism, bringing into the

---

[46] Words of the theologian Paul Tillich, interpreting Paul's concepts about *kairós*, op. cit., p. 667.

[47] II Peter 3, 4 and 8.

[48] Revelations 20: 2.

daily timeframe the experience of the glorious promise of a thousand years in the kingdom of Christ.

Transnationalisation and the future of religions

The fusion of time – the mundane and the millennial – cannot be contained within the limits of a place or church. Space is the Pentecostal vocation, the word its instrument of conquest. It is in the missionary work of the new Pentecostal churches, that the word, space and time best express the meaning of the day of Pentecost. Time and space are recovered through the spoken word 'to all who are far off'.[49] I believe I cite the Brazilian theologian Rubem Alves when he commented on what Karl Mannheim calls the 'esprit de corps'; that is, how the nature of a 'predominant desire' determines the 'sequence, order and sense of value of isolated experiences': 'The reality which a group constructs socially is not limited by time. Desire also builds a physical place. It means not only clocks and calendars, but also maps and roads. It is necessary that not only time but also space become significant. Space and time cannot be separated. Reality is always built as a spatial-temporal synthesis'.[50]

However, the transnationalisation of Pentecostalism is not limited to this model of religion. It is not the only form of a particular culture, as Max Weber insinuates when writing about religion as an important element in processes of modernisation. Is the wave of new religions and their syncretisms, the growth of countless 'New Age' movements at the end of the second Christian millennium, a sign that we are witnessing a return to spirituality? Are secularisation and disenchantment losing their place in history? The current debates between sociologists and anthropologists on this issue cannot deny the reality of a truly global explosion of religious phenomena.[51] The revival of Islam, its renewed missionary zeal, and its radicalisation have dramatically increased the number of its faithful (16 per cent of the world's population, not very far from the Christians' 23 per cent).[52] It can be compared to the enthusiasm of the Pentecostal expansion, especially in its conception of the relationship

---

[49] Acts 2: 39. The text probably refers to pagans, as confirmed in Acts 22:21 and elsewhere.

[50] Rubem Alves, *Protestantismo e repressão* (Protestantism and Repression), São Paulo: Editora Atica, 1979, p. 30.

[51] Antônio Flávio Pierucci, 'Reencantamento e dessecularização' (Reenchantment and De-Secularisation), *Novos Estudos CEBRAP*, São Paulo, November 1997. The author, disenchanted with a sociology of religion based on the 'end of the process of secularisation', even lists the names of authors and writings in favour of and against the theory of secularisation. The long article does not take into account the debate among theologians on 'the death of God' (and of secularisation) and trends which defended the thesis of the return of what is sacred – which could have enriched this interesting piece.

[52] According to UNESCO, in the year 2000 Islam would have surpassed Catholicism by about 100,000 followers.

between the individual and society: 'Islam is not so much a religion but a general way of life. One is a Muslim every day and at every moment.'[53] This personal conviction and its appropriation of every facet of life seems to indicate a revival of fundamentalism (if it actually was in recession) as a consequence of processes of modernisation and globalisation. Most world religions appear to be embracing or reaffirming different versions of religious fundamentalism.

In this 'rebirth' of religion evident today throughout world we cannot ignore the aggressive, even bellicose, nature of both Pentecostalism and Islam. Islam gives a sacred aspect to its struggle through the unification of the state and religion. Pentecostalism, as we have seen, gathers its forces in a battle without respite against the demons which infest society and the bodies and souls of its own followers. Both grow largely among the poorer sections of the population, with the substantial difference that Islam participates in the world scene through a kind of revitalisation of its own characteristics, while Pentecostalism takes over the essence of geographic sub-units (nation, county, region).[54]

What is the future of this unforeseeable expansion in the light of the contrast between the disastrous human experience of the tower of Babel and the manifestation of the holy Spirit on the day of Pentecost? In its plurality, Pentecostal religiosity becomes a personal virtue, making religion 'a characteristic of a person' which nonetheless goes beyond a mere individualistic attitude. Individual religion is a bit less than a contradiction *in terminis*, because religion is an aspect of man in society and an elementary social reality. Its difference in relation to individual religiosity lies in the fact that 'personal religiosity underlines a global interpretation of which it is also an integral part'.[55] In this sense the great individual outpouring of Pentecostalism favours a mission beyond itself. 'My parish is the world', the Methodist revivalist John Wesley said in the eighteenth century. This may be one of the paradoxes of the Pentecostal being.[56] In it, however, is revealed a personal and social meaning of radical view of faith, of intimacy with the transcendental: a life based on the power of the word, a new space of life and a new time which redeems the world. In its utopian view of the future brought into the quotidian, all aspects of life

---

[53] 'O ressurgimento do Islamismo' (The Revival of Islam), *Tempo e Presença*, Rio de Janeiro, March/April 1995, transcribed from *Cadernos Terceiro Mundo*, 182, Feb. 1995. The quotation is from the Zimbabwean Abdul Abdur Rahman, ex-Catholic, converted in 1988.

[54] Peter Beyer, op. cit., pp. 2-3.

[55] I borrow these last ideas from Raimon Panikkar, 'La religion de l'avenir', *INTERculture* (Centre Interculturel Monchanin), XXIII, 2, spring 1990, p. 102.

[56] Philip J. Williams, exploring the growth of Pentecostalism, points out some paradoxes (spiritual refuge versus symbolic protest, authoritarianism versus democracy, submission of women versus liberation, and breaking away versus continuity), stating that this has not stopped its growth during the last few years (Edward I. Cleary, op. cit., pp. 194-7).

are under religious inspiration. Babel, on the contrary, symbolises the control of the world by means of the 'ideology of autonomy', of a 'myth of self-centred development'. Pentecost, showing itself to the world of its time, reveals the beginning of a transnationalisation, today ruled by the universal concept of its mission.

Another paradox lies in its rejection-acceptance of the world. Breaking with the past (worldly life, other Christian denominations or religions) no longer means withdrawing from the world but launching out to save it – what is important is to coexist with the problems of those who have not yet 'given themselves to Christ'. As human existence is the object of salvation, the contradiction between profane and sacred is simultaneously accepted and overcome. A schism in the religious field, according to Weber, arises from the tension between the radical search for salvation and the worldly institutional order.

In the case of Pentecostalism, the activism arising from this deep evangelical responsibility would explain in part the superficial theology and lack of deeper biblical and ecclesiastical reflection. Or will the Pentecostal experience be a basis for a new theology, a new paradigm of salvation?[57] After all, it was from the presence of Christ in the world, and the experience of the apostles in the primitive church, that Paul and others developed the bases of the Christian theology. The Pentecostal theologian Juan Sepúlveda states that Chilean Pentecostalism has its theology, but that it must be sought in the witnessing, in the experience of the Holy Spirit.[58] The theologian Harvey Cox follows the same line of thought when he says that theology should 'follow in the direction of the analysis of the experience and not of the exegesis'.[59]

Babel and Pentecost reveal something of the extreme complexity of human existence. Both events – with all their symbolic force, millennia from each other – widen the field of meanings we can ascribe to the relationship between God and mankind and among human beings

---

[57] The topic – a new paradigm of salvation – is thoroughly treated in the second part of the book *Pentecostalism and the Future of Christian Churches – Promises, Limitations, Challenges* by Richard Shaull, op. cit. (see footnote 1). One should remember the reference by Emilio Willems to the relationship between 'an emotional experience of the individual' and the 'intellectualization' as one of the characteristics of North American Protestantism of the twentieth century, 'weak in theology, but strong in action', according to the words of William Warren Sweet (*Followers of the New Faith,* Nashville: Vanderbilt University Press, 1967).

[58] Juan Sepúlveda, *Na força do Espírito – Os pentecostais na América Latina. Um desafio às igrejas históricas* (The Power of the Spirit – The Pentecostals in Latin America: a Challenge to the Historical Churches) in Benjamin Gutiérrez and Leonildo Silveira Campos (eds), São Paulo: Aipral-Pendão Real-Ciências da Religião, 1996, p. 68. The author quotes the theologian Jürgen Moltmann, who contrasts the theology of revelation, for pastors and priests, with the theology of experience, 'preeminently a theology of laity'.

[59] The affirmation by Cox (*A festa dos foliões* [The Feast of Fools], Petrópolis: Editora Vozes, 1974, p. 171) refers to the book by Peter Berger, *A Rumour of Angels.*

themselves. For the Pentecostal movement, this 'plurality of meanings' reveals itself in a new form of language, opens a new space of action and anticipates the time of 'a new heaven and a new earth.'[60]

[60] Revelation 21:1.

BIBLIOGRAPHY

Alves, Rubem, *Protestantismo e repressão*, São Paulo: Editora Atica, 1979.

Armstrong, Karen, *A History of God – Four Millennia in the Search by Judaism, Christianity and Islam*, London: Heinemann, 1993.

Berger, Peter, *A Rumour of Angels: Modern Society and the Rediscovery of the Supernatural*, London: Allen Lane, 1970.

Beyer, Peter, *Religion and Globalization*, London: Sage, 1994.

Chouraqui, Andrée, *No princípio Gênesis*, Rio de Janeiro: Imago, 1995.

Como ler a Bíblia, São Paulo: Edições Paulinas, 1983

Corten, André, *Os pobres e o Espírito Santo. O Pentecostalismo no Brasil*, Petrópolis, 1996.

Croatto, Severino, *Uma hermenêutica da liberdade,* São Paulo: Edições Paulinas, 1981.

d'Épinay, Christian Lalive, 'Religião, espiritualidade e sociedade', *Cadernos de ISER*, no. 6, March 1966.

Gadamer, Hans Georg, *Verdad y Método*, Madrid: Cristianidad, 1977.

Goldmann, Lucien, *Le dieu caché*, Paris: Éditions Gallimard, 1975.

Gutiérrez, Benjamin and Campos, Leonildo Silveira (eds), *Na força do Espírito - Os pentecostais na América Latina: um desafio às igrejas históricas*, São Paulo: Aipral-Pendão Real-Ciências da Religião, 1996.

Os sentidos da paixão, São Paulo, Funarte / Companhia das Letras, 1989.

Otto, Rudolf, *Sociology of Religion and Theology*, Madrid: Instituto Fé y Solidaridad, Editorial Cuadernos para el Diálogo, 1975.

Pace, Enzo, *Sociologia da religião*, São Paulo: Edições Paulinas, 1990.

Palmer, Samuel, 'Conversão pessoal e a comunidade de afetos como sinais de libertação', Santiago de Chile, 1991 (mimeo)

Panikkar, Raimon, 'La religion de l'avenir', in *INTERculture* (Centre Interculturel Monchanin), vol. 13, no. 2, Spring 1990.

Pears, David, *As Idéias de Wittgenstein*, São Paulo: Cultrix, 1973.

Pierucci, Antônio Flávio, 'Reencantamento e dessecularização', *Novos Estudos CEBRAP*, São Paulo, Nov. 1997.

Ricoeur, Paul, *Freud. Una interpretación de la cultura*, Mexico, Siglo XXI, 1973.

Rolim, Francisco Cartaxo, *Pentecostalismo – Brasil e América Latina*, Petrópolis: Editora Vozes, 1995.

—— (ed.), *A religião numa sociedade em transformação*, Petrópolis: Editora Vozes, 1997.

Sennett, Richard, *Flesh and Stone: The Body and the City in Western Civilization*, London: Faber & Faber, 1994.

Shaull, Richard and César, Waldo, *Pentecostalismo e futuro das igrejas cristãs*, Petrópolis: Editora Vozes, 1999.

Skolimowski, Henrik, 'Poder, mito e realidade', *Humanidades* vol. 16, no. 5. Editora Universidade de Brasilia, 1988.

Tillich, Paul, *Systematic Theology*, London: SCM Press, 1978.

Vieille, Paul, 'Du transnational au politique-monde?', *Peuples méditerranéens*, 35-36, April-Sept. 1986, pp. 309-38.

Vocabulário de teologia biblica, Petrópolis: Editora Vozes, 1984.

Willems, Emilio, *Followers of the New Faith*, Nashville: Vanderbilt University Press, 1967.

GLOBALISATION AND PENTECOSTAL SUCCESS

André Droogers

The characteristic of Pentecostalism that seems to have attracted the most attention is its rapid expansion. The interpretations given to Pentecostal expansion have differed according to each author's paradigmatic preference. Some, for instance, have worked from a modernisation perspective (Pentecostals make good citizens of modern society), whereas others have taken a neo-Marxist starting-point (Pentecostals seek relief from oppression or resist it in their own particular way). In the 1990s, partly as an elaboration and modification of previous approaches, the concept of globalisation has come to the fore (Pentecostalism flourishes under the conditions that globalisation creates, or is even part of that process). In any case, both currently and in the past, whatever the theoretical framework used, most attention is given to factors that are external to Pentecostalism itself. Only rarely are specific characteristics of Pentecostalism taken into account and a more idiosyncratic explanation sought.

In this chapter I take the cultural anthropology of religion as a disciplinary frame of reference, in order to take a closer look at the internal religious characteristics of Pentecostalism and their articulation within the external circumstances of globalisation. I propose to do this because I believe that if the starting point of analysis is the prevailing external social processes, then we will never be able to do justice to the specifics of a particular religion such as Pentecostalism. These social processes usually affect other religions as well, whether they are growing or not, and the particularities of a specific religious situation are usually insufficiently explained in the light of these external processes alone. I suggest that the search for a more complete explanation for the expansion of these religions should start from the particularities of a specific religion and proceed from there to the influence of, and articulation with, external social processes. Only in such a case is it possible to clarify why different religious reactions to similar processes occur and why a new adherent opts for one of the religions on the market, rather than another.[1]

Some theoretical issues

Even when analyses give priority to the typical religious particularities, the complex nature of the connection between religion and society must

---

[1] For a discussion of this problem with regard to Brazilian Umbanda and Pentecostalism see P. Fry and G. Howe, 'Duas respostas à aflição: Umbanda e Pentecostalismo', *Debate e Crítica*, no. 6, 1975, pp. 75-94.

also be taken into account. A plea to use religion itself as the starting point does not necessarily imply either a causal one-way relation between the religious and the social, not even in the case of a religion such as Pentecostalism, with its clearly marked boundaries and large degree of autonomy, or even a relation of opposition with regard to the surrounding culture and society. Any religion can influence non-religious social processes, just as it too can be influenced by them; equally, some degree of correlation, or complementarity, can exist between religion and social processes. My purpose, then, is not to prove that Pentecostal expansion is an internally propelled phenomenon, unfettered by the external social conditions that surround it. That would be as one-sided as a sociological reductionism of religious expansion to those same social conditions, in this case globalisation. To refuse either form of unidirectional explanation means that some view on the mutual implications of the interaction between religion and society must be developed. This would amount to summarising the whole history of the discipline of the anthropology (and sociology) of religion, a task far beyond my scope here. In the light of recent insights, however, I do feel that a few useful remarks can be made.[2]

As long as the discipline has existed, cultural anthropology has struggled with its self-imposed distinctions. The basic questions raised here are: how does the autonomy of cultures relate to contact between them; how are the order and continuity a cultural framework guarantees reconciled with rupture and change; does culture make people (a culturalist view) or do people make culture (a constructivist view); to what degree is a culture homogeneous; how are the universal human and the particular cultural related? These general questions are not valid for cultures alone, but for religions as well, including Pentecostalism, especially when studying their connection with the globalisation process. More specific questions can be added, of course, particularly with regard to religion's relations with the social and cultural context. Does religion reflect society around it, and compromise with it, or does it stand in opposition to its central values? Has this position been inspired by religious views and experiences? Does it determine its adepts' identity or is there room for individual initiative? When Pentecostalism spreads to other cultures, how does its specific character relate to that of those other cultures and to human nature in general? And how does this relate to the internal organisation of that religion?

[2] See for example Stuart Hall and Paul du Gay (eds), *Questions of Cultural Identity*, London, 1996; D. Holland, W. Lachicotte Jr, D. Skinner and C. Cain, *Identity and Agency in Cultural Worlds*, Cambridge, MA, 1998; R. Keesing, 'Theories of Culture Revisited' in R. Borofsky (ed.), *Assessing Cultural Anthropology*, New York, 1994, pp. 301-12; S. Ortner, 'Theory in Anthropology Since the Sixties', *Comparative Studies in Society and History*, vol. 26, no. 1, 1984, pp. 126-66; C. Strauss and N. Quinn, 'A Cognitive/Cultural Anthropology' in Borofsky, *Assessing Cultural Anthropology*, pp. 284-300; C. Strauss and N. Quinn, *A Cognitive Theory of Cultural Meaning*, Cambridge, 1997.

In the culturalist perspective, culture – including religion as a cultural phenomenon – is viewed as a more or less fixed and autonomous complex of ideas and actions shared by the members of a human group and through which they are socialised. It guarantees continuity and order, just as it facilitates identification by individual group members with its central ideas and values, with its standardised behaviour and with their fellow-group members. Correspondingly, identity is understood, in an essentialist way, as a constant and consistent self-understanding, the hard core of the cultural personality. Since Pentecostalism is often depicted as strict and even as fundamentalist, as well as influential in determining a person's attitude to life, a culturalist approach might at first sight seem adequate.

In the globalising setting of the current situation, however, the boundaries of these autonomous cultures are becoming ever more perforated. One might even say that religions have played a major role in perforating cultural boundaries, in spreading their messages to people of cultures not previously primarily associated with them. In any case, the times of splendid cultural isolation, if ever they existed, are now well and truly over. It follows, then, that a constructivist critique of the culturalist view is to be recommended, because it does justice to individual initiatives and to global change, in the same way that it also points to dynamism, flexibility and difference. People construct their identity in an unessentialist and strategic way, depending on the context, and using elements from multiple selves, and a large, and nowadays intercultural, repertoire of scripts.[3] Cultural reality, therefore, is understood to be in a constant state of shift and fragmentation, with an ever-growing library of scripts. New religions, including Pentecostalism, add to it their own scripts, just as do all the other partners in the globalisation process.

However, this constructivism should not swing to the other extreme, where all is in a state of change and profound chaos. Order and dynamism, culturalism and constructivism, therefore, should all be components of a framework that can serve to clarify the relationship between religion and society. In the case under examination here, this means that Pentecostalism should not be thought of as a phenomenon with a constant, more or less fixed, autonomous position, nor as a constantly adapting and changing religion. We will have instead to look for unity in diversity and diversity in unity. Similarly, Pentecostals should not be seen as people with a fixed religious position, nor as champions in adapting to changing circumstances. It is much more a question of studying the localised form which basic Pentecostalism adopts in specific cases.

To this a remark must be added about the relationship between the actors and their social context. Neither the one-sided determinism of

---

[3] e.g. J. Friedman, *Cultural Identity and Global Process*, London, 1994; Hall and Du Gay, *Questions of Cultural Identity*.

culturalism, nor the equally one-sided voluntarism of constructivism, offers very much help in understanding how Pentecostal actors operate in the globalising world. These protagonists are both constrained and empowered by their social context; they submit to socialisation and social control, just as they act in their own idiosyncratic way and may thus take innovative initiatives that will appeal to others and which, in the end, may change those constraining structures, be they symbolic or social.

On a much wider scale, globalisation processes have led to renewed attention being focused on the tension between the common and the particular, between the universally human and the specifically cultural. If everyone in the world were submitted to the same global processes, that which is common to all humanity would obviously receive more attention than that which is exclusively cultural. Contact between people of different cultures exploits the source of common humanity. Whereas both a culturalist and a constructivist approach appear to emphasise particularity, be it at the culture or actor level, the common human element will always need to be taken into account as well. In the case of Pentecostalism, this element is important because, for example, similar trance-like phenomena occur in other religions, and yet they remain typically Pentecostal by virtue of the concrete form they take. Just as the human gift for culture can only be observed in actual cultures, so too, what is universally human can only be studied in the context of its concrete manifestations. Attempts to study the way in which universal human potential is used and interpreted thus in no way contradict the approach advocated earlier in this chapter, that is to embark on an explanation of Pentecostal growth from the premise of its own particular religious characteristics.

Some common characteristics

Despite apparent diversity within the world of Pentecostalism which I will discuss in the next section, something can nevertheless be said in a general, more or less 'culturalist', way about common Pentecostal features. This is particularly so when the ultimate goal is to understand Pentecostal expansion within the context of globalisation and in terms of its internal religious characteristics. There is, of course, some unity in diversity, as is illustrated by the internal characteristics of the churches and other Pentecostal or charismatic groups. Whilst some of these characteristics might readily be mentioned by Pentecostals themselves, some are more striking to the outside observer. In elaborating on these characteristics, it should be clear that they too appear in diverse forms and that we are dealing here with ideal types. Healing through exorcism, for example, is certainly not the same everywhere. I once witnessed how an Argentinian pastor, for instance, exorcised the 'demon of economic problems'. Local variations mean that an over-essentialist picture of Pentecostalism needs to be avoided.

A good starting-point may be the central place given to the presence of the Holy Spirit, as experienced in the gifts of healing, speaking in tongues (glossolalia) and prophecy, all of which have the human body as their locus. These gifts, or *charismata*, are available in principle to all the faithful through conversion and baptism in the Spirit. The constructivist comment, of course, would be that what really matters is what the person actually does with their potential. The generous distribution of the gifts of the Spirit is, of course, the ideal image; the reality might be different, because not all members display the same gifts in the same way, despite doctrinary equality.

Secondly, there is the conversion experience, which is often related to the first experience of the *charismata*. To many Pentecostals, conversion is a dramatic personal event, by far the most important of their lives. And when it is linked to the experience of the Spirit, it has a strong physical component. Its consequences are felt in daily life, twenty-four hours a day, seven days a week. After conversion, the claim of the faith on the lives of its converts is – at least formally – total and absolute. In giving witness to their conversion, most people divide their lives into pre- and post-conversion periods. The watershed is a primal or proleptic spiritual experience that fundamentally changes the parameters of his or her life.[4] The receiving of the gifts of the Holy Spirit usually has the effect of solving an existential problem and continues to be an important and healing resource in the ongoing struggle for life. In this context, healing must be understood in a very wide sense, including non-medical problems such as unemployment or conflicts with others. At the very moment of their conversion, people embark on a new life. The 'rebirth' metaphor is common, and is also implicit in baptism through total immersion as a physical experience. Again, we are dealing here with an ideal image, and we should bear in mind that membership includes believers who have not necessarily gone through such a dramatic experience or who do not succeed in living up to the high claims of the model, full-time, Pentecostal.

Conversion often means that a person takes leave of customs in his or her culture that are considered sinful and demonic. This may lead to the church being seen as an alternative cultural community, that substitutes the dominant culture in important respects and that may even demand the rupture of kinship ties with non-converts. In contexts where ethnic identity is salient, the brothers and sisters of the church may form a new 'tribe', as it were. The original culture will not fully disappear from the lives of such converts, but it will undergo profound changes and only those aspects that are considered harmless remain.

---

[4] I. Hexham and K. Poewe, *New Religions as Global Cultures, Making the Human Sacred*, Boulder, CO, 1997, pp. 59ff; K. Poewe, 'Rethinking the Relationship of Anthropology to Science and Religion' in K. Poewe (ed.), *Charismatic Christianity as a Global Culture*, Columbia, SC, 1994, pp. 234-58.

This leads us to a third characteristic, the so-called duality of the Pentecostal world-view. In a simple and clear manner, just as in the division of a personal life history into pre- and post-conversion phases, so too is the world divided into two parts: that of God and his believers, and that of the devil and his followers. The Pentecostal convert moves from the second to the first and feels saved in consequence. In both the social and the personal sense, the convert takes sides in the war that is said to rage between these two parts of the world. Looking back on the evil world, from whose sinfulness believers are fleeing, they are comforted by having taken the right decision. Once this fundamental choice has been made, the convert's life becomes both transparent and comprehensible. This helpful and therapeutic world-view should therefore be brought to others, indeed to as many as possible. Such a rich experience cannot be kept to oneself. There is a certain 'narrative compulsion'[5] felt by many Pentecostals, and the experience becomes truly self-fulfilling when transmitted to others. The more people accept the message, the better the world will be, until the devil is finally defeated. All people who share in the gifts of the Spirit are, in consequence, obliged to spread the 'good news'.

Pentecostal diversity

The concept of Pentecostalism is, to a certain degree, very much a social scientific construct. The term covers a variety of forms, to such a degree even that it seems difficult to determine exactly what they all have in common. In view of this diversity, the constructivist approach would seem to be more applicable than the culturalist approach discussed in the previous section. Despite their being renowned for their strictness, one's first impression is that of a huge diversity in the types of churches and movements that choose to call themselves Pentecostal.

First of all, there is much historical diversity. The first churches, founded at the beginning of the twentieth century, had a variety of precursors, thus ensuring diversity from the start, and there is no doubt that the segregation of white and black churches contributed in no small measure to this diversity.[6] Within a very short time span, Pentecostal churches were founded throughout the Americas and Europe. They are all recognisable as Pentecostal churches, but at the same time they all have their own particular profiles, depending on their history and their cultural context.[7]

[5] Personal communication from Ruth Marshall-Fratani.

[6] W. Hollenweger, *Pentecost Between Black and White, Five Case Studies on Pentecost and Politics*, Belfast, 1974, pp. 18-19.

[7] D. Míguez, *Spiritual Bonfire in Argentina: Confronting Current Theories with an Ethnographic Account of Pentecostal Growth in a Buenos Aires Suburb*, Amsterdam, 1998; D. Míguez, 'Qué Puede Agregarse a los Clásicos?': Buscando Nuevos Horizontes a los Estudios Sobre el Pentecostalismo Latinoamericano', *Estudios sobre Religión*, no. 6, 1998, pp. 4-6.

The charismatic movement, also worthy of the name 'Pentecostal' despite being part of mainstream churches, including the Roman Catholic Church,[8] emerged from the early 1960s onwards. In the last few decades, a neo-Pentecostal type has also become evident, although in a very different sense, to refer to the charismatic movement referred to above.[9] Others use the term to label so-called Third Wave Pentecostals, who themselves come in a wide variety. One approach is to identify these churches as very actively seeking expansion, as having a middle-class orientation, with an emphasis on prosperity as a fruit of faith, and a 'health and wealth' message.[10]

Besides diversity for historical reasons, therefore, there is also a social and organisational diversity, and the model of the autonomous church is, of course, a very common one. Many followers of the charismatic movement have often opted to remain loyal to their mainstream churches, be they Roman Catholic or Protestant. Even when a church model is adopted, the size may differ enormously. At one extreme, there are the living-room churches with services being held at the leader's home, and at the other extreme we see multinational churches with a strong presence in many countries. A special case, best illustrated in the US, is formed by pastors organising their work as businesses, carrying expressive or personal names such as 'Full Gospel Healing Ministries', or 'John Johnson Exorcist Ministries Inc.' Some make use of modern marketing and PR techniques, a business-type strategy that can also be found in some of the Pentecostal churches. Another significant social type is the organisation surrounding a gifted evangelist who may travel around the world, appearing in huge local campaigns held in sports stadiums, and often in collaboration with local churches, but with his own core group as the real organiser and powerhouse. A good example of this is the Korean Paul Yonggi Cho and his 'Church Growth International'.[11]

There is also diversity with respect to political issues.[12] The almost stereotypical image is that of a Pentecostal church that, in the light of Romans 13, honours the authorities that be, even when they also happen to be dictators. But there have also been churches, albeit a small minority, that have defended a politically progressive stance and have formed part of the opposition against dictatorships. Chile in the 1970s and 1980s is a notorious example of deferment, with the majority of the Pentecostal

---

[8] Hollenweger, *Pentecost Between Black and White*, pp. 76-97.

[9] e.g. S. Hunt, M. Hamilton and T. Walter, 'Introduction: Tongues, Toronto and the Millennium' in S.Hunt, M.Hamilton and T.Walter (eds), *Charismatic Christianity: Sociological Perspectives*, London, 1997, p. 2.

[10] S. Brouwer, P. Gifford and S. Rose, *Exporting the American Gospel: Global Christian Fundamentalism*, New York, 1996, pp. 6, 44, 266.

[11] Brouwer *et al.*, *Exporting the American Gospel*, pp. 44,45.

[12] Hollenweger, *Pentecost Between Black and White*.

churches remaining loyal to the Pinochet regime, while a few took an active dissenting role.[13]

And then there is diversity too in terms of the attitude towards other Pentecostals, let alone other Christians. On the one hand, there may exist a very exclusivist and hostile attitude, especially on the part of Protestant Pentecostals towards Catholics, and this is sometimes reinforced by fundamentalist thinking. On the other hand, there may be forms of cooperation among Pentecostals, such as when a famous evangelist visits various regions. Some Pentecostal churches are members of international organisations and networks, including the mainstream ecumenical World Council of Churches, and several use ecumenical training institutes for the education of their pastors.

A final comment concerns a special source of diversity: Pentecostalism's capacity for the paradoxical combination of opposite characteristics.[14] A variety of seemingly contradictory scenarios are used according to context and need. There are several examples of this. There is an eschatological, even apocalyptic, tendency in Pentecostalism. Pentecostals live in expectation of the imminent coming of the Kingdom of God on earth. They also hold a long-term view of human history, although there is no question of postponing the treatment of affliction in anticipation of that moment, and the Pentecostal faith in the gifts of the Spirit also serves to solve small and large problems, here and now, and within a short-term perspective of human history. Another example of this way of reconciling apparent opposites is the way in which Pentecostal believers despise the sinful world, and yet they participate and have even earned themselves a reputation of being responsible and reliable citizens and workers in it. Similarly, traditional culture may, by and large, be condemned while even Pentecostals cannot escape cultural socialisation completely. The way in which equality and hierarchy are combined also illustrates this facility to maintain a double perspective. Both forms of social management seem to belong to the Pentecostal repertoire and are used according to need and situation.

The combination of opposite characteristics can also be detected in the simultaneous presence of spontaneity and control, or of individual expression and social conformity. The manifestation of the Holy Spirit seems to stimulate the free expression of emotions; people sometimes give tearful witness to their faith. But at the same time, the pastor usually has his own codes for bringing this spontaneous part of the service to an appropriate end.

[13] F. Kamsteeg, *Prophetic Pentecostalism in Chile, A Case Study on Religion and Development Policy*, Lanham, MD, 1998.

[14] A. Droogers, 'Paradoxical Views on a Paradoxical Religion, Models for the Explanation of Pentecostal Expansion in Brazil and Chile' in B.Boudewijnse, A.Droogers and F.Kamsteeg (eds), *More than Opium: An Anthropological Approach to Latin American and Caribbean Pentecostal Praxis*, Lanham, MD, 1998, pp. 1-34.

Contextual factors

Now that Pentecostalism's unity and diversity have been duly sketched, I shall discuss the problem of explaining the Pentecostal success story. The first step is to make an inventory of reductionist explanations put forward since the 1960s. In the next section, we will focus on the recently-introduced concept of 'globalisation'.

Where Pentecostals themselves have attributed the expansion of their churches and movement to the workings of the Holy Spirit, social scientists have looked for other, more secular, explanations. Reference to anomie, therefore, is common to several such explanations, be they economic, social or psychological by nature.[15] For example, the growth of Pentecostalism is presented as a remedy or a compensation for some disorder in society from which people suffer. In this context, modernisation is often mentioned, especially with respect to the developing countries. When modernisation is mentioned, it is usually placed in the context of the city, and urbanisation is seen as an influential manifestation of the modernisation process. The story is told in terms of personal uprooting and the loss of a social and cultural framework. The urban religions, including Pentecostalism, provide a new home and even a new family of brothers and sisters, albeit based on artificial kinship. When that same argument is used to explain the expansion of other religions, it does not represent a sufficient explanation for Pentecostal growth, or for people's preference for it.

Rather more specific is the explanation from modernisation which argues that Pentecostals, because of their reliability and good citizenship, make model participants in the modernisation process.[16] The individualism inherent in the Pentecostal faith – although often lived out within the confines of a closely-knit community – corresponds, in this sense, to the individualism which is regarded as an asset in a liberal capitalist society. Using the Weberian thesis in a selective manner, it can still be argued that, in the case of Pentecostals, their faith, their personal (missionary) initiatives, their desire to make full use of their talents and their labour ethos all contribute to making them strong candidates for upward social mobility in modern society. This argument, in my view, is an example of a more specific interpretation, in that it takes a particular characteristic of Pentecostal religion into account and thereby departs from the level of general social theorising. Again, the question is whether this explanation suffices, and whether it is applicable to all new converts.[17] It may also be that a Pentecostal church attracts successful and socially mobile citizens because the ideology corresponds with their own expectations

15 For a more detailed account, see Droogers, 'Paradoxical Views'.
16 e.g. E. Willems, *Followers of the New Faith*, Nashville, TN, 1967.
17 J. Hoffnagel, *The Believers: Pentecostalism in a Brazilian City*, Ann Arbor, MI, 1978.

and aspirations: the Weberian thesis is thus inverted. This would seem to be the case when it becomes apparent that urban converts are not recent migrants but belong, instead, to the already established middle class.

Some authors[18] have pointed to the fact that the patron role of the rural landlord corresponds with that of the influential Pentecostal pastor, thereby implying that this urban religion is successful because it consolidates a feudal framework that, in itself, is anything but modern; the 'clients' have merely changed their patrons. Viewed from this standpoint, Pentecostalism creates no break between the rural and urban contexts, but represents continuity instead.

A few authors have developed a variation on the modernisation thesis, by focusing on the trend towards cultural and social pluralism typical of today's society. Especially where a monolithic religion such as Catholicism makes itself felt on the Latin American context, the rise of alternative religions is viewed as the emergence of a free social space, a value cherished by societies on the Northern Atlantic axis.[19] Latin American Pentecostals have, in consequence, been presented as radically innovative, in that they develop a new social framework devoid of the traditionally everpresent leadership of some sympathising elite. In this respect, Pentecostals differ from their competitors, the liberation theologians.[20]

The matter can also be looked at from another theoretical – and ideological – perspective, in this case neo-Marxist. In its more vulgar version, religion – and thus Pentecostalism – parades as the opium of the people, serving only the interests of the producing owners. Religions, including Pentecostalism, are said to be growing because they help their converts and adepts to forget the misery that, as workers, they experience in capitalist modernising society. In this view, the new free social space is not free at all, but subject to manipulation and foreign interests. In more sophisticated versions, reference is made to the Gramscian concept of hegemony, which suggests that the oppressed have a part in the acceptance of their own fate. Another, less vulgar, interpretation contends that the disappropriated victims of economic production ultimately gain control over religious production without any control on the part of upper class clergy; in this way, they rehabilitate themselves from anonymity and address their fellow-victims in the language of their own class.[21] Again, it must be observed that the neo-Marxist approaches are partial. The

[18] e.g. Christian Lalive d'Epinay, *El Refugio de las Masas, Estudio Sociológico del Protestantismo Chileno*, Santiago de Chile, 1968.

[19] D. Martin, *Tongues of Fire: The Explosion of Protestantism in Latin America*, Oxford, 1990.

[20] D. Lehmann, *Struggle for the Spirit: Religious Transformation and Popular Culture in Brazil and Latin America*, Cambridge, 1996.

[21] F. Rolim, *Religião e Classes Populares*, Petrópolis, 1980; *idem.*, *O que é Pentecostalismo*, São Paulo, 1987; *idem.*, *Pentecostalismo: Brasil e América Latina*, Petrópolis, 1995.

Marxist perspective does not explain Pentecostal expansion among the middle and upper classes, unless the new prosperity preached by Pentecostalism is legitimised as a blessing from God. Neither does it account for the growth arising from autochthonous 'Southern' initiatives, sometimes even specifically directed, as in the case of some Brazilian churches, towards 'Northern' capitalist societies, including the US. And as we have seen already, Pentecostalism is politically diverse and even includes believers with leftist preferences upon which they act.

We have discussed the predecessors of current globalisation theories, and we have seen that their authors have managed to reduce the religious to the non-religious to the extent that their theories, in consequence, are not sufficiently specific. It has also been shown that their explanations are not valid for all Pentecostals, and in that sense too, they are partial. These contributions from the 1970s and the 1980s are nonetheless relevant to the present debate because several of the insights gained from the modernisation and Neo-Marxist approaches are still in use, as will become clear when we take a closer look at globalisation perspectives.

Globalisation

Globalisation has been referred to in diverse manner. Depending on their disciplinary homeland, some authors focus on the economic and ecological aspects, and others on the social, political and cultural sides of the phenomenon. In all cases, the world is experienced as a single place, or even a non-place, an abstract sign space, or as subject to time/space compression.[22] World society is presented as a system of mutual dependency. People, nations, transnational corporations and religions are all condemned to each other.

But this one world also has its shadow world. There is often talk of a tension between the universal and the particular, the global and the local, the whole and the fragments, and this has led to terms such as 'glocalisation'.[23] Globalisation has stimulated postmodern interest in fragmentation, not so much in relation to the global, but much more in relation to the local translations of the global. In Arizpe's words: 'the new "globality" is, in fact, a new "locality" '.[24] The fascination with globalisation does not stem from the characteristics of the global, but from the attitudes

[22] In order: R. Robertson, *Globalization: Social Theory and Global Culture*, London, 1992, p. 6; M. Augé, *Non-Places: Introduction to an Anthropology of Supermodernity*, London, 1995; P. Vieille, 'Du transnational au politique-monde?', *Peuples méditerranéens*, no. 35-36, 1986, p. 312; Z. Bauman, *Globalization: The Human Consequences*, Cambridge, 1998, p. 2.

[23] Robertson, *Globalization*, p. 73.

[24] L. Arizpe, 'Scale and Interaction in Cultural Processes: Towards an Anthropological Perspective of Global change' in L. Arizpe (ed.), *The Cultural Dimensions of Global Change, An Anthropological Approach*, Paris, 1996, pp. 89-90.

developed locally in order to survive in an era of globalisation. The stereotype is that the local disappears under the influence of Coca-Colaisation or McDonaldisation. A world culture, however, is highly improbable. It would seem better to follow Axford's advice: 'understanding the complexity of the global system requires a multi-dimensional approach that deals with the mediated connections between actors and institutional orders, at whatever "level" they are to be found'.[25] The only solid conclusion that can be drawn from this is that a cognitive global order has come into existence, rather than a political, let alone a moral one.[26]

At the political level, one aspect of globalisation that is often mentioned is the erosion of society as a unity and, more specifically, of the nation-state.[27] The transnational corporations are said to be the new states of the future, no longer confined to a particular territory, but ever-present, especially through the world-wide availability of brand name consumer products. Instead of proclaiming the end of the nation-state, it would perhaps be more interesting to study how the nation-state adapts itself through what might be called an effort at cultural syncretism, thus surviving global erosion at the local or regional level. This means that so-called national cultures share in the transformation of the state, and society's boundaries are redefined along similar lines. Multicultural societies are the result of this process and they represent the wider world within the old national and cultural boundaries, changing former concepts of space and scale. Some authors[28] use a linguistic metaphor to describe the cultural change that is taking place; by taking the example of the Creole languages and speaking of 'creolisation', they imply that people today are increasingly fluent in more than one cultural 'language'. This account bears a striking similarity to the founding myth of Pentecostalism as explained in the story of the first Pentecost, when people were able to understand each others' languages.[29]

Religion sometimes receives a good deal of attention in globalisation debates,[30] and fundamentalist forms, Christian and Islamic in particular, are said to thrive in the new globalising climate. Christian expansion has always been viewed as a transnational phenomenon with globalising

---

[25] B. Axford, *The Global System: Economics, Politics and Culture*, Cambridge 1995, p. 26.

[26] *Ibid.*, p. 27.

[27] *Ibid.*, p. 25; M. Featherstone, 'Global Culture: An Introduction' in M.Featherstone (ed.), *Global Culture: Nationalism, Globalization and Modernity*, London, 1990, p. 2; Vieille, 'Du transnational'.

[28] e.g. L. Drummond, 'The Cultural Continuum: A Theory of Intersystems', *Man*, vol. 15, no. 2, 1980, pp. 352-74; Ulf Hannerz, *Cultural Complexity: Studies in the Social Organization of Meaning*, New York, 1992.

[29] See chapter 2.

[30] e.g. P. Beyer, 'Privatization and the Public Influence of Religion in Global Society' in Featherstone, *Global Culture*; P. Beyer, *Religion and Globalization*, London, 1994.

tendencies, even before the term became popular. For several decades already – and without using the word – Christian missiologists have been very aware of the 'glocalisation' concept, as in the case of local cultural translations of the universal message, stamped as 'inculturation'. Especially in non-Western contexts, Christian converts have shown how people can adopt a global view and at the same time remain faithful to their traditional identities. An African church elder once told me, quite unashamedly, that he regularly asked his ancestors for help in being a good Christian.

The emphasis on globalisation as a cultural process has stimulated interest in the concept of identity. As we saw above, two approaches to identity, formerly presented as mutually exclusive, are now being combined to represent two aspects of the identity phenomenon. On the one hand, identity viewed from a culturalist standpoint is stable, and forms the basis for the experience of continuity; for this view of identity, Hall uses the metaphor of the root.[31] On the other hand, it has also been presented in a constructivist way as contextualised, as a strategic device used by persons according to their particular needs in a particular situation, as a repertoire of multiple selves. To summarise this view Hall suggests the metaphor of the route.[32] People involved in globalisation processes tend, like the above-mentioned church elder in Africa, to protect themselves by trying to remain who and what they are (identity as root), while simultaneously developing their own history, and making strategic use of all new opportunities that present themselves (identity as route).

Though not identical, this distinction can be coupled with that between mechanistic and subjectivistic perspectives, emphasising respectively the autonomy of structures and of actors. The more autonomous the structures are, the more they produce people with similar identities who feel themselves to have the same roots. Actors have their own way of dealing with structures, by means of adaptation or selection, or even by constructing totally new structures, choosing – in short – their own routes. In globalisation processes, actors are confronted with a new stock of structures that seem to impose themselves upon them, but which they use to develop their own routes.

This then is the somewhat murky globalising world within which Pentecostal expansion occurs. Many of the issues raised so far provoke the type of questions relevant to understanding the 'why' and 'how' of Pentecostal expansion. If we move from Pentecostalism's basic characteristics towards the non-religious aspects of the globalising context, how specific and precise can our explanation of Pentecostal expansion then be? What, in this case, is the relationship between the religious and the social? How are the two articulated? What are, in Axford's terms, the mediated connections? Does a religion like Pentecostalism change when it crosses

---

[31] Hall and Du Gay, *Questions of Cultural Identity*, p. 4.
[32] *Ibid.*

cultural boundaries? Is the global message translated into local forms? To what degree does Pentecostalism mark people, and to what extent do Pentecostals form and transform their religion? How are culturalist roots and constructivist routes connected? Does the Pentecostal experience easily combine with universal human characteristics?

Globalisation and Pentecostal commonalty

To find a tentative answer to these questions – the complete answer will require years of research – I will now return to the characterisation of Pentecostalism given above, and confront it with the globalisation process as described in the previous section. I will suggest that these internal religious elements together, as a constellation, make Pentecostalism a religion that fits with the globalising world. In the subsequent section, I will address the relationship between globalisation and Pentecostal diversity.

What then is the value of the experience of the Holy Spirit as a religious element in a globalising world? Experience of the Spirit is personal, embodied and, therefore, dramatically intense. It is not just a message, but more often a message experienced bodily. This very intimate manifestation of the Spirit, however, is not limited solely to the personal universe. First of all, what is felt physically is an experience that the believer shares with the universal body of Pentecostal believers, his or her brothers and sisters, in a world-wide artificial kinship of God's family. The community of believers is the model of the ideal society, and globalisation has made this world-wide fellowship more visible. Secondly, the personal experience of the Spirit underpins a link not only with other Pentecostals but with all people of this one-place world, because the message must, by all means, be transmitted to the whole of mankind. The ultimate perspective is that of a global world that coincides with the Kingdom of God. The Pentecostals have their own scenario for the globalised world. The scope of Pentecostal interest is global; after all, the whole world is under God's authority and all people are potential believers. The language miracle of the first Pentecost is more than a metaphor: Pentecostals behave like cultural polyglots. Whether or not the nation-state will survive the globalisation process, Pentecostals will certainly not allow themselves to be constrained by national boundaries. They preach their own model of a world society, and give it substance within their own communities. They regard fellow believers in other countries as their kin in faith and, as such, part of the world-wide community. Pentecostalism takes advantage of the world-wide change in scale, it normalises the expanded boundaries of people's worlds, and facilitates access to that larger world. Anywhere in this global setting, it provides a place where the believer can feel 'at home', meet fellow believers, and make converts.

'Place' is primarily the Pentecostal meeting-place, and secondly a locus for recruitment, wherever it may be located.

This perspective is reflected in the *charismata*, most clearly in 'speaking in tongues' (glossolalia) as the victory over linguistic differences, and the new universal language of God's worldly Kingdom. Through the gift of prophecy people are instructed, not so much about the future, though this may occur, but about the right path to follow and about the course the world as a whole will follow. This gives certainty to the faithful, who have to bear with the lack of comprehension on the part of non-believers.

Healing is the practical reaffirmation of a prevision of the Kingdom of God. Globalisation is for many often accompanied by pain and suffering – they have not asked for it, and every token of help, therefore, is welcomed with open arms.[33] Interestingly enough, the definition of healing goes beyond purely medical problems, and includes a wide variety of personal problems which people have to deal with in this modern global world.

One of these problems is that of identity. Globalisation creates all kinds of identity crises in all kinds of cultures, societies and persons. The question 'who am I?' becomes more pressing when new repertories of behaviour and conviction enter the market of public opinion. Globalisation brings a solution in the shape of Pentecostalism. Interestingly, as some have suggested the US is the main distributor both of corporate capitalism and of Evangelical missionaries.[34] Though they are by no means the only ones in the field, 'astute Christian entrepreneurs are successfully selling a new international belief system'.[35] Pentecostalism helps to solve the individual quest for a reliable and convincing orientation in life and, in addition, it offers a formula that corresponds to the scale of the globalised world insofar as it links personal and global worlds.

There is, of course, much more that can be said about the way people receive the gifts of the Spirit in very diverse cultures, such as Ghana, Korea and Brazil. Cox has suggested, for instance, that Pentecostalism flourishes on a basis of 'primal spirituality',[36] and he thus takes as his starting-point the importance of physical experiences in Pentecostalism[37] as a reflection of supposedly universal human experiences which include

---

[33] This might give the impression of a functionalist and therefore reductionist interpretation, yet the mere fact that Pentecostalism offers relief cannot be denied, even though its success cannot be explained from this 'function'. The point is that this function depends on religious convictions and the experience of the Spirit.

[34] Brouwer *et al.*, *Exporting the American Gospel*, p. 7.

[35] *Ibid.*

[36] H. Cox, *Fire from Heaven*, New York, 1995, p. 82.

[37] See also T. Csordas, 'Somatic Modes of Attention', *Cultural Anthropology*, vol. 8, no. 2, 1993, pp. 135-56; T. Csordas, *The Sacred Self: A Cultural Phenomenology of Charismatic Healing*, Berkeley: University of California Press, 1994.

glossolalia, trance, vision, dreams, healing and hope. Other authors take paranormal experiences as the universal basis for Pentecostalism.[38] The functional continuity between Pentecostalism and its more traditional, or popular, predecessors also seems to point in the direction of a common human basis, beyond specific times and places. It may well be that the Pentecostal gifts ought to be seen as a specific use and interpretation of a global human body language, doubly adapted to Pentecostal theology and the local cultural context in which it is sometimes helped, as in the African, Brazilian and Korean contexts, by a tradition of similar experiences, albeit critically used and interpreted. The Pentecostal repertoire has coloured human potentialities through the role attributed to the Holy Spirit, thus giving them a unique and exclusive flavour.

Conversion, the second religious characteristic, brings this complex of views and practices 'home' to the new believer. As a dramatic bodily event, expressed in baptism, with water and in (the name of) the Holy Spirit, it is the prototype of an individual's experience of the Spirit. It has drastic consequences at the personal level too, but acts as a mediating force between the person and the community of believers, locally as well as globally. It amounts, in fact, to admission to the new world community of the saved, the prototype of the promised Kingdom of God and an alternative to the prevailing global situation. It also emphasises the commitment to that divine Kingdom. Conversion stories are widely used in spreading the message, and in globally expanding Pentecostalism these stories serve as models open to adoption by potential converts. The narrative discourse offers cross-cultural possibilities of identification, despite cultural differences that may hamper understanding. Basic human experiences of affliction and happiness are easily recognised.

Let us turn now to the third Pentecostal characteristic, duality of worldview. This has the advantage of being a simplistic model of what is happening in the world: God and Satan are at war and Pentecostals are God's proud and committed soldiers. It is a short-hand theory of globalisation, tailormade for the Pentecostal believer. In this way, misery and suffering can be explained, just as the moral choices believers have to deal with are put into a comprehensive and decisive framework, while retaining the belief that the end of the world is expected and understood. At the same time, there is an absolute certainty that God will ultimately win and that the devil will be overcome. Here, too, is a universal dimension that corresponds to the global expansion of Pentecostalism, just as the experience of the spirit and the conversion experience have a universal human component. Dichotomous views have a certain universality, across and despite cultural boundaries, even though each society, or religion, produces its own form of this duality.[39] The expansion of Pentecostalism appears to be

---

[38] Chalfont *et al.*, 1987, mentioned in Hunt *et al.*, *Charismatic Christianity*, p. 6.
[39] R. Needham (ed.), *Right and Left: Essays on Dual Symbolic Classification*, Chicago, 1973.

seconded by a capacity to understand such dual schemas. On the global market, a dualist view stands a good chance of being recognised and accepted, even in its specific Pentecostal form.

It is suggested, in short, that taken together as a constellation, the three characteristics of Pentecostalism currently facilitate Pentecostalism's access to the world's peoples. The message is adapted to the global scale and experienced at the recognisable level of the human body. Precisely because the corporeal experience, through the *charismata*, is so important, it grounds universal human potential in a physical basis, even though it is interpreted in a radically exclusive manner. Similarly, duality can be traced to universal dichotomous thinking. Pentecostalism offers a universal framework that can be amplified and developed within the cultural (and culturalist) as well as the personal (and constructivist) context. It allows for cultural adaptation and for individual initiatives. It combines root and route, commonalty and diversity.

Globalisation and Pentecostal diversity

Having examined the basic Pentecostal constellation of defining religious traits in relation to the human universal potential as applied in the Pentecostal global world-view, it is now possible to concentrate on the other end of the spectrum, the almost fragmented diversity of Pentecostal manifestations. How can this diversity be linked to the globalisation process? What is its relevance for the expansion of Pentecostalism? In my opinion, this diversity can best be seen as an illustration of the capacity of Christianity to bridge the gap between the global and the local. This adaptability may surprise those who have a view of Pentecostalism as static, dogmatic and rigid. Pentecostals have, throughout their history, shown themselves well able to adapt to new circumstances. In social terms, their strong focus on their mission has given them good insights into the most efficient way of organising themselves.

What role then does this diversity play in the context of the globalisation process? Let us look, first of all, at social diversity which may have a weakening effect on that sense of unity. The sheer variety can also be seen as an asset in the globalisation process, especially if this diversity is coupled to flexibility. If globalisation can best be observed at the local level, then Pentecostal diversity matches the local diversity that is the other side of the universalising globalisation coin. Pentecostalism facilitates the translation from the global to the local and *vice versa*. An example of this is the neo-Pentecostal emphasis on prosperity, which fits very well the dream of wealth spread by the globalisation process. As Brouwer *et al.* put it: 'It makes the religious culture compatible with the worldwide commodity culture'.[40] Another example is that conscious choice of

---

[40] Brouwer *et al.*, *Exporting the American Gospel*, p. 9.

a target group, using modern commercial marketing techniques, facilitates Pentecostal penetration into new mission fields. Pentecostalism adapts easily to the contours of the social map.

Two restrictions must be mentioned, however. Firstly, the radical choice converts are expected to make carries obvious consequences for their cultural repertoire. Much of what was normal in pre-conversion times now becomes anathema, in short, demonic.[41] Pentecostalism is able to make short shrift of cultural elements considered contrary to the message. The second restriction is that Pentecostals are ambiguous with regard to modernity. As we have already seen, they apparently fit well into modern society and make good citizens. They also make skilful use of modern communication techniques, although they are not averse to voicing strong public criticism of such phenomena as loss of 'community' and falling moral standards, which they claim are the result of modernity, and which lead to dereligionisation or secularisation. In this sense, Pentecostals are anti-modern.[42]

With regard to political diversity, it could be that political abstinence, based on respect for the established order, actually did much to aid missionary access to dictatorially governed countries. On the other hand, progressive churches may also have served as rallying-points for those opposed to dictatorship, as happened in some Chilean churches.

Ecumenical diversity is linked to globalisation, if only in the sense of the meaning attributed to the word 'ecumenical': concerning the whole inhabited world. Cox has called Pentecostalism 'a kind of ecumenical movement',[43] and indeed Pentecostals have their own world-wide networks and conferences. The intricacies of information technology were quickly grasped, as was clear from the rapid spread of the so-called 'Toronto Blessing' in the early 1990s. The spread of the Roman Catholic charismatic movement presents another example.

The final Pentecostal feature mentioned, the combination of opposite characteristics, exists only within the parameters of a simplistic worldview; it does, however, facilitate access, bearing in mind that whatever the circumstances, every potential convert can find something of value. This may also be linked to the global nature of current world society, notwithstanding cultural differences and whether or not they are taken into account. Globalisation also combines opposite characteristics, especially the global and the local. The combination of a 'happy end' for all believers and a problem-solving capacity in the here and now is undoubtedly very attractive. Similarly, the condemnation of the world as sinful imposes no demands to retreat from it as was the custom in the monastic tradition.

---

[41] An example can be found in B. Guerrero, *A Dios rogando... Los pentecostales en la sociedad Aymara del norte grande de Chile*, Amsterdam, 1995.

[42] Hunt *et al.*, *Charismatic Christianity*, p. 3.

[43] Cox, *Fire from Heaven*, p. 16.

In short, Pentecostal diversity has generally worked towards utilising the opportunities offered by the globalisation process. As a global movement, Pentecostalism can be said to have become part of religious globalisation. As a form of faith, it has spread its message on the wings of more secular sectors of the globalisation process, just as in the traditional churches, both Catholic and Protestant, missionary efforts were the constant companions of colonial expansion.

This chapter has explored the complex articulation between Pentecostalism and globalisation. An effort has also been made to avoid reductionist explanations of Pentecostal expansion that seek to attribute it to effects arising out of non-religious (social, economic, political and psychological) factors. Without denying the importance of these factors, however, the internal religious characteristics of Pentecostalism were taken as the starting-point in order to discover how, taken together as a constellation, they are articulated together with these non-religious factors, thus facilitating Pentecostalism's role in the current process of globalisation. In this way, a more specific explanation has been found whereby the Pentecostal's physical experience with the Holy Spirit, based on a dramatic conversion experience and lived out in the framework of a dualist world-view, serves to situate the believer effectively at the global, local and personal level. The Pentecostal message has the potential to create a religious fellowship that serves as a model, not only for the individual, but for national and global societies as well. Pentecostals have shown themselves well able to use the cultural tools that are at the disposal of all mankind, tools which ensure both continuity and change, combining social control and individual initiative, and making unique use of capacities that belong to the universal human toolkit. Although Pentecostal identity contains outspoken and, as it were, eternal components, believers are able to find a dynamic form that facilitates adaptation to changing personal and cultural situations. Special attention has been given to the way in which unity and diversity are related in Pentecostalism and how this influences its position in the globalisation process. The global scope of the Pentecostal message matches the current global framework. At the same time, the variety of Pentecostal forms corresponds to the local groundedness of the globalisation process.

BIBLIOGRAPHY

Arizpe, Lourdes, 'Scale and interaction in cultural processes: towards an anthropological perspective of global change' in L. Arizpe (ed.), *The Cultural Dimensions of Global Change: An Anthropological Approach*, Paris, 1996, pp.89-107.

Augé, Marc, *Non-Places, Introduction to an Anthropology of Supermodernity*, London, 1995.

Axford, Barrie, *The Global System: Economics, Politics and Culture*, Cambridge 1995.

Bauman, Zygmunt, *Globalization, The Human Consequences*, Cambridge, 1998.

Beyer, Peter, 'Privatization and the Public Influence of Religion in Global Society' in M.Featherstone (ed.), *Global Culture: Nationalism, Globalization and Modernity*, London, 1990, pp. 373-95.

——, *Religion and Globalization*, London, 1994.

Brouwer, Steve, Paul Gifford and Susan D. Rose, *Exporting the American Gospel: Global Christian Fundamentalism*, New York, 1996.

Cox, Harvey, *Fire from Heaven*, New York, 1995.

Csordas, Thomas J., 'Somatic Modes of Attention', *Cultural Anthropology*, vol. 8, no. 2, 1993, pp. 135-56.

——, *The Sacred Self, A Cultural Phenomenology of Charismatic Healing*, Berkeley, CA: University of California Press, 1994.

Droogers, André, 'Paradoxical Views on a Paradoxical Religion, Models for the Explanation of Pentecostal Expansion in Brazil and Chile' in B. Boudewijnse, A. Droogers and F. Kamsteeg (eds), *More than Opium: An Anthropological Approach to Latin American and Caribbean Pentecostal Praxis*, Lanham, MD, 1998, pp. 1-34.

Drummond, Lee, 'The Cultural Continuum: A Theory of Intersystems', *Man*, vol. 15, no. 2, 1980, pp. 352-74.

Featherstone, Mike, 'Global Culture: An Introduction' in M. Featherstone (ed.), *Global Culture: Nationalism, Globalization and Modernity*, London, 1990, pp. 1-14.

Friedman, Jonathan, *Cultural Identity and Global Process*, London, 1994.

Fry, Peter Henry and Gary Nigel Howe, 'Duas respostas à aflição. Umbanda e Pentecostalismo', *Debate e Crítica* no. 6, 1975, pp. 75-94.

Guerrero, Bernardo, *A Dios rogando... Los pentecostales en la sociedad Aymara del norte grande de Chile*, Amsterdam, 1995.

Hall, Stuart, and Paul du Gay (eds), *Questions of Cultural Identity*, London, 1996.

Hannerz, Ulf, *Cultural Complexity, Studies in the Social Organization of Meaning*, New York, 1992.

Hexham, Irving and Karla Poewe, *New Religions as Global Cultures, Making the Human Sacred*, Boulder, CO, 1997.

Hoffnagel, Judith Chambliss, *The Believers: Pentecostalism in a Brazilian City*, Ann Arbor, MI, 1978.

Holland, Dorothy, William Lachicotte Jr, Debra Skinner and Carole Cain, *Identity and Agency in Cultural Worlds*, Cambridge, MA, 1998.

Hollenweger, Walter, *Pentecost Between Black and White: Five Case Studies on Pentecost and Politics*, Belfast, 1974.

——, 'The Pentecostal Elites and the Pentecostal Poor, A Missed Dialogue?' in K. Poewe (ed.), *Charismatic Christianity as a Global Culture*, Columbia, SC, 1994, pp. 200-14.

Hunt, Stephen, Malcolm Hamilton and Tony Walter, 'Introduction: Tongues, Toronto and the Millennium' in S. Hunt, M. Hamilton and T. Walter (eds), *Charismatic Christianity: Sociological Perspectives*, London, 1997, pp. 1-16.

Kamsteeg, Frans H., *Prophetic Pentecostalism in Chile: A Case Study on Religion and Development Policy*, Lanham, MD, 1998.

Keesing, Roger H., 'Theories of Culture Revisited' in R. Borofsky (ed.), *Assessing Cultural Anthropology*, New York, 1994, pp. 301-12.

Lalive d'Epinay, Christian, *El Refugio de las Masas. Estudio Sociológico del Protestantismo Chileno*, Santiago de Chile, 1968.

Lehmann, David, *Struggle for the Spirit, Religious Transformation and Popular Culture in Brazil and Latin America*, Cambridge, 1996.

Martin, David, *Tongues of Fire: The Explosion of Protestantism in Latin America*, Oxford, 1990.

Míguez, Daniel P., *Spiritual Bonfire in Argentina: Confronting Current Theories with an Ethnographic Account of Pentecostal Growth in a Buenos Aires Suburb*, Amsterdam, 1998.

——, 'Qué Puede Agregarse a los Clásicos? Buscando Nuevos Horizontes a los Estudios Sobre el Pentecostalismo Latinoamericano', *Estudios sobre Religión*, no. 6, 1998, pp. 4-6.

Needham, Rodney (ed.), *Right & Left: Essays on Dual Symbolic Classification*, Chicago, 1973.

Ortner, Sherry B., 'Theory in Anthropology Since the Sixties', *Comparative Studies in Society and History*, vol. 26, no. 1, 1984, pp. 126-66.

Poewe, Karla (ed.), *Charismatic Christianity as a Global Culture*, Columbia, SC, 1994.

——, 'Rethinking the Relationship of Anthropology to Science and Religion' in K. Poewe (ed.), *Charismatic Christianity as a Global Culture*, Columbia, SC, 1994, pp. 234-58.

Robertson, Roland, *Globalization: Social Theory and Global Culture*, London, 1992.

Rolim, Francisco Cartaxo, *Religião e Classes Populares*, Petrópolis, 1980.

——, *O que é Pentecostalismo*, São Paulo, 1987.

——, *Pentecostalismo: Brasil e América Latina*, Petrópolis, 1995.

Strauss, Claudia and Naomi Quinn, 'A Cognitive/Cultural Anthropology' in R. Borofsky (ed.), *Assessing Cultural Anthropology*, New York, 1994, pp. 284-300.

——, *A Cognitive Theory of Cultural Meaning*, Cambridge, 1997.

Vieille, Paul, 'Du transnational au politique-monde?', *Peuples méditerranéens*, no. 35-36, 1986, pp. 309-38.

Willems, Emilio, *Followers of the New Faith*, Nashville, TN, 1967.

THE COMPLEX PROVENANCE OF SOME ELEMENTS OF AFRICAN PENTECOSTAL THEOLOGY

Paul Gifford

In these pages I look at some aspects of Pentecostal theology with the aim of relating the African expression to the wider or international scene. The links I would argue are quite complex, but repay careful consideration. I focus on three common theological motifs within Africa's current Pentecostalism, namely the faith gospel, deliverance theology and Christian Zionism, and try to tease out the local and the international strands, the balance between which may be different in each case.

Faith gospel

First, the faith gospel characterises so many of Africa's charismatic churches. According to the faith gospel, God has met all the needs of human beings in the suffering and death of Christ, and every Christian should now share the victory of Christ over sin, sickness and poverty. A believer has a right to the blessings of health and wealth won by Christ, and he or she can obtain these blessings merely by a positive confession of faith. As regularly articulated, several well-known names have helped create it: most notably, E.W. Kenyon, A.A.Allen, Oral Roberts, T.L.Osborn, Kenneth Hagin, Kenneth Copeland, John Avanzini. Each of these has made his own contribution. It was Allen, for example, who first made it an aid towards fund raising; he was the first to teach that God is a rich God, and that those who want to share in his abundance must obey and support God's servant – often the speaker himself. Roberts added the idea of seed faith; the idea that you prosper by planting a seed in faith, the return on which will meet all your needs. The texts that are invariably utilised include: Mk 11:23-23; Dt 28-30; 3Jn 2; Mal 3:8-11; Mk 10:29-30; Phil 4:19; and for health in particular Ps 91; Is 53:4-5 (=1Pet 2:24), Mt 9: 27-31. This faith gospel has proved very functional among the religious entrepreneurs who constitute the media evangelists, for its 'seed faith' idea has helped to bring in the enormous resources needed to sustain these extremely expensive ministries. Indeed, it developed in those circles precisely because it was so functional in this regard. Kenneth Copeland has admitted that only after committing himself to a TV series with no apparent capital did he come to understand the doctrine of 'biblical prosperity' properly.[1] Its widespread diffusion owes much to its pervasiveness

---

[1] Kenneth Copeland, *The Laws of Prosperity,* Fort Worth, 1974, pp. 74-6. Hagin claims he properly understood prosperity in January 1950 (Kenneth E. Hagin; *How God Taught*

on Christian broadcasting. But it is not only its functionality but its general socio-economic context that is significant. It appeared in the boom years of the 1960s and early 1970s in the US. These were the days when living standards were visibly increasing, opportunity was everywhere, and 'success through a positive mental attitude' was the rule. Indeed, the faith gospel's affinities to new age thinking are obvious.

Without some idea of the faith gospel, it is possible to miss some of the complexity of some developments within Christianity globally. Thus a recent study of Korean charismatic Christianity claims that 'Korean Christianity has become almost completely shamanised'. The author proves the 'shamanistic orientation' of the theology of Paul Yonggi Cho by expounding Cho's exegesis of 3John 2 (not John 3:2 as stated). Yet everything Cho understands by prospering has been taught in exactly that form by the faith gospel for years, and 3John 2 has been one of its key texts. The emphasis on this-worldly blessing is too readily attributed to shamanism, with no reference to what is taught in a whole swathe of Christianity in America.[2]

A much more satisfactory approach which attends to both external and local factors, is found in Coleman's writings on *Livets Ord* (Word of Life), a faith church in Sweden. Coleman can write: 'The Word of Life is a cultural product that cannot be understood merely in terms of its local or even national context. It must also be seen as formed from and reacting to international influences, and specifically as a product of North American religious culture'. In this he is surely correct. This church's symbols, hymns, organisation, networks, rituals, technology, order of service, use of the Bible, instrumental music, literature and tapes sold in the bookshop, theology – all of these characteristics, and many more, betray their origins. However, Coleman immediately adds the equally important corollary: 'Its doctrines and forms of worship take on new symbolic resonances as they are transferred almost wholesale from one country to another'.[3]

---

me about Prosperity, Tulsa, 1985, p. 15). The Copelands admit being influenced by Hagin, and started to think in terms of prosperity in 1967-8. See Gloria Copeland, *God's Will is Prosperity*, Fort Worth, 1978, pp. 32-3 and Copeland, *Laws of Prosperity*, p. 9.

[2] Mark R. Mullins, 'The Empire Strikes Back: Korean Pentecostal Missions to Japan' in Karla Poewe (ed.), *Charismatic Christianity as a Global Culture*, Columbia, 1994, pp. 92-3. The author also oversimplifies the complex origins of the Korean theology of illness, much of which is also standard faith gospel. The author's claim: 'Paul Yonggi Cho's theology might best be viewed as a synthesis of Korean shamanism, Robert Schuller's "Positive Thinking", and the pragmatism of the church-growth school of missiology associated with Fuller Theological Seminary's School of World Mission' (*ibid.*), is too simple.

[3] Simon Coleman, '"Faith which Conquers the World": Swedish Fundamentalism and the Globalisation of Culture', *Ethnos*, vol. 56, no. 1, 1991, p. 7; also Simon Coleman, 'Conservative Protestantism and the World Order: the Faith Movement in the United States and Sweden', *Sociology of Religion*, vol. 54, 1993, pp. 353-73. Also: 'In all movements of religious conversion and change there is a dialectic of external influence and local adaptation' (Martin, *Tongues of Fire: The Explosion of Pentecostalism in Latin America*,

I have written elsewhere about the faith gospel in Africa, and I will not repeat myself here.[4] I would argue that in Africa it is obvious that the faith gospel builds on traditional preoccupations. Africa's traditional religions were focused on material realities. Last century, Crowther wrote of the Yoruba religious search for 'peace, health, children and money'.[5] This preoccupation has been noted several times since.[6] But Africa's current Pentecostalism is increasingly articulated in terms of the faith gospel normally associated with a standardised American form: the necessity of proclamation (from which it is derided as the 'name it and claim it gospel'); the idea that possession is prior to belief (from Hagin's unique exegesis of Mk 11:23f); the idea that 'what you speak is what you get'; 'speaking things into existence'; the working out of ineluctable laws of sowing and reaping (an emphasis that does not sit perfectly well with the all-sufficiency of belief); tithing, and offerings generally; the idea that increase is for evangelisation; and (often, from the influence of John Avanzini) that in the end times, God is going to return to the righteous all the resources of the unrighteous. It is likewise expressed in terms of the biblical texts outlined above, especially Deuteronomy. I suggest that in the form in which it is widely heard in Africa the African preoccupation with material realities has been subsumed into this standardised formulation. The external contribution cannot be ignored, and I think Coleman is quite correct when he writes that in this matter the idea of a 'world wide culture' should be used with a degree of caution, for 'faith ideology retains a strong imprint of its North American roots'.[7]

The increasing standardisation of expression is in part explicable through the influence of the media. Faith gospel literature has been abundant across the continent through the 1980s and 1990s. In Zambia, for example, the bookshop of even the Evangelical Fellowship of Zambia has been full of it. Similarly Zambia's TV channel on a Sunday morning

---

Oxford, 1990, p. 282). Peel writes of Africa's 'active engagement' with external influences (J.D.Y. Peel, 'Poverty and Sacrifice in Nineteenth-Century Yorubaland: A Critique of Iliffe's Thesis', *Journal of African History*, vol. 31, 1990, p. 484; and see pp. 482-84).

[4] See Paul Gifford, *Christianity and Politics in Doe's Liberia*, Cambridge, 1993, pp. 146-89. For an account of one of its main avenues into Africa, namely Bonnke's 1986 Fire Conference in Harare, see Gifford, 'Prosperity: A New and Foreign Element in African Christianity', *Religion*, vol. 20, 1990, pp. 373-88. A good account of its origins and specifics is J.N. Horn, *From Rags to Riches: An Analysis of the Faith Movement and its Relation to the Classical Pentecostal Movement*, Pretoria, 1989.

[5] Cited in J.D.Y. Peel, 'An Africanist Revisits Magic and the Millennium' in Eileen Barker, James A. Beckford and Karel Dobbelaere (eds), *Secularization, Rationalism and Sectarianism: Essays in Honour of Bryan R. Wilson*, Oxford, 1993, p. 98, n.15.

[6] Inus Daneel, *Quest for Belonging: Introduction to a Study of African Independent Churches*, Gweru, 1987, p. 46; Monica Wilson, *Religion and the Transformation of Society: A Study in Social Change in Africa*, Cambridge, 1971, p. 37; Okot P'Bitek, *African Religions in Western Scholarship*, Kampala, 1971, p. 62.

[7] Coleman, 'Conservative Protestantism', p. 371.

in early 1996 screened seven successive Christian programmes, almost all foreign products, including *The 700 Club, Benny Hinn, Praise the Lord, Ernest Angley Ministries*, and *Rhema Church Hour* (this last from South Africa) – all faith gospel. This is what is spread through the numerous conventions and revivals which are such a part of Zambian life. In Zambia this faith gospel is so common, so axiomatic, so pervasive that it appears that President Chiluba, a born-again Christian himself, subscribes to this theology. Speaking at the annual conference of Swedish Pentecostal churches in 1994 he told the congregation: 'Give one tenth of your money to (God) and see returns on your capital...The benefits you will receive will astound you.' He takes it somewhat further; if you give to God, you will experience not only personal prosperity, but national prosperity. During the ceremonies celebrating the fourth anniversary of his declaration of Zambia as a Christian nation in December 1991, he actually said that 'because Zambia had entered into this covenant with God, God is blessing this nation to the point where we shall stop borrowing. We shall lend instead.'[8] This expression of Christianity cannot be understood without reference to the faith tradition coming from Hagin and Copeland, even though the greatest reason for the popularity of the faith gospel in Africa is probably that it has proved very functional for pastors. Its stress on seed faith has brought in the revenues that have enabled pastors to survive in a very competitive field, in extremely depressed circumstances.[9]

Deliverance

As a second example, consider the deliverance phenomenon that has become so widespread in the 1990s especially in West Africa. The basic idea of deliverance is that a Christian's progress and advance can be blocked by demons who maintain some power over the Christian, despite his or her coming to Christ. The Christian may have no idea of the cause of the hindrance, and it may be through no fault of his own that he is under the sway of a particular demon. It often takes a special man of God to diagnose and then bind and cast out this demon. Thus, in the mind of many of its exponents, this deliverance is a third stage, beyond being born again, beyond speaking in tongues.[10] A favourite text is Jn 11:1-44, in which Lazarus is called forth to life, but is still bound and must be 'let go' (Jn 11:44). There is some difference of opinion as to whether it is a

[8] Faith Key to Success – Chiluba', *Times*, 11 Dec. 1994; *Mirror*, 7-13 Jan. 1996, p. 2. The *Times* and *Mirror* cited in this chapter are published in Zambia.

[9] For another treatment of the faith gospel in Africa, see David Maxwell, '"Delivered from the Spirit of Poverty?": Pentecostalism, Prosperity and Modernity in Zimbabwe', *Journal of Religion in Africa*, vol. 28, no. 3, 1998, pp. 350-73.

[10] M. Addae-Mensah, in *Step*, vol. 4 no. 5, 1992, p. 12.

strictly 'necessary' stage.[11] Some seem to say yes, but Ghana's most celebrated deliverance exponent Owusu Tabiri cites in explanation another biblical passage, that of Dives and Lazarus (Lk 16:19-31). In that story both Abraham and Lazarus reach heaven, so both are 'saved', but Abraham had been blessed and powerful on earth (Gen 24:1) whereas Lazarus had led a miserable life. All Christians are meant to be like Abraham; deliverance will transform the earthly life of a Lazarus into that of an Abraham.

A clear and systematic exposition of this deliverance thinking is to be found in a popular book by a member of the Evangelical Presbyterian Church of Ghana, Aaron Vuha's *The Package: Salvation, Healing and Deliverance*. Demons, we are told, are former angels, disembodied beings, who when they come to earth 'find themselves rivers, mountains, rocks, trees, humans etc to dwell in'.[12] We are most conscious of what is happening in this spirit world when we are asleep, in dreams. Activities of demons prevent humans from enjoying the abundant life that Jesus came to give. Some effects of their activities are phobias, complexes, allergies, chronic diseases, repeated hospitalisation, repeated miscarriages, non-achievement in life, emotional excesses, and strikingly odd behaviour. In discussing the work of demons he gives special place to the inability to contract or maintain a happy marriage. The cause of this is a prior 'spiritual marriage' to a 'spiritual spouse', which is often manifested through dreams of sexual intercourse with this person. These spiritual marriages are often contracted when people are dedicated to family gods, stools or shrines. Spiritual marriages are detected through a lack of desire for marriage, the cessation of monthly periods, impotence, the end of a marriage (for a spiritual spouse can kill a rival), childlessness or an unsatisfactory sexual life. Demons enter human beings through 'doorways' or openings, such as: ancestral gods; traumatic childhood experiences (such as sexual abuse or an accident); curses (not only on an individual, but on one's family or clan); covenants (agreements 'made on behalf of a family or clan members with shrines or gods or stools are binding on all members whether they actively took part or not'); involvement in 'wrong churches' (which include any using candles, incense and so on); eastern cults; sex ('Satan has agents around seeking to deposit demons in people; sex with such an agent lets in demons'); sin; names (demons associated with names 'make good' the meanings of the names); pornography; addiction; and contaminated objects (so one should avoid rings, earrings, clothes and shoes of others). The demons must first be identified (by discovering the names of shrines or stools, by noting effects in one's life like sickness or poverty, by noting the doorways opened to them), and then Vuha gives an elaborate procedure for casting them

---

[11] Abamfo Atiemo, 'Deliverance in the Charismatic Churches in Ghana', *Trinity Journal of Church and Theology*, vol. 4, no. 2, 1994-5, p. 41.

[12] Aaron K. Vuha, *The Package: Salvation, Healing and Deliverance*, Accra, 1993, p. 36.

out, involving exhaling slowly. Sometimes this will be accompanied by yawning, coughing, spitting, vomiting or convulsions. Even a born-again believer is never perfectly delivered: 'No matter your spiritual standing, you are under constant attack and demons often make incursions into you only to be thrown out', although (confusingly) he can also write that 'demons cannot come back unless you positively invite them back or you go back into the very sins you confessed which amounts to reopening the doors'.[13] The book is full of testimonies of casting out demons of childishness, of divorce, of sleep, of sadness, of poverty.

As an illustration of a specialised deliverance ministry, consider Christian Hope Ministry, just outside Kumasi. In 1997 this was not a church, and all activity ceased on Saturday morning after Friday's all night session. Here about 5-10,000 people came every week, with about 2,000 attending the Thursday afternoon deliverance session. Those who came on any day were divided into four groups, according to whether their problems had to do with marriage, sickness, general (normally financial) constraints or deliverance. Those with marital problems filled in their own questionnaire. All others filled in a questionnaire which asks the petitioners, after personal details and Christian affiliation, questions like the following: have they attended any spiritual or Aladura church, 'palmist, fetish priest, card reader, dwarf worship or witch doctor'; have they ever been given any ring, amulet or talisman for protection; have they been bathed by a prophet or prophetess, malam or fetish priest; have they had any incisions, and how many, on what part of the body; have they undergone puberty rites; have they slept with anyone they have never seen afterwards; do they maintain a stool or seat or shrine in the family; have they been adopted by or named after any river, god, tree; have they made any covenant with 'secret society, transcendental group, lodge, Buddhism, Krishna'; have they received beads, ornaments or chains from anyone; do they experience excessive or useless dreams or nightmares; do they experience 'invisible presence'; do they easily lose personal property or money, hear voices, feel heaviness or a burning sensation; have they had sex with any family member; have they had an abortion; have they had an 'enema with any native medicine' from a fetish priest; have they applied nasal drops or concoctions from a malam or fetish priest; have they made a vow to any object beside God; have they taken a spiritual bath with the blood of a dove, sheep or animal; have they had sex with any spiritual advisor; do they have excessive menstrual pains; or are they addicted to alcohol, drugs, sleep or food. The answers to this questionnaire enable the full-time team of sixteen to establish whether the problem is demonic, and if so, to identify the demon.[14] In a special building with a

---

[13] *Ibid*, pp. 82, 95.

[14] Similar questionnaires, with only minor variations, are used by Gospel Light International Church, and the Fountain of Life International Church in Accra.

sunken floor, the patients (overwhelmingly women) lie fully clothed on tables, and those involved in the deliverance ministry amid praying and shouting and often physical pummelling drive out the demon.

This deliverance thinking has since about 1993 led to the emergence of institutions which promote and cater for the needs it addresses. The first of these institutions is the deliverance or prayer camp. Five major camps are now in operation, all of them run by lay members of the Church of Pentecost. They are at Edumfa (Cape Coast), Sunyani, Sefwi, and (in Accra) Macedonia and Canaan.[15] Macedonia began in March 1993. By mid-1995 it held four days of revival near the beginning of each month, which about 10,000 attended. Also, every Saturday, about 5,000, over-whelmingly women, attended a deliverance session. At these sessions women came out to the front where either they told, or more usually, had drawn from them, the nature of the demonic blockage afflicting them. These sessions could be quite physical, with women, speaking in the name of some demon, rushing around the open space, sometimes pursued by a team of about twenty fit men who physically restrained them. The evangelist often indulged in almost lighthearted banter with the spirits speaking through the women, before casting them out. Besides these camps, special deliverance ministries have appeared, such as the Christian Hope Ministry outside Kumasi which we have just described. Besides these institutions which have grown up to cater for this development, other institutions have changed their nature to cater for it. For example, crusades have moved from occasions for making a decision for Christ, or a combination of that and healing sessions, to fully fledged deliverance rituals. In Koforidua, Evangelist Owusu Tabiri's May 1995 crusade was advertised as deliverance. As well, the charismatic churches have in general moved in this direction – even those churches which initially resisted the current craze for deliverance. Thus by 1995 two of Ghana's most prominent leaders of the new paradigm churches, Mensa Otabil and Nicholas Duncan-Williams, had deliverance teams alongside all the other groups that characterise their churches. Deliverance thinking has now come to dominate many of these churches, reshaping the faith gospel which throughout the 1980s was their characteristic theology.

The origins of this outbreak of deliverance in Ghana are complex. Matthew Addae-Mensah, the pastor of Gospel Light International Church

---

[15] Bethel and Macedonia both produce magazines of testimonies: *Bethel News* and *Macedonia News*. The testimonies tell of cures from barrenness and all kinds of sickness, obtaining visas and green cards, and often involve dreams, Muslims, fetish priests or false churches. *Bethel News* places great stress on overseas visits, and selling cassettes and raising money, and even in 1995 one could sense the tension between the camp and the Church of Pentecost. For the importance of overseas connections for these camps, see Rijk A. van Dijk, 'From Camp to Encompassment: Discourses of Trans-subjectivity in the Ghanaian Pentecostal Diaspora', *Journal of Religion in Africa*, vol. 27, no. 2, 1997, pp. 135-59.

in Accra, claims that he brought this thinking to Ghana in 1986, after attending Benson Idahosa's Bible school in Benin City, Nigeria, and then pastoring churches for three years in Nigeria. When he returned to Ghana he began a deliverance outreach, which attracted considerable criticism from most, including Otabil and Duncan-Williams. There was quite a split in charismatic-pentecostal Christianity. Addae-Mensah 'feared persecution', and he told people coming to him to stay in their own churches. It was a visit to Ghana by Florida's Derek Prince that 'salvaged my reputation'. After Prince had conducted a seminar on deliverance, many began to say: 'Now we understand what that young man is saying'.

Addae-Mensah speaks both of Nigeria and Derek Prince; both influences are important. Obviously a traditional or 'enchanted' world-view underlies this deliverance thinking. However, as Addae-Mensah indicated in acknowledging his debt to Derek Prince, that is not the full story. We noted the resistance he experienced, until Derek Prince came to Ghana on a lecture tour. Then others were prepared to accept deliverance – in the words Addae-Mensah's attributed to them: 'Now we understand what that young man is saying'. It was the same with the evangelist Owusu Tabiri. When I asked him if his preoccupation with deliverance from spirits and demons was derived from traditional conceptions, he demurred, saying he got it all from American authors Derek Prince, Marilyn Hickey and Roberts Liardon, whose books he promptly fetched from his bedroom: 'I got the foundation from them. I develop it in the light of experience, as I go round, to African conditions'.[16] Cox has written of such a dynamic in Korea: 'Korean pentecostalism has become a powerful vehicle with which hundreds of thousands of people who might be embarrassed to engage in the "old-fashioned" or possibly 'superstitious' practice of shamanic exorcism can now do it within the generous ambience of a certifiably up-to-date religion, one that came from the most up-to-date of all countries, the USA'.[17] A similar perception is suggested for Pentecostalism in Ghana by Max Assimeng, Professor of Sociology at Legon. 'Things are truer if un-African, so we quote Americans. It is traditional, but projected in modern dress. The more foreign, the more serious, true, powerful it is.'[18]

---

[16] Interview, 21 May 1995. Derek Prince, *Blessing or Curse: You can Choose!*, Milton Keynes, 1990; Marilyn Hickey, *Break the Generation Curse*, Denver, 1988; Roberts Liardon, *Breaking Controlling Powers*, Tulsa, 1987. Tabiri also brought Kwaku Dua-Agyeman, *Covenant Curses and Cure*, no publication details, 1994. The latter had been an Anglican priest, but in 1995 was with Rhema Temple, Kumasi. Marilyn Hickey has also written *Devils, Demons and Deliverance*, Denver, 1994.

[17] H. Cox, *Fire from Heaven: The Rise of Pentecostal Spirituality and the Reshaping of Religion in the Twenty-First Century*, London, 1996, p. 225.

[18] Interview, 26 May 1995. He continued: 'In the eyes of many, "African Christianity" is offensive, a denigration of the real thing. Not many want it.' See also J.M. Assimeng, *Salvation, Social Crisis and the Human Condition*, Accra, 1995.

In fact, it is noteworthy that many Ghanaian church leaders, including Addae-Mensah, positively reject many African elaborations of deliverance as dangerous. There has been a spate of Nigerian literature on demons, the most famous individual book being Emmanuel Eni's *Delivered from the Power of Darkness*.[19] When Eastwood Anaba, pastor of Broken Yoke Foundation in Bolgatanga, told me that his particular charism was demonology, I asked, encouraging him to elaborate, whether his demonology was something like Eni's. I was surprised by the force and speed of his reaction: 'No, I don't have that attitude so much'. He criticised the general Nigerian tendency to attribute everything to demons, and by name; understandably, his training as a pharmacist made him less ready to attribute every illness to demons. He listed the people who best expressed his understanding of demons as the Americans Lester Sumrall, Kenneth Hagin and Gordon Lindsay.[20] Not long afterwards I had the opportunity to ask the resident pastor at World Miracle Bible Church in Tamale whether his demonology was anything like Eni's. Again, a rather similar answer was forthcoming: 'No, some of those Nigerian books are not well based, frightening. Some are so weird and exaggerated. We don't take them as true, especially Nigerian books. We just concentrate on Frank Hammond's book.'[21] Even Addae-Mensah distances himself from Eni as 'extreme'.[22]

I would suggest that both poles have to be attended to. American charismatic Christianity has a strand which gives enormous prominence to demonic beings. This has been evident in Paretti's best selling novels, in Wagner's *Territorial Spirits,* in books like Rebecca Brown's – and at the beginning of 1995 Rebecca Brown and the equally demonic Mark I. Bubeck were the fastest selling authors in Accra's evangelical Challenge Bookshop.[23] (Rebecca Brown illustrates too that the American strand is just as preoccupied with sex, cannibalism and child sacrifice as Eni.) These two strands – the African and the Western – reinforce one another, even feed off one another, and in certain circles tend to coalesce.[24]

---

[19] Emmanuel Eni, *Delivered from the Power of Darkness,* Ibadan, 1987. Eni is discussed in Birgit Meyer, '"Delivered from the Powers of Darkness": Confessions of Satanic Riches in Christian Ghana', *Africa,* vol. 65, 1995, pp. 236-55; and in Stephen Ellis and Gerrie ter Haar, 'Religion and Politics in Sub-Saharan Africa', *Journal of Modern African Studies,* vol. 36, no. 2, 1998, pp. 175-201.

[20] For his Christianity, see Eastwood Anaba, *God's End-Time Militia: Winning the War Within and Without,* Accra, 1993; *Releasing God's Glory from Earthen Vessels,* Accra, 1994: and *Elevated Beyond Human Law: Through the Touch of the Spirit,* Accra, 1995.

[21] Frank and Ida Mae Hammond, *Pigs in the Parlor: A Practical Guide to Deliverance,* Kirkwood, MI, 1973.

[22] Interview, 30 May 1995.

[23] Atiemo, 'Deliverance', p. 39. For further illustrations see Paul Gifford, 'Ghana's Charismatic Churches', *Journal of Religion in Africa,* vol. 24, 1994, pp. 241-65.

[24] Thus a Christian magazine, in advertising a forthcoming conference, could categorise Rebecca Brown and Eni as the same thing. It states simply: 'The evangelist Emmanuel

We outlined above Vuha's 1993 book *The Package*. At the end of 1994 Vuha published a sequel, *Covenants and Curses: Why God Does Not Intervene*, to address the question why deliverance does not solve all medical, emotional, spiritual and financial problems. The answer is that covenants and vows 'seemingly tie up God's hands'.[25] One vowed to a demon (even by one's parents, or before becoming a Christian) would be affected: 'God is powerful enough to set (the person) free but would not, since the demons have a "legal" right to oppress him'.[26] Likewise blessings and curses affect us, according to Dt 28-30. 'Those who qualify for curses cannot escape or avoid them. They would suffer setbacks, failure, no reproduction, defeat in all spheres of life, a life that can simply be described as a life of frustration'.[27] People come under curses through things like inheritance (up to the fourth generation, Ex 20:5), worship of idols, murder, wrong worship, sexual sin, divorce, robbing God (not paying tithes, Mal 3:8-10), cursing Israel (Gen 12:1-3). Vuha writes that 'Nobody comes under a curse unless he/she deserves it', yet (confusingly) also writes: 'He is also under a curse, if he belongs to a nation that is under a curse, or lives in an area or home whose inhabitants have been cursed.'[28] The way out is to examine one's life: 'If there is a curse or if there is a covenant entered into against the will of God, or if there is a broken covenant or if a bad seed is sown or if any of the above is inherited from ancestors, unless they are revoked or cancelled they will each run their full course of consequences.'[29] Curses or covenants must be identified and revoked, and Vuha gives prayers which effect this.[30] All the theological ideas contained here ('openings' of 'doorways' for demonic intrusion, the

---

Eni and Rebecca Brown *who were Satanists before converting to Christ*, are scheduled to attend'.

Among the Western books and booklets on demons widely available in Ghana in 1995 were Frank E. Paretti, *This Present Darkness*, Wheaton, IL, 1986; Frank E. Paretti, *Piercing the Darkness*, Westchester, 1989; Rebecca Brown, *He Came to Set the Captives Free*, Springdale, PA, 1989; Rebecca Brown, *Prepare for War*, Springdale, PA, 1990; Bill Subritsky, *Demons Defeated*, Chichester, 1986; Lester Sumrall, *Three Habitations of Devils*, South Bend, 1989; Stuart Gramenz, *Who are God's Guerrillas?*, Chichester, 1988; Stephen Bransford, *High Places*, Wheaton, IL; Elbert Willis, *Exposing the Devil's Work*, Lafayette, LA, n.d.; John Osteen, *Pulling Down Strongholds*, Houston, 1972; Frank and Ida Mae Hammond, *Pigs in the Parlor: A Practical Guide to Deliverance*, Kirkwood, MI, 1973; Lester Sumrall, *Alien Entities: Beings from Beyond*, South Bend, 1984, and the pamphlets of Kenneth Hagin and Gordon Lindsay.

[25] A.K. Vuha, *Covenants and Curses: Why God does not Intervene* (Accra [1994], p. 3.

[26] *Ibid.*, p. 31.

[27] *Ibid.*, p. 54.

[28] *Ibid.*, pp. 55, 57.

[29] *Ibid.*, p. 67.

[30] This second book contains much anti-Catholic material, proving that 'Mary' and the saints are spirits that need exorcising. They enter at Catholic baptism or on Ash Wednesday, or through anointing with oil (*ibid.*, pp. 79-83). Another Ghanaian book which illustrates this whole deliverance phenomenon, but written by a Catholic, the founder of Christian

'legal rights' of demons, curses lasting till the fourth generation, the power in the uttered word, a 'superior's' control over an inferior through speech, the ambiguity surrounding whether a person can be possessed through no fault of his own but because of a curse on his group) can also be found in, for example, Derek Prince.[31]

Besides books, Ghana's parachurch institutions have played a large role in spreading this teaching. Scripture Union organises two separate programmes every year to train people and to enable those involved in deliverance ministry to share experiences. Their first in 1984 attracted about fifty people. In 1992 eighty-four teams participated in the programme at Aburi, and in the same year 1,244 participated in their Kumasi meeting.[32] The Full Gospel Businessmen's Fellowship International (FGBMFI) has begun to promote this too. At a meeting at Accra's Labadi Beach Hotel on 27 May 1995, a pastor of one of the new deliverance churches was the guest speaker. He had begun his church in 1992, and by mid-1995 had over 1,000 members. He found spirits responsible for all kinds of rejection, including 'societal machinery of rejection', by which he meant continually being passed over for a top position: 'Find the root cause; there must be a spiritual reason.' He could identify spirits responsible for recurring conditions in families: if everyone is poor; if many are divorced; if many of the women have difficulty in childbearing; if many in the family have mental or emotional illnesses; if there has been a history of suicide. The bulk of his address was on curses. He insisted that when a superior person (a pastor, teacher, husband or parent) pronounced something over you, 'it will come to pass, unless you walk under the blood of Jesus'. He cited as biblical evidence the story of Jacob and Laban; Jacob's innocent statement that the guilty person 'shall not live' (Gen 31:31) had to be fulfilled, and thus Rachel had to die in childbirth. In many of his examples spirits came to enjoy sexual intercourse with women at night, thus causing them to be barren or to have difficulty in bearing children. In another, an eight-year-old boy was paralysed, and prayer could achieve nothing. Then the pastor had asked the boy's name. He asked his mother what the name meant. Even the mother had no idea. 'I discovered it referred to a spirit, and cast it out. Then I told him to walk, and he is perfect now.' Of course the motifs of barrenness, intercourse in dreams, a name indicating a spirit's control seem totally African; but the basic ideas, even up to using the biblical example of Rachel, are equally prominent in Derek Prince's writing.[33]

Hope Ministry outside Kumasi, which we discussed above, is Francis Akwaboah, *Bewitched*, London, 1994.

[31] Derek Prince, *Blessing or Curse: You Can Choose*, Milton Keynes, 1990.

[32] Atiemo, 'Deliverance', p. 39; Paulina Kumah (ed.), *Twenty Years of Spiritual Warfare: the Story of the Scripture Union Prayer Warriors' Ministry*, Accra, 1994.

[33] A book on deliverance by a Nigerian Catholic Priest and seminary lecturer contains the

It is possible to view the rise of deliverance theology as a response to or mutation in the face of the shortfall of faith preaching. Faith preaching in so many cases cannot be said to have worked. Faith did not bring about all that was promised. Deliverance still allows the emphasis on success, as long as something more than faith is added. The FGBMFI speaker just referred to actually quoted the standard faith gospel text Dt 30:28, but this time to add a crucial rider. Yes, he said, there are some curses that are purely a result of your choice. (According to the faith gospel, you *choose* whether to receive blessing or curse.) But he went on to say that there is another set of curses that come not a result of choice but come from other sources, namely demonic influences. It has not been difficult to combine the two strands.

Through the 1990s deliverance thinking grew to such a degree that it caused widespread alarm in Ghana, mostly on the grounds that Satan had become far more central to Christianity than Christ. Otabil has privately expressed concern – privately because he preferred to use his influence to moderate excesses rather than lose all influence by denouncing it openly. His concern has arisen for a characteristic reason; that because in practice deliverance bears on idols, local spirits, ancestors, stools and face markings, it hardly applies to whites and is really tailored for blacks, and is thus one more way of alienating blacks from their culture.[34] Even Addae-Mensah was trying to set up a fellowship of deliverance pastors 'to regularise, to bring sanity'.[35] The Church of Pentecost, the church most closely associated with the prayer camps, became seriously alarmed. Deliverance became a major source of tension within the church, all the more so because, with their traditional lack of interest in theology, they have difficulty in deciding the issue one way or the other. At the same time as the church authorities moved to regulate the practice, the five major prayer camps announced that they would begin a nation-wide crusade, conducted by the five camp directors, in Ghana's major cities. Tabiri in particular had become too big for the Church of Pentecost. His wealth became a matter of comment in the national press. For his part, Tabiri attacked the church

following acknowledgement to Derek Prince and his wife: 'Their video tape recording on "Release from the Curse" provided the initial tonic I needed to write this book. Their format helped me to put together more clearly what I had been doing in an unclear manner' (Stephen Uche Njoku, *Curses: Effects and Release*, Enugu, 1993, p. iv).

[34] 'African Christians especially, still carry the spiritual influence of their cultural practices most of which are steeped in idol ancestral worship', Atiemo, 'Deliverance', p. 41. Rebecca Brown, in addressing an almost entirely black church in London, expressed it thus: 'You folks are under even greater attack than other cultures, because your cultures (are involved in demon worship). 100% of your background is involved in demon worship... In the USA there is a mass movement for Africans to go back to their roots, but their roots are demon worship...Almost every single thing done in African culture is to do with demon worship' (London's First Born Redemption Church of God, 14 Dec. 1995).

[35] Interview, 30 May 1995.

leadership.[36] In October 1995 Tabiri split from the Church of Pentecost and became Bethel Prayer Ministries International.

The point I am making is that deliverance thinking is complex in its origins. It obviously is African (or more generally 'enchanted'), in its sensitivity in daily life to ubiquitous spiritual forces working in the universe. But in its articulation it has obvious links with the West. It is made all the more complex because in its expression it often totally demonises African traditions. But as Cox has noted, it is often most indigenous when inveighing against the local most strongly.[37] (Is further complexity suggested in that the acknowledged guru of Ghana's deliverance thinking, Derek Prince, was himself a missionary in Kenya for some years?[38])

Christian Zionism

As a third element within African Pentecostal theology, consider Christian Zionism. Part and parcel of pre-millennialist dispensationalism is the idea that God has never abandoned Israel: God works through two agents on earth, the church and Israel.[39] Thus so many biblical references to Israel refer to precisely that – the modern state of Israel established in 1948. Since God will accomplish his end-time purposes through Israel, and Israel is a prerequisite of Christ's return, Israel must be defended by every means possible. This leads to unquestioning support, on supposedly biblical grounds, for everything the modern Israeli government wants or attempts.

Yet far from being the teaching of the Bible, this Christian Zionism is a product of contingencies in America's recent history. Geopolitically, Israel has functioned as a proxy for furthering American interests in the Middle East. Christian Zionism provides a religious justification for pursuing these interests. It has been suggested that another reason for the widespread diffusion of this passionate Zionism in America is the 'macho or muscular' Christianity so admired by Middle America. Israel's 1967 six-day victory, when America was mired in the Vietnam War and filled with defeat, helplessness and despair, made many Americans turn worshipful glances towards Israel.[40] And there is no doubt that Christian

[36] *Free Press*, 20 Oct. 1995, p. 3.

[37] Harvey Cox, 'Into the Age of Miracles: Culture, Religion and the Market Revolution', *World Policy Journal*, Spring 1997, p. 91.

[38] For another case of a Western missionary writing of deliverance in Africa, see Gordon Suckling, *Casting out Demons: the Ministry of Casting out Demons in the Name of Jesus in the Context of the African Republic of Zambia*, Southampton, 1992.

[39] As found in America today, this thinking stems from the dispensationalism of John Nelson Darby. Its most popular expression is Hal Lindsey, with C.C. Carlson, *The Late Great Planet Earth*, New York, 1970, which in selling about 20 million copies was in the 1980s (according to some estimates) America's best selling book of non-fiction (if such it can be called).

[40] Grace Halsell, *Prophecy and Politics: Militant Evangelists on the Road to Nuclear War*, Westport, CT: 1986.

Zionism has come to occupy a crucial place in American Christianity. It spans all sectors – fundamentalists like Falwell, Pentecostals like Robertson and Sumrall, Southern Baptists like Criswell and has even permeated the mainstream churches through the charismatic movement. Christian Zionism is obviously rooted in modern American history. Even when transposed elsewhere, it can also be put to good use, as is evident from a case we have mentioned earlier, *Livets Ord* in Sweden. Christian Zionism, embodying support for Israel and opposition to Russia, often fosters a keen antipathy towards the European Union, for the Antichrist of the last days is supposed to arise from a reconstituted Roman Empire, which in this thinking is understood to be the EU, created by the 1957 Treaty of Rome. In the 1990s Sweden was seriously split on the issue of joining the EU, and its Christian Zionism enabled Word of Life Church to adopt a very high profile in this debate, in the vanguard of the anti-EU forces. Thus, in Sweden, Christian Zionism has proved very functional. Another aspect of Christian Zionism (the belief that the Jews of the diaspora must return home to Israel to usher in the return of Christ) has proved invaluable to the church itself. Word of Life had laboured for some years in East Asia, with virtually no success at all. Their evangelistic outreach (which effectively holds the church together) was in danger of collapse. At just the right time for them, the Soviet Union disintegrated, enabling Word of Life to switch its missionary thrust to a much more responsive area. Their phenomenal success in opening churches and Bible colleges and running crusades in former Soviet lands has not only revitalised the church but enabled them to focus on repatriating Russian Jews to Israel. This task has almost come to define the church; Word of Life has bought and refitted an ocean-going ship solely for the purpose of transporting Jews to Israel – a Christian 'duty' that anyone who does not share their Christian Zionism could hardly credit. Of course this, too, sharpens the local church's identity. Sweden generally has been consistently pro-Palestinian in foreign policy; this Zionist orientation is one more way of standing out in Sweden. Thus an element of a total religious package, which (I would argue) is hardly comprehensible outside its American roots, has in Sweden, because of its functionality both in the nation generally and within the church itself, helped to establish the church's particular identity.[41] In this matter, too, Sweden's adopton of Christian Zionism exhibits both continuity and adaptation.

In parts of Africa, Christian Zionism can be functional too. The obverse side of Christian Zionism is frequently a marked hostility to Islam. (Again, this highlights its roots in recent US history, for this Christianity rose to prominence in the period when Gaddafi and the Ayatollah

---

[41] For Word of Life's prosperity gospel, see Ulf Ekman, *Financial Freedom*, Uppsala, 2nd edn 1993; for its Zionism, see Ulf Ekman, *The Jews: People of the Future*, Uppsala, 1993, and especially the church's magazine, *Word of Life, passim*.

Khomeini were being demonised.) In a place like Nigeria the battle lines are being drawn, and much of the antagonism is expressed in terms of religion. But in a place like Zambia, when many Pentecostals preach about the Muslim threat, it seems totally out of place. Zambia is about seventy per cent Christian, and less than one per cent Muslim – and most of them are the Asians that dominate the retail sector. Here, the anti-Islamic aspect of Christianity arises less from any local experience, and more from the external input.

On 25 December 1991, about the same time that Zambia's new born-again President declared Zambia a Christian nation, Chiluba established diplomatic links with Israel. This seems to stem from Chiluba's Christian Zionism, a belief pervasive in Zambia's Evangelical churches. During the Gulf War four pastors prominent in the Evangelical Fellowship of Zambia (EFZ) had all argued on ZNBC TV that the Gulf War was linked to biblical prophecies, and that 'since the Israelis were God's chosen people all world affairs were supposed to be centred around Israel'. They argued that the Middle East problem could not be solved by the UN, but 'through religious means'.[42] The EFZ issued a press release on 7 February 1991 stating: 'The Bible is clear that God will bless those that bless Israel. This may imply that those who oppose Israel can only expect the wrath of God. Some of the present difficulties experienced in our country can be attributed to a direct result of rejecting Israel.' Another born-again pastor wrote: 'We know that our nation will only prosper if it changes its stand against Israel.' Writing just before the election, he stated that Christians 'shall only vote for a party whose foreign policy would strive to promote Zambia's relations with the international community...This shall include a diplomatic relationship with Israel above all.'[43] Zambia's high-profile evangelist Nevers Mumba called for a review of Zambia's Middle East policy on the basis of Christian Zionism.[44] In a later article, Mumba wrote: 'Zambia has cursed Israel in both word and attitude and we are still reaping the curse on our nation. God's word is final. By being against Israel we are standing up against God and his will...No wonder we lack progress.'[45] Another pastor set the establishing of diplomatic links with Israel as the first priority of any new government.[46] Such Christian Zionism often goes unnoticed by Catholics and the Christian Council of Zambia who seem

[42] *Times*, 3 March 1991; the pastors were Sexton Chiluba of City Community Church, Ernest Chilelwa of Assemblies of God, Helmut Reutter of the Apostolic Faith Mission and Gabriel Schultz of Abundant Life. See also *Mirror*, 16 March 1991, p. 4.

[43] Rev. Mpundu Mwape, 'Church lobbies for Israeli Ties', *Times*, 6 May 1991. In this article he writes, 'The West as well as the East Bank belongs to Israel historically' (thus ceding Israel Gaza and the Golan Heights).

[44] 'Zambia faces Religious Invasion', *Times*, 24 Feb 1991.

[45] *Times*, 13 Oct 1991. He ostensibly derives his Zionism from Mal 3:6; Dt 28:64-7; 2 Chron 7:19-22; Is 43:5-7; Mt 24:32.

[46] *Mirror*, 30 March 1991, p. 5.

totally unaware that such views are possible. Yet, because these views are so important in the born-again camp, it seems likely that, before the 1991 election which brought him to power, Chiluba made them the promise that he would restore such links with Israel, perhaps also break them with Iran and Iraq (which he later did). In these circles, this was bound to be a great vote winner, and would have had the effect of distinguising clearly between the challenger Chiluba and the incumbent Kaunda, who was in these same circles considered to be too close to the Arabs. Israel has increased its influence in Chiluba's Zambia. It may be that Zambia is one country for which Christian Zionism is a key determinant of foreign policy.[47]

It seems to me that in all three examples – the faith gospel, deliverance thinking, Christian Zionism – we have to take into consideration both the local and the external element. The balance is different in each case. In the first two, the balance might be viewed more as a local conceptualisation expressed in a standardised foreign form. In the third, at least in a place like Zambia, the Christian Zionism must surely be explained as essentially an import. In teasing this out, we must give due importance to Africa's marginalisation. That is why Cox, in his discussion of international Pentecostalism, is perhaps misleading in placing his chapter on Korea next to his chapter on Africa with no suggestion that the context of Christianity in these countries is entirely different.[48] Korea for four decades prior to 1997 was being transformed through an economic miracle. Africa over the same period was undergoing an economic collapse, and in serious danger of total marginalisation. Many Africans are acutely conscious of this. Afropessimism is a reality for them too. Ghana's influential Pentecostal preacher Mensa Otabil began a series of talks in Zambia in 1994 with these words: 'Look around the continent, the situation seems almost hopeless. It seems one big continent of war, strife, hunger, malnutrition, pain, famine, killing, ignorance. If you look at CNN it seems all the bad news comes from Africa...When you look at yourself as an African, it is easy to think that God has cursed you.' Consequently, he claims,

[47] In July 1994 Chiluba made a state visit to Israel. The visit was covered by a TV programme screened on ZNBC TV on 2 Aug. 1994. The documentary was in the form of a pilgrimage. Besides the state functions, Chiluba visited Bethlehem, the Garden Tomb, Temple of Solomon, Galilee, Capernaum, the place of the baptism in the Jordan. All the footage of these scenes was accompanied by appropriate biblical references. The increasing Israeli involvement was deplored in *Mirror*, 3-9 Dec. 1995, p. 14. In April 1996 Chiluba called clergymen to State House to pray for Israel on the grounds that 'All who curse Abraham will be cursed; all who bless Abraham will be blessed'. An AME pastor attacked Chiluba for not understanding that Israel's fate is clearly laid out in the Bible, and cannot be changed (*Mirror*, 28 April-4 May 1996, p. 6).

[48] Cox, *Fire from Heaven*.

Africa's biggest problem now is its inferiority complex: 'We are a people who feel inferior and wallow in our own inferiority.' This is frequently the context in which Africa's Pentecostalism is developing. In many countries, this despair and sense of powerlessness has to be factored into any discussion of the dynamics within Christianity.

This makes Africa's case somewhat special in a discussion of global or transnational Pentecostalism. This particular dynamic is largely overlooked in Beyer's work on religion and globalisation. He argues that on one level, religious networks function in the same way as the new global industries like banking, law, health, sport, technology and science, or higher education. But Africa tends to be bypassed by most of these.[49] Beyer argues that the emerging global system both corrodes inherited or constructed cultural and personal identities, yet at the same time also encourages the creation and revitalisation of particular identities as a way of gaining more power or influence in this new global order. Religion has been and continues to be an important resource for such revitalisation movements. Thus Beyer explains the rise of Islamic fundamentalism – but also religious movements in places as diverse as Ireland, Israel, Iran, India and Japan. But the dynamics of Africa's burgeoning Christianity are very different. Africa is not reacting to globalisation by revitalising African traditional religion; movements like Afrikania in Ghana and Godianism in Nigeria have very little popular appeal.[50] Much of Africa is responding to globalisation by opting into exotic religions. Africa's newest form of Christianity, while in many ways reinforcing traditional beliefs, also serves as one of Africa's best remaining ways of opting *into* the global order.[51]

It must be stressed, however, that such links with the outside are quite compatible with a considerable creativity on the part of African Christians. It is widely acknowledged today that Africa's Christianity was always the creation of Africans rather than of missionaries.[52] The creativity is

---

[49] That Africa is in danger of being bypassed by the processes of globalisation was well caught in Paul Kennedy's 1996 BBC Analysis Lecture 'Globalisation and its Discontents' (30 May 1996) which was in reality elaborated in reference to all the globe except Africa; the lecture was really about incorporating Middle Eastern and Asian (and to a lesser degree, Latin American) countries into the formerly overwhelmingly Western networks. I think the only mention of Africa was a passing reference to the 'hopeless countries of Africa'.

[50] *Pace* Bediako's chapter 'The Afrikania Challenge' in Kwame Bediako, *Christianity in Africa: the Renewal of a Non-Western Religion*, Edinburgh, 1995, pp. 17-38.

[51] Peter Beyer, *Religion and Globalisation*, London, 1994. It is another sign of the marginalisation of Africa that Beyer elaborates his globalisation theory without reference to the particularities of Africa.

[52] 'The fate of Christianity depended upon its ability to be reread in terms and with implications for the most part unimagined by its propagators' (Adrian Hastings, *The Church in Africa 1450-1950*, Oxford, 1994, p. 306; see also p. 591).

even greater in the case of Africa's newer charismatic forms. Cox offers a suggestive image in his discussion of the parallels between Pentecostalism and jazz. Jazz and Pentecostalism share 'the near abolition of the standard distinction between the composer and the performer, the creator and the interpreter'.[53] Africans in their current plight are being even more creative with Christianity – it is perhaps a sign of how deeply rooted Christianity is in Africa that it can be put to such myriad uses.

[53] Cox, *Fire*, p. 157.

MEDIATING THE GLOBAL AND LOCAL IN NIGERIAN PENTECOSTALISM [1]

Ruth Marshall-Fratani

Introduction: transnationalism, the nation-state and the media

All world religions are 'transnational', and have been long before the idea of nation took on its modern significance as the privileged space for the construction of political identity and as a new form of 'imagined' community. Christianity in particular, despite its often intimate historical connections with the internal politics of nation-states, its multitude of denominational and institutional forms, has at its core an evangelical message which is to be spread to all peoples, and which seeks to impose a truth which subordinates all other forms of allegiance and identification. However, the transnational character of contemporary Pentecostalism takes on a new significance in the context of what is called 'globalisation' and refers to recent and profound changes in the structure of the international scene. [2]

I will begin with the definition of transnationalism offered by Badie and Smouts in their study of changes in the international order, *Le retournement du monde: Sociologie de la scène internationale.* [3] They define transnationalism as "any relation which, deliberately or by its nature, constructs itself within a global space beyond the context of the nation-state, and which escapes, at least partially, the control or mediating action

---

[1] A longer version of this paper was published in: *Journal of Religion in Africa*, Leiden: Brill, vol. 28, Fall 1998.

[2] There is a growing literature on the subject of globalisation, and often heated discussion over the definition of the phenomenon. The term 'transnationalism' seems more often used in the francophone literature to distinguish the phenomenon from 'globalisation' or *'mondialisation'* which is often understood as involving a process of the 'homogenisation' or 'Americanisation' of global culture. I do not share this position, arguing with Appadurai and others that globalisation involves both processes of homogenisation as well as heterogenisation, as explained in the introduction to this volume. In this paper, I will use the terms more or less interchangeably, and will make my definition clear in the discussion below. See M. Featherstone, S. Lash and R. Roberston (eds), *Global Modernities*, London: Sage, 1997; R. Robertson; *Globalization: Social Theory and Global Culture*, London: Sage, 1992; Peter Geschiere and Birgit Meyer, 'Globalization and Identity: Dialectics of Flows and Closures', *Development and Change*, vol.29, no.4, October, 1998; M. McLuhan and B. Powers, *The Global Village: Transformations in World, Life and Media in the 21ˢᵗ Century*, Oxford University Press, 1989.

[3] B. Badie and M.-C. Smouts, *Le retournement du monde: Sociologie de la scène internationale*, Paris: Presses de la Foundation Nationale des Sciences Politiques/Dalloz, 1992.

of States'.[4] They argue that while transnational flux among organisations has always existed, citing the case of the Roman Catholic Church, it take on 'in the world today, a particular importance and weight which gives [it] a totally different stature and function than [that] observed in the past.'[5] The transnationalism Badie and Smouts refer to takes on its new significance in a context where nation-states and nationalism no longer necessarily constitute the primary physical and ideological contexts in which identity and community are imagined and political allegiance expressed. They argue convincingly for the fragmentation of the unitary space of the nation-state with the enormous growth of multiple forms of transnational flux, which are intimately connected to the sophistication of communications and media networks. Nicolas Garnham likewise associates the 'crisis' of the nation-state with the growth of global media systems and an increasingly integrated global market, a growth which 'appears to be undermining the key locus of democratic power and accountability within the liberal model – namely, the nation-state'. He links this to 'the development of "identity politics", including the recrudescence of ethnic particularism in nationalistic forms and of religious fundamentalism'.[6] Religious identity also takes on a particular significance in Badie and Smouts' analysis, as the crisis in the old mechanisms of identification 'gives back to the "sacred realm" an importance and a social function which the construction and diffusion of the state model, as rational and secular, had helped it to lose'.[7]

The theme of a 'post-national global order' is taken up by Arjun Appadurai in his book *Modernity at Large: Cultural Dimensions of Globalization.*[8] In this subtle and penetrating analysis of the dynamics of global culture Appadurai likewise draws attention to the crisis of the nation-state, recognising that while the nation-state is not yet 'out of business', its crisis is related to the emergence of strong alternative forms for organising global traffic in resources, images and people; forms that either contest the nation-state directly, whether invested with 'nationalist' ambitions or not, or constitute peaceful alternatives for large-scale political loyalties. At the same time, he notes that the capabilities of the nation-state to monopolise the 'moral resources of community' and command political loyalty are being steadily eroded. In his analysis, he privileges the processes of mass mediation and migration, examining the ways in which they affect 'the imagination as social practice'.[9]

[4] *Ibid.*, p. 70.

[5] *Ibid.*, p. 73.

[6] Nicolas Garnham, 'The Mass Media: Cultural Identity and the Public Space in the Modern World' in *Public Culture*, 1993, p. 251.

[7] *Ibid.*, p. 53.

[8] A. Appadurai, *Modernity at Large: Cultural Dimensions of Globalization*, Minneapolis: University of Minnesota Press, 1996.

[9] *Ibid.*, p. 31.

The relationship between the media and the process of 'imagining' new communal identities has been demonstrated by Benedict Anderson in his study of nationalism,[10] but as Appadurai argues, 'the revolution of print capitalism and the cultural affinities and dialogues unleashed by it were only modest precursors to the world we live in now' – a world of communications explosion which involves 'an altogether new form of neighborliness, even with those most distant from ourselves' and yet one which is characterised by media-created communities with 'no sense of place'.[11] In contrast to the communitarian idealism behind McLuhan's notion of a 'global village' and in rejection of those theorists who express fears of the homogenisation or 'Americanisation' of global culture, Appadurai stresses the non-isomorphic character of transnational flux. The speed, scale and volume of flows of money, people, machinery, images and ideas have become so great that 'disjunctures have become central to the politics of global culture'.[12] In particular, mass-mediation results in the circulation of images, ideas and symbols which, as they move through global space, break free from their context of production and are appropriated in endless, inventive processes of cultural *bricolage*.

The importance of global media is not limited to the technological possibilities it offers for the production and dissemination of ideas, images, and narratives. The circulation of these media-produced 'strips of reality' has two important related consequences for the formation of identity in the context of the crisis of the nation-state. Firstly, such images, ideas and narratives provide 'a series of elements (such as characters, plots and textual forms) out of which scripts can be formed of imagined lives',[13] scripts which, while interpreted in terms of local, everyday experience, are taken from global repertoires, and as such, provide means for imagining communities outside or in defiance of the nation-state's bid to monopolise the resources of community formation. Such imagined communities are not the stuff of wistful longings or fantasies, even given the disjuncture between the flow of images and the flow of goods, finance and technologies which such images evoke. As we shall see in the case of Pentecostalism in Nigeria, it is not simply access to globalised media images in general which fuels the imagination of actors, but the ways in which access to mediated images, narratives and ideas produced by specific transnational 'imagined communities', such as Pentecostal Christianity, connect local actors to global networks on the one hand, and on the other, the ways local access to media technology enables the dissemination of

[10] B. Anderson, *Imagined Communities*, London: Verso, 1983. See also K. Deutsch, *Nationalism and Social Communities*, Cambridge University Press, 1966.

[11] J. Meyerowitz, *No Sense of Place: The Impact of Electronic Media on Social Behaviour*, New York: Oxford University Press, 1985, cited in Appadurai, *Modernity at Large*, p. 29.

[12] Appadurai, *Modernity at Large*, p. 29.

[13] *Ibid.*, p. 35.

local appropriations of these images, and narratives nationally and globally, creating a constant process of circulation between global and local, in which it becomes more and more difficult, even on an analytical level, to separate these two spaces.

Added to this circulation of images and narratives is the movement of people in connection with these transnational communities. In the case of Pentecostalism, evangelists from Korea, Brazil, Nigeria preach at conferences in Manila, Atlanta, and Accra; indigenous Nigerian Pentecostal 'missions' or 'ministries' (as their transnationally ambitious leaders now call them, invariably adding 'International' to the name, even if the mission comprises only a handful of members) open branches not only in the heart of Nigeria's Muslim north and just next door in Benin, Liberia or Ghana, but as far afield as London, Manchester, New York and Toronto, their congregations peopled by an ever-growing diaspora. Rijk van Dijk's examination of exchanges between Ghanaian Pentecostal communities in Ghana and Holland provides evidence for his claim that: 'Pentecostalism is historically a transnational phenomenon, which in its modern forms is reproduced in its local diversity through a highly accelerated circulation of goods, ideas and people. The new charismatic type of Pentecostalism creates a moral and physical geography whose domain is one of transnational cultural inter-penetration and flow.'[14]

This 'deterritorialisation' of culture via mediation and migration leads us to the second consequence for identity formation, insofar as it facilitates the delocalisation of identity and community formation, resulting in, as Appadurai argues, a disjuncture between the production and reproduction of 'locality as a property of social life', and its realisation in the in the form of 'neighbourhoods as social formations' made up of '*local subjects*, actors who properly belong to a situated community of kin, neighbours, friends and enemies'. In this 'battle between the imaginaries of the nation-state, of unsettled communities, and of global electronic media...the production of locality – always...a fragile and difficult achievement – is more than ever shot through with contradiction, destabilised by human motion and displaced by the formation of new kinds of virtual neighbourhoods.'[15] One of the questions to be taken up in this paper is the extent to which the current wave of Pentecostalism sweeping Nigeria provides an example of the creation of 'delocalised' subjects, or at least, of subjects whose individual and collective identities seem to have been formed in terms of a new type of negotiation between local and global, one in which the media has a privileged role.

The second issue that will be addressed is the way Pentecostalism positions itself *vis-à-vis* the Nigerian nation-state. As mentioned above,

---

[14] R. van Dijk 'From Camp to Encompassment: Discourses of Transsubjectivity in the Ghanaian Pentecostal Diaspora', *Journal of Religion in Africa*, vol. 27, no. 2, 1997, p. 142.

[15] Appadurai, *Modernity at Large*, pp. 178-81.

transnationalism offers possibilities for identification and political allegiance that may allow groups to bypass or confront the nation-state, and erode its attempts to monopolise such identification and allegiance. As Appadurai argues, 'electronic mass mediation and transnational mobilization have broken the monopoly of autonomous nation-states over the project of modernization. The transformation of everyday subjectivities through electronic mediation and the work of the imagination is not only a cultural fact. It is deeply connected to politics, through the new ways in which individual attachments, interests and aspirations increasingly crosscut those of the nation-state.'

The 'demise' of the nation-state and its consequences discussed by Badie and Smouts rely largely on evidence from the industrialised West, yet one can argue that the failure of nationalism and the 'developmentalist' state in post-colonial countries to provide a stable reference for the construction of identity likewise opens the ground for this 'explosion' of multiple identities. Those identities which are part of transnational movements have a particularly important and powerful position within these societies, not simply because of their access to what Bayart calls 'resources of extraversion',[16] that is, important material and symbolic connections with global networks which enable them to erode the state's historical monopoly on such resources, but also because the access to these resources enables them to provide an alternative vision of 'modernity', and the means by which individuals and communities may inscribe themselves within it. In the Nigerian context, Pentecostalism and new Islamic movements present a challenge to the state's monopoly over the public sphere, and pose one of the greatest ever threats to its goal of national unity and ideologies of development. Pentecostalism is attempting to colonise the national public space and reconceptualise the structure and normative basis of the nation, and it is doing this largely not through the institutionalisation of churches, but through the production and dissemination of a multitude of discourses via the media.

Conversion and agency: negotiating 'local pasts' and 'global modernities'

The wave of conversions to Pentecostalism which has swept across urban Nigeria in the past decade or so has brought a number of changes in doctrine, membership, organisation and transnational affiliation to the already existing Pentecostal churches which expanded or were established in the earlier revival of the 1970s. Unlike these older churches, typically denominational, emphasising a doctrine of 'holiness' and anti-materialism, expressed in the eschewal of fancy clothes, expensive commodities and modern media such as television, and peopled by

[16] See J.-F. Bayart, *L'Etat en Afrique. La politique du ventre*, Paris: Fayard, 1989.

relatively disadvantaged social groups, these new organisations place themselves firmly in the 'world'. Typically young, upwardly mobile, relatively well-educated, their leaders privilege international contacts and experiences, incorporating, as van Dijk notes of their Ghanaian counterparts, this international image in the operation and symbolism of their organisations. The gospel of prosperity offers a doctrine of morally controlled materialism, in which personal wealth and success are interpreted as the evidence of God's blessing on those that lead a 'true life in Christ'. Membership comprises largely young members of the now struggling middle classes, even if most organisations boast at least a few conspicuous elites. The structure of organisation of these new missions and ministries tends to be less denominational; despite the need for leaders to create a solid clientele, there is perpetual movement from one group to another on the part of the converted, and the formation of a multitude of interdenominational groups ranging from intimate 'house' or 'prayer' fellowships to larger professional, gender-based, educational, or political organisations. This tendency for movement among converts is related in part to doctrine, which stresses the importance of the individual conversion experience over belonging to a given institution as the marker of identity; but, as we shall see below, it is also closely linked to the transnational character and mediation of the Pentecostal message. The media, both print and electronic, play a central role in this 'new wave'. More shall be said on this below.

This new form of Pentecostalism responds to and helps resolve the fear and uncertainty which have come to mark social relations over the past decades. The anxiety created by the continued influx of 'dangerous strangers' to urban centres as a result of increased rural-urban migration, the extreme instrumentalisation of social relations, as well as the breakdown of many patron-client networks during the past decade have introduced a kind of urban paranoia about 'evil doers' who are out to cheat, deceive, rob and kill. A kind of Hobbesian sense of 'all against all' prevails; the old forms of community – ethnic, kinship, professional, home town, neighbourhood – have proved unreliable sources of support. New Pentecostal networks, both spiritual and material, extend beyond local, ethnic, regional and even class considerations. At the local or national level, these networks not only offer an overarching sense of belonging and common purpose, but also provide material benefits such as employment opportunities, exchanges of goods and services, and even access to officialdom without the usual costly red tape and inevitable 'dash'. Networks extend beyond the national to the global, and even if the particular mission or ministry to which a believer belongs is small, it carries with it the sense of belonging to a global movement and access, if not immediately to financial or technological support, to resources such as literature and ideas. While the actual amount of material resources any given church or ministry receives from abroad is difficult to estimate, I would argue that most revenues are generated locally. The importance of international ties may be largely symbolic, but they certainly have real material consequences in mobilising local wealth and creating vital connections via the media, and in certain cases through international travel, with millions of other Pentecostal Christians the world over.

Conversion does not necessarily imply a rejection of other identities, but involves their assimilation within a complex of discourses and practices governing all aspects of social, cultural economic and political life which enable them to be mediated through and subsumed within a collective system of representations. One is always a born-again first, and this implies of course that being born again is simply incompatible with certain other forms of identification – most obviously religious. But one can learn how to be a born-again woman, Yoruba, businessman, politician, southerner, husband, rich or poor man, youth or elder. The success of Pentecostalism in converting massive numbers is clearly related in part to the opportunity it provides for the mediation of conflicting and often unmanageable situations of multiple identification. Issues which are addressed in Pentecostal discourses also form the locus for the creation of interdenominational groups which address problems relating to other modes of social identification – women's groups, professional or business groups, lawyers, doctors, journalists, students, businessmen, singles, neighbourhoods – enabling people to articulate practices which address the particular demands of a given social identity within the strictures of Pentecostal doctrine.

The model of agency implicit in the born-again conversion depicts a lone individual struggling to achieve selfhood in a world full of evil forces which seek his undoing at every turn. True conversion means cutting the links with one's personal past; not simply the ungodly habits and sinful pastimes, but also friends and family members who are not born-again. Such individuals provide the greatest threats to a 'new life in Christ', precisely because of the power in ties of blood and amity, and if they cannot be brought to give their lives to Christ, they must be cut surgically from the lives of the new convert. Friends, family and neighbours become 'dangerous strangers', and strangers, new friends. The social grounds for creating bonds – blood, common pasts, neighbourhood ties, language – are forsworn for the new bond of the brother or sister in Christ.

It is not simply the past life of the convert which is seen as a potential avenue through which evil forces will attempt to reclaim him, but also the communal past in whose shadow he lives. Even a born-again Christian is not free from such evil influences, as this writer on 'Demonology' attests:

The spirit of sin from the ancestors can enter subsequent generations. Worshipping of traditional idols, masqurades [*sic*], family shrines and other family traditions can be passed down to other generation. Ancestral sinful practices of blood convenant with evil spirits may tie their children's children to that spirit. Generation can be affected with the curses and sin of their forefathers unless there is true and genuine repentance and turning to God for forgiveness.[17]

The 'sins of the fathers'[18] are often represented in terms of 'traditional' religious practices – shrines, masquerades, covenants – but it is not simply the fact that this religious 'otherness' represents a danger to Pentecostalism which projects itself as the only 'true' religion. Religious 'Others', in particular Muslims, are typically demonised in Pentecostal discourse; however, this demonisation of the past is less about the contemporary threat that traditional religion poses in terms of religious competition (unlike Islam) and more about its connection with a cultural past that failed to provide the moral grounding for a 'good' society in the present. Another preacher makes this clear. He begins by speaking about various rites, such as naming ceremonies, puberty rites, circumcision, and goes on to explain how such rites are specified by the spirits of the land, with the purpose of bringing people under control. These 'territorial spirits' affect the minds of the people living in the land:

There are certain people who are prone to violence, there are certain that love money a lot; if you want to check up if a man is dead, you could just chuck money round his ears and if he doesn't wake up, then he's dead. And there are certain people, they are never straightforward, you could never rely on them, if you relied on them, you would break and pierce your heart. And then there are some others who manipulate everything. [...] There are others that are violent, if there is an argument, it ends with blows. Then there are those that, by this hour, they are drunk. There are certain parts of this country that if you went now, the men would be gathered in places just lounging around and drinking, the women would be in the farms. The women would come back and pound the yams and the men would have the audacity to eat. It affects people, this is the way territorial spirits operate. [...] Now you look at certain parts of the country, people have a disposition to lie, and I mean they lie by the second. Now if you had them on a church committee, whenever there's going to be a scandal, notice they will be at the end of it. They will trade gossips between these ones and the other ones, they are the people who know who and who, what is doing what. Now you know, there are certain types of deliverances that may not, I'm using the word may, that may not come through, unless you deal with the thing that is on the land, the particular powers that hold the people.[19]

What the convert must be delivered from is the history that makes these anti-social practices commonplace. It is not so much the missionary view of the evils of 'paganism' that Pentecostals are echoing here, but the

[17] *Ibid.*, p. 10.
[18] This term was the title of another address given by Emeka Nwankpa at the conference cited below.
[19] Emeka Nwankpa, 'Territorial Spirits', Address given at Pentecostal conference on 'Combatting the Powers of Darkness', National Theatre, Lagos, April, 1993.

idea that all moral orders have their spiritual counterparts, that there is no real distinction to be made between the natural and supernatural. Clearly if things have come to such a pass, it is because the wrong sort of spiritual-moral order has held sway. The same theme is taken up again below, this time in more 'secular' language:

'*Be not deceived; God is not mocked: for whatsoever a man soweth, that shall he also reap*' (Gal. 6:7). What is it that we sow that could be responsible for the unfavourable conditions that prevail in this country presently? Why is the truth relegated to the background or completely obliterated while unrighteousness, ungodliness, and injustice reign supreme? Why do we advertise or publicize mediocrity at the expense of excellence? Why do we rejoice at spiritual elimination? Why should anyone hinder the spread of the Gospel and ban early morning devotion at schools? What is basically wrong with us as a people? Why do we massacre in cold blood our defenceless [*sic*] students at the slightest excuse? Why do we have such a large number of juvenile delinquents? Why is armed robbery a very 'profitable' profession in our midst? Why do we have deceit in governments and high places? Why do we have instability in government to the extent that anybody in uniform can occupy the 'hot' seat and pronounce himself Head of State even when he has nothing to offer? Why do Christians obey man rather than God when we know that Isa. 10:1 says 'Woe unto them that decree unrighteous decrees and that write grievousness which they have prescribed'.[20]

This poignant questioning is followed by a response expressing the Pentecostal conviction that it is not simply present day individual sin which has lead to this state of things, but the 'sins of the fathers'. Pentecostal discourses engages with the 'history of the present', questioning the social, political and cultural forms that they see as historical ground for the present crisis. This questioning focuses not on external interventions such as colonialism, or capitalism, but rather focuses on the local; on the *practices* of local agents – 'What is basically wrong with us as a people?' Pentecostalism's fierce rejection of all forms of socio-cultural practice which are seen as particularly 'Nigerian', 'traditional' and 'local' not only expresses a form of socio-political critique which emphasises individual agency – it is individual sin and the personal rejection of Christ that open up the space in which the failure of the nation is manifested – but also reinforces its resolutely 'modern', transnational character.

The view of Christian conversion as a mode of collective socio-political advancement is not new in Nigeria, as John Peel has eloquently argued.[21] Nineteenth-century missionaries among the Yoruba likewise managed to present Christianity in terms which linked the issue of personal salvation to collective progress in a time which was marked by war and great social upheaval. Contemporary Pentecostalism inserts itself in a way that builds

[20] F. Tayo, *Nigeria Belongs to Jesus*, Ibadan: Feyistan Press, 1988, pp. v-vi.

[21] J.D.Y. Peel, 'For Who Hath Despised the Days of Small Things? Missionary Narratives and Historical Anthropology', *Comparative Studies in Society and History*, vol. 37, no. 3, 1995.

upon the historical experience of Christianity as a mode of bringing about social change, but introduces something quite novel at the same time. This novelty refers to the ways in which Pentecostalism in Nigeria is part of a transnational movement, one in which the circulation of narratives via the media plays a central role. What is new is the way in which this break with the past goes hand in hand with a new role for the imagination in the creation of new identities and communities. Although he rejects the definition of 'modernity' as it has been typologised by the social sciences in terms of the difference between traditional and modern societies, Appadurai rightly observes that the world in which we all live does involve 'a break with all sorts of pasts'. The theory of rupture that he sketches involves a different way of looking at agency and social change than that entailed in modernisation theory, one which, as noted above, concerns the effects of media and migration on the 'work of the imagination as a constitutive feature of modern subjectivity'.[22] In this sense, it is not so much the individualism of Pentecostal conversion which leads to the creation of modern subjects, but the ways in which its projection on a global scale of images, discourses and ideas about renewal, change and salvation opens up possibilities for local actors to incorporate these into their everyday lives.

As Appadurai argues, the work of the imagination 'is neither purely emancipatory nor entirely disciplined but is a space of contestation in which individuals and groups seek to annex the global into their own practices of the modern'.[23] As he puts it, what is new about the role of the imagination in today's world is that the imagination

has broken out of the special expressive space of art, myth and ritual and has become part of the quotidian mental work of ordinary people in many societies. [...] Of course, this has precedents in the great revolutions, cargo cults, and messianic movements of other times, in which forceful leaders implanted their visions into social life, thus creating powerful movements for social change. Now, however, it is no longer a matter of specially endowed (charismatic) individuals, injecting the imagination where it does not belong. Ordinary people have begun to deploy their imaginations in the practice of their everyday lives.[24]

The new wave of Pentecostalism – with its multiple organisational forms, its interdenominationalism, relatively loose ritual structure, its emphasis on the individual converts' own actions in gaining salvation, the idea that the 'gifts of the spirit' may be within the reach of anyone, not just specially anointed, charismatic leaders, and the production *by converts* of a multitude of narratives (testimonies, evangelism, booklets etc.) – provides a particularly powerful example of the ways in which the imagination of the individual is given a new role in the everyday lives of converts.

[22] Appadurai, *Modernity at Large*, p. 3.

[23] *Ibid.*, p. 4.

[24] *Ibid.*, p. 5.

At the same time, Pentecostalism provides an example of the ways in which the 'new power of the imagination is inescapably tied up with images, ideas and opportunities that come from elsewhere, often moved around by the vehicles of mass media'.[25]

To embrace the idea of linear progress via human agency which is at the heart of the idea of 'modernisation', individuals and collectivities must 'domesticate' and subdue the past. The 'invention of tradition' which accompanies the rise of nationalism in the West is central to this process of domestication. It is in this sense perhaps that Pentecostalism provides a version of 'modernity' which is more compelling and more accessible; one which 'delivers the goods' in contexts where so many experience modernity as a series of unfulfilled promises and broken dreams. The 'breach' between past histories, everyday realities and the promises of 'development' is narrowed not only in Pentecostal discourse, but the very spaces where people come to worship reflect a conscious project of creating - modern, functional spaces and forms of association. It is not simply the way these spaces are 'delocalised', with their emphasis on cleanliness, order and punctuality, the use of modern technology such as computers, electrical instruments, video recorders, televisions, but the way in which, in particular through the use of modern media, a sense of 'delocalised' community is created one in which members are 'brothers' and 'sisters' in Christ before being members of different age groups, ethnic groups and social classes.

At the same time, the use of the mass media provides examples of the ways in which, as Appadurai argues, 'consumption of the mass media throughout the world often provokes resistance, irony, selectivity, and, in general, *agency*...Part of what the mass media make possible, because of conditions of collective reading, criticism and pleasure, is what I have elsewhere called a "community of sentiment", a group that begins to imagine and feel things together.'[26] Citing Anderson's reference to the ways in which print capitalism creates communities of national sentiment, he argues that 'electronic capitalism' has similar and even greater effects, since they go beyond the context of the nation-state. As he puts it, 'it is the imagination, in its collective forms, that creates ideas of neighbourhood and nationhood, of moral economies and unjust rule, of higher wages and foreign labour prospects'[27] or, if you are a born-again, of health, wealth, happiness and salvation. Indeed, collective experiences of the mass media can create 'sodalities of worship...communities in themselves which are always potentially communities for themselves, capable of moving from shared imagination to collective action'.[28]

[25] *Ibid.*, p. 54.
[26] *Ibid.*, pp. 4-5.
[27] *Ibid.*, p. 7.
[28] *Ibid.*, p. 8.

Mediatisation and 'delocalisation'

In recent years, nearly all ministries or missions in Nigeria have become producers of some form of print and/or audio and video production. More and more services, rallies, revivals and assemblies are videotaped as well as audiotaped, and sold to members, distributed to various shops, inter-denominational groups, or simply passed from hand to hand. Born-again weeklies or monthlies appear, circulate for a period, sometimes breaking off production, or being replaced by new editions, and a huge quantity of Nigerian as well as foreign booklets and tracts can be found in the grow-ing number of private Christian bookshops, sold by itinerant sellers at large assemblies and stocked in church or ministry bookshops. Videos of local revivals, rallies and plays, as well as many 'born-again' films or religious broadcasts from the US and other countries, can be rented from a grow-ing number of born-again video rental outfits. Those lucky enough to have satellite television can watch and record foreign evangelical programmes, but even terrestrial television will enable born-again viewers to tune into a variety of local televangelists, especially on beleaguered state networks. In the apartment where I lived, my flat-mates had a video machine, and our sitting room was often full of young born-agains come to watch the latest video that one of my friends' uncles had brought back from his trips to preach or attend born-again seminars in the US or Britain.

While religious doctrine and ritual proper (prayer, bible study, guides to salvation, deliverance from evil spirits, testimonies of miracles and healing, sermons) make up a significant part of these media discourses and images, they by no means exhaust them. A dizzying quantity of dis-courses on subjects ranging from history, politics, development, economics to family life, sexual behaviour, professional conduct, dress codes, cul-ture and lifestyles can be found in the form of tracts, articles, lectures, discussion groups, sermons, taped or televised messages, testimonies, music, public rallies, bumper stickers, plays in theatres or video movies, radio broadcasts, public preaching or 'street evangelism'. The 'official' press, admittedly one of the freest and most critical in Africa, speaks to issues which most people see as irrelevant to their social reality; as Oluyinka Esan shows, popular responses to news and information programmes characterise them as 'lies'; 'a nauseating business'.[29] Pentecostalism, on the other hand, expends enormous resources on the dissemination of its messages in forms which excite and inspire, bringing technologies of modern media to bear on the issues and idioms central to popular urban culture.

Yet the media is not simply a tool for the dissemination of representa-tions, but central to the imagined form of the community. Firstly, the

[29] O. Esan, 'Receiving Television Messages: An Ethnography of Women in a Nigerian Context', PhD diss., Department of Sociology, University of Glasgow, 1994.

media allow for internal debate among members, and the working out of a relatively coherent sort of Pentecostal 'public opinion' A born-again 'community of sentiment' is formed through reading, watching and discussing together tracts, magazines, videos: interchanges which entail the articulations not only of models of 'correct' behaviour, and new regimes of personal and collective discipline, but also new attitudes towards consumption, new dress styles, aesthetics, ways of speaking and moving. These articulations are made with reference, often self-consciously, to a global Pentecostal community and its perceived modes of worship, models of behaviour, styles and culture. I remember attending a birthday party thrown by a group of born-again friends in a small Lagos flat. Someone had brought an amplifier and speaker, although the space was easily small enough for those 'preaching' to be heard without them. A young women led the praise and worship, speaking with an odd American accent. My friend with whom I had come started to giggle, and when I asked him what was funny, he told me that the nearest the girl had been to the USA was Ikeja (where the airport is). My friend was forced to retire outside so as not to disturb the praying group when the girl started to preach in Yoruba with an American accent. Rather than being evidence for the 'Americanisation' of local culture, what this anecdote points to is the way in which these new forms of social behaviour express new kinds of prestige, new grounds upon which social hierarchies can be established, and new models for social interaction which draw their social power, not simply among members, but in the eyes of broader Nigerian society as well, from global images of wealth and success. Access to such registers has in Nigeria typically been the privilege of a small elite, particularly those in government. Part of Pentecostalism's success in Nigeria is related to the community's ability not only to give regular people access to these global repertoires, but also to use this in its self-representations to an outside which has not yet been saved; an outside which comprises a potential threat, but also a challenge. Increasingly intense competition in the religious field means that 'resources of extraversion' are more and more essential for success.

The increasing use of the media also means that the locus of identification and signification is no longer the church or congregation as a 'situated community' which provides the place and context of the message's enunciation. Messages and images are sent out to a public which is not defined according to denominational, ethnic, gender, geographic or social markers. Nor are they designed simply to reach confirmed members of the church, or even the Pentecostal community. Even before its mediation, every message, no matter how precise its theme, how circumscribed the original audience, is an evangelical message. That is, it is designed to reach beyond the saved, to incorporate a theoretically unlimited group of potential converts. This expansionist, evangelical position is fundamental to Pentecostalism everywhere, and central to its transnational character.

In the West, in particular the United States, televangelism and the intense mediatisation of the Pentecostal message seem somehow in keeping with the totalising grip the media has on popular culture. But its use has particular significance in cultures where the media still represent 'islands of modernity' in a sea of local 'artisanal' culture.[30] Here the media, and the technology behind them can often imply a magical, almost supernatural power of their own.[31] In the hands of the 'anointed', electronic media can work their of their own special miracles. I often heard references made to those who were healed by touching the television, or who were moved to conversion after watching a broadcast. Below is an example of the re-diffusion via the media (a taped message) of an indirect experience of the miracle of the mediated word:

'I always share this testimony everywhere I go. This happened some years back. I was preaching on television in Benin City and a man watched my programme. As he watched, this man, according to his testimony, he had been sick for five years and had been on his sick bed at home. When I was done preaching I said – now you see, I didn't even know he was there – I said, "Get out of that bed in the name of Jesus. Do what you couldn't do before." He believed me. He jumped out of his bed. His relative grabbed him and said "No, you can't do that. Listen to me, your relatives will love you to death. They will love you and kill you." They said, "You can't do that. For five years you've been on the bed, you can't. Oh Uncle, stay on the bed." And he said, "Thank you, I've listened to you for five years and it didn't help me. I like what that man just said." He said, "Get me some water, I want to take a shower." For five years they were dry-cleaning him on the bed. He got up, staggered to the bathroom, took a shower, a good shower, after five years. He said, "Put my food on the table." He got down and ate his food on the dining table for the first time in five years. And you know what he did next? He got out of the house, he walked to the T.V. station and he said, "I want the manager." And they took him to someone there. And he said "You know, I don't know that man that just preached, but I want you to let him know that it works.'[32]

The message conveyed in this testimony is not simply one of the powers of televangelism, nor God's mysterious ways in the world of electronic media. The miracle occurs in a 'virtual' relationship between the preacher and the sick man, total strangers. The sick man identifies immediately the televised message as a personal, intimate call. His family, who have been caring and ministering to him for five years – feeding and 'dry-cleaning' him on his bed – are depicted as the obstacles to his healing,

[30] I thank Karin Barber for this apt expression, used in comments she made on one of my papers in progress.
[31] See A. Lyons and H. Lyons, 'Magical Medicine on Television: Benin City, Nigeria', *Journal of Ritual Studies*, vol. 1, no. 2, 1987.
[32] A. Oritsejafor, 'Jesus on the Offensive', Preached Message, Lagos National Theatre, Lagos, 13 May 1993.

salvation and personal success. They may love him, but it is a dangerous love, one that thwarts and ultimately kills. The space of intimacy is thus displaced, and the story finishes with the recognition by the healed to the healer not in a person-to-person contact (although we must imagine that such a contact subsequently took place) but rather via the television station manager.

The use of the media allows for the multiplication of narrative forms, and the delocalisation of messages. Sermons preached to local congregations are video- or audio-taped, and then circulated among members not only of the given church or ministry, but among Pentecostals and their unconverted friends, relatives and neighbours, or taken by missionaries to different parts of the country and even the world. Taped sermons are often transcribed and published in a variety of magazines, tracts and leaflets with an equally wide circulation. The organisational structures of many new ministries which have many local 'parishes' or branches, as well as many associated groups, such as youth, women's or professional associations which are often interdenominational in membership, also ensures the circulation of discourses dissociated from a specific social 'place'. The growth of new religious complexes such as ministry headquarters or prayer camps in what was previously socially empty space – bush land, recuperated swamp, industrial urban areas, or spaces which are not claimed or 'colonised' by a determinate social group, such as cinemas, national stadiums and sports grounds – reinforces the delocalisation of identity and community.

The case of Bethel church in Lagos provides a striking example of how the media penetrates even the intimate space of the congregation and also demonstrates how new places are built from spaces without creating localised social formations. Bethel Church is an impressive Pentecostal complex developed in the late 1980s on reclaimed swampland along the Leki Peninsula, about 10 miles from Victoria Island (where the rich and powerful live) and at least half an hour by car (on a Sunday) from the Lagos mainland. Proudly presenting itself as the only air-conditioned born-again church in Lagos, it boasts a large and beautifully decorated central church surrounded by well-appointed offices worthy of any of the off-shore banks which are found in neighbouring Victoria Island. The church has a fleet of new buses, which it sends out early on Sunday mornings to various parts of Lagos to bring the faithful to worship. The service itself is extremely high-tech, even by Pentecostal standards, the most striking aspect being the closed-circuit televisions dotted throughout the congregation, which numbers about three or four hundred. What I remarked immediately upon entering was the incongruity of these televisions in a space which, while large, still appears relatively intimate in comparison with the many other new 'converted warehouse' churches which can hold congregations of several thousand. One can see the pastor on the raised stage from all points within the church; clearly the televisions are not there to ensure everyone can see as well as hear the message. But people do watch them. The congregation is socially mixed – people from all different areas of Lagos, different social classes, different ethnic groups. Many are young and fairly middle class, but there are middle-aged businessmen who arrive in Mercedes, their beautifully groomed wives on their arms. I spoke with a couple of older market women in traditional attire, and shared a pew with a young man in a worn suit who told me he was a vulcaniser. In this example of the mediation of the message, the performance staged by the preacher on his closed-circuit televisions takes to an extreme the tendency for the church to become less the site for the formation of 'local' communities, and more and more a stage for a performance whose audience is elsewhere. One could almost say that at Bethel, the physical audience is already only virtually present.

If we compare these organisations with other older, more established churches, both among mainstream or orthodox denominations, the Aladura churches, and earlier Pentecostal churches even, we find striking differences in the ways in which congregations are set up as communities, and in the ways in which they identify themselves as co-religionists. As André Corten argues with reference to Pentecostalism in Latin America: 'Through the media, transversal relations [among churches] are formed. The community of the church still exists as a reference, but is transformed from a place of praise and cohesion to a "show place" [*lieu de spectacle*] where deliverance and divine healing are staged. In this staging of a "show", there is a change of imaginary [*imaginaire*]."[33] This change of 'imaginary' involves the ways in which Pentecostalism inserts itself into a situation of urban crisis, where 'local' identities and social relationships in Appadurai's sense of 'neighbourhoods' are harder and harder to maintain and reproduce. This is in part due to the ways in which identities are imposed and manipulated by the Nigerian state, but is also related to the economic crisis and the strains it puts on local networks and social relationships, increased rural-urban migration, and perhaps most importantly, the ways in which the global images, ideas, commodity forms, technologies have been absorbed by local culture. As Appadurai argues, in this context identity appears less and less as something tacitly accepted and reproduced as 'natural', and more and more a question of conscious choice, justification and representation.[34] Pentecostalism offers forms of identification and community formation which are extremely well-adapted to this context, enabling individuals to recreate their personal and social lives in a way that helps them overcome the social anxiety and economic hardship of everyday life in the city, but also allows them to master this

[33] A. Corten, 'Pentecôtisme et Politique en Amérique Latine', *Problèmes d'Amérique Latine*, no. 24, 1997.

[34] Appadurai, *Modernity at Large*, chaps 2 and 7.

new context by providing their own account of it which inscribes itself
into the logic of displaced communities and transnational identities.

For Pentecostalism, the media are triply powerful – not simply as a
tool which assists the spread of the message, and as a new mode of
imagining the self and the community in terms of transnational identity,
but also as a mode of appropriating modernity, and the material and
symbolic goods it offers. Although the 'megarhetoric' of developmental
modernisation is still being spouted by the Nigerian state, we may see
Pentecostalism as an example of one of the 'micronarratives and other
expressive forms which allow modernity to be rewritten more as vernacular globalization and less as a concession to large-scale national and
international policies'.[35] This is one aspect of Pentecostalism's relationship with the Nigerian state; the other evokes the dangerously volatile
relationship between a nation-state in crisis, and the rise of more than
one community of 'postnational Others', groups which, as they compete
for 'a piece of the nation, and the resources of the state…inevitably enter
into the space of potential violence'.[36]

Winning Nigeria for Jesus: the political mobilisation of identity

In the light of brief remarks made at the beginning of this paper on the
'crisis' of the nation-state, what can we say about the Nigerian context?
One can hardly talk about the loss of a fundamental national identity in
places where it has never been fully established, or at least, where its
existence reveals a radically different history from its Western counterparts. Despite convincing arguments for looking more closely at the
historicity of the African state, and rejecting the image of the 'imported'
state which hangs like a 'balloon' suspended above society, the mode in
which the modern nation-state is 'grafted' onto indigenous political
forms unsurprisingly results in something quite different than the liberal
model.[37]

Nationalism in Nigeria, and more particularly the socio-cultural content of citizenship and normative notions such as civic virtue, have always
been the weakest aspect of the Nigerian nation-state. From the colonial
period on, forms of 'public space' develop outside the unified community of the nation, that is, as multiple 'publics' or multiple, competing
identities. Pluralism in Nigeria does not mean, as theorists of liberal democracy explain it, a plurality of interests meeting in a public sphere
whose underlying cohesion is determined by a principle of citizenship
captured by the ideology of juridical equality and the symbolic force of

---

[35] *Ibid.*, p. 10.
[36] *Ibid.*, p. 156.
[37] See J.-F. Bayart (ed.), *La Greffe de l'Etat*, Paris: Karthala, 1996, especially his contribution, 'L'historicité de l'Etat importé', pp. 11-39.

'the nation'. Rather, it means a plurality of 'citizenships', each with its own moral vision, invented history, symbolic forms, models of power and authority, and institutional expressions, all interacting in the context of an authoritarian power whose control over public goods and accumulation is constantly under the pressure of their claims, and whose legitimacy is challenged by their alternate visions.[38] The official public space is a 'monologic' one which, as Ekeh argues, is 'morally empty'.[39] The state retains its monopoly over discourses of social progress and development and attempts to ensure that competing identities remain fragmented and politically unmoblised. Groups negotiate under the form of 'political tribalism', attempting to colonise this space and appropriate the state's power for their own in a struggle of all against all.

Attempts by the post-colonial state to moralise the political economy, to link power with virtue and thus legitimate its exercise, reveal not the officially stated ambitions extolled in the press – a just society, a thriving economy, prosperity for all, and other such official cant – but the dissimulation, the 'unreality' that Mbembe places at the heart of post-colonial relations of power.[40] While continuing to plunder shamelessly the coffers of the state, living lifestyles and publicly displaying their power in a manner that reflects well Mbembe's characterisation of the African state in terms of excess and obscenity, various leaders with the aid of the national press have attempted to impose 'morality' and 'discipline' by fiat. Shagari's 'Ethical Revolution' during Nigeria's Second Republic and General Buhari's 'War Against Indiscipline' are two examples of the outrageous sort of 'doublespeak' that those in power have used to try and impose a version of civility and disciplined behaviour on the population, one completely at odds with the real activities of powerful men.

As Appadurai points out, states 'are everywhere seeking to monopolize the moral resources of community, either by flatly claiming coevality between nation and state, or by systemically museumising and representing all the groups within them in a variety of heritage politics that seems remarkably uniform throughout the world'.[41] In Nigeria, the state has used a combination of these two strategies. In the aftermath of the civil war, ethnic forms of identification become officially proscribed, 'tribalism' is trumpeted in the press as the great enemy of the people – ethnicity, officially speaking, does not exist. However, budget allocations and the apparently endless spate of state creations, political appointments and election strategies show that the taxonomies of ethnicity are very much alive in state rationality and strategy. Judicious deference paid by

---

[38] J. A. Mbembe, *Afriques Indociles*, Paris: Karthala, 1988, p. 161.

[39] P. Ekeh, 'The Constitution of Civil Society in African History and Politics' in Caron, Gboyega and Osaghae (eds), *Democratic Transition in Africa*, Ibadan: CREDU, 1992.

[40] A. Mbembe, 'Provisional Notes on the Postcolony', *Africa*, vol. 62 (1), 1992.

[41] Appadurai, *Modernity at Large*, p. 39.

government leaders and dignitaries to 'local customs', the staging of
'traditional' dances and the wearing of traditional regalia during official
visits and ceremonies which are often televised, the funding of cultural
events, such as Festac,[42] the television and radio productions or drama-
tisations of local ceremonies, stories and fables, are all part of a 'heritage
politics' which seeks to abrogate and control the content of such identity,
to reduce the potentially volatile differences among groups to a series of
'traditions' which are portrayed as the 'same', insofar as they are boiled
down in state rhetoric to the 'Africanness' or the 'Nigerianness' of the
nation. Religion has its official uses as well – leaders make much of their
'devoutness' as Christians and Muslims, calling publicly on God to help
them in their task of national redemption, and bargaining with, or buying
off prominent religious leaders,[43] yet all the while denouncing 'fanaticism' and the evil machinations of those who seek to use religion to 'political
ends' whenever it appears that groups or individuals have placed their
loyalty in their faith above their obedience and allegiance to the nation-
state. The national press' reporting on religion rarely deviates from this
official line; religious riots are inevitably the work of 'fanatics' under the
grip of foreign doctrines and finance, which 'corrupt' and 'distort Nigerian Islamic [and Christian] culture';[44] Pentecostal leaders in particular
have been portrayed recently as money-grabbing manipulators who
dupe their congregations into believing foreign doctrines for their own
personal profit and to serve their political ambitions.

As Mbembe points out, the signs, narratives and vocabulary that the
state produces

> [....] are not meant merely to be symbols; they are officially invested with a sur-
> plus of meanings which are not negotiable and which one is officially forbidden
> to depart from or challenge. So as to assure that no such challenge takes place,
> the champions of state power invent entire constellations of ideas; they adopt a
> distinct set of cultural repertoires and powerfully evocative concepts; but they
> also have resort, if necessary, to the systematic application of pain.[45]

One of the central cultural repertoires that the state evokes, if not in so
many words, is the realm of the supernatural. The developmentalist
state must pay lip-service to its Western model; official public discourse
remains secular, and rational, in particular its forms in the official media.
And yet the outrageous excess of personal accumulation, the extrava-
gance and obscenity of elite lifestyles, the arbitrary uses of terror and

---

[42] The Festival of Black Arts and Culture hosted by Nigeria in 1977. I often heard Pentecostals make reference to the demonic influence this festival had on Nigeria.

[43] See J.-F. Bayart, 'Les Eglises Chrétiennes et la Politique du Ventre', *Politique Africaine*,
no. 35 (1989).

[44] 'Funtua, Izombe; How Religious Fanatics Unleashed Terror', *African Concord*, vol. 7,
no. 38, 8 Feb. 1993, p. 17.

[45] Mbembe, 'Provisional Notes', p. 4.

violence, all of these immediately refer in popular imagination to the idiom of occult powers and witchcraft. J.-F. Bayart's analysis of the 'politics of the belly', in which he locates elites' strategies of accumulation and consumption in an historical system of 'extraversion' where rents from their privileged connection with the 'outside' enable elites to maintain their positions and 'eat' their fills. This idiom of the belly also evokes the relationship between eating and the world of occult forces, in particular, witchcraft.[46] As Peter Geschiere argues, in Africa, 'the problem of power has reached unprecedented proportions. This is one of the reasons why ideas like *evu, djambe* or *sem* [forms of witchcraft] seem to impose themselves when one attempts to understand modern relationships...[T]he association between power and eating (and thus witchcraft) serve to express a profound anxiety, but at the same time an obsession *vis à vis* power, and its new forms.'[47] The official discourse about governance is seen as mendacious and unconvincing to most people since it fails to address those issues which are central to the idioms that make up popular political consciousness – in particular the unseen world of spiritual forces. The popular press is full of stories of witchcraft, 'money medicine', evil spirits such as 'Mammy Wata'; in urban centres, rumour and panic about uncontrolled spiritual forces abound (such as the 'missing genitals' scare of 1990, where people were lynched after having 'spirited' away the private parts of others by casual contact). In Nigeria, power is itself the evidence of strong spiritual connections; all 'big men' that have 'eaten well' are understood to have links to secret and occult forms of power. The state, with its references to Nigerian 'culture', its uses of evocative symbols and language, reinforces, not unconsciously, the popular understanding of a whole world of occult and dangerous dealings behind the scenes.[48]

Mission Christianity took a strong position about ties with 'traditional religion' and cultural practices, but failed to develop a discourse which would address the continued *reality* of the forces expressed through these cultural forms. The discourse it developed about civic virtue and allegiance to the state was a purely secular account. The secular discourse about civic virtue simply misses the mark, since in Nigeria 'virtue', or normative issues about the uses of authority, are indissociable from supernatural matters. What is novel about Pentecostalism is that it directly addresses the problem of the forces of evil and incites public testimony about the workings of evil forces,[49] producing discourses which expose

[46] Bayart, *L'Etat en Afrique.*

[47] P. Geschiere, *Sorcellerie et Politique en Afrique: La viande des autres*, Paris: Karthala, 1995.

[48] See *ibid.*

[49] These are extremely popular and widely circulated booklets, which are often also circulated in audio form as well as reprinted by instalments in a variety of Pentecostal

these forces and show the individual how to overcome their dangerous and destructive influence. These narratives enable the individual to constitute himself as an historical agent who is not only empowered in his personal life but, with other believers, has the strength to do battle with 'powers and principalities', 'raising up an army for God in the Land'.

Pentecostal discourse on the current economic and political situation in Nigeria entails a fairly bold attack on the Nigerian state. In its engagement with local forms of knowledge and practice it develops an ongoing critical debate about government, one which not only indicts the immorality and inequality at the heart of domination, but does this by using a language and imagery that resonates in the imagination of the dominated. It is, in part at least, through this 'intellectual response to social process...[this] contest of moral knowledge'[50] that the community constitutes itself politically. Pentecostalism is a political force not merely as a result of successful competition within the religious field – providing the spiritual and material benefits others did not. Its radical success in conversion has as much to do with the fact that it reconceptualises the moral order, claiming a redemptive vision of citizenship in which the moral government of the self is linked to the power to influence the conduct of others. To align oneself with the wrong sort of supernatural and material powers, and to regulate one's conduct according to the wrong set of precepts opens up the space in which the 'failure of the nation' is manifested.[51] Kehinde Osinowo, when asked why he had started his organisation 'Christians for the Regeneration of the Nation', explained that: 'without spiritual change, no programme will have its effect. The sin of the nation is based on the sin of the individual...we shall restore Nigeria to moral probity, godliness and prosperity.'[52]

---

magazines. They often mirror very closely stories which circulate in the popular 'tabloid' press, with themes such as 'How my search for a baby led me into witchcraft' and 'My wife is initiating my children into witchcraft'. The titles of these booklets are themselves very suggestive: 'How I Served Satan Until Jesus Christ Delivered Me: A true account of my twenty-one years experience as an agent of darkness and my deliverance by the powerful arm of God in Christ Jesus' and 'Former Satan Deputy in the World Turned Follower of Christ' and 'Exposition on Water Spirits'. Similar accounts, though usually less detailed, can be heard in services and revival rallies during the time consecrated to conversion testimonies.

[50] J. Lonsdale, 'The Moral Economy of Mau Mau' in J. Lonsdale and B. Berman, *Unhappy Valley: Conflict in Kenya and Africa*, Book 2: *Violence and Ethnicity*, London: James Currey, 1992.

[51] R. Marshall, 'Power in the Name of Jesus: Social Transformation and Pentecostalism in Western Nigeria Revisited' in T. Ranger and O. Vaughan (eds), *Legitimacy and the State in Twentieth Century Africa* (Oxford: Macmillan, 1993), p. 215. See also R. Marshall, ' "God is not a Democrat": Pentecostalism and Democratisation in Nigeria' in P. Gifford (ed.), *The Christian Churches and the Democratisation of Africa*, Leiden: E.J. Brill, 1995).

[52] Interview, Lagos, April 1993.

Pentecostalism engages directly with the state, but in a manner which I would like to argue is novel. Winning Nigeria (Africa, the world) for Jesus means the projection into the national public space of a highly political agenda. The image of the 'invading army', sweeping all unbelievers in its path, expresses the political ambition on the part of Pentecostals for material and political autonomy from the state, all the time using the state's own images of armed leaders waging war, with the ultimate goal of replacing one 'theocracy' with another. As one pastor puts it:

Clearly, we will have to contend and conflict with wicked spirits in heavenly places and rulers of the darkness of this world and wrest their control over entire cities, region, nations and continents to enable us to do our job of preaching the gospel to all nations of the world. The Holy Spirit has recently been calling the Church (the body of Christ) to prepare for unprecedented warfare through many Christian leaders. The 1990s will *definitely* witness the most intence (*sic*) spiritual warfare the Church has ever been involved in over its entire 2,000 year history. There is no de-militarised zone. *You* will have to fight. Be of good cheer our Lord has already given us the victory.[53]

And at the same time, this new image places Nigerian Pentecostalism at the heart of the global battle against Satan being fought by all Pentecostals throughout the world. As I discussed above, it is the access Pentecostals have to 'resources of extraversion' and the way that the communities are constructed as part of a transnational movement that gives it its particular position of strength *vis à vis* the state. Firstly, because it has access to completely new repertoires of images and narratives about 'modernity' and 'modernisation' which are quite different than those monopolised by the state. Local appropriations of global Pentecostal narratives about the course of world history, about the workings of evil spirits in the global political arena, about models of domesticity and family life, of aesthetics and lifestyles, of consumption and accumulation, provide a new site from which to evaluate the past and imagine the future. Moreover, these narratives and images adapt themselves so easily to local concerns and problems, in a way that mission Christianity did not, that they immediately appear to have that 'naturalness' and plausibility that is so vital for belief. American Pentecostals are completely at home using the Internet to discuss how demons enter the body and how to make sure deliverance is complete. Nigerian Pentecostals identify immediately with the way that what have typically been presented as two separate registers – 'modernity' (the computer) and 'tradition' (the evil spirits) – find their untroubled marriage in this new form of global modernity.

Secondly, communities which do not have a fixed 'sense of place' or defined locality present a particular challenge for the state. The Nigerian government may refuse visas to visiting evangelists, may close down

---

53 Excerpt from Bible School lesson, Voice of Faith Ministries International, Lagos, Oct. 1992.

churches or refuse building permits for new ones, may wage war against them in the national press; Pentecostalism can work around such constraints in ways that other identities or groups may not. With its own media network, its 'delocalised' forms of community and networks which extend well beyond a neighbourhood church, or specific physical site, the state has a much more difficult time policing its activities. At the same time, it provides a form of overarching identity which makes the government's manipulation and control over other forms of identity much less traumatic and consequential for individuals. Because they occupy a space of relative exteriority *vis à vis* the state, Pentecostals can afford to reject 'complicity' – refusing to bribe, refusing all sorts of excess, rejecting well-established hierarchies and social relations, refusing to compromise their beliefs for many of the other competing identities they may have access to.

Yet at the same time, such engagement with the state inevitably involves the politicisation of identity, one which, in the context of their transnational links, demonstrates the limits of integration within the nation-state and the dangers to national unity. Pentecostals are fighting what they see as a life and death battle with the enemy – a zero sum struggle for existence. The enemy is whatever cannot be assimilated to the born-again articulation of reality. Now clearly a nation whose population is half Muslim, and whose Muslim population includes similar movements with a similar political agenda, cannot easily hold itself together under the weight of such opposing forces. Despite the intensified authoritarianism of the Nigerian state over the past decade, this newly volatile political fault line presents perhaps the greatest threat ever to its grip over Nigerian society. The increasingly violent religious riots in Northern Nigeria over the past decade must be seen as directly related to Pentecostals' evangelical strategies and their use of the media to disseminate their messages.

Central to their strategy of winning Nigeria is the demonisation of Islam. The competition that Islamic movements represent, not only in terms of the religious field but also in terms of the appropriation of the state-dominated public sphere, results in the linking in Pentecostal discourse of the evil spiritual forces at work behind Islam to the current state of economic and political decline, capitalising on the resentment felt widely among Southern Christians about the Northern (read Muslim) domination of national politics since independence, and growing fears about the 'Islamisation' of the nation-state. In Pentecostals' bid for political mobilisation, the internal debate about the proper form of government is conflated into a Manichaean struggle between two religious complexes, rendered in terms of a global battle between spiritual forces of good and evil. The growing importance of this representation of the global at the heart of local religious practices has potentially extremely real and dangerous consequences. Winning Nigeria for Jesus entails a national strategy which does not so much express the process of mobilising identity in terms of local 'invented traditions' which typically characterises ethnic nationalisms, but rather involves the localisation of a transnational conflict between what are global religious identities. The localisation of global identities inevitably brings into the context of local politics pressures and conflicts from a much wider arena, with the result that local political imagination increasingly brings such events and conflicts to bear on the interpretation of mundane occurrences as well as state policy. In the kind of large-scale 'delocalised' identity which Pentecostalism seems to foster, face-to-face everyday relationships are reinterpreted such that everyday certainties about 'others' are subverted, and one's Muslim neighbour or brother-in-law suddenly becomes a dangerous agent of the devil. At the level of national politics, state decisions and activities are likewise interpreted in terms of larger conflicts; for example, the Nigerian state's decision to break diplomatic relations with Israel was seen by many Pentecostal leaders as a principal reason behind Nigeria's economic decline, and more evidence for the 'Islamisation' (read 'demonisation') of the nation.

Islam is itself increasingly transnational in the same ways as Pentecostalism, and the symbolic and material networks of Nigerian Muslims, the ways in which identity is formed, community imagined and the media implicated in these processes, are remarkably reminiscent of the discussion above. In this sense, the nation is not so much the prize of political mobilisation as the stage upon which it is acted out. This situation may seem paradoxical, especially in the light of the highly 'nationalistic' language which is used in Pentecostal political discourse and its stated ambitions for 'national regeneration'. However, Appadurai points out that this sort of expression is less about the hegemony of territorial nationalism, and more to do with the fact that

no idiom has yet emerged to capture the collective interests of many groups in translocal solidarities, cross-border mobilizations, and post-national identities. Such interests are many and vocal, but they are still entrapped in the linguistic imagery of the territorial state.[...] Postnational or nonnational movements are forced by the very logic of actually existing nation-states to become antinational or antistate and thus to inspire the very state power that forces them to respond in the language of counternationalism.[54]

This 'linguistic trap', which of course goes well beyond just 'words', but involves the internalisation of an historically realised political form, seems to describe well Pentecostalism's apparently paradoxical project of personal and collective emancipation *as well as* sectarian violence and theocratic ambition.

[54] Appadurai, *Modernity at Large*, p. 166.

We are witnessing the construction in Nigeria of what might be called a 'postnational' form of religious identity, in which global images, ideas and forms are locally appropriated and used in the creation of new subjectivities and collectivities whose forms and activities appear to reflect a new role for the imagination in changing the everyday lives of individuals, one which is intimately linked to the use of the media and processes of globalisation. Yet such a construction inevitably engages these groups into the vicious circle of conflict which results when the Nigerian state as well as other large-scale movements, unable to tolerate the challenge Pentecostalism represents, respond with aggression, censure or violence, provoking in turn a 'counternational' response. This vicious circle can, particularly in the context of violence, hardship and precarity which marks urban life in Nigeria, easily become an escalating spiral of violence, and indicates the very real danger that this new form of imbrication between local and global presents not only to the nation-state, but to the lives of those who are caught up in it.

BIBLIOGRAPHY

Adekola, S., *Understanding Demonology*, Ibadan: Scripture Union Press, 1993.

African Concord vol.7, no.38, 8 February 1993.

Anderson, B., *Imagined Communities*, London: Verso Press, 1983.

Appadurai, A., *Modernity at Large: Cultural Dimensions of Globalisation*, Minneapolis: University of Minnesota Press, 1996.

Badie, B. and M.-C. Smouts, *Le retournement du monde. Sociologie de la scène international*, Paris: Presses de la Fondation Nationale des Sciences Politiques & Dalloz, 1992.

Bayart, J.-F., 'Les Eglises Chrétiennes et la Politique du Ventre', *Politique Africaine*, no. 35, 1989.

——— (ed.), *La Greffe de l'Etat*, Paris: Karthala, 1996.

——— *L'Etat en Afrique: la politique du ventre*, Paris: Fayard, 1989.

Bongo, K., *Christianity in Danger (As Islam Threatens)*, Nigeria: Diquadine Admiral Productions, 1989.

Bourgault, L., *Mass Media in Sub-Saharan Africa*, Bloomington: Indiana University Press, 1995.

Corten, A., 'Pentecôtisme et Politique en Amérique Latine', *Problèmes d'Amérique Latine*, no. 24, Jan.-Mar. 1997.

Deutsch, K., *Nationalism and Social Communities*, Cambridge University Press, 1966.

Ekeh, P. P., 'The Constitution of Civil Society in African History and Politics' in Caron, Gboyega and Osaghae (eds), *Democratic Transition in Africa*, Ibadan: CREDU, 1992.

Esan, O., 'Receiving Television Messages: An Ethnography of Women in a Nigerian Context', PhD diss., Department of Sociology, University of Glasgow, 1994.

Falola, T. and Ihonvbere, J., *The Rise and Fall of Nigeria's Second Republic 1979-84*, London: Zed Books, 1985.

Featherstone, M., S. Lash, and R. Roberston (eds), *Global Modernities*, London: Sage, 1997.

Garnham, N., 'The Mass Media, Cultural Identity and the Public Space in the Modern World', *Public Culture*, 1993.

Geschiere, P., *Sorcellerie et Politique en Afrique: La viande des autres*, Paris: Karthala, 1995.

—— and Birgit Meyer, 'Globalization and Identity: Dialectics of Flows and Closures', *Development and Change*, vol.29, no.4, October 1998.

Hacket, R., 'Mediating the Miracles: The Charismatic Appropriation of Media Technologies in Ghana and Nigeria' [forthcoming].

Lonsdale, J., 'The Moral Economy of Mau Mau' in B. Berman and J. Lonsdale, *Unhappy Valley: Conflict in Kenya and Africa*, Book 2: *Violence and Ethnicity*, London: James Currey, 1992.

Lyons, A. and H. Lyons, 'Magical Medicine on Television: Benin City, Nigeria', *Journal of Ritual Studies*, vol.1, no.2, 1987.

Marshall, R., 'Power in the Name of Jesus: Social Transformation and Pentecostalism in Western Nigeria Revisited' in T. Ranger and O. Vaughan (eds), *Legitimacy and the State in Twentieth Century Africa*, Oxford: Macmillan, 1993.

——, ' "God is not a Democrat": Pentecostalism and Democratisation in Nigeria' in P. Gifford (ed.), *The Christian Churches and the Democratisation of Africa*, Leiden: E.J. Brill, 1995.

Mbembe, J.A., *Afriques Indociles*, Paris: Karthala, 1988.

——, 'Provisional Notes on the Postcolony', *Africa*, vol. 62 (1), 1992.

McLuhan, M. and Powers, B., *The Global Village: Transformations in World, Life and Media in the 21st Century*, Oxford University Press, 1989.

Meyer, B., 'Translating the Devil: An African Appropriation of Pietist Prostestantism: the Case of the Peki Ewe in Southeastern Ghana, 1847-1992', PhD diss., Univ. of Amsterdam, 1995.

——, 'Commodities and the Power of Prayer: Pentecostalist Attitudes Towards Consumption in Ghana', *Development and Change*, vol.29, no.4, Oct., 1998.

Meyerowitz, J., *No Sense of Place: The Impact of Electronic Media on Social Behaviour*, New York: Oxford University Press, 1985.

Nwankpa, E., 'Territorial Spirits', address given at Pentecostal conference on 'Combatting the Powers of Darkness', National Theatre, Lagos, April 1993.

Oritsejafor, A., 'Jesus on the Offensive', preached message, Lagos National Theatre, Lagos, 13 May 1993.

Peel, J.D.Y. 'For Who Hath Despised the Days of Small Things? Missionary Narratives and Historical Anthropology', *Comparative Studies in Society and History*, vol. 37, no. 3, 1995.

—— *Ijeshas and Nigerians: The Incorporation of a Yoruba Kingdom 1890s-1970s*, Cambridge University Press, 1983.

Robertson, R., *Globalization: Social Theory and Global Culture*, London: Sage, 1992.

Tayo, F., *Nigeria Belongs to Jesus*, Ibadan: Feyistan Press, 1988.

Van Dijk, R., 'From Camp to Encompassment: Discourses of Transsubjectivity in the Ghanaian Pentecostal Diaspora', *Journal of Religion in Africa*, vol. 27, no.2, 1997.

TRANSNATIONALISED RELIGIOUS NEEDS AND POLITICAL DELEGITIMISATION IN LATIN AMERICA

André Corten[1]

In Latin America today, instead of a return of the religious, new religious needs, produced by transnationalisation, are emerging. These needs are expressed in the form of externalised emotion, a pursuit of the sacred through the representation of fear-inspiring powers and fantasies of radical transformation. They are constructed by transnationalised discursive strings (chains) and involve the recombining of elements of popular culture that are beyond the control of the national elite. Theological expressions (Methodist theology, the theology of prosperity and that of spiritual warfare, etc.) and ritual phrases ('Alleluia', 'go away Satan!', glossolalic words, etc.), at times heterogeneous, circulate. They come from both within and outside society, appearing primarily in sermons and testimonies of miracles. Local particularities aside, the effects, defined here as religious needs, establish Pentecostalism as a transnational belief. Pentecostalism[2] is the name given to new religious needs tied to the transnationalisation of living conditions.

These needs take shape through a new mode of operation of discourse, which affects the legitimacy of political systems. How? Not through the specific content of discourse, which remains religious, but through logico-linguistic mechanisms. By articulating utterances, these mechanisms fashion a certain emotional and cognitive order. This order then clashes with the foundational categories which legitimise Latin American political systems. In the second part of this chapter, it will be demonstrated that political delegitimisation operates on at least three levels: the public/private equivalence, 'exclusive participation' instead of faithfulness to the Church, and a criterion of 'plausibility' instead of 'truth'. At all levels, the logico-linguistic mechanisms brought into play in the expression of new religious needs (a certain correspondence also exists between mechanisms and needs) run counter to the order which founds political legitimacy. Although populism has left its mark in Latin America, it has not been the basis of legitimacy in the region for over a quarter of a

[1] The research for this chapter was funded by the Social Science and Humanities Research Council of Canada.

[2] Also known as Charismatic churches, movements or Christendom. See Karla Poewe (ed.), *Charismatic Christianity as a Global Culture*, Columbia, SC: University of South Carolina Press, 1994.

century. Similar to the presidentialism of political liberalism, the current legitimacy of Latin American political systems is a compromise – even more unstable than in the past – between a rational-legal order and a traditional order (neo-patrimonial).

Transnationalised religious needs

Transnationalised Pentecostalism is neither a combination, nor even a reinterpretation of pre-existing elements. It is rather the catalyst for the emergence of new religious needs. Through theological and ritual elements, which circulate between regional and national spaces, Pentecostal discourse constructs in each society a new reality expressed through new religious needs. These needs assert themselves through an overall recombination; it is a recombination of popular elements, which eludes the control of the elite.

Popular elements. Pentecostalism is usually understood to have originated from a combination of Methodist elements – a religiosity which is less cognitive and assigns less importance to the clergy (and from this perspective a more 'popular' religiosity) – and African elements – the bodily manifestation of emotion. This combination is thought to have occurred in the nineteenth century in 'camp meetings' and North American black churches. However, it is more accurate to say that Pentecostalism is composed of popular elements transformed by intercontinental circulation, and is in this sense 'new'. Speaking in tongues, for instance is quite different from the trance of African religions. It is new as a mass phenomenon (not counting second-century Montanism and a few localised movements).

1980s Pentecostalism[3] extends the 'popular' character of religious expression by way of an increase in heterogeneity. The Universal Church of the Kingdom of God (*Igreja Universal do Reino de Deus*), a Brazilian multinational, is a typical example of this phenomenon. There is, on the one hand, the (piecemeal) incorporation of elements of traditional Catholic popular religiosity[4] and Afro-Brazilian religions and, on the other

---

[3] On the 'third wave of Pentecostalism', see Paul Freston, 'Pentecostalism in Brazil: A Brief History', *Religion*, no. 25, 1995, pp. 119-33. Depending on the society, one can date this wave back to the 1970s. See Virginia Garrard-Burnett and David Stoll (eds), *Rethinking Protestantism in Latin America*, Philadelphia: Temple University Press, 1993, pp. 66-110; David Martin, *Tongues of Fire. The Explosion of Protestantism in Latin America*, Oxford: Blackwell, 1990. The phrase '1980s Pentecostalism' not only designates what some authors call 'neo-Pentecostalism', but also conveys the sense of a general evolution of Pentecostalism. See André Corten, 'Pentecôtisme et "néo-pentecôtisme"', *Archives des sciences sociales des religions*, no. 105, Jan.-Mar. 1999, pp. 163-83.

[4] Pierre Sanchis, 'O repto pentecostal à cultura "católico-brasileira"' in Alberto Antoniazzi et al., *Nem anjos nem demônios. Interpretações sociólogicas do Pentecostalismo*, Petrópolis: Editora Vozes, 1994, pp. 34-66.

hand, the adoption (in snatches) of modern traits characteristic of an urban environment. Elements of Catholic popular religiosity include the manipulation and circulation of sacred objects (for example, water rituals, where a glass of water is placed on a television set)[5] and the organisation of time according to the principle of the novenas (the *correntes*). One finds elements of Afro-Brazilian religions in the staging of entities and spirits as satanic manifestations.[6] As for modern traits, new churches are opening in places of heavy traffic (near bus stations), often in old movie theatres; wireless microphones and synthesisers are used and the premises have fans and bathrooms, but rarely air conditioning. The discourse refers to modern problems: drugs, unemployment, family break-up, etc. Commercial-type advertising is used, including the distribution of leaflets in the street. Instead of preaching in the street, proselytism is carried out on radio and television.[7] An industry of music records, CDs, cassettes, evangelical videos, and musical instruments is developing. The Internet has also been appropriated: on the top left-hand corner of the front page of the Universal Church (*Folha Universal*) newspaper, an Internet address[8] has replaced the traditional biblical verse.

These elements become objectified in their circulation through multipolar transnational networks. In addition to the Igreja Universal do Reino de Deus (IURD), there are several other multinational churches based in non-Western countries (notably in Latin America).[9] However, although multipolar, Pentecostalism continues to be heavily influenced by North America.

The multipolar agglomeration of heterogeneous elements (coming from other regions of the Third World as much as from the United States, but including elements of local origin – notably the 'war' against Afro-Brazilian religions) does not correspond to the popular culture recognised by the elite.[10] After sustained persecutions, this same elite has today integrated certain elements of Afro-American religions in its liturgy (such as

[5] Waldo César, 'Linguagem, Espaço e Tempo Cotidiano Pentecostal' in *Pentecostes e nova era: fronteiras, passagens, religião e sociedade*, vol. 17, nos 1-2, Aug. 1996, pp. 110-23.

[6] Patricia Birman, 'Males e malefícios no discurso pentecostal' in Patricia Birman, Regina Novaes and S. Crespo (eds), *O mal à brasileira*, Rio de Janeiro: Ed. UERJ, 1997, pp. 62-80; Ari Oro, 'Neopentecostais e Afro-brasileiros: Quem vencerá esta guerra?', *Debates do NER*, vol. 1, no. 1, 1997, pp. 120-37; Véronique Boyer, 'Possession et exorcisme dans une Église pentecôtiste au Brésil', *Cahiers des sciences humaines*, vol. 32, no. 2, 1996, pp. 143-54.

[7] Alexandre Brasil Fonseca, 'Evangélicos e Mídia no Brasil', MA diss., UFRJ, Rio de Janeiro.

[8] http://www.folhauniversal.com.br.

[9] In Brazil the *Deus é Amor*, in Chile the *Iglesia evangélica pentecostal de Chile* (IEPC), in Bolivia the *Ekklésia* and in Puerto Rico the *Iglesia Pentecostal de Dios*.

[10] David Lehmann, *Struggle for the Spirit: Religious Transformation and Popular Culture in Brazil and Latin America*, Cambridge: Polity Press, 1996.

the adoption of the drum at High Mass). As Gramsci would say, it is an external and mechanical integration. However, this same elite views Pentecostal popular culture as vulgar, in poor taste and as a Mafia device which turns religion into a business by taking advantage of the gullibility of the least educated. As in past heretical attempts, 'the official religion of the intellectuals' was unable to prevent, in Gramsci's terms, the formation of 'two distinct religions'.[11] Religion is popular in the sense that it eludes the control of the national elite without generating (notably because of its multipolarity), in its transnational networks, a competing elite (neither American, nor international); present-day 'popular' is characterised by cultural heterogeneity and 'crass materialism'.[12]

New religious needs. Much is being said about the return of the religious,[13] but what characterises the contemporary period is the construction of new religious needs. Yet what is meant by needs? Agnès Heller,[14] an important figure of the Budapest School (formed around Lukàcs), distinguishes (more or less successfully) between qualitative and quantitative needs in her development of young Marx's conception of 'man rich in his [qualitative] needs'. Proletarianisation is not, in this conception, a non-satisfaction of needs, but the transformation of qualitative needs into quantitative needs. It is the reduction of all needs to one: the worker's need to reproduce his own labour. This need is presented as quantifiable on the basis of a subsistence level; it is a minimum natural need. Following Hegel, Heller proposes a non-naturalised conception of needs. Qualitative needs, from a Hegelian perspective, are social objectifications; they designate the indefinite knowledge of the subject and enable its exteriorisation.

From the perspective of discourse analysis, in which discourse is defined as a 'linguistic process of reality construction',[15] the need said to be natural (religious need itself is viewed by the theodicy as part of human nature) is, *par excellence*, a reality constructed through discourse. It appears natural while in fact being an entirely 'supernatural' fabrication. In discourse, need is a heterogeneous construction. New religious needs are constructed through a discourse that recombines traits of traditional religions and elements of modern religiosity; the former are also constructed in the crude recycling of imported elements.

[11] *Gramsci dans le texte*, Paris: Éditions Sociales, 1977, p. 261.

[12] *Ibid.*, p. 259.

[13] For de Rosny, there is no need for a return of the religious in Africa, as the Charismatic movement renewed African emotionality. Eric de Rosny, *L'Afrique des Guérisons*, Paris: Karthala, 1992.

[14] Agnès Heller, *La théorie des besoins chez Marx*, Paris, 1978. See also Cornelius Castoriadis, *L'institution imaginaire de la société*, Paris: Seuil, 1975.

[15] Eve Seguin, 'Unité et pluralité de l'analyse du discours', *Langage et Société*, no. 69, Sept. 1994, p. 52.

These needs are new. Although they are not necessarily opposed to old needs, they are opposed to the idea of reducing all religious needs to one, that defined by orthodoxy. These needs are constructed through a discourse that blends 'traditional' and 'modern' elements and is traversed by phrases circulating transnationally. The issue is not what aims to pass off as eternal religious need, but of the construction, through this discourse, of a multiplicity of needs.

The religious is still too often placed in an evolutionist perspective (including in the Marxist account). It is associated with the 'traditional'. Religious discourse itself emphasises the idea that all human beings possess a fundamental religious need,[16] either because human beings recognise an order – the Thomist vision; because they must give meaning to the difficulties of human existence, perhaps to express Marx's[17] 'protest against human misery'; or because human beings necessarily experience a 'feeling of absolute dependency'.[18] This vision is popularised and reinforced by the naturalised conception of needs (to eat and drink to sleep, etc.), and supplemented by the need for the 'supernatural'. Hence the paradox of the 'natural' need for the 'supernatural'! There are presumably 'necessary' (or essential) needs and, in contrast, luxury or artificial needs (generated by imitation and advertisement manipulation).

The new religious needs that characterise the remarkable expansion of Pentecostalism are constructed. However, they do not directly depend on the heterogeneous elements in circulation. They are needs which respond to extremely diverse situations and yet are endowed with a certain characteristic coherence. To borrow a Durkheimian problematic, they are the expression of a collective consciousness. Within Pentecostalism, three new religious needs can be identified: a strong externalised emotion; a pursuit of the sacred through the representation of frightening powers; and fantasies of dramatic transformation. Mystical emotionality, at the origin of Pentecostalism is still widespread in present-day Pentecostalism. Pentecostalism is emotional insurrection; it is a reaction of society upon itself. This insurrection gives itself legitimacy by repeating the original utterance of praise in the para-discourse of glossolalia. It requires no mastery of speech and is understood by the poorest. The second trait – the staging of fear-inspiring powers – gives a new popular root to religious need.[19] While the elite identifies the sacred with purity and beauty, contact with the sacred within popular circles is less sanitised. Hence 'conversion' is

---

[16] Note the entire discussion as to whether Christianity is a 'religion', Bonhoeffer's 'a-religious Christianity' or Gauchet's 'end of religion'. Marcel Gauchet, *Le désenchantement du monde: une histoire politique de la religion*, Paris: Gallimard, 1985.

[17] Peter Eicher (ed.), *Dictionnaire de théologie*, Paris: Cerf, 1988, pp. 643-4.

[18] See Frederich Schleiermacher, *La foi chrétienne*, Paris: Boccard, 1988.

[19] Rudolf Otto, *Le sacré. L'élément non-rationnel dans l'idée du divin et sa relation avec le rationnel*, Paris: Payot, 1969.

associated with deliverance – liberation – from evil forces. It actualises in everyday life the sense of the sacred, constitutive of society. Thirdly, fantasies of life transformation are central to the modern version of salvation; they are omnipresent in the narratives of conversion and, the often corresponding, narratives of miracles. Salvation is not deferred to the future – to another life; it is brought about in the life of the believer who, thanks to his 'encounter with Jesus', has his life transformed (and in possibly healed). It corresponds to an immediate need. Is this a secularisation of spirituality? Only if one concludes that the character of religious joy experienced in actual life is non-transcendental.[20]

Political delegitimisation

Legitimacy, understood in its Weberian sense, is based on the belief in the validity of a certain order (rational-legal, traditional, charismatic). In Latin American political systems, the presidential system rests on a Hobbesian conception of sovereign power. The sovereign arbitrates in terms of 'truth'. According to Hobbes, he decides 'in truth' which are the good and bad prophets.[21] He is placed above ecclesiastical authority. Truth is also opposed to the diversity of human opinions from which, in Hobbes' view, the fear of violent death (characteristic of the state of nature) necessarily arises. On theses two accounts, truth founds a new form of political institution.[22] While not excluding other forms, Hobbes preferred a sovereign power placed with the hands of only one man. In modern political liberalism, the president is the 'representative' *par excellence*, for he symbolises a perfect chain of mediations going all the way to the top.

In Latin America, the president must constantly barter for parliamentary support (particularly obvious in Brazil where Congress seats are divided among eight important political parties).[23] A neo-patrimonial type of traditional order based on clientelism coexists with the rational-legal order (prefigured by Hobbes). In neo-patrimonialism, the political develops on the basis of personal relationships. The legitimacy of Latin American political systems is the result of a compromise between two contradictory orders, and as such, extremely fragile. Populism, with its

[20] Richard Shaull and Waldo César, *Pentecostalismo e futuro das igrejas cristãs*, Petrópolis: Editora Vozes, 1999.

[21] Thomas Hobbes, *Leviathan*, chapter 36.

[22] Truth ruled by the sovereign transcends both reason (which, when non-controlled, ends in the uncontrollable diversity of opinions) and ecclesiastical interpretations of the word of God. It ensures that the earthly/Godly Republic duality is overcome; it founds, in this respect, the modern form of the State. See Pierre Manent, *Naissance de la politique moderne. Machiavel, Hobbes, Rousseau*, Paris: Payot, 1977; Hobbes, *Leviathan*, chapter 2.

[23] In 1999, at least twenty seats each. The government coalition comprises five parties.

André Corten

confusion of the private and the public and its identification of the people with the leader, is a form of compromise that had gained a certain tradition in Latin America. Overturned by military regimes, populism has been replaced today by a liberal presidential system with a strong clientelist component.

The mode of operation of Pentecostal discourse has accustomed part of the population to an order other than that which founds the legitimacy of the (post-populist) political system. It does not, however, provide a political alternative. In this sense, it delegitimises the political system. By mode of operation, we mean the logico-linguistic mechanisms[24] that articulate utterances and shape a certain cognitive and emotional order. These mechanisms contribute to determining which utterances and phrases are acceptable. Firstly, Pentecostal discourse operates through chains of equivalence. In these chains, the confusion between private and public, characteristic of populism,[25] is reinscribed. Secondly, Pentecostalism generates a participation that exceeds by far the 'piety effect' produced by theological discourse. The believer comes to have only one participation, that in the neo-community of the church. In this *exclusive participation*, which partly obeys the logic of commercial success, mediation procedures of political representation by association of interests or ideologies are no longer possible.[26] Viewed from another perspective, it is fear (to find oneself alone at the mercy of fear-inspiring forces) rather than a calculation of interest that prevails. Representative legitimacy is thus undermined. Thirdly, in its appraisal of total transformation, Pentecostal discourse does not rest on foundational modalisations in terms of *truth*, but in terms of *plausibility*. The logico-linguistic ordering of utterances is carried out according to the plausible. Plausibility is what makes a narrative of 'miracle' acceptable. Thus, a certain correspondence exists between the three logico-linguistic mechanisms and the three needs. This correspondence, moreover, continues in the processes of delegitimisation.

The private/public chains of equivalence of Pentecostal discourse. Private and public are modern categories. As Habermas has shown, the classical age is the 'ideal type' not only because of the distinction between the two spheres but also because of their peculiar development. The public claims to be publicity in the sense of visibility and transparency; it is necessary for the operation of the market and political representation. A completely distinct private sphere is necessary for the proper operation of the public sphere. At the economic level, suffering can be

[24] Uli Windisch, *Le raisonnement et le parler quotidiens*, Geneva: L'Age d'Homme, 1985.
[25] However, cohesion through identification with the leader, on which populist legitimacy was founded, is lacking.
[26] Chantal Mouffe, *The Return of the Political*, London: Verso, 1993.

denied because a private sphere exists, where love combines with sacrifice.
In the world today, the two domains, private and public, 'overlap constantly like waves in the incessant stream of life'. As Arendt says, the social domain, which 'devours the old spheres of the political and the private', comes to 'cover evenly all members of a given society'.[27] The 'social' corresponds to the reality of mass society. In the literature on Latin America,[28] the 'social' also designates the reality of populism. Populism is a confusion of the two operates under the hegemony of a populist leader.[29] In populism, the leader took charge of the suffering of the *'descamisado'* people, while the sphere of the private remained shapeless under the effect of family disintegration. Meaning was organised by the relationship between the leader and the people.

Today, at least for a certain section of the population, meaning is organised by the evangelical religious domain and by narratives of divine healing (a new popular culture of health). Religious discourse produces a valorisation of intimacy of (personal) 'conversion', while treating this 'conversion' as a public 'solution'. Religious discourse produces a substitute for the private in order to treat it afterwards as the 'social'. Evangelisation is administered in the same way that the State was supposed to administer society, like a 'collective household'.[30] The 'religious' occupies a field left empty, but does provide a political substitute. When the Evangelical participates in the political, it forms neither a political opposition (even though it sends elected members to national or local assemblies),[31] nor a theocratic project.

Traditionally, Protestantism has contributed towards the enclosure of suffering within the private sphere. The great success of Pentecostalism is linked in part to this capacity to give an externalised form to suffering. In 1980s Pentecostalism this capacity is reinforced; the same theological categories used in previous waves of Pentecostalism are in place. As in the general tradition of Protestantism, current Pentecostalism proposes a theology of 'justification', that is a theology of salvation and conversion. In the specific tradition of Pentecostalism, Pentecostalism is, above all, praise[32] and an opening up to the gifts of the Holy Spirit. Yet the very success of the popular language adopted by the Pentecostal wave of the

[27] Hannah Arendt, *Condition de l'homme moderne*, Paris: Calmann-Lévy, 1983, pp. 71, 85, 80.
[28] *Los populismos. Críticas de la economía política*, Edición Latinoamericana, 20/21, July-Dec. 1981.
[29] Ernesto Laclau, *Politics and Ideology in Marxist Theory*, London: New Left Books, 1977.
[30] Arendt, *Condition de l'homme moderne*, p. 76ff.
[31] Note the cases of Brazil, Bolivia, Peru, Ecuador, Venezuela and Central America.
[32] André Corten, *Pentecostalism in Brazil: Emotion of the Poor and Theological Romanticism*, Basingstoke: Macmillan, 1999 (updated translation, Karthala, 1995), chap. 5.

1980s brings about a displacement effect. Chains of equivalence[33] cause the different to be at once identical. What made religion a private affair (of individual consciousness) in historical Protestantism is transformed in 1980s Pentecostalism to become collective effusion. Distinctions are blurred. Three equivalences are established in the preachings and testimonies of miracles: salvation is at the same time solution; conversion is liberation; and praise is prosperity. The first equivalence is illustrated in the omnipresent phrase, painted on the walls of cities and villages: 'Jesus is the solution' or 'Jesus: the only solution'.[34] 'Solution' evokes a public policy in the face of (social) 'problems'. The effect of the second equivalence is to remove guilt. Sin becomes possession by a demon. Inward repentance becomes spectacular exorcism. The third equivalence, between praise and prosperity, is surprising but can be explained nonetheless. Praise is a discourse with a syntax from which 'doing' is absent.[35] Praise is free; it cannot 'do' anything in relation to God, for he cannot let himself be corrupted by praise. As for the prosperity in question, it is not that of the self-made man; it belongs to the domain not of 'doing' but of '*posse*' (to take possession of what has been freed). Jesus has already freed the world; we must '*take*' it. Praise and '*posse*' are at once different and identical. From a public point of view, praise is expressed in an incomprehensible language; '*posse*', on the other hand, is to make public what God has freed, hence the importance of testimony. Yet to take what God has freed (*posse*) is to praise God.

The discourse of 1980s Pentecostalism reinforces the equivalences between intimate feeling and public manifestation. These equivalences elude the discursive control of the theological elite. There is indeed a 'piety effect', that is a 'meaning effect' typical of theological discourse. Yet these equivalences also operate through the implementation of a popular language which functions with and through success. This point will be developed later. Popular language is not sanctioned by recognition from an elite, but by its own success. These equivalences are established in chains of utterances.[36] For example, the praise/prosperity equivalence functions by associating praise with the 'joy of the encounter with Jesus', happiness, bliss, conjugal and family happiness, well-being and domestic and financial prosperity. In the testimonies given in church or on television, prosperity is associated with the denial of tormenting elements: denial of debt, unemployment, drug-consuming children, discord,

[33] Ernesto Laclau and Chantal Mouffe, *Hegemony and Socialist Strategy: Towards a Radical Democratic Politics*, London: Verso, 1985, pp. 127-34.

[34] André Corten, 'Jésus, la solution égalitaire et autoritaire du pauvre', Communication au Congrès de l'association canadienne d'études latino-américaines, Ottawa, 10-11 Nov. 1994.

[35] Corten, *Pentecostalism in Brazil*, chap. 5.

[36] Laclau and Mouffe, *Hegemony and Socialist Strategy*.

family divisions, prostitution, vices, loss of control over one's life and oppression; denial of problems, difficulties, pain, anguish, suffering, sadness; denial of a life in ruins, of the opposite of being abandoned, lost, hurt, wounded, desperate, betrayed. In general terms, family and financial prosperity are associated. Taken up in sermons, prosperity is placed in a chain of tranquillity, help, strength to fight, love, peace, outburst, solution, power and being touched by the Holy Spirit. In testimonies, as in sermons, the chain is epitomised in this phrase: spiritual healing, physical healing, financial healing.

In the popular language adopted by the faithful and by the pastors, a language repeated incessantly in various terms throughout services and radio and television programmes, 'chains of equivalence'[37] are developing. These chains pass imperceptibly from the private to the public sphere. Continuity is established between emptiness of the soul, a life in ruins, conjugal break-up, disease and financial collapse. In the discourse of prosperity, continuity is also established between the intimate joy of the encounter with Jesus and the possession of ostentatious material goods. There is a certain coherence in these chains that can be interpreted in terms of the theoretical distinction between the private and public.

The new religious needs are constructed through these chains of utterances. Externalised religious emotion is, in the context of Protestantism, a paradox. Traditionally, in Protestantism, emotion is internal and even the cause of anguish. The need for a sacred, appraised in the spectacular manifestation of fear-inspiring forces, prolongs the sense of sin, yet simultaneously cuts off guilt from Protestant as much as Catholic. The need for a radical transformation conveys a quest for intimate joy and, at the same time, for a lifestyle transformation. It is constructed, like the other two needs, through strings of utterances which establish equivalences.

According to Laclau and Mouffe, the distinguishing characteristic of these chains is to make differences disappear, while simultaneously giving the quality of realness to negativity.[38] In Latin America, this negativity is expressed in a particularly empty term, post-populism. This is often the case when it is a question of *post*. The thesis on the end of populism in Latin America, and even the thesis on the 'necessity' of its end, is common in current literature.[39]

Post-populism is defined in purely negative terms. It is characterised by a withdrawal of the State from the 'social'. The State reduces its nurturing role (cutting the subsidies of basic necessities). The 'social' was mystified by the image of the populist leader. In post-populism,

---

[37] *Ibid.*, pp. 127-34.

[38] *Ibid.*, pp. 127-8.

[39] Alain Touraine, 'Amérique latine. La sortie de la transition libérale', *Problèmes d'Amérique latine*, no. 25, April-June 1997, pp. 131-50.

demystification encompasses not only the figure of the leader, but also the corresponding figure of the 'people'. The confusion between private and public persists, nevertheless, due to a lack of development of these spheres; in post-populism, this confusion strikingly accentuates the withdrawal of the State from the 'social'.

Pentecostal discourse, through its mode of operation in the form of a private/public chain of equivalence, brings this withdrawal from the 'social' to the fore; it makes the 'social' live in terms of a 'void'. It is in this sense that Pentecostalism is said to occupy the void left by populism. If populism had certain legitimacy – based on mystification – post-populism appears to be devoid of legitimacy. Pentecostal discourse, by occupying the space left empty by populism, delegitimises the current political system.

Religious need and 'exclusive participation'. The intensity of the need for mystical emotionality, for the staging of fear-inspiring powers and for a radical life transformation demands a high degree of participation. Such enthusiasm is the typical driving effect of theological discourse. As the Romantic theologian Schleiermacher noted, the peculiarity of theological discourse is to incite participation through the 'piety effect'[40] and to bring about attachment and fidelity to one church.[41] It is in this sense that one commonly speaks of the faithful. In Pentecostalism, however, participation becomes almost compulsive, transformed into 'exclusive participation'. Concrete participation in evening services three or four times a week plus Bible school on Sunday mornings, all for two hours at a time, eventually takes up the entire social life of participants. One can also – housewives in particular – tune in to all-day Evangelical radio. Evangelical television, broadcasting all night and early morning, is like a virtual window, always open on a rather odd amalgam of the profane and sacred.[42] By bringing even the non-converted into an enunciative contract,[43] from the moment that they watch or pick up the habit of watching (in case of insomnia) this television, a soft proselytism enters the home. In 'neo-communitarianism',[44] it is impossible not to participate in all the activities – non-involvement is a source of anguish. The context is one

[40] Perry Miller, *The New England Mind, The Seventeenth Century*, Cambridge, MA: Harvard University Press, 1939, ch. 1. On 'piety' see also Schleiermacher, *La foi chrétienne*.

[41] See Schleiermacher, *La foi chrétienne*.

[42] Razelle Franckl, *Televangelism: The Marketing of Popular Religion*, Carbondale and Edwardsville: Southern Illinois University Press, 1987.

[43] André Corten, 'Miracles et obéissance: le discours de la guérison divine à l'Église Universelle', *Social Compass*, vol. 44, no. 2, June 1997. On the concept of the enunciative contract, borrowed from Greimas, see Patrick Charaudeau, *Langage et discours. Éléments de sémiolinguistique (Théorie et pratique)*, Paris: Hachette, 1983.

[44] Jean-Pierre Bastian, *La mutación religiosa de América latina: Para una sociología del cambio social en la modernidad periférica*, México: FCF, 1997.

of compulsion. Compulsion, anguish and 'need' for fear-inspiring forces go together. Yet 'exclusive participation' is not only typical of 'fanatics' gathering together. To counter the caricatural conception of 'sects', it should be stressed that this 'exclusive participation' paradoxically enters the life of everyone, in much the same way as going to the supermarket or watching soap operas. Hence this 'exclusive participation' suggests such expressions as the marketing of faith. One recognises in it the character of soft totalitarianism found in commercial advertising.[45]

It is a general effect of theological discourse to view participation as confused with the image of artificially fabricated needs and of consent obtained through manipulation. The great narratives of salvation are put in publicity spots thanks to the implementation of successful narrative machines. The private/public chains of equivalence contribute to this. Consent is no longer obtained solely through 'enthusiasm' induced by the 'specula effect'[46] of sacred verses, which causes current events to be viewed as 'signs of the times'; it is obtained through the demonstrated success of the narrative machine.[47] The successful narrative machine, comparable to that which Umberto Eco discovered in James Bond novels,[48] is the second mode of operation corresponding to 'exclusive participation'. The success of this machine is demonstrated in part by its transnational volatility. There is indeed enthusiasm, but it is not temporary. On the contrary, the belief is spreading in a proselytism which until now has never been challenged. For the past fifty years, Pentecostalism has been in constant expansion and continues to enter new countries. While in the artificial fabrication of economic needs products are being promoted, in these new religious needs it is an imaginary that is being pushed.

'Exclusive participation' characterises religious needs as they are expressed in the imaginary new form of living together. This imaginary is called 'neo-communitarianism'. 'Neo-communitarianism' rests neither on the belief in the sacred character of tradition, nor on the principle of representation through interest association. Rather it rests on an urge to

---

[45] Leonildo Silveira Campos, *Teatro, Templo e Mercado. Organização e Marketing de um Empreendimento NeoPentecostal*, Petropolis: Editora Vozes e Simpósio Editora, 1997.

[46] André Corten, 'Catégories politiques et discours théologique', *Discours social/ Social Discourse, Discourse Analysis and Text Socio-Criticism*, vol. 4, nos. 3-4, 1992, pp. 119-44.

[47] In the narratives of miracle, four discursive operations ensure the success of the machine: 1) narrative simplification, 2) polarisation in the semantic axes; 3) isotopy: the 'glorification' of an individual subject; 4) fascination with the figurative motif of complete transformation. André Corten, 'Miracles en Amérique latine', *Mots*, no. 55, June 1998, pp. 60-73.

[48] Umberto Eco, 'James Bond: une combinatoire narrative', *L'analyse structurale du récit*. (Communication 8), Paris: Seuil, 1981, pp. 83-99. The narrative machine analysed by Eco functions with myths and is market by a Manichaean bipartition.

be together without an objective of 'doing together'. It is a social form which corresponds to the proto-politics of praise.[49] People do not come together in order to do; they do not join forces in order to pursue interests. Neither fear nor panegyric are dealt with through pragmatic calculation. 'Exclusive participation' confronts the legitimacy upon which the Latin American political system rests. It thwarts the procedural mechanisms of interest mediation inspired by political liberalism. These mechanisms presuppose that political representation is neither on the basis of an essentialist position (ethnic, racial, and so on), nor on the basis of a 'comprehensive doctrine'[50] (religious, philosophical, or moral). 'Exclusive participation' does not allow the procedural mediation of interests because it combines precisely these two principles of exclusion: compulsion causes the individual to stop judging in function of his interests; the individual thus comes close to an essentialist position. Neither does it correspond to the clientelist type of mediation, which, without being essentialist, is particularist; fidelity is given to an invisible force as opposed to a person. 'Exclusive participation' is incompatible with these two forms of mediation. Most of all, it opposes a strong principle of cohesion to political systems which suffer from a deficit of legitimacy.

Religious needs: modalisations in terms of the plausible. The new religious needs expressed in 'exclusive participation' make one think of fanaticism. They are nevertheless organised by a form of 'experimentalism', by a form of knowledge relativism. Hence it is only inappropriately that one can speak of fundamentalism.[51] The narrative of miracle is characteristic of this 'experimentalism' and is where the third mode of operation of Pentecostal discourse is distinguished. Repeated *ad nauseam* in the Pentecostal discursive machines, the miracle (the image of dramatic transformation) is not ruled 'in truth' by an authority (ultimately the truth of the sovereign); it is presented as a 'plausible' reality.[52] It is no longer exceptional but, on the contrary, made commonplace by the discursive machine. Healing is assessed in medical terms in order to show the limits of medicine. The narrative of miracle produces a post-scientific vision of the world: one accepts the achievements of science but relativises their importance. This narrative expresses a religious need justified by

[49] André Corten, 'La glossolalie dans le Pentecôtisme brésilien. Une énonciation proto-politique', *Revue française de science politique*, vol. 45, no. 2, Apr. 1995, pp. 250-81. See also Bastian, *Mutación religiosa*.

[50] John Rawls, *Libéralisme politique*, Paris: PUF, 1993, pp. 67-70.

[51] Percy Miller, 'Fundamentalism: A Problem for Phenomenology?', *Journal of Contemporary Religion*, vol. 10, no. 1, 1995, pp. 83-91 and vol. 10, no. 3, 1995, pp. 173-282.

[52] André Corten (with the collaboration of Viviana Fridman and Anne Deret), *Alchimie politique du miracle. Discours de la guérison divine et langue politique en Amérique latine*, Montreal: Balzac, Collection Univers des Discours, 1999.

an immediate spiritual satisfaction (evidently criticised by the 'doctors of theology'!).

In the Pentecostal context, the religious and the political do not confront one another according to a principle of truth. In Hobbes, the principle of truth was necessary in the context of a frontal struggle between the theological and political plane. The principle of truth is placed above the opinion of the theologian and the reasonable opinion of each individual in order to avoid war. This principle designates the political forces and orders them in relation to one another (for Hobbes, this principle subordinates ecclesiastical power to the Christian sovereign). This principle of truth remains the essence of sovereign power in contemporary societies. It is Carl Schmitt's reformulation of the Hobbesian principle of truth which states that 'the sovereign is he who decides as to whether a situation is exceptional'.[53] The political is above the legal; it is also above the reasonable opinion expressed by economists (who claim to establish laws of society on the model of laws of nature).[54] From a liberal point of view, the legitimacy of this political is nonetheless threatened by the influence of the 'social' and the administration of society as a collective household.

Returning to the Latin American political context. The assertion of strong religious needs, which monopolise the attention and energy of 10 to 15 per cent of the population (in 'exclusive participation'), reduces the political to a field devoid of significance, to which one simply responds formally. The very logic of a representation (denied in terms of truth, as is the case in the logic of sovereign power)[55] of political forces escapes this section of the population. These people, through their indifference towards politics and their passion for religious participation, compel the political personnel to assess their existence in terms of forces which the latter neither control nor understand. At first, the political system considered the Evangelicals as a non-existent force which formed a world apart and was without political significance. The Evangelicals, for a long time, adopted this vision of exclusion as their own: what Lalive d'Epinay, the pioneer of the study of Pentecostalism in Latin America, calls 'withdrawal from society'.[56] The major Latin American political parties later became aware of the potential of Pentecostal votes. Nevertheless, they have shown a tremendous failure to understand the Pentecostal conception of the 'moralisation of political life'.

A tremendous failure to understand remains, not only because some of the agents escape the representative political model (through 'neo-

[53] Carl Schmitt, *Théologie Politique 1922, 1969*, Paris: Gallimard, 1988, p. 15.

[54] Romain Laufer, 'Rhétorique et politique' in Michel Meyer (ed.), *De la métaphysique à la rhétorique*, Éditions de l'Université de Bruxelles, 1986, pp. 189-203.

[55] Hobbes, *Leviathan*, chap. 18.

[56] Christian Lalive d'Épinay, *El Refugio de las Masas*. Santiago de Chile: Ed. Pacífico, 1970.

communitarianism'),[57] but also because they support a different reality principle. It is a principle which these agents share with other sectors of postmodern society (that is more or less linked up with the 'virtual' through computer technology and the mass media). As much as it is a discourse of passion, Pentecostal discourse has also overcome the idea of a principle of truth. Pentecostal discourse, archaic in several respects, appears to be able to tell the political that its discourse of truth no longer holds, that it is obsolete. It brings to the fore the fact that political representation governed by a transcending principle is no longer accepted.[58]

Pentecostal discourse undermines the representation of the political to the extent that it introduces foundational modalisations in terms of the *plausible* instead of the *true*. It thus affects the classical (Hobbesian) basis of (national) 'sovereign power' defined in terms of truth.[59] Pentecostal discourse (of plausibility) does not, of course, have access to the authorities which determine political forces (the terrain of political representation); from this perspective, it cannot directly affect political legitimacy. Yet it can spread to other spheres by encircling, as it were, political language, sometimes entering political discourse itself. Research on this point has barely begun.[60] Pentecostal discourse can also undermine the compromises made, at the core of political language, between the principle of a representative sovereign power (embodied in the presidential system) and that of neo-patrimonialism (manifested in Brazil, through fragmented party support).

Religious needs cause the emergence of a reality unaccountable by political language. Labelled as grotesque, fanatical, superficial, hypocritical, charlatans, sectarian, etc., Pentecostals nevertheless impose themselves as a reality: the 'unacceptability'[61] of Pentecostalism. Until now, political language, when confronted with the expression of historically new religious needs, was able, during persecutions against Protestantism or anti-superstition campaigns against Afro-American religions (still widespread in the 1940s), to judge in function of a principle of truth between superstition and reason. When it does so today, it risks losing its legitimacy, for it is no longer supposed to intervene given the separation between church and state.[62] It must then face the sceptical yet obedient gaze of a section

---

[57] And of what we called elsewhere 'neo-clientelism'. See André Corten, 'Pentecôtisme et politique en Amérique latine', *Problèmes d'Amérique latine*, no. 24, Jan.-Mar. 1997, pp. 17-32.

[58] If it were only the transcendence of the law; or if it were in the form of an abstraction as in Lefort's conception of the political as an 'empty place'. See Claude Lefort, 'Permanence du théologico-politique', *Essais sur le politique*, Paris: Seuil, 1986, pp. 251-300.

[59] Hobbes, *Leviathan*, p. 460. See also Pierre Legendre, *Le désir politique de Dieu*, Paris: Fayard, 1988.

[60] Corten *et al., Alchimie politique.*

[61] *Ibid.*, chap. 7.

[62] Nevertheless, it still intervenes as in the event of the '*chute na santa*' which generated

of the population (according to 'believers', whatever the judgement passed on politics, authority is willed by God). Gathered together on 'neo-communitarian' bases and on a principle of plausibility in reading reality, the population reached by Pentecostalism represents another social imaginary. This population is a counterbalance which, with its other imaginary, does not legitimise the political system. On the contrary.

Religious needs are not immutable. They are, to paraphrase Marx, historically determined. This was demonstrated above by showing how these needs combine, beyond the control of the elite, popular elements (characterised precisely by their heterogeneity) drawn from within and outside these societies, from the 'traditional' and the 'modern'. The contemporary world and transnationalisation cause the emergence of new religious needs. This chapter has examined the consequences of the emergence of these new religious needs at the theologico-political level. As the legitimacy of political systems rests on the belief in the validity of an order considered to be, in spite of everything, transcendent (the rational-legal refers to the transcendence of the law; tradition refers to the sacred), the emergence of new religious needs is likely to disrupt political legitimacy.

What some have called the 'Protestant Reformation of Latin America'[63] does not produce a new economic 'spirit'. On the other hand, it does exert a major influence at the political level. The reality of new needs imposes itself without offering a political alternative. As its development is not controlled by a national (or international) social and intellectual elite, this reality affects the legitimacy of Latin American political systems all the more, and this in a (post-populist) historical period when the contradictions inherent in the system's foundation are exposed. The unstable compromise between a representative sovereign power and neo-patrimonialism is laid bare before the eyes of a population inhabiting a universe marked out by new needs.

---

in the Brazilian press a true *'guerra santa'* for several months (1995). A Universal Church (IURD) bishop had given a blow to a statue of the Virgin, in the context of a fight against idols. Executive power, embodied in the person of 'atheistic' Fernando Henrique Cardoso – President of the Republic – and judicial power intervened.

[63] Virginia Garrard-Burnett, 'Conclusion: Is This Latin America's Reformation?' in Garrard-Burnett and David Stoll (eds), *Rethinking Protestantism*, 1993, pp. 199-210.

BIBLIOGRAPHY

Arendt, Hannah, *Condition de l'homme moderne*, Paris: Calmann-Lévy, 1983.

Bastian, Jean-Pierre, *La mutación religiosa de América latina: Para una sociología del cambio social en la modernidad periférica*, México: FCE, 1997.

Boyer, Véronique, 'Possession et exorcisme dans une Église pentecôtiste au Brésil', *Cahiers des sciences humaines*, no. 32(2), 1996, pp. 143-54.

Campos, Leonildo Silveira, *Teatro, Templo e Mercado: Organização e Marketing de um Empreendimento NeoPentecostal*, Petrópolis: Editora Vozes e Simpósio Editora, 1997.

Castoriadis, Cornelius, *L'institution imaginaire de la société*, Paris: Seuil, 1975.

César, Waldo, 'Linguagem, Espaço e Tempo Cotidiano Pentecostal' in *Pentecostes e Nova Era: fronteiras, passagens, Religião e Sociedade*, no. 17(1-2), Aug. 1996, pp. 110-23.

Charaudeau, Patrick, *Langage et discours. Éléments de sémiolinguistique (Théorie et pratique)*, Paris: Hachette, 1983.

Corten, André, 'Catégories politiques et discours théologique', *Discours social/ Social Discourse, Discourse Analysis and Text Socio Criticism*, no. 4(3-4), 1992, pp. 119-44.

——, 'Jesus, la solution égalitaire et autoritaire du pauvre', Communication au Congrès de l'association canadienne d'études latino-américaines, Ottawa, 10-11 Nov. 1994.

——, 'La glossolalie dans le Pentecôtisme brésilien. Une énonciation protopolitique', *Revue française de science politique*, vol. 45, no. 2, Apr. 1995, pp. 250-81.

——, 'Pentecôtisme et politique en Amérique latine', *Problèmes d'Amérique latine*, no. 24, Jan.-Mar. 1997, pp. 17-32.

——, 'Miracles et obéissance. Le discours de la guérison divine à l'Église Universelle', *Social Compass*, no. 44(2), June 1997, pp. 283-303.

——, 'Miracles en Amérique latine', *Mots*, no. 55, June 1998, pp. 60-73.

——, 'Pentecôtisme et "néo-pentecôtisme" ', *Archives des sciences sociales des religions*, no. 105 (Jan.-Mar. 1999), pp. 163-83.

——, *Pentecostalism in Brazil: Emotion of the Poor and Theological Romanticism*, Basingstoke: Macmillan, 1999 (updated translation, Karthala, 1995).

—— (with the collaboration of Viviana Fridman and Anne Deret), *Alchimie politique du miracle: Discours de la guérison divine et langue politique en Amérique latine*, Montréal: Balzac, Collection Univers des discours, 1999.

Eco, Umberto, 'James Bond: une combinatoire narrative' in *L'analyse structurale du récit* (Communication 8), Paris: Seuil, 1981, pp. 83-99.

Eicher, Peter (org.), *Dictionnaire de théologie*, Paris: Cerf, 1988, pp. 643-4.

Fonseca, Alexandre Brasil, 'Evangélicos e Mídia no Brasil', MA diss., UFRJ, Rio de Janeiro.

Franckl, Razelle, *Televangelism: The Marketing of Popular Religion*, Carbondale and Edwardsville: Southern Illinois University Press, 1987.

Freston, Paul, 'Pentecostalism in Brazil: A Brief History', *Religion*, no. 25 (1995), pp. 119-33.

Garrard-Burnett, Virginia and David Stoll (eds), *Rethinking Protestantism in Latin America*, Philadelphia: Temple University Press, 1993.

Gauchet, Marcel, *Le désenchantement du monde: une histoire politique de la religion*, Paris: Gallimard, 1985.

Gramsci dans le texte, Paris: Éditions sociales, 1977.

Heller, Agnès, *La théorie des besoins chez Marx*, Paris: 10/18, 1978.

Hobbes, Thomas, *Léviathan: Traité de la matière, de la forme et du pouvoir de la république ecclésiastique et civile*, Paris: Sirey, 1971.

Laclau, Ernesto, *Politics and Ideology in Marxist Theory*, London: New Left Books, 1977.

Laclau, Ernesto and Chantal Mouffe, *Hegemony and Socialist Strategy: Towards a Radical Demoncratic Politics*, London: Verso, 1985, pp. 127-34.

Lalive d'Épinay, Christian, *El Refugio de las Masas*, Santiago de Chile: Ed. Pacífico, 1970.

Laufer, Romain, 'Rhétorique et politique' in Michel Meyer (ed.), *De la métaphysique à la rhétorique*, Brussels: Éditions de l'Université de Bruxelles, 1986, pp. 189-203.

Lefort, Claude, 'Permanence du théologico-politique', *Essais sur le politique*, Paris: Seuil, 1986, pp. 251-300.

Legendre, Pierre, *Le désir politique de Dieu*, Paris: Fayard, 1988.

Lehmann, David, *Struggle for the Spirit: Religious Transformation and Popular Culture in Brazil and Latin America*, Cambridge: Polity Press, 1996.

Manent, Pierre, *Naissance de la politique moderne: Machiavel, Hobbes, Rousseau*, Paris: Payot, 1977.

Martin, David, *Tongues of Fire, The Explosion of Protestantism in Latin America*, Oxford: Blackwell, 1990.

Miller, Percy, 'Fundamentalism: A Problem for Phenomenology?' *Journal of Contemporary Religion*, vol. 10, no. 1, 1995, pp. 83-91, Vol. 10, no. 3, 1995, pp. 173-282.

Miller, Perry, *The New England Mind, The Seventeenth Century*, Cambridge, MA: Harvard University Press, 1939.

Mouffe, Chantal, *The Return of the Political*, London: Verso, 1993.

Oro, Ari, 'Neopentecostais e Afro-brasileiros: Quem vencerá esta guerra?', *Debates do NER*, vol. 1, no. 1, 1997, pp. 120-37.

Otto, Rudolf, *Le sacré: l'élément non-rationnel dans l'idée du divin et sa relation avec le rationnel*, Paris: Payot, 1969.

Poewe, Karla (ed.), *Charismatic Christianity as a Global Culture*, Columbia, SC: University of South Carolina Press, 1994.

Los populismos. Críticas de la economia política, Edición latinoamericana, 20/21, July-Dec. 1981.

Rawls, John, *Libéralisme politique*, Paris: PUF, 1993, pp. 67-70.

de Rosny, Eric, *L'Afrique des Guérisons*, Paris: Karthala, 1992.

Sanchis, Pierre, 'O repto pentecostal à cultura "católico-brasileira"' in Alberto Antoniazzi *et al., Nem anjos nem demônios. Interpretações sociólogicas do Pentecostalismo*, Petrópolis: Editora Vozes, 1994, pp. 34-66.

Schleiermacher, Frederich, *La foi chrétienne*, Paris: Boccard, 1888.

Schmitt, Carl, *Théologie Politique 1922, 1969*, Paris: Gallimard, 1988.

Seguin, Eve, 'Unité et pluralité de l'analyse du discours', *Language et Société*, no. 69 (Sept. 1994), pp. 37-58.

Shaull, Richard and César, Waldo, *Pentecostalismo e futuro das igrejas cristãs*, Petrópolis: Editora Vozes, 1999.

Touraine, Alain, 'Amérique latine. La sortie de la transition libérale', *Problèmes d'Amérique latine*, no. 25 (April-June 1997), pp. 131-50.

Windishc, Uli, *Le raisonnement eilt le perler quotidiens*, Geneva: L'Age d'Homme, 1985.

Part II. LATIN AMERICA AND THE CARIBBEAN

PENTECOSTALISM AND TRANSNATIONALISATION IN THE CARIBBEAN

Laënnec Hurbon

Since the 1970s, religious movements have experienced spectacular success throughout the Caribbean and Latin America. Jehovah's Witnesses, Adventists, Mormons as well as Evangelicals, Baptists and Pentecostals have grown to the point of challenging the traditional hegemony of Catholicism. At the same time, new religious movements mixing Far Eastern and Christian origins, such as Mahikari and Moonism, have found the Caribbean a propitious place for expansion, while local syncretic systems, often politico-religious, such as Rastafarianism, exercise a greater and greater influence throughout the islands. I have analysed these developments in a number of earlier articles, attempting to grasp the reasons for these movements' growing success. These analyses have been based on lengthy periods of fieldwork in the Caribbean, especially in the French Antilles, Puerto Rico, the Dominican Republic and over the last ten years in Haiti. In closely following the evolution of certain sects and new religious movements across the region, I have not only been concerned to discover the common denominator among these religions, but above all, what within the societies themselves has served as their launching pad.

This paper will focus on the Pentecostal movement and its relationship to what is called transnationalisation. I argue that Pentecostalism is the religious movement most adapted to the social, cultural and political changes occurring in the Caribbean, and that it also is the movement which, paradoxically, assures a transition to the modern world by a process of transnationalisation of the individual; in other words, in enabling him both to escape the limitations of the framework of the nation-state, and to enter into a confrontation with traditional culture.

I will begin by briefly reviewing some of the findings from my earlier research on sects and new religious movements in the region.[1] Firstly, I argue that it is not possible to produce a monograph of a given religious group without integrating it into the broader religious field of the coun-

[1] See my articles written between 1977 and 1989. I employ the word sect in the non-pejorative sense in keeping with the definitions given by E. Troeltsch and M. Weber.

try. Secondly, I discovered that in the Caribbean, many sects have a double role. In other words, beyond the practices and discourses of conversion one can identify a revival, presented under the form of a negation, of the very forms of traditional religious systems. A resistant symbolic core endures, despite assaults from a victorious modernity, through the new systems of interpretation offered by the groups. The theme of transnationalisation gives us an opportunity to deepen the analysis of this religious movement. Pentecostalism is precisely the movement which proposes most clearly a new lifestyle and an ethic which, to a certain extent, offers new converts an opportunity to liberate themselves from the yoke of family, town and nation, and places them at the level of the universal, or, more precisely, transnationalises them. In this paper I will examine the extent to which the movement honours its promises, and why converts claim to find satisfaction, not simply on the symbolic level of meaning, be it of individual or collective life, of history and the world, but also at the level of economic and social life.

The constant progression of Pentecostalism

Which sections of the population are most affected by Pentecostalism in the Caribbean? How does conversion occur? What are the motives and factors behind conversion? What are the images it portrays with respect to social relations, politics, family organisation, religious systems and traditional culture, in particular Afro-American? It is in seeking responses to these questions that I will approach the process of transnationalisation induced by Pentecostalism. At the same time, I will develop a discussion of recent theses which have been proposed in response to the success of the movement in Latin America and the Caribbean.

Without yet being able present precise quantitative data, it is nevertheless clear that Pentecostalism is expanding everywhere in the Caribbean. In Guadeloupe and Martinique, it is the newly de-ruralised social groups that are the most open to Pentecostal preaching: the petty traders and small shop owners, factory workers, lower level civil servants, and in particular, Haitian immigrants, but also those from St Lucia and the Dominican Republic. It is not in the villages, where local forms of social control are still strong, that Pentecostal expansion can be observed. Almost everywhere in the Caribbean and Latin America it is among the most mobile sections of the population, those recent arrivals living on the periphery of large cities, that one finds in Pentecostal congregations. In the case of Haiti, this tendency is marked, according to recent surveys[2] undertaken on changes in religious belonging. Whereas in 1972 the surveys counted 80.8 per cent Catholics in Haiti, in 1997 this percentage

---

[2] See F. Houtart and A. Rémy, *Les référents culturels à Port-au-Prince*, Port-au-Prince: Cresfed, 1997, p. 47 and p. 50. On the other hand, statistics published by the Haitian Catholic Bishops in *Présence de l'Eglise en Haiti: Messages et documents de l'Episcopat*

had been reduced to 55.5 per cent during which time the Protestant population went from 15.3 per cent in 1972 to 28.7 per cent in 1997. In the capital, Port-au-Prince, there are 39 per cent Protestants as opposed to 49.6 per cent Catholics; in rural areas, the figures reveal 14.9 per cent Protestants in 1972 as against 25.7 per cent in 1997. It is the informal traders and the artisans who form the sector most affected by Protestantism with 51.8 per cent of their population in the capital, while only 37.0 per cent profess to be Catholic; in rural areas, Protestantism has gained ground among agricultural workers, of whom 47.1 per cent now belong to a variety of Protestant organisations. This progress of Protestantism should above all be related to the increase in Pentecostalism, whose churches steadily multiply as soon as slums develop under the pressure of rural exodus. On the other hand, statistics published by the Catholic hierarchy in 1988 seem founded on the belief in, rather than the fact of, the stability of Catholic hegemony in Haiti: the proportion of the Catholic population varies between 80 and 90 per cent according to these statistics, which show no evidence of corresponding to any survey. In referring as well to the data presented by J.P. Bastian[3] cited in *Christianity Today* and *Operation World* from England, we are reminded that these sources concern the general progression of Protestantism throughout the Caribbean and Latin America. In the Dominican Republic, Protestantism went from 1.5 per cent in 1960 to 6.4 per cent in 1985, in Puerto Rico, from 6.9 per cent to 27.2 per cent, to cite a few examples. In Jamaica, Pentecostalism accounted for only 3 per cent of religious affiliation in 1943, but reached 13 per cent in 1960 and 20 per cent in 1970. These developments have been reproduced throughout the Caribbean. Of course other religious denominations, such as the Jehovah's Witnesses and Adventists, have also prospered by directing their energies at the same socially mobile groups, but it is without a doubt Pentecostalism which is the religion apparently closest to the aspirations of certain social groups: those relatively disadvantaged sectors of the population which are in constant augmentation and growing confusion as the processes of globalisation increasingly make their effects felt.

The loss of traditional symbolic references

One does not find representatives of the middle class or the intellectuals,

1980-1988, Paris: S.OO.S., 1988, p. 13 are not based on anything but belief in the stability of Catholicism in Haiti: according to them, the actual percentage of the Catholic population varies between 80 and 90 per cent. Regarding the general progression of Protestantism in Haiti, see the remarkable study by Ch. Poisset Romain *Le protestantisme dans la société haïtienne: Contribution à l'étude sociologique d'une religion*, Port-au-Prince: Henri Deschamps, 1986. This study shows how Protestantism, especially Pentecostalism, readily adapts to Haitian cultural profiles, in spite of the diabolisation of voodoo in pastors' preaching.

[3] See J.P. Bastian, *La mutación religiosa de América Latina. Para una sociología del cambio social en la modernidad periférica*, Mexico: Fondo de Cultura Económica, 1997, p. 52.

nor upper level civil servants in Pentecostal congregations in the Caribbean. But it would be wrong to rely solely on economic criteria in trying to account for their success. It is very difficult to compare standards of living among countries such as Puerto Rico, Jamaica, Cuba and Haiti. But these are all countries that provide a large migrant population to the United States especially, but also to Britain. A significant modification[4] thus occurs in social and cultural relations. Of course, it is the most economically vulnerable groups which leave, but a deep crisis appears at the level of traditional symbolic points of reference: the structure of the family is modified as the new conditions of living abroad impose a radical separation from the extended family, from the village and the neighbourhood, which itself breaks down to a large extent, even if it is partially reconstituted in the big city ghettos. Isolation and solitude are felt not as the price to pay for social mobility but as a situation of vulnerability to all sorts of danger. The large Caribbean cities are the final step before leaving for abroad, or, when departure is not possible, the migrant installs himself in the provisional life of the shanty towns. The changes which are produced at the level of individual life styles do not have their origins in the home country itself, or at the local level. We must look elsewhere, and yet this 'elsewhere' is not some identifiable centre from which all these changes are tele-guided. It is rather a question of understanding that we are facing a broad deregulation of the modern economy, as well as political life and symbolic systems. Locally, one can feel the repercussions of the flow of information pouring out of radio and television stations, of the anonymous international institutions, the assembly factories, or the upheaval of systems of communication. One no longer knows whom to hold responsible for contemporary living conditions. One only knows that people are seized by new desires that cannot be satisfied, and that at the same time, they have no way of explaining or justifying their exclusion from the spheres of wealth and consumption. This context shows the processes of transnationalisation at work, processes which render obsolete all connections to a particular location (neighbourhood, village or country), and to a nation-state which has

---

[4] See Paul Vieille, 'Du transnational au politique-monde?', *Peuples méditerranéens*, no. 35-36, April-Sept. 1986, pp. 309-38 and, more recently, M. Revelli, 'Crise de l'État-Nation, territoire, nouvelles formes du conflit et de la sociabilité', *Futur antérieur*, vol. 38, no. 4, 1996, pp. 59-79. Revelli's study shows how the nation-state changes status with the current transformation in the world economy under the domination of the financial sector and by the 'the distribution of work cycle in many countries' (pp. 63-4), resulting in the loss of power of any one region to decide its future. C. Parker has analysed the relationship between popular religion and modernisation in Latin America, and emphasises that the poor classes are increasing throughout the region: of 270 million inhabitants, 62 per cent live in poverty. C. Parker, *Popular Religion and Modernisation in Latin America: A Different Logic*, Maryknoll, NY: Orbis, 1996, p. 51. See also A. Giddens, *Les conséquences de la modernité*, Paris: L'Harmattan, 1994 for a sociology of the consequences of modernity and globalisation.

become powerless to propose the least solution for the crisis in confidence people have *vis à vis* their own country. What, then, does the individual find in his conversion to Pentecostalism?

Firstly, Pentecostalism is not easily identified in terms of the churches in which is it practised, nor by the names that groups of believers adopt. Seen from the outside, they could be confused with Baptists, in part because their influence is widely felt in numerous Baptist and Catholic congregations. But each church is supposed to be an independent church that belongs to the pastor who directs it. There are only a few church networks which are established in Haiti itself and linked with a church abroad, especially those in the US. It is because of this that Pentecostal congregations often register themselves separately with the Ministry of Culture, although in certain cases a number of them may try to register under the umbrella of a mission. In fact, the Ministry of Culture does not have sufficient resources to account for all of the Pentecostal churches, which are created most often through schism and located in remote and inaccessible areas. Pentecostals are however identifiable by their white clothes in particular, the women wear a white scarf tied around the head as well as their services which are distinguished by musical instruments such as cymbals, and by behaviour similar to trance or possession which is a regular feature of testimonies, and finally by the practice of glossolalia, that is, speaking in tongues or incomprehensible languages.

The account of conversion: a new imaginary and symbolic field

My purpose here is not to give a detailed description of Pentecostal rites, but to try to understand what these numerous conversions mean in Haiti and in the Caribbean in general, in the light of processes of transnationalisation that I have briefly outlined above. The testimony of a young Haitian woman recently converted to Pentecostalism will serve as our guide in the examination of the sources of this movement's success. I will endeavour to discuss this testimony in the context of ritual and social practice. In forming a comparison of the forms of conversion in Haiti with those found in Jamaica, I will show that the relationships with writing, via the Bible, then with graven images (as a forbidden practice) as they are developed in the church are signs of a desire to re-evaluate the relationship with the local culture and the traditional symbolic system and to create a new identity.

'I started out as a Catholic', Maguy told me. 'I learned from reading the Bible that graven images are forbidden. But, since some believers go to the *oungan* (voodoo priest), I thought that I could do it, too, and I didn't want to convert. Nevertheless, God had a plan for me. Before converting, I went to an evangelical school. One day, the teacher said he used to know how to eat people, fly in "werewolf" form, turn people into animals; a pig, for example. At night he had out-of-body experiences, he practised evil. He said he could make someone die, that is, stun him so that he appears to be dead, they bury him in the cemetery and afterwards wake him up, dig him out and cut his body into pieces and make each piece of his body turn into some kind of animal, like a goat. He ended up by getting converted. They could have done the same thing to me, today nothing has power over me. I had asked my father to let me convert. My father, he knew how to call the *lwa* ("spirits" or voodoo gods) and how to make animal sacrifices. He wanted to see us participate in the services he was conducting. He said that he needed his children because they were the ones who had to get water for the sacrifices. My guardian wanted the *lwa* to dance inside my head and he beat us so that we would have a *lwa* fit.

But God has a plan for me. One Sunday morning there was a distribution of meat parts from animal sacrifices done in voodoo ceremonies. It was then I felt that I was not at home in this environment. I understood that this wasn't good for me. I asked to convert. I read Psalm 115: "There is only one God". [...] One must invoke the good Lord before all the sacrifices in voodoo; for me, the only thing to do was to go directly to the good Lord himself.

My life changed. Today, I would have had several children without a father. After my conversion, my parents were angry. But my mother converted with all of her nine children. We organised prayer services at home.

A initial observation imposes itself: conversion to Pentecostalism is above all a break with established religions. In Jamaica, testimonies collected by Nicole Rodriguez Toulis show us that converted Jamaicans say they do not succeed in feeling at home within religious systems[5] that do not take into account their everyday problems. However, it is not in stopping at this rather superficial level that we will be able to understand the meaning of conversion, since conversion is an unconscious psychological process which puts into play the relationship between the imaginary and the symbolic. The individual does not enter into the church in one fell swoop, even if he claims to have been seized by 'grace' overnight. Although it is often in a dream or following an accident or during illness that the message to convert is received, the individual must, in one way or another, have been prepared, or been caught within a network of influences. Maguy explains that she had tried to convert, but that her father did not want her to and that it was one day, during a sacrifice in honor of voodoo gods, that she finally felt the moment had come. Her life was upside down and she realised she aspired to another way of living, because if she had stayed within the voodoo symbolic system, she would have passed her time having children without a father, this is to say she would have lived in 'disorder' (*le désordre*), as they say in Haiti. She no longer felt comfortable with voodoo, even through it was the environment in which she was raised. The entire family, except the father, chose to convert. One could say,

---

[5] Nicol R. Toulis shows that the dominant religions (Episcopalian, Roman Catholicism, Methodism etc.) in England and in Jamaica do not succeed in satisfying religious needs of the poor social classes and of migrants at the same time because of doctrine and their silence on or their indifference to racism. N. Toulis, *Believing Identity: Pentecostalism and Mediation of Jamaican Ethnicity and Gender in England*, Oxford: Berg, 1997.

then, that the traditional system no longer corresponded to the family's aspirations.

Maguy's account tends to show that she went through long periods of reflection and questioning of voodoo. She says that she took Bible courses and that a teacher told of how he had left his body to commit crimes of witchcraft, such as becoming a werewolf, turning himself as well as other people into animals in order to eat them.[6] The act of witchcraft, according to voodoo beliefs, is the result of an evil spiritual force that works within the body of the presumed witch. Everything happens as if one does not know at which moment one becomes a witch or is bewitched. The *imaginaire* of witchcraft begins to run away with itself, as it were, and is no longer able to be mastered and controlled. It is not at all the case that voodoo is a false religion, but rather, in this context, is ceases to be operative. The decisive triumph of witchcraft is a symptom of the difficulties encountered in everyday life: impoverishment, unemployment, no future in agricultural work, no prospects for oneself, no hope from the school system, and above all, no way of relying on the state or any authority in the country. Pentecostalism goes and meets individuals at the heart of their distress, and this is why they have the impression, during conversion, of being relieved of a burden; the yoke of a world and a lifestyle veiled in obscurity gives way to a world of light in which the whole of life can now be taken up. The account of conversion is a new imaginary and symbolic plot into which individuals succeed in inserting themselves. It offers a different view on the past, on life before converting, not rejecting it, but giving it a new meaning by integrating it under a new sign within the church.

The written, the image and the body

It must be understood that new converts no longer belong, in the strict sense of the term, to their family or village, yet neither are they fully integrated with a modernity which, in any case, also fails to satisfy. It is this issue that I will examine in more detail in terms of what Pierre Legendre calls in *Le désir politique de Dieu* (1988), the triple relationship of the individual to the written, the body and the image. These are themes which are strongly linked to the question of the construction of identity as well as of the state and authority in general. Legendre's reflections are

---

[6] One finds in a number of African countries avowals of witchcraft practices of this type. During testimonies which are demanded by pastors in Pentecostal services, certain converts in Haiti recount the details of their previous witchcraft activities in practically the same terms as confessions studied in Côte d'Ivoire, where before their conversion, individuals practised witchcraft by sucking the blood of their victims. See my analysis in L. Hurbon, *Le Barbare imaginaire*, Paris: Cerf, 1988. On the development of witchcraft beliefs in Africa (as a result, in my view, of a deregulation of the traditional religious systems see P. Geschiere, *Sorcellerie et politique en Afrique. La viande des autres*, Paris: Karthala, 1995.

extremely suggestive because they claim to go to the heart of what is constantly occulted in the West, namely that the Reference given as the founding instance of law (*droit*) must be understood as a 'mythical construction'.[7] This expresses a political-theological relation that is never totally resorbed and dissolved. Among newly converted Pentecostals, one finds the desire to confront not only what they believe to be the foundation or the source of the modern Western world but also the symbolic cultural system that is the heritage of slavery and conquest. Pierre Legendre argues that 'the institutional system of the West is founded on the separation of the ancestral and the divine',[8] the origins of which one finds in the image of power as it appears in Roman law. The Roman image of power, he explains, is found in a 'ritual representation of the ancestors'. This is illustrated in funeral ceremonies for illustrious individuals, in which the person's image is carried in the funeral procession. From this develops the declaration that any reparation or correction of an imperial statue constituted a crime against sovereignty. Thus a distinction was established between the true image, which incarnated legitimacy, and the false image, or the idol, which corresponded to the lie. True image, power and truth form a single chain of meaning.

What we may retain from these theoretical suggestions is above all an invitation to rethink that which grounds the modern West and which Pentecostal converts somehow intuit by re-founding their life on the written word and placing it in radical opposition to the image. For the convert, the graven image which the Bible speaks about is a pure lie and the work of idolatry; since worshipping the voodoo gods no longer allows individuals access to their society's origin or foundation, they must therefore change their direction. Although the good Lord was invoked at the beginning of voodoo sacrifices, now believers want to avoid losing themselves in the world of 'spirits' and intermediate gods, and instead go directly to God. Indeed, participation in voodoo sacrifices, called approximately *mangé-lwa* (eaten-lwa), consists of entering into communion with the gods. Maguy told us that they wanted to force her to be possessed by the voodoo gods, and that they even beat her. It was little by little, as her decision came to be made and as she removed herself from this heritage, that she

---

[7] P. Legendre, *Le désir politique de Dieu*, Paris: Fayard, 1988, and *Dieu au miroir*, Paris: Fayard, 1994.

[8] Legendre, *Le désir politique*, pp. 232ff. See also S. Gruzinski's work *La guerre des images. De Christophe Colomb à 'Blade Runner'*, Paris: Fayard, 1990, pp. 76ff for a very pertinent analysis of the production of idolatry by evangelisation of conquest during the colonial period which sought to destroy 'the reference to the divine' of its adversary. We may ask ourselves whether this 'confrontation of images' (p. 78) which occurs during colonial conquest does not repeat itself in Pentecostal converts, with the difference that the latter claim to choose for themselves using a strategy of offence, between idolatry and the good image or referent. It is as if the original globalisation which is brought by colonial conquest is still at work in the region.

refused the authority of tradition and fell back entirely on a modern form of authority that is grounded in the written word. It is as if Maguy's individuality (that is, her autonomy) emerged, in the sense that she was able to decide to reject the ancestral heritage of voodoo for a new religion that she had chosen. At first, she had hesitated to ask her father for permission. But when she converted, she had to leave the village with her mother and four of the other children who had converted. The key phrase of her conversion story – 'God has a plan for me' – refers to her leaving a group in which her life had been already mapped out: before 'I was just like everyone else, some believers go to see the *oungan* (voodoo priest) and I thought I could do it too'. Today, she adds, 'nobody has power over me'. In saying this, she claims to have attained a new status, that of someone who has move to a new symbolic system. From this point on, she submits herself to the written word: the Bible which declares that there is but one God and that graven images are nothing but falsehoods. This is the meaning of the Psalm Maguy read to me, in order to prove the truth and rightness of her conversion. The Bible is thus all knowledge, all truth and all power. Here, the written is like the image, but the true image which presents itself against the falsehood of the graven image which become idols. This new relation to the divine which conversion instigates leads to a retrospective view of voodoo, in terms of which it is seen by the interpreter as a whole field given over to evil. In other words, the diabolisation of voodoo only occurs after conversion. Evil and witchcraft are real, and yet they could be defeated by sacrifices in honour of the voodoo gods. These sacrifices have now become powerless to control evil.

Pentecostalism and Afro-American religions

In this sense, Pentecostalism has been viewed as a religious form which creates a total rupture between converts and their previous religion, which is rendered responsible for all the misfortune they are experiencing or have experienced (unemployment, illness, poverty, etc.). Pentecostalism thus opens the door to a social mobility which pushes the convert to adapt to a modern world, with its social hierarchies and political system oriented to serve the wealthy dominant classes. Rather, I would like to argue that Pentecostal converts, through the very forms of their conversion and ritual practices, enter into a permanent confrontation with the traditional symbolic system. This system undergoes a negation only at the moment when the graven image are rejected: a rejection which implies the loss of this system's legitimacy.

In her study of Jamaicans immigrants in Great Britain, Nicole Toulis[9] argues that converts reject their Afro-American culture in order to be-

---

[9] See Toulis, *Believing Identity*, p. 169, where she shows how Rastafarianism and Pentecostalism are both messianic and millenarianist movements but differ with respect to solutions they

come integrated in the modern Western world, and that Rastafarians, on the other hand, seek to develop an identity which distinguishes them from the dominant culture. This sort of analysis is not incorrect at a basic level, since converts undoubtedly recognises the futility of their attachment to their past culture and profoundly desire to be seen as worthy of respect, no longer identified in terms of colour, social origin or level of education. Yet this analysis must be nuanced in a deeper examination of Pentecostalism and sects in general in the Caribbean. Of course, it is not difficult to argue that the case of Haiti is an exception, because of the strong presence of voodoo. And yet nearly everywhere, whether it be the French Antilles, Cuba or Jamaica, the enthusiasm for Pentecostalism grounds itself on an explicit confrontation with the ensemble of beliefs and practices inherited from the period of conquest and slavery. What appears as the total rejection of this ensemble must rather be understood as a reinterpretation in the course of which the convert reappropriates the ensemble of past beliefs; it is as if they receive a new legitimation. Naturally, not every element is integrated into Pentecostal worship, and yet many elements are redeployed without hesitation. We might say that the traditional symbolic system undergoes a veritable purification process which rids it of its harmful elements, or those aspects which are powerless to respond to the convert's distress.

What strikes the observer of the Pentecostal congregation is the believers' search for a bodily union with the Holy Spirit, mirroring in many ways Afro-American religions in which the gods manifest themselves to their followers through trance and possession. In proclaiming their attachment to the letter of the Bible, Caribbean Pentecostals turn, paradoxically, the written word into full speech (*parole pleine*), which, by definition, is not understood as a simple mediator leading to contact with God; rather, it is directly from within this speech that they experience the truth of worship. Strictly speaking, this notion of truth is experiential rather than dogmatic; expressed firstly through the experience of trance, which is the bodily gratification offered by the Holy Spirit, and then through the practices of healing and the various miracles accomplished by the Holy Spirit. This is why Pentecostalism is not the least bit concerned by either doctrinal purity or dogmatic truth. It is from God's recognition of the self, obtained through the power of the Holy Spirit acting in the body, that the individual receives complete material and spiritual salvation. In

---

propose. The Rastafarians seeks to have their ethnic identity recognised in a radically divided society, whereas the Pentecostals seek to overcome racial differences. The author recognises that the Pentecostal position is subtle and complex. J.-F. Bayart in a recent book demonstrates convincingly that there exist not identities, but only strategies of identification, which are employed according to context and needs (J.F. Bayart, *L'illusion identitaire*, Paris: Fayard, 1996). See also the excellent book by D.J. Austin-Broos, *Jamaica Genesis: Religion and the Politics of Moral Orders*, University of Chicago Press, 1997 on the distinction between Rastafarianism and Pentecostalism.

fact, many conversions occur in cases where the individual is afflicted with an illness that both the *oungans* (voodoo priests) and doctors have been incapable of curing. The testimonies given by followers during Sunday services tell of miraculous healings worked by the Holy Spirit. Some churches even provide more long-term care, welcoming the sick, who may spend from one to three months in hangars that resemble hospitals. Saturday is the day reserved for healing sessions, using baths of leaves and medicinal plants accompanied by the recitation of Psalms. These healings are above all practices of deliverance (exorcism), which expel from the body the evil spirits responsible for illness, bad luck and all manner of misfortune.

Pentecostalism is a religion of emotion, and it is so above all because it is grounded in an anthropology of the body which is different from that of Catholicism or historical Western Protestantism, which remain dominated by the distinction between the terrestrial and celestial order, between the body and the soul. In Afro-American cultures, the body can be traversed by spiritual forces, either beneficial or evil, and requires protection at all times. During the Pentecostals' Sunday services, the visits to the sick in their homes, or the periodic fasting and night vigils in the church, manifestations of the Holy Spirit abound. The clapping of hands and the swaying bodies induce a state close to trance, but the whole service is under the control of the pastor, who works to intensify the emotion which grips the faithful. The height of the service is marked by the breaking into tongues (glossolalia). Everyone begins to pray aloud, or make loud proclamations in an incomprehensible language: a language, they say, unknown to humans, and which, as a result, expresses the greatest possible proximity to the Holy Spirit, or is even seen as the very words of the Spirit manifesting themselves through the bodies of the faithful. It is at these moments that the healings occur. The testimonies proving God's power reinforce the bonds among the faithful; individual confessions made in subdued tones are heard and accepted by the congregation. One might say that the Holy Spirit enflames the whole congregation, which becomes akin to the meeting of the followers of the voodoo gods (*Iwa*).

However, Pentecostalism is not a substitute for voodoo. For the new convert, the Holy Spirit subsumes the voodoo gods, producing a hierarchical ranking of the two religious systems to the benefit of Pentecostalism. This is precisely what occurs among the groups within Pentecostalism known as the Heavenly Army.[10] These groups rarely identify themselves under this name, but know each other and develop links among themselves. They represent a sort of superior grade within congregations, as

---

[10] It is not possible here to dwell on the history and sociology of the Heavenly Army in Haiti. For more detail see A. Corten, 'Un mouvement religieux rebelle en Haiti. L'Armée céleste', *Conjonction. La revue franco-haïtienne de l'Institut français d'Haïti*, no. 203, 1998, pp. 53-62.

if, and it can be said without exaggeration, they were initiates. Their mission is to do battle with demons, not single-handedly, but with the help of a whole celestial army that they know how to call upon using songs and dances apparently appropriated from the structure of voodoo religious ceremonies. During services they mime battles, in the course of which trance, glossolalia and miraculous healings occur. The members of the Heavenly Army make free use of traditional medicinal plants and healing remedies used by healers known as *doetè-fey* (or *docteurs-feuilles*, leaf-doctors) who are believed to have received the gift of their knowledge through dreams.

However, if these gods can still do miracles with God's permission, they remain dangerous, since, according to Maguy, they may persecute their agents who no longer have the financial means to honour their often exorbitant demands. Once converts enter into direct contact with the Holy Spirit, they are offered what they had hoped for from the gods of voodoo, but which the gods can no longer provide. Confronted with this interpretation of Afro-American religion, as it is received by converts themselves, one might be inclined to think that Pentecostalism places converts in modernity, adapting them to an idea of social mobility which leads them to believe that salvation is nigh, that soon the miracles which will bring them out of his poverty, joblessness and vulnerability will be accomplished. And yet, once again, this should not lead us to imagine that the convert looks upon the modern world with an uncritical eye.

The place of the political

That the weakening of traditional symbolic markers is provoked by the appearance of new desires does not mean that the convert is unaware that such desires remain inaccessible. Granted, one could reasonably argue that conversion prepares the individual for entry into modernity, but on the condition that we understand that for the Pentecostal convert, modernity does not deliver what it promises. Indeed, the present misery in the world, the growing number of accidents and natural catastrophes are so many signs that this world is dominated by Satan and that the end is near. The apocalyptic vision is continually invoked in sermons and preaching so that converts ready themselves while waiting for Christ's second coming. The world cannot be changed by human or political will. There develops a sort of despair *vis-à-vis* the political (*le politique*) which is expressed through the act of conversion. In his analysis of Pentecostalism in Brazil, whose social and cultural context is close to that of Haiti, André Corten employs the concept of the 'anti-political' to describe what he calls the politics of the poor, which is characterised by the refusal of any compromise with political parties, judged to have little interest in bringing about the changes desired by the poorer sections of the population.

The anti-political does not, in itself, lead to a conservative or authoritarian political vision, but, according to Corten, through the social boycott it expresses, it applies pressure to the 'political syntax' and appears as 'a force for transformation'. This perspective appears to take up the notion of the sect as a form of implicit protest that has not managed to find the ideal conditions for its political efficacy. The oscillation of Brazilian and Chilean Pentecostals between the refusal to participate in political life and the willingness to mount the political stage to defend their churches' interests shows that these churches do not express a clear desire to shut themselves off from the world. In order to understand this, we need to sharpen our understanding of the conversion process.

It is important to note that the separation between the religious and the political which is characteristic of modernity is not found clearly in Pentecostalism.[11] Hence one does not find the desire for a total exclusion from the political field; while Pentecostals declare that they are still citizens, at the same time they make it clear that they have little faith in human justice, which they consider subject to error. What is being sought here below can be found through God above; thus the political is juxtaposed upon, and subsumed within, the theological. Having experienced what we might call a veritable deterritorialisation, the members of the poorer sections of the population remain excluded from the world of the written word, which to their mind is the source of the strength and domination of the wealthy. This world is only rediscovered metaphorically, through the Bible, which is understood as representing all wisdom and

---

[11] The theological-political problem raised by Pentecostalism is the subject of a number of studies. See, for example, F.C. Rolim, *Pentecostalismo. Brasil e América Latina*, Petrópolis: Vozes, 1994, who describes the movement's thoroughly conservative orientation and the support it gives to dictatorial governments; J. Sepulveda, 'Características Teólogicas de um Pentecostalismo Autóctone: o caso chileno' in Benjamin Gutiérrez and Leonildo Silveira Campos (eds), *Na força do Espírito – Os pentecostais na América Latina. Um desafio às igrejas históricas*, São Paulo: Aipral-Pendão Real-Ciências da Religião, 1996, pp. 63-75, who emphasises that the political position of Pentecostalism in Chile expresses the desire to find a non-marginal place in global society which up till now has been dominated by Catholicism. On the same theme, C. Parker, *Religião Popular e Modernização Capitalista. Outra Lógica en América Latina*, Petrópolis: Vozes, 1996, reports that Pentecostalism supported the Pinochet dictatorship. Many studies, however, focus their discussion on secularisation. Thus, for example, Bastian, *La mutación religiosa*, shows how the success of Pentecostalism opens on an era of religious pluralism that is the road to Latin America and Caribbean modernity, until now marked by the hegemony of Catholicism. The pluralisation of beliefs leads to a reinforcement of the private nature of belief, and their individualisation, and eventually, to the separation between religion and politics. In his theoretical analysis of contemporary spiritual renewal, D. Hervieu-Leger in Françoise Champion and Danièle Hervieu-Léger (eds), *De l'émotion en religion. Renouveaux et traditions*, Paris: Centurion, 1990, p. 244, sees in 'the flood of affective expression of the religious experience something of a protest against the bureaucratisation of the personal belief experience' and discovers that it is the middle class who are attracted by these spiritual communities.

all knowledge. During the trance induced by the Holy Spirit, converts manage to place themselves in that very space where all inequalities are abolished: 'God has a plan for me', says Maguy, echoing the many songs which tell of God's plan of salvation for each and every one. This is a verse from a song I heard sung during a service:

> *Quelle assurance, je suis joyeux,*
> *Déjà mon nom est écrit dans les cieux.*
> [What assurance, I am joyful,
> My name is already written in Heaven.]

Equality before God is a promise of the actual equality which is expressed in the way in which each convert is personally welcomed into the church and in the solidarity among members in the face of everyday life's difficulties: for example, those who fall sick are visited by their 'brothers' and 'sisters in Christ'. More importantly, as the traditional symbolic system disintegrates, conversion offers an opportunity for the reconstruction of identity. In the last instance, the church itself provides a sort of intermediate space which enables the convert to surmount the difficulties of both the traditional and modern worlds. To begin with, converts are provided with a general explanation of the current social and economic situation in the context of world history which enables them to undertake the struggle to create a place in society. At the same time, they are able to freely express their suffering in a liturgical context in which emotion is sought after and valued, making them feel at home within the Pentecostal church, when everywhere else they are rejected and excluded. A new family, a new community, and a new form of solidarity; these are the promises redeemed by Pentecostalism.

It appears that it is the political order itself, in the ways in which it is experienced within the limitations of context of the nation-state, which is out of touch with the demands of the poorer sections of the population. These sections of the population, far from being a-political, are literally steeped in politics and demonstrate a hunger for a symbolic realm that the political order cannot respond to. When, for example, the masses of poor from the shanty towns and the countryside began to ally themselves with Aristide (who styled himself as a religious leader in the service of the poor), it was not because he offered them any rational discourse on democracy or any programme for economic development, but rather because the emotion he knew how to arouse was sufficient to guarantee their support. Small Christian communities called *Titegliz* (from *petites églises*), all manner of Protestant groups, as well as members of the Charismatic Revival of the Catholic Church put their various religious differences aside in order to give their votes to this priest-candidate in the presidential election. Once their initial enthusiasm had given way to disappointment, the social and economic demands retreated once more into the churches. 'Now we have nobody, no president to speak in our name, Jesus is our only captain' proclaimed a pastor from the Heavenly Army during a service. It is as if nothing more may ever be expected from the political sphere. In Pentecostal congregations, one finds the hope for the resolution of social and economic difficulties, but the resolution of problems remains subordinate to a quest for the symbolic which cannot be reduced to a simple decor surrounding conversion, as I have argued above.

Pentecostalism as an intermediate space

In summary, Pentecostalism seems to embody both an expression and an implicit criticism of the transnationalism process. During conversion individuals manage to tear themselves deliberately from their traditions, and from its values which are considered obsolete, and which are even understood as the source of their misfortunes. We may wonder whether this amounts to a sort of local perfecting of transnationalisation which, in the eyes of the convert, represents an irreversible process. And yet conversion does not imply the obliteration of local values and traditions; rather, after having been transformed into 'floating signifiers', to use Lévi-Strauss' term, they are made available to be redeployed in diverse ways, from a nationalist, ethnic or fundamentalist perspective. In the case of Pentecostalism, it is clear that the diabolisation of the traditional symbolic system does not imply that, for example, voodoo gods no longer exist; rather, they reappear in the form of a heavenly army which accompanies converts in their battles against Satan; likewise, the Holy Spirit is now expected to deliver that which was asked of the voodoo gods; and finally, visions, dreams, trance and possession by the Holy Spirit presuppose an anthropology of the body which has its roots in Afro-American religion.

However, we should be cautious in speaking about the implicit criticism made of transnationalisation. The modern world is considered bad because it is still under Satanic control, until all evil is vanquished with the second coming of Christ. In other words, evil arises not only from values which predate conversion, but also from the modern world itself, and since this world cannot be changed overnight, one must adapt to it as something which is inevitable. Thus Pentecostalism prepares the individual to accept the social hierarchies and conditions determined by the dominant classes as part of the process of achieving a better socio-economic situation.

By way of conclusion, I would like to return to the question of relationship between transnationalism and the central place given by Pentecostalism to the body and the trance induced by the Holy Spirit. An excellent study has been undertaken recently by Paul Brodwin[12] on medical pluralism in

---

[12] See P. Brodwin, *Medicine and Morality in Haiti: the context for reading Power*, p. 199. We are entirely in agreement with Austin-Broos, *Jamaica Genesis*, p. 242 when she states

Haiti and the choices which individuals from rural and poor urban areas are driven to make when faced with illness. According to Brodwin, the body becomes the site for a battle waged at the level of individual subjectivity between the different interpretations of social reality available and the different norms to which individuals are called to submit themselves. These norms originate from voodoo, from Catholicism (both of which dominated village life from slavery throughout the nineteenth century) and more recently from Protestantism, and more particularly, Pentecostalism. The majority of the cases of illness/healing studied by Brodwin tend to show that the converted individual is 'flung into a transnational space, with its political center in North America'.[13] The conflicts experienced by the sick in the face of the diverse appeals made by voodoo or Pentecostalism are an indicator of the crisis in their habitual symbolic points of reference. In seeking a resolution to this crisis, Pentecostalism has the advantage of offering a window on the future and inciting criticism of both traditional and modern systems.

On the other hand, Brodwin does not discuss the relation that exists between the Heavenly Army and voodoo. It is clear that a conception of the body which closely resembles that of the voodoo symbolic system is at work in Pentecostal services. With this observation in mind, a few authors have launched into speculation about the voodoo, or at least Afro-American, origins of Pentecostalism. Thus G. Barthélemy argues that it is voodoo itself which, having become transnationalised, provides the basis of Pentecostalism's success among whites and blacks alike, in the US, the Caribbean and Africa.[14] According to this perspective voodoo, until now discredited and ill famed in the US, manages by a sort of sleight of hand to impose itself on the international scene via Pentecostalism. However, not only is voodoo only one of many Afro-American religions, but there is little reason to invest it with such importance as to imagine it, together with Methodism, at the origin of Pentecostalism. More importantly, it seems very hard to defend the idea that the experience of trance is exclusive to voodoo and to Haitian blacks. On the other hand, if the

---

that Pentecostalism is 'a total way of life, a comprehensive moral order that sustains coherence in their lives. This transnational and metropolitan world, rather than Jamaica's nation-state, becomes the Pentecostal milieu.'

[13] Brodwin, *Medicine and Morality*.

[14] G. Barthélemy, *Dans la splendeur d'un après-midi d'histoire*, Port-au-Prince: Henri Deschamps, 1996, p. 410. 'This is the New Orleans voodoo cult which constituted the source of Seymour's [one of the first Pentecostal preachers in 1906] inspiration. Indeed, the particularity of voodoo is its ability to master profound emotional impulses and mystic trances, phenomena which the Protestant churches had only just timidly begun to try. It appears that voodoo alone, this Afro-Catholic near-schism, possessed the necessary knowledge to assure the correct manipulation of these type of phenomena. One only needs to change the names to realise to what extent the content of both are close, or, at least, of the same order.' This vision of voodoo as an Afro-Catholic schism easily leads to the confusion on both the origin of voodoo and Pentecostalism.

same forms of Afro-American religion from both Haiti and Jamaica are found in the ritual practices of Pentecostals, we can only go as far as saying they have some 'elective affinity'. Afro-American beliefs and practices as such are rejected and diabolised and yet they continue to signify as a witness and denunciation of the past in the Pentecostal context. Such is the paradox of conversion. C. Chivallon[15] puts it well in her study of Jamaican Pentecostalism when she writes that Pentacostalism aims to overcome racial categorisations, rather than conserving or exacerbating them in terms of a black ethnic identity which is continually pressed on the convert by global society and by institutions. What converts ultimately desire is an intermediate space, almost a sort of virtual[16] world, from which they can confront the challenge of a transnationalised world that they know only through its illusions and devastating effects.

[15] C. Chivalion, 'La diaspora antillaise et le religieux: appropriation d'um espace symbolique, déconstructions etreformulations identitaire', Communication au colloque de la SISR à Toulouse, July 1997.

[16] Virtual, as Weisberg defined it in 'Réel et virtuel', *Futur antérieur*, vol. 11, no. 3, as that which helps one to face reality.

BIBLIOGRAPHY

Austin-Broos, Diane J., *Jamaica Genesis: Religion and the Politics of Moral Orders*, University of Chicago Press, 1997.

Barthélémy, Gérard, *Dans la splendeur d'un après-midi d'histoire*, Port-au-Prince: Henri Deschamps, 1996.

Bastian, Jean-Pierre, *La mutación religiosa de América Latina. Para una sociología del cambio social en la modernidad periférica*, Mexico: Fondo de Cultura Económica, 1997.

Bayart, Jean-François, *L'illusion identitaire*, Paris: Fayard, 1996.

Brodwin, Paul, *Medicine and Morality in Haiti: The context for healing power*, Cambridge University Press, 1996 .

Champion, Françoise and Danièle Hervieu-Léger (eds), *De l'émotion en religion: Renouveaux et traditions*, Paris: Centurion, 1990.

Chivalion, Christine, 'La diaspora antillaise et le religieux: appropriation d'un espace symbolique, déconstructions et reformulations identitaires', Communication au colloque de la SISR à Toulouse, July 1997.

Corten, André, *Le pentecôtisme au Brésil: Émotion du pauvre et romantisme théologique*, Paris: Karthala, 1995.

——, 'Un mouvement religieux rebelle en Haiti: l'Armée céleste', *Conjonction. La revue franco-haïtienne de l'Institut français d'Haïti*, no. 203, 1998, pp. 53-62.

Derrida, Jacques, *De la Grammatologie*, Paris: Minuit, 1967.

Geschiere, Peter, *Sorcellerie et politique. La viande des autres en Afrique,* Paris: Karthala, 1995.

Giddens, Anthony, *Les conséquences de la modernité,* Paris: L'Harmattan, 1994.

Goody, Jack, *Entre l'oralité et l'ecriture*, Paris: PUF, 1993 .

Gruzinski, Serge, *La guerre des images: De Christophe Colomb à 'Blade Runner'*, Paris: Fayard, 1990.

Gutiérrez, Benjamin and Silveira Campos Leonildo (eds), *Na força do Espírito - Os pentecostais na América Latina. Um desafio às igrejas históricas*, São Paulo: Aipral-Pendão Real-Ciências da Religião, 1996.

Houtart, François and Anselme Remy, *Les référents culturels à Port-au-Prince*, Port-au-Prince: Cresfed, 1997.

Hurbon, Laënnec, 'Sectes religieuses, loi et transgression aux Antilles' in CARE (Centre Antillais de Recherche et d'Etudes), Pointe-à-Pitre, May 1981, pp. 79-107.

——, 'New religious movements in the Caribbean' in J. A. Beckford (ed.), *New Religious Movements and Rapid Social Change*, Paris: Sage/UNESCO, 1986, pp. 146-76.

——, *Le Barbare imaginaire*, Paris: Cerf, 1988.

——, *Le phénomène religieux dans la Caraïbe* (collective work edited by L. Hurbon)

——, 'Mahikari in the Caribbean', *Japanese Journal of Religious Studies*, no. 18, June-Sept. 1991, pp. 241-64.

——, 'La crise de la culture et les nouvaux mouvements religieux aux Antilles' in *Culture, développement et identité dans la Caraïbe*, Conseil Général de la Guadeloupe,1992.

——, 'Pratiques de guérison et religions dans la Caraïbe' in F. Lautman and J. Maître (eds), *Gestion religieuse de la santé*, Paris: L'Harmattan, 1994.

Legendre, Pierre, *Le désir politique de Dieu. Étude sur les montages de l'État et du Droit*, Paris: Fayard, 1988.

——, *Dieu au miroir. Étude sur l'institution des images*, Paris: Fayard, 1994.

Parker, Christian, *Popular Religion and Modernization in Latin America: A Different Logic*, Maryknoll, NY: Orbis, 1996.

Présence de l'Eglise en Haïti. Messages et documents de l'Episcopat 1980-1988, Paris: S.OO.S., 1988.

Revèlli, M., 'Crise de l'Etat-Nation, territoire, nouvelles formes du conflit et de la sociabilité', *Futur antérieur*, vol. 38, no. 4, 1996, pp. 59-79.

Rolim, Francisco Cartaxo, *Pentecotalismo: Brasil e América Latina,* Petrópolis: Vozes, Coll. Teologia e Libertação, 1994.

Romain, Charles-Poisset, *Le protestantisme dans la société haïtienne. Contribution à l'étude sociologique d'une religion*, Port-au-Prince: Henri Deschamps, 1986.

Seguy, Jrean, 'La socialisation utopique aux valeurs', *Archives de sciences sociales des religions*, vol. 50, no. 1, 1980, pp. 7-21.

Toulis, R.N., *Believing Identity: Pentecostalism and the Mediation of Jamaican Ethnicity and Gender in England*, New York and Oxford: Berg, 1997.

Vieille, Paule, 'Du transnational au politique-monde?', *Peuples méditerranéens*, no. 35-36, April-Sept. 1986, pp. 309-38.

Weber, Max, *Sociologie des religions*, Paris: Gallimard, 1996.

Weisberg, J.-L., 'Réel et virtuel', *Futur antérieur*, vol. 11, no. 3, 1992, pp. 19-28.

JAMAICAN PENTECOSTALISM

TRANSNATIONAL RELATIONS AND THE NATION-STATE

Diane J. Austin-Broos

Many Pentecostals in Jamaica have close links with the US. These connections stem from the fact that the churches that first brought a Pentecostal message to Jamaica emerged in the US in the first and second decades of the twentieth century.[1] In Jamaica, the very identity of being Pentecostal is associated with these transnational links. Evidence of this can be found at numerous Sunday morning services where it is common, not only in Kingston but also in the countryside, for 'foreign' visitors to be asked to identify themselves. Occasionally these visitors are foreign nationals who are not and never have been Jamaican. More often, the visitors are returned nationals or else Pentecostals of Jamaican origin who now reside permanently overseas and may even have taken up an overseas citizenship. Typically, visitors are asked to stand and to share 'a wave' with the congregation, a movement of the arm indicating appreciation of the presence of the Holy Spirit. Visitors may also be asked to testify either by giving their testimony of faith or by singing a hymn or by offering a vocal prayer. Less often, and more commonly in Kingston, a visiting pastor 'from foreign' will sit beside the pastor on the dais of the church. The visitor may participate by offering a sermon, a Bible reading, a vocal prayer, or simply a reflection on the work of the church. Enacting and underlining these relations is integral to Pentecostal practice. It contrasts with the practice of Zion Revivalists, Jamaica's earlier revival religion stemming from the American and British revivals of 1858 and 1859. This development came to Jamaica as the Great Revival of 1860 and 1861 and involved the first major breakaway movement of Jamaican Christians from the missionary churches that had been prominent in the anti-slavery movement. This revival was enthusiastic, placed emphasis on spirit possession and healing, and also invoked a pantheon that suggested a compromise between notions of African and European cosmology.[2] Zion Revivalist churches today, with their principal emphasis still on healing, are distinctive, local organisations linked in a Jamaican network but with very few associations with an extra-national world. These revival churches

---

[1] The three most important churches in this regard are the New Testament Church of God, the Church of God of Prophecy and the United Pentecostal Church. For an account of the history of these churches and others in Jamaica and of their early evangelism see Diane Austin-Broos, *Jamaica Genesis: Religion and the Politics of Moral Order*, Chicago, 1997.

[2] *Ibid.*, pp. 34-71.

represent a mode of Jamaicanised Christianity stemming from a time during which communications beyond Jamaica were very limited, especially for country people. Pentecostalism in Jamaica, a no less indigenised form, has nonetheless been indigenised in a period marked by prolific communication, through a variety of media, with a world beyond Jamaica's shores.

In this important sense, Pentecostalism is a 'modern' religion of the twentieth century whereas Zion Revival is indicative of the relative isolation experienced by rural people in a pre-twentieth-century Jamaica. Pentecostal enacting of transnational links is a way of putting claim to a modernity that is not identified with Zion Revival, which for this reason is often associated with backwardness or superstition. For their part, Zion Revivalists identify their revival colleagues in the Pentecostal movement as being part of 'the church business', as being part of a commodification of religion thought to be rampant in the US. In part, this identification is due to the fact that large Pentecostal organisations in the US have helped to fund the building of branch churches in Jamaica. This is a form of assistance unknown to the Zion Revival movement by virtue of its largely domestic concerns. In part, the perception that Pentecostals are part of 'the church business' is also a product of the fact that Pentecostal practitioners are people more likely to have access to foreign earnings and remittances than their colleagues in Zion Revival who tend to be drawn from the poorest sectors of Jamaican society. Transnationalism, and indeed internationalism, are part of Pentecostalism's identity. This is not so for Zion Revival, Jamaica's most popular folk religion prior to the rise of Pentecostalism.

In this transnational identity Pentecostalism does not stand alone, however. Most Jamaican 'denominational' churches also have extensive links 'with foreign'. Anglican and Roman Catholic churches in Jamaica still recruit some of their priests from overseas and, if this is less common for Jamaica's Baptist and Methodist churches, these churches nonetheless also have extensive transnational contacts as much with Britain as with the US. These links represent a different history from that of Pentecostalism. They reflect the colonial history of the denominational churches and of their mainly middle class congregations whose transnational links have stood witness to their higher education and engagement with the state, sometimes in an oppositional mode of politics. The defining historical period for these churches is a different one from Pentecostalism's. If Pentecostalism's style has been set by conditions of the early twentieth century, and Zion Revival's by those of the mid-nineteenth century, the denominational churches can be understood by reference to their role in Jamaica in the early to middle nineteenth century.[3] The ambiguous

---

[3] The two best sources on the denominational mission churches in nineteenth-century Jamaica are Mary Turner, *Slaves and Missionaries: the Disintegration of Jamaican Slave*

relations between these latter churches and the Jamaican state are summed up best by the different positions which the churches adopted as Jamaica moved from emancipation in 1838 through revival and rebellion to Crown Colony rule in the aftermath of the 1865 Morant Bay rebellion.[4] The Methodists and especially the Orthodox Baptists had been strong advocates of slave emancipation in the face of a reluctant Jamaica Assembly. Crucial in their respective campaigns were links with their home churches in England and with the political pressures that those churches could bring on the British parliament during the slavery debate.[5] After the emancipation and as the economy worsened, however, the churches in Jamaica were disappointed by diminishing attendance.[6] To this disappointment was added the consternation of the Great Revival that, although it brought many new converts into the churches and encouraged backsliders to return, it also marked the departure of many Jamaicans from orthodoxy and into their own forms of enthusiasm. As political unrest followed spiritual turbulence, the original missionary churches grew even more uneasy. Far from sustaining their role as alternative representative of the people that could intercede on their behalf at the seat of colonial power, these churches turned to support the colonial state and its structure of authority within Jamaica. Clergy from Britain who had once been radicals became clergy endorsing the colonial way, and the denominational churches in Jamaica, albeit as they grew in independence, became missionary training grounds for foreign clergy rather than sites of critical theology. This uneasy movement between critic of and handmaiden to the Jamaican state has since been typical of the denominational churches, and in both these roles the links of Jamaican churches with the metropolitan world have been quite crucial.

In its particular transnational identity, twentieth-century Jamaican Pentecostalism shares more with these denominational churches than it does with Zion Revival. On the other hand, Pentecostalism was never part of the 'civilising mission' pursued by the denominational churches during the colonial era.[7] The denominational churches typically were involved in education and especially nineteenth-century primary education as a way of assisting state and church with the production of good colonial citizens.[8] Their role and positioning within the society marked a political

---

Society, 1787-1834, Urbana, IL, 1982, and Robert Stewart, *Religion and Society in Post-Emancipation Jamaica*, Knoxville, TN, 1992.

[4] For the significance of the Morant Bay rebellion see Stewart, *Religion and Society*, pp. 153-70 and Austin-Broos, *Jamaica Genesis*, pp. 59-62.

[5] Turner, *Slaves and Missionaries*, pp. 102-31.

[6] Austin-Broos, *Jamaica Genesis*, p. 56.

[7] See Diane Austin-Broos, 'Redefining the Moral Order: Interpretations of Christianity Post-Emancipation Jamaica' in F. McGlynn and S. Drescher (eds), *The Meaning of Freedom*, Pittsburgh, 1992, pp. 221-44.

[8] See Elsa Goveia, *Jamaica, 1830-1930*, Manchester, 1961, pp. 326-37.

moment of imperialism in which good citizens were a necessary ingredi-
ent of colonial nation-building.[9] Pentecostalism's growth in twentieth-
century Jamaica marks, rather, the expansion of a regional market system
and the indirect political and cultural influence of the US through intensified economic activity in the region.[10] The opening of the Caribbean
and Central America to North American investment both in rural industry
(bananas and sugar) and in communications (shipping and construction
of the Panama Canal) was also a very significant moment in the development of Caribbean and especially Jamaican urbanisation, wage-labour
and labour migration: a nexus that had previously much more reliant on
rural subsistence production. These developments changed the world in
which Jamaicans lived and also changed their sense of self and person.
Numerous Jamaicans whose previous world had been bracketed by the
relations between a site of plantation labour and the sites of small, independent farming surrounding emancipation villages were thrown into a
world of regional, transnational labour and sometimes highly urbanised
environments.

The focus of Pentecostalism on personal salvation and interior experience manifested in embodied and highly portable forms of speaking in
tongues and ritual dancing matched in religious terms these early twentieth century forms of economic individuation. Whilst there was always a
political dimension to this process, it is nonetheless a good example of
Robin Horton's proposal for Africa, that 'conversion' takes place as the
world in which a people lives actually changes and they come to experience themselves in different ways.[11] Pentecostalism in twentieth century
Jamaica has been responsive not so much to the process of nation-building
that engaged the denominational churches, but rather to the process of
individuation that marked the incorporation of the Caribbean and Central
America in a modern, transnational capitalist order.

Where Pentecostalism involves teachings which can morally legitimate
some of the presumptions of regional capitalism, Rastafarianism, Jamaica's
other religion of transnational modernity, tends to challenge some of these
presumptions.[12] The characteristic common to both Pentecostalism and

---

[9] On the cultural significance of 'education' in Jamaica see Errol Miller, *Jamaican Society and High Schooling*, Kingston, 1990; also see Diane Austin-Broos, *Urban Life in
Kingston, Jamaica*, New York, 1984 and also 'Educating Jamaica: Diaspora Culture and
the "Old" Middle Class', Paper presented to the African Diaspora conference at the Australian National University, 7-9 April 1998, organised by Barry Higman and James Walvin
for the Humanities Research Centre, Australian National University.

[10] See Austin-Broos, *Jamaica Genesis*, pp. 17-33.

[11] Robin Horton, 'African Conversion', *Africa*, no. 41, 1971, pp. 85-108. See also Jean
Comaroff and John Comaroff, *Of Revelation and Revolution: Christianity, Colonialism
and Consciousness in South Africa*, Chicago, 1991.

[12] The best account of Jamaican Rastafarianism is Barry Chevannes, *Rastafari, Roots
and Ideology*, Syracuse, NY, 1994.

Rastafarianism is a marked emphasis on redemptionism. Each of these religions looks to the time when its practitioners will transcend their current circumstances in a new role in the world as ritually felicitous beings. Each therefore emphasises a transcendental God who will intervene in the lives of believers and towards whose mode of being believers should strive. Beyond this redemptionism and transcendentalism, however, the religions are very different.[13] Pentecostalism in Jamaica tends to replace a Jamaican history of suffering with a history of sin. In other words, the disorders of social and emotional life encountered by the individual are attributed not to a social-historical milieu thrust on Jamaicans by their accident of birth, but rather to a chosen personal history of spiritual and moral being which can be changed and will be changed only through commitment to a saving God. In Jamaica, accepting God as one's 'personal saviour' also means accepting personal responsibility for the difficult and often demoralising conditions in which many Jamaicans live. Issues of employment, housing and especially physical health are seen to be dependent not so much on a socio-economic condition but rather on the spiritual strength of the person. History is rewritten in individual and moral-spiritual terms that propose that redemption and individual transcendence 'through Jesus Christ' is the route to a felicitous life. Rastafarian belief is closer to these forms than one might suppose.[14] Like liberation theology, however, Rastafarian redemptionism takes secular history and the language of the political as its medium of articulation. As a consequence, and at different times, either removal 'back to Africa' or removal through the reconstitution of Jamaican community - an ambition that many Pentecostals share - is seen as the precondition of transcendence. Rastafarianism allows criticism of the temporal order as relevant comment on the everyday moral and spiritual circumstance of Jamaican people. Pentecostalism, on the other hand, draws a radical contrast between religion and politics and thereby frequently adopts a quietistic stance in relation to the political that can and often does become conservative.

Both these religions play with the intimate relation in Western thought between Christian redemptionism and histories of progress on which much of the West's political thought has rested for centuries.[15] The close

---

[13] For comparisons of Rastafarianism and Pentecostalism see Austin-Broos, *Jamaica Genesis*, pp. 239-42; see also Diane Austin-Broos, 'Pentecostals and Rastafarians: Cultural, political and gender relations of religious movements', *Social and Economic Studies*, no. 36, 1987, pp. 1-39 and 'Religion and the Politics of Moral Order in Jamaica', *Anthropological Forum*, no. 6, 1991-2, pp.287-319.

[14] See, for instance, Chevannes' account of the 'Revival' aspects of contemporary Rastafarianism, Chevannes, *Rastafari*, pp. 171-88, 208-30.

[15] I have sought to deal with this issue both in a general theoretical way and in relation to Jamaican understandings of history and theology. See Diane Austin-Broos, 'Religion and Rationalism: a Hegelian Revival?', *Mankind*, no. 19, pp. 53-64, and 'Politics and the

association in Jamaican culture between histories of progress and notions of moral progress hark back to the role of early missionaries in conversion and their concurrent fight against the evil of slavery. In these theologically informed readings of history and historically informed renderings of theology both Pentecostalism and Rastafarianism call on transnational links to give weight to the redemptions they recommend. Pentecostalism's modes of spiritual redemption are given plausibility by its organisational breadth as a world-wide religion with its power base in the US, the world's sole superpower. If people there, and everywhere, heed the Pentecostal message it must be taken seriously. Notwithstanding the very clear line drawn by Pentecostals between the political and the religious, the sheer organisational scope of Pentecostalism is influential among rank and file Jamaicans. Rastafarianism draws on a different type of transnationalism to augment its status in Jamaica. Through the music and poetry of many Jamaicans but most notably the late Bob Marley, Rastafarianism has become an internationally accepted medium of representation for protest against human injustice. In its performative aspect as poetry, music and song, it is one of the major representations of the enduring exploitative relations perceived to obtain between North and South and between the developed world and the less developed world.[16] Rastafarians in Jamaica know this not so much through their own transnational travels but, rather, through the numerous young visitors to Jamaica who come to engage with Jamaican life and to attend famous concerts and culture-fests where Rastafarian themes prevail.[17] To watch Rastafarians dealing with enthusiastic tourists is to watch seasoned transnationals exercising an urbane knowledge within their own domain. If Pentecostalism's transnational medium is organisation, Rastafarianism's is performance. From both these media the respective religions draw strength, including financial strength, to propagate with heightened conviction their particular forms of redemptionism.

In this brief introductory survey I have sought to suggest the manner in which modes of transnationalism, or their critique, are important to all of Jamaica's major religions. In fact, a more extensive historical survey of Christianity in Jamaica could not but show it as one of the society's principal media of transnational relations over a period of at least 200 years. Understanding Jamaican culture requires that one understand the poetics and politics of its Christianity.[18] Understanding the politics of

---

Redeemer: State and Religion as Ways of Being in Jamaica', *Nieuwe West-Indische Gids*, no. 70, pp. 1-32.

[16] See Stuart Hall, 'Negotiating Caribbean Identities', *New Left Review*, no. 209, pp. 3-14.

[17] An example of these events is the annual 'Reggae Sunsplash' concert. That these events are famous reflects the transnational popularity of reggae music and performers including Jimmy Cliff and the bands Third World and Burning Spear.

[18] I have made an extended argument for this view in *Jamaica Genesis*.

Jamaican Christianity requires that one understand its extensive and enduring transnational dimensions. Transnationalism therefore is not defining for Pentecostalism alone. At the same time, there is a crucial association between the nature of Jamaican Pentecostalism, a Jamaican experience of modernity, and the particular form of transnationalism in which Jamaican Pentecostals engage. In the discussion that follows I shall investigate this nexus in more detail. First I propose to consider a number of different ways in which Jamaican Pentecostals that I met in the course of fieldwork in Jamaica and North America were involved with or sustained or hoped for transnational relations as part of their religion.[19] Then I will place these forms of practice, hope and aspiration in the historical context of twentieth-century Jamaica. These two considerations will reveal how transnational and even global dimensions of Pentecostalism are absorbed into a local religion and how, in turn, the local is invariably, in Jamaica, informed by transnational concerns. While the mode of Pentecostalism's transnationalism in Jamaica is specific in its modernity, at a more general level it might be observed that Jamaica's entire religious spectrum partakes of this modernity to some degree. Religion in general, and especially Pentecostalism, conforms to Daniel Miller's designation of Caribbean cultures as being, in their dualism which registers both rapid change and desire for moral transcendence, paradigms of the modern in the New World.[20]

Jamaican Pentecostals as transnational religious

While tracing the history of Unitarian (Jesus' Name) churches in Jamaica I met a retired Unitarian bishop who lived in a pleasant three bedroom brick house in the small northern coastal town of Discovery Bay. The circumstances of his retirement and of his beginnings in the Pentecostal church constituted a striking contrast. He had grown up with his mother in one of the poorest areas of Kingston and recalled as a child attending large and rowdy gatherings at Emmanuel Tabernacle, an early Unitarian church. He recalled sleeping on or underneath the pews as his enthusiastic mother praised and sang to the Lord well into the early hours of the morning. His clothes were threadbare and he was often hungry. The bishop had never known his father. As a young man the bishop joined the United Pentecostal Church (UPC) established in Jamaica in 1947. The parent organisation, he believed, rejected him for study in the US owing mainly to the colour of his skin. In 1971 he left the UPC and developed his own ministry in the northern rural parish of St. Anne where the town

---

[19] I have been a field worker in Jamaica since 1971. The research for my writings on Pentecostalism was done mostly in 1986, 1987, 1990 and 1991.

[20] See Daniel Miller, *Modernity, an Ethnographic Approach: Dualism and Mass Consumption in Trinidad*, Oxford, 1994.

of Discovery Bay is located. He supported himself as an electrician while building his church organisation. Ultimately he established a strong Jamaican base and made contact in the US with black Unitarians who were associated with the integrated but increasingly black Pentecostal Assemblies of the World. His own Jamaican 'fellowship' grew to 26 churches, with one additional church in Fort Lauderdale, Florida. He became part of an international mission organisation sponsored by black Unitarians in the US. He was involved in a lecture circuit which passed through many major towns in the south-east, mid-west and west of the US, and even through parts of Canada. In all these places he was paid to lecture on missionary practice in the Caribbean and Central America and, for a time, these activities meant that he was based in Fort Lauderdale. Nonetheless, the principal object of his activities was the nurturing of his church network at home. His activities within the US provided needed support for his churches in Jamaica and alleviated the trials he had experienced as a young pastor in St. Anne. In his words, 'I built church with pick axe and crow-bar. Brethren would come to work and you pick up the tools after they left. I used to cry, I was so alone. I had no facilities. Then I walked nine miles to go to service and nine miles back. But when a person caught the Spirit I always feel such a thrill. Even with the suffering, you just enjoy it.' The bishop had made his initial contacts with US brethren through the UPC in Jamaica. Despite the early setback, racial solidarity led sympathetic supporters to sponsor him to the US as his own church work in Jamaica flourished. An excellent basic education in Jamaica augmented by aptitude gave him a compelling preaching and lecturing style. His career developed from these beginnings.

Importantly, this transnational career did not involve subservience towards his US colleagues. The bishop had his own organisation in Jamaica and in fact tended to judge quite harshly the spiritual credentials of visitors from the US. In conversation he observed to me that he did not see why Americans less educated and of lesser social standing, and also less inspired by the Holy Spirit, should come in and be placed over Jamaicans. These people would come and sit at one's table and behave as though they had no manners. They would look at Jamaican food and push it aside. They insisted that church choirs be robed and that everything be done in an American way. In Jamaica, the bishop observed, the attitude was different. If a person received the Holy Spirit, even if he had come barefooted to church, Jamaicans would praise the Lord for him. Jamaicans, the bishop said, accepted Pentecostalism because they already lived in a spirit-filled world. They were Africans. They were emotional. They liked rhythm in their worship and they knew what it was to be spirit-filled from the days of the Great Revival. Notwithstanding his extensive transnational connections, the bishop observed that Jamaicans therefore did not need 'Americans' to tell them about a spirit-filled world.

The bishop therefore saw his role as one of taking needed enlightenment to the US, a place where the power of large-scale organisation was manifest but where the spiritual enlightenment of Jamaicans was not always equalled. The bishop attributed his own success to the blessings of 'God-Jesus' who had prevailed over both his foreign initiatives and also the growth of his church in Jamaica. Clearly an astute and talented man, as well as a devout Pentecostal, the bishop in his youth had been touched by the extent of discrimination in the US and yet had found in the interstices of its Pentecostal order an amenable course for his own life's work.

Like the bishop from Discovery Bay, the Jamaican Trinitarian Pentecostal that I met in Cleveland, Tennessee stood in no awe whatsoever of the colleagues with whom he worked in his church's 'world mission department'. This man had grown up and become a Pentecostal in Jamaica where his parents had been devout members of the Holiness Church of God. The family had migrated to Miami in the late 1950s and the man had completed his secondary education in Miami. His college education had been pursued in Cleveland where, after graduation as a minister, he had entered the bureaucracy of the church and remained there to become the general secretary of his department. Despite a long residence in the US, the man still identified as a Jamaican and visited his homeland annually. Although our acquaintance was fleeting, the general secretary discussed with me his church's attitude in the past to matters of race. He related how, after early visits to the US in the mid-1930s, a Jamaican bishop of the church in Jamaica refused to return owing to the prejudice of places like Cleveland. He mentioned various incidents in the history of the American church in the Caribbean and especially in the Bahamas where both he and other church members from the Caribbean believed that the church had been discriminatory. Nonetheless, he observed to me that Jamaicans were well represented in the central bureaucracy of this particular church and of others in Cleveland and elsewhere in the US. He observed that especially in the 'missionary' field, Caribbean Pentecostals were more able than others to 'handle' Americans and give them some effective instruction in how to proceed in unfamiliar cultures. His observations to me were delivered with a considerable dash of humour and distance from the more troubling aspects of his stories. He said that he was content living in Cleveland and was happy to see his children raised there rather than in Jamaica where opportunities were few.

In the course of my research on Pentecostalism in Jamaica, I interviewed four bishops of large Trinitarian churches, three from one church. All had spent significant time abroad either as students or in the ministry of their respective churches. The three bishops had all lived in the United States: in Cleveland, Tennessee, Michigan, Indiana, and Miami or Fort Lauderdale. One of these bishops had published two modest volumes of Bible commentary. For many years after his term as bishop in Jamaica he had been pastor to a church in Miami. Although he owned a house in that same city, he had retired to Kingston, Jamaica. The other two bishops of the same church, which maintains a fixed term of office for bishops, had gathered their American experience mainly as students in Cleveland with briefer sojourns in other American cities. Nonetheless, all of these men exhibited an acute understanding of the regional politics of their church organisation. The New Testament Church of God to which they belonged did not sustain a regional conference in the Caribbean but, rather, drew representatives from Jamaica and other islands to its annual US conference. There, the bishops were well aware of the possibilities available to them through alliances with various sets of voters within the US body. No less than Unitarian ministers, these men were alive to the element of racial tension in American churches. One of them observed that while the structure of authority of the church was predominantly 'white' the rank and file members were, in the majority, 'black'. This circumstance meant that it was unlikely that the base church would agree to a separate Caribbean conference. Were the Caribbean churches allowed to break away, black churches in the US would soon wish to follow suit. The American organisation would be decimated. The same bishop noted that the Caribbean churches did receive organisational support from the United States, and advanced theological training for their more talented students which the Jamaicans could not afford to sustain themselves. Therefore his judgment was that while in theory a separate conference would be preferable the practicalities of the moment did not allow it. He and the other two bishops observed that the prospects for a retiring bishop in Jamaica were not good. The differential in income and opportunities between the positions of bishop and pastor, even in a well-established Kingston church, was considerable. One of the bishops complained that there was no clear career path for a retiring bishop in Jamaica.

The last of these four bishops headed the Church of God of Prophecy in Jamaica. This church stood in the unusual position of having been a major Pentecostal missionary church to the United Kingdom. This missionary activity reached its height during the 1960s following large-scale emigration from Jamaica to England in the 1950s.[21] The emigrants were mainly rural Jamaicans who had sold their farming land to or were compensated by North American bauxite companies investing in Jamaica. A significant number of these migrants were Pentecostals and many of them members of the Church of God of Prophecy, the Trinitarian church which has remained strong in particular rural areas of Jamaica. The bishop, who had grown up in Jamaica, went to England as a young pastor and

---

[21] See Nancy Foner, *Jamaica Farewell: Jamaican Migrants in London*, London, 1979. On their Pentecostalism see Malcolm Calley, *God's People: West Indian Pentecostal Sects in England*, London, 1965, and Nicole Rodriguez Toulis, *Believing Identities: Pentecostalism and the Mediation of Jamaican Ethnicity and Gender in England*, Oxford, 1997.

lived there for many years rising in the church organisation. He welcomed his return to Jamaica, a position he saw as a senior one, but kept close ties with the church organisation in England which he quite clearly saw as a missionary outreach from Jamaica. The church in Jamaica had never received the same support from the US that had been given to the New Testament Church of God, its fellow Trinitarian organisation based like the Prophecy church in Cleveland, Tennessee. Financially, it was Jamaicans who had 'grown' early Church of God of Prophecy organisations in England. Therefore this bishop did not focus on the resource issues that concerned the New Testament bishops. He did, however, designate the Jamaican church as the spiritual wellspring of the transnational organisation with which he had been involved throughout his career.

In some of the cases already described, individual migrations, often involving an immediate family, have intersected with the transnational reach of a church organisation and thereby shaped a career. Research in small independent churches both in Kingston and the countryside suggests that transnational links can be formed by energetic proselytisers in their own right. One local Trinitarian church with which I was familiar in a slum area of East Kingston had a partner church in rural Florida and a missionary outreach in West Kingston. The partner church was pastored by the bishop of the East Kingston church who also earned a living as a carpenter on building sites. He had migrated to the US in the mid-1970s as Jamaica passed through a period of political instability and of considerable violence in the neighbourhood where his original church stood. Migrating with his family, he left a young pastor and the senior woman evangelist in charge of his church in Kingston, promising that he would assist them financially once he established a base in the US. He moved from Miami to a smaller town, established a Pentecostal church there, and was modestly successful both as a pastor and in the local building industry. Aid sent from the US helped the congregation in Kingston to purchase a building site and begin construction of a new church. The congregation also felt confident enough to embark on its own missionary activity. Periodically, possibly two or three times a year, the bishop returned to preach at his original church. Both his material support and the spiritual power of his preaching meant that he stood in little danger of losing his pre-eminence in the Kingston church while the central personnel remained unchanged. Once again, there was in this circumstance no simple one-way relation between foreign and Jamaican practice. Though the bishop used his North American activities as a source of support for his Jamaican church, at the same time church members in Jamaica described his work in the US as no less a 'missionary outreach' from East Kingston than their own activities in West Kingston.

The woman pastor of a large East Kingston church was also a prominent figure in the city of Kingston, having been a custos of the city and also a prominent civil servant.[22] She, too, had begun her Pentecostal career as a member of the Unitarian United Pentecostal Church and with her husband had split from that church to found an independent organisation at the East Kingston site. The woman had studied to be a pastor in Kingston, guided in no small part by her husband who died at a relatively early age. Well-educated, she had taken a Master's degree in public health at a university in California. Although the woman had devoted her life to work and preaching among the poor in East Kingston and had never pastored a church in the US, nonetheless her pre-eminence in Unitarian circles and her urbanity in secular affairs and ease with visiting dignitaries meant that her church was a site for regular visits from a range of foreign Unitarian notaries, many of them women pastors who came simply to 'fellowship' or to preach at her church. Sometimes these visits were marked by 'teas' or other forms of reception following a church service. The pastor encouraged her congregation to 'mix with' these visitors and through their presence sought to give the members of her congregation, many of whom had hard lives, a sense of their own presence in the world. In discussions with her she often observed to me that Jamaicans needed to know who they were; not everything that seemed desirable overseas necessarily worked in Jamaica. Jamaicans, she proposed, had their own forms of social organisation and very often these were the best for them. This comment was made, among other things, regarding the fairly strict child rearing practices that she advocated for Jamaicans.

Transnationalism was present in another way in Jamaican Pentecostalism. Just as it was common for visitors from 'foreign' to be recognised in Jamaican churches, so it was common for Jamaicans visiting relatives overseas, or on reaching a site of migration whether in the US, Canada or England, to find a relevant church to attend or join as a way of establishing themselves in a community.[23] Pentecostal parents in Jamaica described to me situations in which children in a new locale had changed from one Trinitarian church to another and, in a few cases, between Trinitarian and Unitarian organisations, as they sought an appropriate church to attend. Jamaicans giving accounts of their visits overseas frequently related how, at the outset, they had been to a church dominated by American or English participants but had felt uncomfortable with the 'style' of proceedings. Typically, if relatives could not help, a search took place between friends and associates, that could even involve a telephone call home to Jamaica, in order to find an appropriate church within the relevant locale. Far more than citizens' groups or friendly associations, churches seemed to be the principal secondary groups called on by many Jamaicans and especially Jamaican women to support them overseas.

---

[22] 'Custos' is an old (Latin-derived) English term for a position similar to mayor.
[23] See Calley, *God's People* and Rodriguez Toulis, *Believing Identities.*

Transnationalism permeated Jamaican Pentecostalism not only at the level of practice but also in imagination. When I was seeking a field location in rural Clarendon parish, one of the initial sites of Pentecostal evangelism in Jamaica,[24] I encountered a young pastor keen to be of assistance because he was eager to find in me a transnational link to a wider world. We met at a pastors' conference in the regional centre of May Pen. There was an air of heightened excitement at the conference for the church's Jamaican bishop had just returned from overseas with his wife and was reporting on his experiences there. In addition, a white American representative from the US was there to speak on pastors' superannuation schemes and introduce a new scheme of life assurance into the local church. These issues interested the pastors greatly not least because an early death could leave the wife of a rural pastor especially almost destitute. In addition, there was a guest black American preacher who had spent many years as a missionary in East Africa. She was there to preach the amazing story of how, in a famine and through God's grace, she had brought a young child back from the dead in Kenya. The conference was held in a large church hall in dry, hot and chaotic May Pen, a trading and service town to surrounding agricultural regions. The site of the conference was on a dusty road leading out of May Pen towards the Clarendon hills where I was hoping to locate. The Clarendon hills is a prime food producing area dotted with remote villages serviced by dirt roads and tracks often rendered impassable by torrential river floods during the rainy seasons. Pastors had come from all over the island to the conference and, despite the rather unpropitious site, there was a definite excitement and even glamour about proceedings due to the transnational links that were manifest.

This glamour was augmented by the bookstalls outside the hall which carried numerous Pentecostal tracts and leaflets, published mainly in the US, being sold as aids in evangelism. Pastors spent a long time examining these offerings and, if not very many were bought, they were a major topic of conversation among younger pastors especially as they discussed the use of literature in bringing the unsaved to God. There was also a session in the conference devoted to radio and television ministry that once again attracted the young but drew some criticism from older pastors who advocated their own immediate methods of evangelism and complained of the drain on their churches' tithed incomes created by these ventures into electronic media. In the midst of this heady environment, the young pastor invited me to be a guest in his family's house and at his church. In the course of my stay with him, he confided his ambition to become a full-time evangelist, preferably overseas. He imagined himself as a tele-evangelist renowned for his guitar playing and compelling religious songs. He had an acute sense of the numbers he might bring to

[24] See Austin-Broos, *Jamaica Genesis*, pp. 93-7.

God by adopting various evangelical methods that relied heavily on music and his own quite beautiful singing voice. Although his first ambition was to get to Kingston, he believed he could be successful in the US and even, he thought, in Australia (where I had come from) where he had heard that the Assemblies of God were successful, but not so successful as his own New Testament church.

My experience was that pastors who incorporated extensive transnational links in their careers were people with higher levels of education or else good basic education on which they themselves had built in an informal capacity. This young pastor had come from a very underprivileged background and had struggled through theological college at Mandeville in Jamaica. Although he had had a successful parish career, becoming an overseer of a number of churches in Clarendon at a young age, it seemed unlikely that he would be successful in his transnational aspirations. Nonetheless, they were a serious ambition and the young pastor's sense of his own career in the Clarendon hills was informed by a continuous world, both rural and remote within Jamaica and urban and urbane beginning from Kingston and extending to other cities of the world. The annual pastors' conference which he attended regularly was a major medium for sustaining this particular experience of his own career.

There were also those in Jamaica who eschewed transnational links and preached against transnational influence on Jamaican Pentecostals, especially as manifest through television. One well-known Unitarian pastor preached ferocious sermons on the evils apparent in US Pentecostal congregations. He criticised the dress of women, that fact that they wore lipstick and that some painted their nails. He was especially critical of hair styles and of the obvious fact that if hair styles could be seen it meant that women were attending church hatless. He also proposed that these US saints could not be filled with the spirit in the same fashion that Jamaican saints were. When asked by their 'preacher' to testify to the spirit of the Lord these congregations did no more than 'offer a little wave'. The hearty speaking in tongues and dancing in the spirit that contorted bodies in Jamaica, both women's and men's, was absent in these televised churches. When some notable evangelists in the US were involved in highly publicised 'backsliding' and 'falling from grace' this pastor was reported as observing that these events were predictable given the state of these men's congregations. Sinful pastors fostered sinful congregations and one had proved to be an index of the other. This particular pastor, from a regional centre on the southwest coast of Jamaica, led a successful but highly localised life albeit in proximity to the famous tourist town of Negril. Observers who knew of his preaching in Kingston suggested that it was this juxtaposition of local life and tourist excess that dictated the tone of his sermons. Where the young Clarendon pastor embraced a transnational world in his imagination, this critic turned away from it and yet used that world as the Armageddon of his evangelical message.

Indigenised religion and transnationalism

In _Jamaica Genesis_ I have argued for the Jamaicanness of its people's Pentecostalism in terms of that religion's specifying history and the specifying history of Christianity in general, in the hands of Jamaican people. Pentecostalism has become Jamaican because its values and symbols are used by Jamaicans in ways that are specifically responsive to their history and cultural environment. Transnationalism has been used by Jamaicans in particular ways as well and this is how transnationalism can be part of an indigenous religion in spite of its extra-local features. Jamaicans used Pentecostalism to legitimate popular revival religion in a turn of the century Jamaica dominated by a colonial order. This domination had been realised through a literate and credentialed denominational religion based in England. It affected the status of Zion Revival. Unable to be recognised as accredited ministers of religion, it was difficult for Zion Revival's leaders to build significant church organisations. In addition, preaching and practices that breached denominational orthodoxy opened Zion Revivalist leaders to charges of _obeah_-ism or witchcraft, punishable in the colonial state by imprisonment.

The Zion Revivalists' practice of Christianity placed them beyond established religion as illiterate, fragmented and possibly dangerous purveyors of superstition. The tone of the establishment's view is conveyed in the comments of Abraham Emerick writing in 1915 of Jamaican 'Mialism' or Zion Revival.

To attempt to describe Jamaica Mialism, a superstition imported from Africa, is like trying to describe the intricacies of the most cunningly devised Chinese puzzle. Mialism is so mixed up with Obeahism and Duppyism and other cults of African warp, together with whatever in Protestant and Catholic ritual that may appeal to the bizarre African imagination, that it is hard to tell which is which and what is what. But for all that it is a most interesting study for the student of folk-lore. The interest becomes great when we find this pagan wolf frisking about in the Christian pasture, among the true sheep.

It was this environment of scorn and scepticism that popular religionists faced as the first Pentecostal evangelists began to arrive in Jamaica in the 1910s. Yet conditions were also changing in Jamaica as this process unfolded. One change involved the spread of literacy, speeded by denominational churches and government efforts in the last three decades of the nineteenth century.[25] Another change was the increasing transnationalism of the region that was sending Jamaicans out as a workforce and drawing cultural brokers in, including Pentecostalists.[26]

[25] See Goveia, _Jamaica_.
[26] See Austin-Broos, _Jamaica Genesis_, pp. 17-24, 97-130.

In these circumstances, there were three aspects of Pentecostalism that Jamaicans took up and used to circumvent the colonial religious order. As Jamaican evangelism rapidly supplanted foreign missionaries in the 1920s, they used the resources of the foreign churches to spread their message effectively.[27] These resources came in the form of modest financial support and also church newsletters and tracts that, with the new literacy, allowed these preachers to connect themselves with the US. Literacy allowed a text-based religion often described as 'fundamentalist'. The importance of this text-based religion was that for Jamaicans it prised apart the authority of the texts from the authority of the colonial social order. No longer was it the case that access to authority in the text could be sought only through colonial institutions, including the denominational churches and the schools and colleges they controlled. Jamaicans with basic literacy could read the Bible for themselves and refer to religious tracts and to the Church of God newsletters that circulated in the countryside. Through these means they could anchor in the text practices of enthusiastic religion that in Zion Revival had floated free from a text-based Christianity controlled by the mission-*cum*-denominational churches. Via fundamentalism, 'African superstition' became a rival orthodoxy backed ultimately by a rival social order. As Pentecostalism challenged the dominance of denominational mission churches in Jamaica, it also drew implicitly on the power of a US market system which was eating away at the stability of Britain's imperial order in the region.

The literacy presumed by fundamentalism influenced popular religion in a second way. It legitimated the focus on healing that had been integral to Zion Revival and to all popular Jamaican religion. Implicit faith in the healing power of God was thoroughly endorsed by the Bible and this endorsement was now brought to bear on everyday Jamaican practice. An elderly Pentecostal in northern Clarendon said of the 1920s:

'Why people flowing to the New Testament Church of God the more, it was divine healing. Anywhere we went and preached, that brought people that was sick and we prayed for them, and they got healing you see. Then the people them, believe the church for the healing more, even more than the preacher. That goes a lot to the physical, you know, because many of the people them, want that power. Yes man, when the Spirit preaches you feel it, you feel it all over your body, the body feel good. I mean, if you go in the church and the Spirit of God is not in the church you can operate. You just sit down listening, but when the Spirit of God come in, you can turn the body in the Spirit.'

To 'turn the body in the Spirit' here means not only, as in Zion Revival, to enter that world where heaven and earth conjoin but also to transform the body so that it becomes a vessel of the Holy Spirit. The total faith that transformed a person was also a faith that realised healing: one would be a sign of the other in the new Pentecostalism.

---

[27] This argument is developed in more detail in my *Jamaica Genesis*, pp. 79-83.

Finally, the power of the US and the accepted bona fides of its organisations allowed Pentecostal churches to accredit Jamaican pastors. In
colonial Jamaica, ministers of new churches were recognised through a
process of peer nomination that required support from other ministers of
religion in a parish. The status quo had effectively debarred Zion Revivalist preachers from recognition. As the Pentecostal movement grew,
whether or not local ministers endorsed Pentecostalism, it became increasingly difficult not to confirm Pentecostals as recognised Christian
pastors. By the 1950s, when Pentecostalism began to take over as the
dominant popular religion in Jamaica, its major Unitarian and Trinitarian
churches were recognised in Jamaica and, by the early 1960s, were all
fully incorporated. Jamaicans had used the transnationalism of the US
churches, in conjunction with the growth of literacy in Jamaica, to circumvent the dominance of religion by a British colonial order. Whilst
this circumvention locked Jamaicans into other authority and power
structures closely connected with a regional capitalism, it did allow them
broader scope for autonomous religious practice in Jamaica responsive
to needs and desires as defined by a popular culture. Transnationalism in
Jamaica therefore served an indigenous project and, in the ways described,
strengthened the local even as it connected Pentecostals with an order
that is global in its reach.

Pentecostal transnationalism and the state today

Since the late 1960s, Jamaican society has been on a roller coaster ride of
economic instability, fluctuating currency and high levels of local unemployment. Public services including basic education have deteriorated
as public employees, and especially teachers, have become increasingly
demoralised. The high expectations of an alternative social democratic
order as represented by the late Michael Manley have been dashed. But
neither have the new-born forms of local capitalism offered long-term
solutions to the needs of Jamaican people. Scepticism concerning politics is much debated in daily newspaper columns. Crimes against property
and people are widespread and local intellectuals express grave concern
regarding the collapse of community.[28] The violence of drug trade connections with the eastern seaboard of the US has penetrated lower class
neighbourhoods to a degree that was difficult to imagine even at the beginning of the 1970s. The per capita income of Jamaica is currently the
lowest in the Anglophone Caribbean.[29] As the state apparatus proves itself unable to effectively protect its people from the vagaries of a regional
capitalism, some of the less attractive aspects of black nationalism are

[28] See Donald Robotham, *Vision and Volunteerism: Reviving Volunteerism in Jamaica*,
Kingston, 1998.
[29] Personal communication, Dr Donald Robotham, Kingston, Jamaica, 7 Dec. 1998.

evident. An understandable but nonetheless destructive element of jingoism is abroad.[30]

These circumstances are, perhaps, typical of numerous other nation states at the end of the twentieth century. With its capacity to shift both capital and labour from place to place in the world, global capitalism has undermined the ability of poorer states to support effective nation-building among their peoples. A previous condition of negotiated or imposed uniformity has, in many places, broken apart into multiple fractious voices as previously silenced minorities give expression to their own specificity and claims on the state. Jamaica is only specific to the extent that for much of its history its black majority was rendered as a silenced minority in the face of a colonial order with its power base located in a white metropolitan world. Most of all, this process underlines the subordination of state structures to transnational processes of the market and media of communication that inform and are supported by these market relations. States as mediators for nations with the world no longer provide stable or fulfilling structures of sociality for many peoples, including many Jamaicans. Being a citizen no longer ensures well being.

This is perhaps the downside of a global modernity about which Arjun Appadurai has written so eloquently.[31] For those unable to access in secure and felicitous circumstances the cosmopolitan offerings of this global modernity, its advent can be frightening. Forms of global fundamentalism that, as I have discussed, employ an authority of texts not located in particular status orders seem to be an alternative mode of transnational sociality to which people are turning as they move away from engagement with their own nation states. The two central examples of this process are Pentecostal Christianity with a geographical and financial anchor in the US, and Sunni Islam with a geographical and financial anchor in the Middle East. It is important to note that as these global movements offer a textual authority independent of the nation-state orders in which they are taken up, they are not themselves simply anonymous. In the two cases cited, these transnational forms of religion do have identifying locales that constitute their power bases grounded in forms of economic and political pre-eminence. Just as the market with its modes of communication has not become entirely de-stated, so these religious organisations that provide alternatives to identification with a local nation state, such as Jamaica, are themselves not entirely de-stated.

As the previous discussion demonstrates, for those equipped to realise the opportunities, engagement with these alternative structures can be

---

[30] See Robotham, *Vision and Volunteerism*, and also Charles Carnegie, 'The Dundas and the Nation', *Cultural Anthropology*, no. 11, pp. 470-509.

[31] Arjun Appadurai has published extensively on this issue but see, for instance, the early statement in 'Global Ethnoscapes: Notes and Queries for a Transnational Anthropology' in R. Fox (ed.), *Recapturing Anthropology*, Sante Fe, 1991, pp. 191-210.

an effective way to re-locate one's citizenship. And that is certainly one of the attractions of the large Pentecostal churches with their local hierarchies and transnational networks within a Jamaican milieu. Through identification with Pentecostalism some Jamaicans can relocate themselves to sites in the US where the benefits of citizenship are more apparent. In the over-used terms of Benedict Anderson, then, transnational fundamentalist religion becomes an alternative imagined community in the face of the failure of the weaker nation states. Pentecostalism in Jamaica currently plays this role and is indicative of a modernity, enmeshed with capitalism, that in both the colonial and the current period has sought to circumvent the Jamaican state. This analysis perhaps gives a new meaning to the opposition that Daniel Miller proposes between the ephemeral and the transcendental as indicative of modernity.[32] Many Jamaicans past and present have sought to escape the rootlessness of a history of slavery, waged exploitation and unstable national politics through the transcendence of religion. As I have discussed above, this is a central feature of both Pentecostalism and Rastafarianism in Jamaica today. However, this transcendence possibly is no more than peoples' desire for secure sociality and moral order: a wish to find a different (but probably equally politicised) route to social equanimity in a world of unequal nations states. The market and communications have made these forms of transnationalism possible in the late twentieth century. Yet the forms of religion that these forces support have not, except in imagination, dispersed the order of capitalism that has supplied their conditions of existence. The transnationalism of Jamaican Pentecostalism is, therefore, in more than one sense a modern phenomenon: a form of transcendence seeking to combat constant change, and also a social form indicative of the relations of international capitalism.

In the foregoing I have sought to underline that whilst transnationalism has always been a dimension of Jamaican religion, the modernity of Pentecostal transnationalism is rooted in its relations with a regional market order and the links between these market relations and a relatively weak nation state. As these relations extended in the Caribbean they gave new roles to literacy, and also encouraged the forms of migration typical of transnationalism today. The Jamaican case suggests that there are important connections between five much discussed phenomena: global capitalism, the continuing inequalities between nation states, transnational migration and communication, the rise of ethnic or essentialist politics within nation states, and the rise of fundamentalist religion as a new, imagined, global order. Where the politics of ethnicity makes exclusionary claims on the resources of often embattled states, fundamentalist

[32] Daniel Miller, *Modernity*, esp. p. 16.

transnationalism moves beyond local states to seek resources in a different structure, but ultimately in more powerful states. Where one form of politics renders social order as indicative of relations between nations, more than one of which may be encompassed by a state, the other renders social order as indicative of forms of moral and cosmological relations proposed to exist beyond nation state boundaries. Each of these responses, nonetheless, is a response to the ordering of nation states that limits the capacity of some to render in a definitive way the experience and being of their citizens. In Jamaica, black nationalism and Pentecostalism can and often do embody these different responses to life within the confines of a relatively poor and weak nation state. The clarity with which this process is revealed may be heightened by Jamaica's proximity to the US. That Jamaica and its Pentecostalism are indicative of a more general phenomenon, however, rather than being unique seems very likely.

BIBLIOGRAPHY

Appadurai, Arjun, 'Global Ethnoscapes: Notes and Queries for a Transnational Anthropology' in Richard Fox (ed.), *Recapturing Anthropology*, Sante Fe, 1991, pp. 191-210.

Austin-Broos, Diane, *Urban Life in Kingston, Jamaica*, New York, 1984.

——, 'Religion and Rationalism: A Hegelian Revival?', *Mankind*, vol. 19, no. 1, 1989, pp. 53-64.

——, 'Politics and the Redeemer: State and Religion as Ways of Being in Jamaica', *Nieuwe West-Indische Gids*, no. 70, pp. 1-32.

——, 'Pentecostals and Rastafarians: Cultural, Political and Gender Relations of Religious Movements', *Social and Economic Studies*, no. 36, 1987, pp. 1-39.

——, 'Religion and the Politics of Moral Order in Jamaica', *Anthropological Forum*, no. 6, 1991-2, pp. 287-319.

——, 'Redefining the Moral Order: Interpretations of Christianity in Post-Emancipation Jamaica' in Frank McGlynn and Seymour Drescher (eds), *The Meaning of Freedom*, Pittsburgh, 1992, pp. 221-44.

——, *Jamaica Genesis: Religion and the Politics of Moral Order*, Chicago, 1997.

——, 'Educating Jamaica: Diaspora Culture and the 'old' Middle Class''.' Paper presented to the African Diaspora conference at the Australian National University, 7-9 Apr. 1998, organised by Barry Higman and James Walvin for the Humanities Research Centre, ANU.

Calley, Malcolm, *God's People: West Indian Pentecostal Sects in England*, London, 1965.

Carnegie, Charles, 'The Dundas and the Nation', *Cultural Anthropology*, no. 11, 1996, pp. 470-509.

Chevannes, Barry, *Rastafari, Roots and Ideology*, Syracuse, 1994.

Comaroff, Jean and John Comaroff, *Of Revelation and Revolution: Christianity, Colonialism and Consciousness in South Africa*, Chicago, 1991.

Foner, Nancy, *Jamaica Farewell: Jamaican Migrants in London*, London, 1979.

Goveia, Elsa, *Jamaica, 1830-1930*, Manchester, 1961.

Hall, Stuart, 'Negotiating Caribbean Identities', *New Left Review*, no. 209, 1995, pp. 3-14.

Horton, Robin, 'African Conversion', *Africa*, no. 41, 1971, pp. 85-108.

Miller, Daniel, *Modernity, An Ethnographic Approach: Dualism and Mass Consumption in Trinidad*, Oxford, 1994.

Miller, Errol, *Jamaican Society and High Schooling*, Kingston, 1990.

Robotham, Donald, *Vision and Volunteerism: Reviving Volunteerism in Jamaica*, Kingston, 1998.

Rodriguez Toulis, Nicole, *Believing Identities: Pentecostalism and the Mediation of Jamaican Ethnicity and Gender in England*, Oxford, 1997.

Stewart, Robert, *Religion and Society in Post-Emancipation Jamaica*, Knoxville, TN, 1992.

Turner, Mary, *Slaves and Missionaries: The Disintegration of Jamaican Slave Society, 1787-1834*, Urbana, IL, 1982.

PENTECOSTALISM, MARKET LOGIC AND RELIGIOUS TRANSNATIONALISATION IN COSTA RICA

Jean-Pierre Bastian

With a population of around 3.8 million inhabitants in 1997, Costa Rica is one of the smallest countries in Latin America. Roman Catholicism still enjoys the status of official religion, and even though there is complete freedom of worship, the Catholic church maintains a privileged relationship with the state. The religious situation of the country has nevertheless evolved rapidly over the last twenty years, and is characterised by a growing diversification of religious identities, so that today, while 78 per cent of Costa Ricans define themselves as Catholic, 18 per cent now belong to the evangelical movement and 3 per cent participate in other religious movements. Far from being homogeneous, the non-Catholic religious community is fragmented, and a few large Pentecostal organisations play a prominent role in the new religious landscape. This new reality is worth analysing in term of the accelerating process of transnationalisation of religion which can be observed elsewhere in the Latin American region.

Religious transnationalisation involves a process of multilateral dissemination which crosses borders without springing from any specific point, and without being determined by any state interests, and it is grounded in networking strategies. The network, functioning as a set of interconnected junctions, facilitates the circulation of discourse and the translocal construction of religious identities. In a context of growing religious plurality, the circulation of discourses and the translocal construction of identities are determined and structured by a 'market situation'.[1] The statistics given above indicate a process of religious differentiation which indeed stimulates the elaboration, the dissemination and the consumption of new religious products in a situation of generalised competition between religious agents or bodies. I take transnationalisation to mean the delocalisation of practices and beliefs that are linked with the fluid and immaterial dimension of religion, and will thus examine the relations between transnationalisation and market logic within the framework of the dynamics produced by the dissemination and the expansion of Pentecostal religious movements in Costa Rica. In order to achieve this, I intend to follow three lines of observation with first an examination of the evolution of Pentecostal movements from international to multilateral

[1] Peter Berger, *The Sacred Canopy. Elements of a Sociological Theory of Religion*, New York, 1969, p. 138.

patterns of dissemination; then an analysis of their shift from the use of imported models to the use of hybrid models, and finally a discussion of their resort to the most sophisticated forms of modern media. On the basis of the results of field work,[2] three characteristics of Pentecostal transnationality will be outlined: multilaterality, hybridity and the networking of practices and beliefs in a 'market situation'.

From international to multilateral patterns

While the rest of Latin America has seen the growth of a liberal form of Protestantism equipped with important educational means, Costa Rica and the rest of Central America have attracted, since the end of the nineteenth century, a form of fundamentalist and pietistic Protestantism which is relatively lacking in educational means and intellectual qualities.[3] This tendency became more pronounced from the 1950s onwards, when various forms of Pentecostalism began to spread throughout the Central American region following a successful implantation in Salvador. Some Pentecostal movements of North American origin had indeed established themselves in Salvador during the 1930s and had rapidly propagated towards neighbouring Guatemala and Honduras.[4] The Iglesia Santidad Pentecostal was the first Pentecostal society to become organised in Costa Rica (1949). Other societies took the same path shortly afterwards, such as Iglesia de Dios, Cleveland, Tennessee, Iglesia Cuandrangular, Iglesia de Dios Pentecostés, and above all the Asambleas de Dios (1951). In particular, the latter organisation grew spectacularly throughout the whole country during the 1960s, beginning in 1951 with some 225 members distributed in three assemblies, and reaching in 1972 the figure of 2,841 members participating in 68 assemblies. At that time, the only group with a higher membership were the Adventists (who had arrived in 1927), with a total of 5,700 members. However, through the 1980s and 1990s, Pentecostal movements continued to grow at an accelerating pace, with a particularly spectacular increase among the Asambleas de Dios, going from 12,466 members in 205 assemblies in 1982 to 78,777 members in 603 assemblies ten years later.[5]

This movement of expansion was made possible through the propagation of North American models and techniques of religious

[2] This article translated from the French by Christopher Sinclair is based on field research carried out in July-August 1997 as part of the survey conducted by the Bergstraesser Institut at Freiburg im Breisgau and Borge y Asociados in San José, Costa Rica, the results of which appear in Bastian *et al.*, 'Sekten und religiöse Bewegungen. Fallstudie Costa Rica', Freiburg im Breisgau: Arnold Bergstraesser Institut, 1998, 267 p. (unpublished).

[3] Wilton Nelson, *Historia del protestantismo en Costa Rica,* San José, 1983.

[4] Douglas Petersen, *Not by Might, Nor by Power: A Pentecostal Theology of Social Concern in Latin America*, Oxford, 1996, p. 73.

[5] *Ibid.*, p. 77.

revival.[6] From the 1950s onwards, Costa Rica became a testing-ground for the strategy of 'in-depth evangelism', a phrase coined by Kenneth Strachan, the son of the founder of the Latin American Mission (1921), when he became the founding director of the Latin American Biblical Seminary of San José in 1948. This movement linked itself with other initiatives of saturation evangelism elaborated by 'missiologists' specialised in 'church growth strategy' who were based at Fuller Theological Seminary (1947) in Pasadena.[7] Large-scale evangelical campaigns were systematically organised, with visiting preachers from North America. These North American evangelists, soon to be imitated by some Latin Americans, had developed aggressive methods for the propagation of their beliefs, drawing inspiration from the evangelical campaigns led by Billy Graham in the post-war United States, which were rooted in the fundamentalist tradition of 'revival'. These campaigns, so characteristic of the 'Bible belt' of rural America, relied on marketing techniques and modern means of communication, while displaying at the same time an emotional and enthusiastic religiosity. With the beginnings of the Cold War and Senator McCarthy's witch-hunt against communists, Billy Graham combined anti-communist declarations with the biblical message during his 1959 'crusades' in the West Indies, Central America and Mexico. Burgeoning Pentecostal churches resorted to the same proselytising means for their own expansion. Pentecostal preacher T.L. Osborn, for instance, led a campaign of '*sanidad divina*' at the 'Plaza de Toros' of San José in March 1952, with the support of the Asambleas de Dios and other Pentecostal groups.[8] As for Billy Graham, he visited Costa Rica in 1959. Around the same time, Kenneth Strachan was using his foothold in Costa Rica to spread the 'evangelism in depth movement' throughout Latin America as a whole, with the aim of mobilising on a permanent basis the energies of the churches in the countries where campaigns were to be held.[9] Evangelists Billy Graham, Luis Palau, Paul Finkenbinder and Yiye Avila, among others, led 'crusades' in Costa Rica during the 1960s and 1970s, boosting burgeoning evangelical organisations by infusing them with the dynamics of expansion. Raúl Vargas, who was to become the founder and 'pastor general' of one of today's largest Pentecostal churches in Costa Rica (the Oasis de Esperanza in Moravia), was converted during a campaign led by Luis Palaù in San José in 1972.

[6] Jean-Pierre Bastian, *Le protestantisme en Amérique latine. Une approche socio-historique*, Geneva, 1994, pp. 217-22.

[7] George Marsden, *Reforming Fundamentalism: Fuller Seminary and the New Evangelicalism*, Grand Rapids, MI, 1987, pp. 263-76.

[8] Nelson, *Historia del protestantismo*, p. 277.

[9] William Dayton Roberts, *Strachan of Costa Rica. Missionary Insights and Strategies*, Grand Rapids, MI, 1971; William Dayton Roberts, 'El movimiento de cooperación evangélica de San José 1948 a Bogotá 1969', *Pastoralia*, no. 2, 1978, pp. 33-42.

In the aftermath of the 'revival' initiated by evangelical campaigns, dissenting Pentecostal societies were formed, such as the Sin Corvata, a movement which broke away from the Iglesias Cuadrangulares originating from neighbouring Panama. But, above all, new Pentecostal organisations founded by Costa Rican religious leaders were born. For instance, in 1976 the Misión Cristiana Mundial Rosa de Sarón was created in a humble home of the Barrio Luján in San José. In 1978, the Iglesia Roca del Pedernal was founded by 'prophet' Zacharias Pérez in Barrance, Puntarenas province, while in the suburbs of the neighbouring town of Ezparza the Iglesia Manantial de Vida was being established, following a split in the local Methodist church. Still in the provinces, Costa Rican Pentecostal leaders set up the Iglesia Ríos de Agua Viva in Cartago (1977), and the Ministerio Casa del Banquete in San Isidro del General (1979). During the 1970s and the 1980s, there also appeared on the outskirts of San José small Pentecostal groups which, thanks to a period of steady growth, have become very large communities, with to-day more than 1,000 members each: Oasis de Esperanza in Moravia (1975), Iglesia de la Luz del Mundo in Hatillo (1975), Comunidad Cristiana Shalom in Hatillo (1978), Centro Cristiano in Tibás (1983), Centro Evangelístico in Zapote (1985), Casa del Banquete in Pavas (1986), Iglesia Cristo Viña in La Urunca (1989), Iglesia del Tabernáculo in San Sebastián, among a few others. At the same time, North American methods of religious propaganda continued to be put to use in the campaigns led by a new wave of evangelical celebrities, among whom Pentecostals were prominent. North American Pentecostal preachers Nicky Cruz, Alberto Motessi, Jimmy Swaggart, Benny Hinn, Franklin Graham and Moris Cerrullo all made regular visits to Costa Rica in the 1980s and 1990s. Their methods of religious activism were rapidly taken over and adapted by the most dynamic local Pentecostal leaders, such as Raúl Vargas, Ronny Chávez and Hugo Solis, who during the same years made full use of a similar process of media communication on a national and even international scale by way of 'crusades' and systematic evangelical movements.[10]

All these initiatives have led to exponential growth among Evangelical organisations in a context of economic changes and demographic explosion. Indeed, during these same years the capital, San José, and the other main towns of the country were being deeply transformed by processes of urbanisation, metropolisation and suburbanisation. In the early 1940s, San José was still a relatively small town, with 70,000 inhabitants (10 per cent of the total population of the country), and the villages which were later to become the capital's suburbs were still separate from it.[11] In 1996, the metropolitan region numbered 1,773,374 inhabitants,

[10] *Maranata*, no. 177, 1996, p. 18.

[11] Mavis Hiltunen de Biesanz, Richard Biesanz and Karen Zubris de Biesanz, *Los costarricenses*, San José, 1979, p. 100.

amounting to half the total population of the country.[12] Throughout the last forty years, migration flows from the countryside to the capital have increased so dramatically that the former villages surrounding the capital have been turned into disordered suburbs, made up of *'precarios'* (shanty towns) and pauperised neighbourhoods. Evangelical and more particularly Pentecostal movements started to grow in the suburbs of large towns, and they continued to expand in parallel with the process of disorganised urbanisation in response to the state of anomie and the absence of religious leadership among recently displaced populations. It is also likely that the migrant population was attracted primarily to Pentecostal places of worship because of the failure of the Roman Catholic church to adapt quickly enough to new population patterns. This can be explained by the fact that the Catholic church was suffering from a personnel deficit, due to its partial inability to recruit a national clergy. In 1960, out of the 293 Catholic priests serving in Costa Rica, 115 were foreigners.[13] Thus, a combination of various factors – an international evangelical effort of foreign origin, the structural effects of socio-economic upheavals, the taking over of imported models by local movements, and finally the inadequate response of the Catholic church to the needs of a migrating and mobile population – can explain the spectacular expansion of Evangelical movements from the 1960s onwards, which is summed up in Table 1.

Table 1. PROTESTANT POPULATION IN COSTA RICA 1892-1997[14]

	Total population	Protestant population	% of total	% of Catholics
1864	120,499	286	0.2	99.7
1883		1,392	n.d.	
1892	243,205	2,245	0.9	98.9
1921	476,581	1,000	0.2	
1940	656,031	4,000	0.6	
1955	933,033	8,340	1.0	
1960	1,149,537	18,250	1.3	
1974	1,905,338	57,930	3.0	
1983	2,403,781	163,020	6.8	
1989	2,886,990	256,900	8.9	81.7
1991	3,063,608	329,100	10.6	82.8
1995	3,347,000	408,000	12.2	78.8
1997	3,680,000	n.d.	18	77.8

These figures make clear that Evangelicalism began to expand following the harsh transformation of the urban landscape between the mid-1970s

[12] *Costa Rica: Datos e indicadores básicos*, San José: INICEM, 1997.

[13] Nelson, *Historia del protestantismo*, p. 322.

[14] J.I. Gómez *El crecimiento y la desección en la iglesia evangélica costarricense*, San José, 1996, p. 35; *Demoscopia*, 1996, p. 16; Bastian *et al.*, 'Sekten', p. 176.

168   *Jean-Pierre Bastian*

and the mid-1980s, and that Evangelical growth has been accelerating even more since the beginning of the 1990s, with the multiplication of various religious enterprises. Evidence of such growth can also be seen in the fact that in the early 1980s the state (and the Catholic church) put great pressure on Evangelicals by endeavouring to stem the continual opening of new places of worship by shutting them down under the pretext that they did not conform with planning or sanitary laws.[15] In the mid-1990s, according to the yearbook of Evangelical churches in Costa Rica,[16] more than 29 Evangelical organisations were active in the metropolitan area, and on a national level, some 104 Evangelical Christian associations were affiliated to the 'Alianza Evangélica' (on 5 October 1996).

By observing diachronically the evolution of Pentecostal movements in Costa Rica, a decisive change can be noticed during the 1980s. Up to then, Pentecostal organisations had developed under the logic of a unilateral internationalisation of the Evangelical faith. Pentecostalism was the fruit of the missionary work of mother churches situated in the US, whose expansion was part of the North American strategy of political influence in Central America, within the context of the Cold War. The imported religious models were taken over wholesale by Costa Rican Pentecostal organisations, which functioned as mere subsidiaries of North American parent organisations. However, in the 1980s, this pattern was radically altered with the appearance of new indigenous leaders endowed with charisma. While forming their own religious organisations, these leaders engaged their churches in multilateral strategies of expansion through networking, directed towards the US as well as towards other Latin American countries, and even towards Europe and Africa. Exogenous influences still remain, but North America has ceased to be their only source. Some Latin American religious organisations are now expanding following Brazilian (Igreja Universal) and Korean (Yonggi Cho) models of propagation. In the same way, since the 1970s, Costa Rican Pentecostal organisations founded by indigenous leaders have been exporting their own models of growth, whereas before, they were only at the receiving end of North American initiatives. The present change is therefore characterised by a process of religious pluralisation and by the development of multilateral exchanges. This process of religious multilateralisation is determined by market logic, by which is meant a situation of competition between religious agents or enterprises struggling for the accumulation and distribution of symbolic goods which are likely to arouse the interest and the demand of ever widening sectors of the population[17]. The intensification

[15] *Maranata*, no. 18, 1983, p. 2; no. 19, 1983, p. 8; no. 21, 1983, p. 4.

[16] *Donde está la iglesia? Un directorio de las Iglesias evangélicas costarricences*, San José, 1995, p. 7.

[17] Pierre Bourdieu, 'Genèse et structure du champ religieux', *Revue française de sociologie*, Dec. 1971, pp. 295-334.

of exchanges and the process of religious transnationalisation make it possible today for practices and symbols produced anywhere in the world to be adopted instantaneously by Costa Rican religious agents and enterprises. Pentecostal organisations have become above all enterprises developing strategies of multilateral commercialisation and distribution of symbolic goods. Market logic induces a transformation of the type of product which is being supplied.

From importation to hybridity in the context of market logic

The 'Latinisation' of Pentecostal practices and beliefs conditioned by market logic is the second characteristic of the process of religious transnationalisation. This kind of hybridisation process has nothing to do with syncretism. The concept of hybridity is not identical to that of syncretism, for the latter, in a culturalist approach to religious phenomena, is based on the idea that there exist pure religious entities which can be normatively classified. The notion of hybridity refers on the contrary to the juxtaposition of various sources of borrowing, among then the contents of beliefs, patterns of transmission and communication, the recourse to the most archaic as well as the most modern mediations, and finally the eclectic and pragmatic use of models linked to market logic. At the same time, in Latin America, the notion of hybridity helps to describe how various social sectors appropriate the multi-temporal and heterogeneous religious heritages and influences which are present in the region. Hybridity is determined by a demand which retains a relation with the diversity of existing traditions, while revealing itself capable of capturing new practices and discourses likely to arouse growing interest. Hybridity is a way of adapting to the market, but also of creating a religious demand which the hybrid product seeks to anticipate by arousing it. While until the 1970s Costa Rican Pentecostal societies continued to reproduce the Northern American model, since that time an endogenous hybrid religiosity has been developing, by putting to use in an eclectic way elements drawn from various local, national and international sources.

For a long time in Costa Rica, Pentecostal worship remained discreet, except for the big campaigns led by North American preachers. Today, on the contrary, Pentecostal churches use market saturation commercial strategies and imitate Catholic practices. The foremost Pentecostal leaders of the country offer non-stop religious services in their churches, organise procession-like marches and come out on public squares to celebrate common prayer days for the nation. In the case of large Pentecostal communities, they offer a succession of worship services every two or three hours throughout the day, especially on Sundays. In other instances, '*cadenas*' or thematic days are offered all through the week. At the same time, Pentecostals have shed their anonymity and have come down into the streets by organising huge processions known as 'Marches for Jesus'. This 'coming out' from the private sphere and this occupation of the public space are ways of competing with Catholic national processions, of establishing one's respectability by displaying numerical strength, and of being present in society on an equal footing with the Catholic church.

Secondly, Costa Rican Pentecostal churches, taking over imported North American models, have emphasised emotion, collective trance and praise. However, while till around the 1970s most of the hymns in use were of British or North American origin, since then great care has been taken to incorporate latino music and rhythms, which has led to transformations in the forms of worship. These rhythms have been borrowed from the various national musical traditions of Latin America, and can be inspired for instance by Mexican ranchera music, Dominican merengue, Colombian cumbia, Puerto Rican salsa or Brazilian samba, as well as by North American rock music. Worship meetings have become real musical shows led by rock bands and small choirs. Such 'ministries of musical praise' have played a great role in the success of worship shows, making them more competitive in the context of market logic. The development of an indigenous hymnology has given rise to dynamic forms of worship which are articulated with Pentecostal expressions of North American origin. The audience participates by clapping their hands, by beating the rhythm, by swaying their bodies in dancelike movements, by shouting *'alleluia'* and *'gloria a Dios'* in response to the appeals of the leaders. Through this emotional piety always in search of new worship 'gadgets', through the rhythms, the songs, the clapping of hands and the controlled swaying of hips, there emerges a communion of praise[18] which is rooted in the popular musical culture and modes of communication of Latin America.

In this atmosphere of praise, individuals become immersed in the group, as they participates in a collective ecstasy which is reflected on the faces of the whole audience, and which helps worshippers to transcend the hardships of everyday life. Through the medium of praise, such worship services act as an outlet for a population plagued by the many family problems which are the consequence of the economic and social problems of a rapidly changing society. Slogans such as *'No sufras más'*, of the Iglesia Cristiana del Espíritu Santo, or *'Ven a gozarte en la presencia del Señor'*, of the Rosa de Sarón church, provide a good summary of the kind of message that is put forward in these movements. What most Pentecostal worship services offer and what their audiences are in search of is a religiosity based on experience and on a physical encounter with the divine. For example, in his sermon during the main service at the

---

[18] André Corten, *Le pentecôtisme au Brésil. Émotion du pauvre et romantisme théologique*, Paris, 1995.

Centro Evangelístico of the Asambleas de Dios in Zapote on Sunday 22 February 1998, Pastor Hugo Solis compared the service to a football match, and asked his 1,500-strong enthusiastic audience, who were already spontaneously whistling, shouting and clapping their hands, to acclaim God just in the same way as a crowd in a football match cheers the winning team. Worship services become a means of collective expression for believers, as rock concerts are for young people. Theological discourse in these services is usually very thin, for, in the very words of the 'pastor general' of the Rosa de Sarón church, 'Jesus is practical'.

One only needs to consider one of the main Pentecostal practices, namely exorcism, to perceive at the same time both the hybrid character of such a phenomenon and the fact that practices of this kind are part of a marketing strategy. Religious trance and spiritual possession, which manifest themselves during exorcisms, belong to the mentality of popular religion. They contribute to reinforcing the image of the religious leader as an intercessor who is the holder of revealed knowledge, for it is through him that the anointing which casts out demons is made active. This may explain why Pastor Alvarado (66 years old), of the Luz de un Nuevo Día church, of the '*precario*' of Los Diques, Cartago, is above all fond of 'evangelising, teaching, healing the sick and confronting demons'. The pastor places himself in the continuity of traditional shamans, who have the power to discern, address and expel evil spirits, to communicate with the numinous and to bestow strength, liberation and healing. Since the 1990s, the practice of exorcism in Costa Rica has become enriched with that of 'spiritual warfare', which has become a prominent theme in the discourse of Costa Rican as well as Latin American Pentecostals these last years. This latest innovation originated in certain currents of North American Evangelicalism, and was put on the agenda by a number of leaders (Peter Wagner, Cindy Jacobs, Kenneth Copeland). But it has been taken over, reformulated and put to use within the mental and physical context of Costa Rica. Pastor Ronny Chávez has turned himself into the national specialist in this form of popular theology known as 'spiritual warfare', which he has put into practice during the 'international meetings of the Word of God' that he has been organising every year since 1990. It takes the form of 'a struggle to be carried out against Satan, the demons and occult practices', by setting up 'a strategy aiming at cleansing occupied territories', but also with the purpose of attracting more attention from the media.

In 1996, some Costa Rican pastors attempted to 'conquer the gates of the cities' by setting out to 'visit the high places of every town and pray for the problems of the country'.[19] With a similar aim in mind, on 26 January 1996 the foremost Evangelical leaders of the country gathered in the 'Templo bíblico' in the centre of San José, and from there 'took a private

---

[19] *Maranata*, no. 179, 1996, p. 12.

aeroplane and flew several times over the metropolitan region, anointing it on the way'. Their action was broadcast by the Evangelical television channel, Canal 23. In the afternoon of the same day, the public effect of this media event was reinforced by giving it a political dimension, for six Pentecostal leaders were received by the President of the Republic, José María Figueres Olsen, in order to inform him about the action that had taken place in the morning.[20] Earlier, in 1994, Pastor Ronny Chávez had performed a spectacular action of the same kind by flying over the whole country 'from the border of Nicaragua to the border of Panama, and from Puntarenas to Limón, sprinkling oil every six kilometres' with the purpose of 'liberating the national territory to make it easier to evangelise'. His goal was also to 'confront the forces of evil': first, he intended to 'break the alliances formed between the devil and the witches who have the habit of meeting on the summits of the important mountains of Costa Rica to offer sacrifices to Satan'; secondly, he wished to 'fight Catholic idolatry, which consists in offering estates, cars, families, football teams and even personal objects to the idols of official religion'. In a formula which sums up very well the fundamentalistic outlook which inspires such actions, he went on affirming that 'if taking Jericho was possible in the past, there is no reason why it shouldn't be possible today'.[21] That is why in early 1995 a group of 200 people gathered near Cartago, the symbolic centre of the country and of the Catholic church, and walked seven times round the Catholic basilica, hoping that it might collapse, or at least with the symbolic goal of circumscribing 'enemy territory'.[22]

Such practices may come as a surprise to observers who are used to interpreting Latin American Evangelical movements through their original North American models. These practices testify to the fundamentally hybrid character of Latin American Pentecostal movements. However, it must be remembered that in Costa Rica, as well as in the rest of Latin America, Pentecostal glossolalia, healing practices and exorcisms have developed in a receptive milieu, which has been fashioned by what can be called 'a culture of miraculous images' also found in neighbouring Mexico, as Gruzinski[23] has shown. As Marzal[24] has pointed out in the case of Peru, 'people have learnt that the saints comfort, listen and perform

---

[20] *Maranata*, no. 169, 1996, p. 15.

[21] *Maranata*, no. 155, 1994, p. 8.

[22] *Maranata*, no. 156, 1995, p. 20.

[23] Serge Gruzinski, *La guerra de las imágenes. De Cristobal Colón a 'Blade Runner' (1492-2019)*, Mexico City, 1994. For example, p. 190: 'el imaginario que acompaña el culto de las imágenes ejerce, pues, un papel motor en la restructuración cultural que funde la herencia indígena con los rasgos introducidos por los colonizadores, y después en la reproducción del patrimonio que ha brotado de esta fusión'.

[24] Manuel Marzal, *Los caminos religiosos de los inmigrantes en la gran Lima*, Lima, 1989 (1st edn,1988), p. 163.

miracles, and this has become a central feature of their spirituality'. The whole population is immersed in this thaumaturgical culture and has learned to venerate those who possess the divine force which expresses itself through prophylactic and therapeutic interventions. This force can manifest itself through a variety of religious traditions: the apparition of the Virgin in 1993 at Sarepequi, in the north-eastern region of Costa Rica;[25] the Pentecostal 'intercessor' who practises 'divine healing'; Edith Brown, a black Baptist woman from the village of Cahuita, in the Atlantic province of Limón, whose ancestors were Jamaican and whose religiosity is a mixture of Evangelical 'old time religion' and popular healing powers believed to bring about miracles and cures. One can even ask whether Pentecostalism is not helping to trivialise the belief in the miraculous. Indeed, far from disappearing, belief in the supernatural is becoming stronger in Costa Rican evangelical communities, with belief in the devil, hell, ghosts, witchcraft and the end of the world being much more widespread among the Evangelical than among the Catholic population, according to a 1996 *Demoscopia* survey.[26] (See Table 2)

Table 2. BELIEFS OF COSTA RICANS

Belief in	*Catholic (%)*	*Non-Catholic Christians (%)*
The Devil	69.3	90.5
Hell	65.1	85.7
Ghosts	24.9	40.8
Witchcraft	40.8	67.3
The end of the world	65.0	87.1
End of the world imminent	30.4	80.3
Purgatory	65.1	25.2
Reincarnation	34.6	20.4
Extraterrestrial beings	44.6	24.5

Even if certain beliefs which are peculiar to Catholicism, such as purgatory, seem to be in sharp decline, and even if belief in reincarnation or in extraterrestrial beings seems to be less prevalent among Evangelicals, the universe of popular religion appears to have gained strength from the rise of Evangelical movements, as the first four items of Table 2 make clear. This may explain the relatively high rate of desertion among Evangelicals,[27]

[25] *Maranata*, no. 139, 1993, p. 3.

[26] *Demoscopia s.a., fe y creencias del costarricense,* San José, Feb. 1996, mimeo, p. 13.

[27] Jorge I. Gómez. *El crecimiento y la deserción en la iglesia evangélica costarricense,* San José, 1996.

which has become a matter of concern for the leaders of the movement. Many causes can be found to explain this trend, but it is somehow a correlative to spectacular religious growth taking place in a fluctuating religious universe. A kind of migrant religiosity has emerged, with a proportion of believers tending to move from one worship centre to the next in search of miraculous and spectacular events. Pentecostal Pastor Jiménez Tabash[28] gives a clear picture of the situation:

There are thousands of people in our Pentecostal and charismatic movements who attend religious services only to 'see something' which can help them to believe. In order to experience emotions, they go from one service to another, from one campaign to another, while lacking any doctrinal certainty. They just go where the services are the most attractive, where the music has the best rhythm and where the seats are the most comfortable.

Significantly, North American Protestant missionaries stationed in Costa Rica, while belonging for the most part to Evangelical pietistic and Pentecostal movements, have voiced their concern about such practices, which they consider 'a deviation from the central message of the Gospel, replacing it with particular teachings, prophecies, revelations, experiences and interpretations'.[29] In their view, 'spiritual warfare' is nothing but 'a revival of the old Animism'.[30]

However, the dynamic character of transnationalised religion is due not to its assimilation of the archaic religious universe, but to its capacity to combine archaic and hypermodern features within the context of a fluctuating universe of references. This fluidity of practices and beliefs is reflected in the absence of firmly rooted belonging to any specific identity, with believers moving easily from one religious expression to another, and finally feeling at home in all of these expressions. The Pentecostalisation of practices and beliefs covers indeed a wide spectrum, from Pentecostalised Evangelical movements to charismatic Catholicism. This kind of delocalisation of beliefs and practices is made possible above all by resorting to the media, which allows an immediate connection to networks in the context of an open religious market. The taking over of religion by the media, and above all by the television image, is probably the main factor behind the present development of religious transnationalisation, while being at the same time a central expression of the hybridity which has made possible 'a powerful return of the all-pervading miraculous images of the baroque period', as Gruzinski has observed in the context of Mexican commercial television.[31]

[28] Yamil Jiménez Tabash, *Dios quiere prosperarte,* San José, 1997, p. 118.

[29] *Maranata,* 178, 1996, p. 24.

[30] Robert J. Priest, 'La guerra espiritual o el viejo animismo', *Apuntes pastorales*, vol. 14, no. 3, 1997, p. 32.

[31] Gruzinski, *La guerra de las imágenes.* Mexico City, 1994, p. 211.

The media and networking

One of the main characteristics of Costa Rican Pentecostal movements is the juxtaposition of their discourse, which draws upon traditional religion, with their use of hypermodern media techniques. Even though the message is very often transmitted through the testimony of relatives and neighbours, the role played by modern means of communication is probably as important. It is quite easy to trace how 'media culture' has penetrated the Costa Rican Evangelical movement. In the 1940s, pioneer Evangelical radio stations were set up in the Central American region. The best known among these is Radio Faro del Caribe, which was founded in 1949 in San José. Since 1982, a second Protestant radio, Sendas de Vida, has been broadcasting regularly, specialising in Christian rock music programmes. More recently, other stations with smaller audiences have been launched (such as Radio Viva in 1993). Beyond this the appearance of Evangelical television channels has helped to increase the visibility of Protestant movements. Canal 23, linked with Trinity Broadcasting Network based in Miami,[32] and Canal 31, both inaugurated in 1989, complete the national and international audio-visual communications network of Costa Rican Evangelicals, while other Evangelical programmes, made in the US, are broadcast on other national channels (for instance the *700 Club* on Canal 4). These initiatives have even prompted Catholics to build up their own broadcasting network, which has become quite developed (with for instance Radio Fides, launched in 1952, and Telefides/Canal 40, set up in 1993). As Piedra Solano, a shrewd observer, has noticed, 'Costa Rica now has its own electronic church, a church on the air which is entering into competition with the formal church'.[33] In this context, it comes as no surprise that many Evangelicals regularly watch religious programmes on television or listen to Evangelical radio, and that a media audience has even formed independently from church attendance. This media religious culture seems to develop independently from specific religious identities. According to the Bergstraesser Institut-Borges survey of June 1997,[34] 'the personality who plays the most important role in the lives' of Costa Rican Evangelicals belongs to the world of the media; surprisingly, this figure is a charismatic Roman Catholic priest, Father Maynor Calvo, who is mentioned by 16.3 per cent of the respondents. The next most important personality (coming far behind with 8.5 per cent of the vote) is another great communicator, the Evangelical 'El Hermano Pablo', manager of an Evangelical radio station which broadcasts from Salvador. The other media figures mentioned are American televangelists Yiye Avila (3.4 per cent), Billy Graham (3.1 per cent), Benny

---

[32] *Maranata*, no. 150, 1994, p. 4.
[33] Arturo Piedra Solano, 'El protestantismo costarricense entre la ilusión y la realidad', *Senderos*, May-Aug. 1994, p. 89.
[34] Bastian *et al.*, 'Sekten'.

Hinn (2.3 per cent) and Luis Palau (1.8 per cent), as well as the Catholic Costa Rican lay preacher Salvador Gómez (2.6 per cent). Jesus Christ comes in quite a good position (10.6 per cent), and so does the Pope (7.5 per cent) (the Pope's is nonetheless a surprising score, since one would expect the Evangelical constituency to be more hostile towards him). Archbishop Roman Arrieta, Primate of Costa Rica, is almost ignored, along with the Virgin of Los Angeles (0.8 per cent) and Martin Luther (1 per cent).

The obvious appropriation of religious references by the media has led to changes in worship patterns, with preachers increasingly adopting theatrical attitudes, the emergence of religious presenters on radio and television, and the setting up of religious musical concerts in public spaces. Such a phenomenon is not restricted to Costa Rica and can be found elsewhere, for instance in Brazil, as Silveira Campos (1997) has recently shown about the Igreja Universal do Reino de Deus, a movement which reformulates the communication of the sacred by combining theatrical effects and religious marketing. Traditional religious discourse in the form of sermons has given way to marketing techniques, ranging from presentations of 'electronic preachers' and spiritual counsellors to religious rock concerts and religious talk shows hosted by professional journalists. This phenomenon can be observed not only in new Pentecostal religious expressions, but also in traditional Evangelical churches and the Catholic church, which attempt to imitate Pentecostal media practices.

This evolution is also reflected in the fact that former cinemas (Antiguo ciné California) have been purchased by religious organisations in a position to use hypermodern means of communication to propagate their message. Pentecostal churches display bare walls devoid of any Christian symbols, and the altar and the choir usually found in traditional churches have been replaced by a platform, as is the case of the churches Oasis de Esperanza in Moravia and the Centro Evangelístico in Zapote, both belonging to the Asambleas de Dios.

The appropriation of the religious message by the media also appears through the recourse to celebrities from the world of mass communication who have been converted to the Evangelical movement. They include former secular rock stars who have begun a new career in Evangelical rock music, such as the Mexican singer Yuri, or the Torre Fuerte band (the accompanists of the famous Mexican singer Luis Miguel), who gave a concert in San José in 1994 during which they shared testimony about their new faith. Other celebrities who combine singing with personal testimonies include the Dominican singer Juan Luis Guerra, North American and Costa Rican football stars (Benjamin Mayorga, Roy Cassiter) and even the Costa Rican former fashion model Alexandra Zamora. Consequently, it comes as no surprise that even secular shows are imbibed with stereotypes of Pentecostal origin, as was the case in the concert given by the Argentinian singer Leo Dan in August 1997 at the Tobogán dancehall of San José, which was interspersed with phrases such as *'Gracias a la Vírgen y al Espíritu Santo'* and which displayed the same forms of communication between the public and the singer as can be found in charismatic and Pentecostal services, such as raising the right hand to greet or approve a spiritual declaration made by the singer.

However, the media network is first and foremost used to broadcast the activities of international evangelists who spread their message during 'crusades' and mass gatherings, which take place on a permanent basis in Costa Rica. This was the effect of maintaining the uninterrupted and continually renewed activity of mass communication and stardom. Most North American and Latin American televangelists[35] have led campaigns in Costa Rica during the last twenty years, gathering thousands of people in the national stadium. On each visit, they bring along with them the latest communication techniques from the international Evangelical universe. For instance, the phenomenon of *'risa santa'*, an experience of encounter with the sacred which makes one fall to the ground 'dying of laughter', which appeared for the first time in 1994 in a community situated near Toronto airport in Canada (hence the name 'Toronto blessing'), was promptly reproduced in Costa Rica the following year. In the same way, the practice of 'spiritual warfare', whose main proponent is North American evangelist Benny Hinn, spread to Costa Rica and to the rest of Latin America immediately after being launched in 1990. The methods of evangelism of Korean preacher Yonggi Cho, the founder of a megachurch in Seoul, are now well known in Costa Rica, following their introduction in the country on one of his visits in the early 1990s.

The process of globalisation' leads to the simultaneous imitation of behaviour, foreign models being taken over as soon as they appear by national evangelists who are constantly in need of providing new products within the context of a competitive culture of religious shows. The activities of Ronny Chávez or Raúl Vargas, or the less spectacular activities of numerous minor evangelists, take place in a constant to and fro between national and international spheres, in a persistent effort to promote their message by staging media events. The media-image of a successful evangelist involves the embarking on frequent visits and campaigns abroad. This may explain why leading Costa Rican Pentecostal pastors attempt to cultivate an image of themselves as international leaders, thus participating in the globalisation process. Pastor Cháves (Centro Cristiano) has travelled to places as diverse as Peru, Spain, Ghana and India. Pastor Madrigal (Rosa de Sarón) maintains close contacts with Colombia and Venezuela, while Pastor Vargas (Oasis de Esperanza) proudly

---

[35] Among them Jimmy Swaggart, Nicky Cruz, Moris Cerullo, Benny Hinn, Yiye Avila, Luis Palau, Franklin Graham, Alberto Motessi, Claudio Freidzon, César Castellanos, Marco Barrientos.

declares that he has preached in more than 26 countries. Even provincial stars like Pastor Yamil Jiménez (Casa del Banquete) aim at reaching an international audience, and the Iglesia Manantial de Vida of Esparza (founded twenty years ago), is 'reaching out to the nations' ('*va a las naciones*') by setting up an international missionary team to assist its associate churches at Seville in Spain, at David in Panama, at San Pedro Sula in Honduras, and in Peru.

Until the 1980s, North American preachers were predominant on the religious television market; but since the 1990s, Latin American preachers, including a few Costa Ricans, have been making spectacular progress in a media universe which is approaching global dimensions. At the same time, the image projected by the religious leader is becoming more and more that of a 'professional' and an 'executive', with a particularly busy timetable, and surrounded by the aura conferred upon him by his capacity to attract a massive audience '*urbi et orbi*'. This process of networking on an international level and the use of hypermodern communication techniques explain the spectacular gains of the Evangelical and Pentecostal movements especially among the middle and even upper middle class. After having long been despised by dominant social groups, Pentecostalism is acquiring a new legitimacy, and is coming out of its sectarian ghetto thanks to the transnationalisation process made possible by the media. It is doing so by integrating into its practices the traditional culture of the miraculous image, which has now taken the form of the television screen (often touched by believers to receive a blessing, or in front of which objects are laid in expectation of a '*limpia*'), while its use of hypermodern means of communication provides its message with greater technical capacities and greater selling potential. Pentecostalism derives from this a double profit and an increased commercial efficiency in the context of a market characterised by ever intensifying competition.

Today, while '*alleluias*' can still be heard in the pauperised suburbs of Costa Rican cities, for the first time Pentecostalism seems to be attracting middle class social sectors in search of a religiosity combining emotion with modern media techniques, which they do not find in the bureaucratised ritual of traditional Catholic services. Why is this happening? The answer is to be found in the recent evolution of Pentecostal movements, which are subsequent to market logic within the context of increasing religious pluralisation. The Pentecostal universe is characterised by improvisation, weak theological regulation and fissiparousness (schisms being frequent) which together bring great flexibility and adaptibility to Pentecostal movements as the bearers of a popular religious culture. By managing at the same time to root themselves in 'archaic' traditional religiosity through the practice of healings and exorcisms, and to use hypermodern musical and media techniques to their own profit, Pentecostal movements have become a hybrid form of religiosity. One can even affirm that they embody a particular expression of the 'hybrid cultures' which compose contemporary Latin American modernity. This process appears as a 'a reconversion in which the lower classes adapt their knowledge and their customs'.[36]

This reformulation of expressions and means of communication takes place within the framework of the transnationalisation of religion and in the context of a market logic. In Costa Rica, transnationalisation is reflected first in the multilateral character of religious exchanges, and then in the hybrid character of messages and practices which are not deeply rooted in particular institutions and which display a high degree of fluidity. This transnationalisation is informed by a market logic which, by creating a competitive environment, forces religious agents and organisations to innovate unceasingly, in order to create or stimulate demand. The resort to the most modern means of communication has become a privileged instrument to achieve this, because it is set within the framework of the miraculous image, of which it is also an extension. It also facilitates, on a national and on an international level, the promotion of a delocalised religiosity which of course has different uses according to the circumstances, but which responds above all to a religious *habitus*, a set of pre-existing dispositions which filter exogenous offerings. At the same time, transnationalisation stimulates creativity and reinforces the respectability of religious movements of national origin. It bestows upon them a symbolic legitimacy and appears as an indispensable frame of reference for the development of a hybrid religious expression drawing simultaneously from a variety of sources. It enables these movements to capture and to put to use immediately any innovation produced or accelerated by the network to which they belong. This probably explains why the middle classes are attracted to this religious expression. The visibility and the legitimacy acquired in this way by Pentecostal movements enable them to emerge into the public space, leading to perceptible social and political effects.[37]

---

[36] Hector García Canclini, *Culturas híbridas. Estrategias para entrar y salir de la modernidad*, Mexico City, 1989, p. 223.

[37] In February 1998, for instance, for the first time in the history of Costa Rica, an Evangelical deputy was elected to the Costa Rican parliament, thanks to Pentecostal voters, who had been rallied to his support by the Partido Renovación Costarricense (clearly defined as Evangelical).

BIBLIOGRAPHY

Bastian, Jean-Pierre, *Le protestantisme en Amérique latine. Une approche socio-historique*, Geneva, 1994.

——, Ulrich Fanger, Ingrid Wehr and Nikolaus Werz, 'Sekten und religiöse Bewegungen. Fallstudie Costa Rica', Freiburg im Breisgau: Arnold Bergstraesser Institut, 1998, 267 pp. (unpublished).

Berger, Peter, *The Sacred Canopy: Elements of a Sociological Theory of Religion*, New York, 1969.

Bourdieu, Pierre, 'Genèse et structure du champ religieux', *Revue française de sociologie*, Dec. 1971, pp. 295-334.

Corten, André, *Le pentecôtisme au Brésil. Émotion du pauvre et romantisme théologique*, Paris, 1995.

Costa Rica. Datos e indicadores básicos, San José, *INICEM*, 1997.

Dayton Roberts, William, *Strachan of Costa Rica: Missionary Insights and Strategies*, Grand Rapids, MI, 1971.

——, 'El movimiento de cooperación evangélica de San José 1948 a Bogotá 1969', *Pastoralia*, no. 2, 1978, pp. 33-42.

Demoscopia s.a., *'Fe y creencias del costarricense'*, San José, Feb. 1996, mimeo.

Donde está la iglesia? Un directorio de las Iglesias evangélicas costarricences, San José, 1995.

García Canclini, Hector, *Culturas híbridas. Estrategias para entrar y salir de la modernidad*, Mexico City, 1989.

Gómez, Jorge I., *El crecimiento y la deserción en la iglesia evangélica costarricense*, San José, 1996.

Gruzinski, Serge, *La guerra de las imágenes: De Cristobal Colón a 'Blade Runner' (1492-2019)*, Mexico City, 1994.

Hiltunen de Biesanz, Mavis, Richard Biesanz and Karen Zubris de Biesanz, *Los costarricenses*, San José, 1979.

Jiménez Tabash, Yamil, *Dios quiere prosperarte*, San José, 1997.

Maranata, San José, 1983-98.

Marsden, George, *Reforming Fundamentalism: Fuller Seminary and the New Evangelicalism*, Grand Rapids, MI, 1987.

Marzal, Manuel, *Los caminos religiosos de los inmigrantes en la gran Lima*, Lima, 1989 (1st edn, 1988).

Nelson, Wilton, *Historia del protestantismo en Costa Rica*, San José, 1983.

Petersen, Douglas, *Not by Might, nor by Power: A Pentecostal Theology of Social Concern in Latin America*, Oxford, 1996.

Piedra Solano, Arturo, 'El protestantismo costarricense entre la ilusión y la realidad', *Senderos*, May-Aug. 1994, pp. 77-96.

Priest, Robert J., 'La guerra espiritual o el viejo animismo', *Apuntes pastorales*, vol. 14, no. 3, 1997, pp. 32-9.

Silveira Campos, Leonildo, *Teatro, templo e mercado. Organiçao e marketing de um empreendimento neopentecostal*, Petropolis, 1997.

Tercera conferencia internacional de la palabra de Dios en Costa Rica. El Espíritu Santo señor de la Iglesia, San José, 1992.

BRAZILIAN PENTECOSTALISM CROSSES NATIONAL BORDERS

Ari Pedro Oro and Pablo Semán

One of the most important characteristics of current Brazilian Pentecostalism, especially in its neo-Pentecostal form, is its crossing of national frontiers to establish branches in other countries. The main, although not only, example is the Igreja Universal do Reino de Deus (Universal Church of the Kingdom of God - UCKG). The UCKG and its expansion to Argentina will be dealt with here.

The transnationalisation of the UCKG is taking place in a 'globalisation context'[1] which has been gathering pace in Latin America since the 1970s and 1980s.[2] We shall attempt to show that the UCKG's beginning and adaptation in Argentina does not represent a mere addition to the growing number of Pentecostal churches and members in that country, but a specific way of being Pentecostal that (as derived from the circulation and adaptation of a discourse) generates subjectivities which constitute a novelty in the transnational religious panorama of the southern part of the Americas.

The chapter is divided into two parts. In the first, we briefly describe the Brazilian and Argentine Pentecostal arena, and then present a profile of the UCKG. In the second part, we analyse the expansion of this church and its reception in Argentina.[3]

The Universal Church of the Kingdom of God and Brazilian and Argentine Pentecostalism

At the current time, Pentecostalism's followers account for around ten per cent of the Brazilian population and six per cent of the Argentine

---

[1] The terms *transnationalisation, globalisation* and *internationalisation* are related but will be distinguished here along the lines suggested by Paul Vieille. For him, *internationalisation* refers to external exchanges between two or more countries and implies a power relationship within an inter-state system. *Globalisation* refers to the effect of economic, legal, cultural and institutional homogenisation which produces a (total) world of standardised material and non-material objects in the context of struggle between economic blocs. *Transnationalisation*, on the other hand, escapes from the logic of the state and does not refer directly to objects but to needs which transcend frontiers and are not necessarily imposed (P. Vieille, 'Du transnational au politique-monde?', *Peuples Méditerranéens*, no. 35-36, April-Sept., 1986, pp. 309-338).

[2] C. Parker, 'Globalização e religião: o caso chileno' in A. P. Oro and C. A. Steil (eds), *Globalização e Religião*, Petrópolis: Editora Vozes, 1997, pp. 117-46.

[3] Our data were gathered by means of field research over the last two years in southern Brazil and in Argentina, using participant observation and interviews.

population, and represent approximately seventy per cent of all Protestants in those countries.[4] In both countries, notable characteristics are its being an option of the poor above all, an initiative which does not depend on social elites and a national religion undergoing rapid expansion.[5]

In both countries, the history of Pentecostalism can be portrayed through the metaphor of three successive waves, each with its own theological, ecclesiastical and social characteristics, have swelled together to produce today's situation.[6] The first wave from the 1910s to 1940 coincides with the arrival of churches from the United States, and is characterised by an emphasis on glossolalia and baptism in the Holy Spirit. The second wave is from the 1940s to the 1960s, during which time the Pentecostal field fragments and the first national churches emerge. There is emphasis on the use of mass media and above all divine healing rituals. The third wave begins in the late 1970s and accelerates in the 1980s, and is characterised by exclusivism towards other Pentecostal and evangelical forms, and by an emphasis on the prosperity gospel and the theology of spiritual warfare.

Both in Brazil and Argentina, the churches of the second and especially the third waves have come to be called neo-Pentecostal,[7] as a result of the changes they have introduced into Pentecostalism.[8] The two most important representatives of this sector in Brazil are Deus é Amor (God is Love) and the UCKG. Both are famed for their bold proselytism, leading to their having thousands of churches in Brazil and world-wide.

[4] A. F. Pierucci and R. Prandi, *A realidade social das religiões no Brasil*, São Paulo: Hucitec, 1996. N. Saracco, 'Argentine Pentecostalism: Its History and Theology', PhD diss., University of Birmingham, 1989.

[5] R. C. Fernandes, 'Governo das Almas' in *Nem anjos nem demônios*, Petrópolis: Editora Vozes, 1994, pp. 163-203.

[6] P. Freston, 'Protestantismo e política no Brasil: Da Constituinte ao Impeachment', Ph.D. diss., UNICAMP, Campinas, 1993; P. Semán and P. Moreira, 'La Iglesia Universal del Reino de Dios en Buenos Aires y la recreación del diablo a través del realineamiento de marcos interpretativos', *Sociedad y Religión*, Buenos Aires, 1998, pp. 95-110.

[7] The main characteristics of Brazilian neo-Pentecostalism are said to be: leaders with strong personalities (often charismatic); stimulus to emotional expressivism; exclusivism with regard to other forms of religion (including Evangelical ones); intensive use of the mass media; emphasis on divine healing and exorcism; liberalisation of customs; and ritual centrality of money. Alejandro Frigerio ('Estudios Recientes sobre el Pentecostalismo en el Cono Sur: Problemas e Perspectivas', in A. Frigerio (ed.), *El Pentecostalismo en la Argentina*, Buenos Aires: CEAL, 1994, pp. 10-28) perceives that in Argentina the ritualistic and ideological centrality of money is not as intense as in Brazil, and that the churches there are less exclusivistic owing to the greater integration of neo-Pentecostals in the Protestant field and the reduced relevance of preaching against Afro-Brazilian religions.

[8] R. Mariano, 'Neopentecostalismo: os pentecostais estão mudando', MA diss., FFLCH/USP, São Paulo, 1995; C. L. Mariz, 'Etica e magia: uma analise do significado da libertação entre os pentecostais', Paper presented at the Congress of ANPOCS, Caxambu, Brazil, October 1995; A. P. Oro, *Avanço pentecostal e reação católica*, Petrópolis: Editora Vozes, 1996.

Similarly, the best known Argentine cases are Pastor Héctor Giménez's Ondas de Amor y Paz (Waves of Love and Peace), Carlos Annacondia's Mensaje de Salvación (Message of Salvation) and Omar Cabrera's Visión de Futuro (Vision of the Future).

The UCKG is a phenomenon of religious growth and success. Founded in 1977 in Rio de Janeiro by a civil servant called Edir Macedo, then 33 years old,[9] the UCKG now has 2,014 churches in Brazil and 236 in 65 other countries. About 4 million people are assisted by its bishops, pastors and *obreiros* (unpaid helpers) in its five daily services.

At the same time, in its short existence the UCKG has become worth an estimated $400 million. Among its property we find a television network (Rede Record de Televisão, with thirty channels and considered the third largest in Brazil), about thirty radio stations, publishers, recording studios, a newspaper, a magazine, a construction company, a furniture factory, a bank, a travel agency and a holding company which administers all the church's business.

Besides its entrepreneurial organisation, sophisticated marketing, direct participation in Brazilian politics[10] and aggressive use of the media, the UCKG has always carried out unremitting daily ritual combat against Afro-Brazilian religions (*candomblé, macumba, umbanda*), especially through the ritual of exorcising their gods (*orixás, exus, pombagiras*) in the daily services in its churches. This 'holy war' is one of the 'doctrinal pillars of the UCKG'[11] and one of its identity markers. The UCKG does not deny the Afro-Brazilian religions; rather it resignifies the rituals and the pantheon of competing religions in the market of symbolic solutions among the lower levels of the population.

Since the UCKG is one of the key exponents of Spiritual Warfare Theology in the countries we are examining,[12] its attack is not limited to Afro-Brazilian cults; it includes Kardecist spiritism and New Age and Catholic devotions and reaches an intensity that leads to tensions and conflicts that agitate the religious field and public opinion.

Similarly, the UCKG is one of the key religious institutions in the southern part of the Americas that has adopted the prosperity gospel.[13] This

[9] From a poor family, Edir Macedo was converted to Pentecostalism in 1963 when 18 years old. Until then he had frequented the Catholic Church and *umbanda*.

[10] In the general elections of 1994, the UCKG elected 12 deputies. In the 1998 elections, it elected 28. At the present time, it is working towards the formation of a political party, the Social Action Party (PAS).

[11] Mariano, *Neopentecostalism.*.

[12] Devised in American theological and evangelistic circles in the 1980s, Spiritual Warfare Theology emphasises, exacerbates and systematises the belief in demonic forces, in practice putting them on a level with the foundational belief in the baptism in the Holy Spirit. The logic of these forces is projected into human history and eschatology, transforming them into a battle against evil.

[13] The adoption of the prosperity gospel (generally known in Brazil as *Teologia da*

theology defines giving as an affirmation of subjection to God and as part of a process of liberation which allows one to receive blessings. This is what legitimates the insistence on monetary offerings; at the same time, these are built on antecedent Catholic traditions such as 'promises' and the logic of reciprocity in relation to the saints.[14]

Both in Brazil and Argentina, the discourse and message of the UCKG finds acceptance mostly among the higher levels of the lower classes and the lower levels of the urban middle classes. In both countries, these sectors are suffering greatly from the recessive effects of neo-liberal policies, and adherents hope to find through the UCKG (although not exclusively through this church) a chance of overcoming the socio-economic crisis and of realising the dream of well-being which has eluded them in the social sphere. This fact shows the articulation between the local and the universal, specifically between the UCKG and the phenomenon of 'globalisation'. This is true in two ways: first, in the sense that this church, stressing the prosperity gospel, entrepreneurial organisation and the use of modern media technology and marketing, has adopted the parameters of neo-liberal ideology; and secondly, in the sense that the preferred members of the UCKG are those negatively affected by globalisation.

In other words, the UCKG makes use of the resources and ideals of neo-liberal modernity in its evangelistic action, taking into account the anxieties and frustrations generated by the destructuring caused by neo-liberal reforms and ideology, especially in the southern countries of the American continent.

The Universal Church of the Kingdom of God in Argentina

Having started in Argentina in 1990, the UCKG had twenty churches by 1994, 22 by 1995 and 46 by 1997. The numbers show the speed of growth in that country, above all in Greater Buenos Aires and environs where most of its churches are situated.

Three distinct but interconnected ideological nuclei are at the heart of the transnational project of the UCKG: deliverance (in Portuguese *libertação,* the same word used to refer to Liberation Theology) as the solution to 'evils'; deliverance as the specific solution to 'evils' caused by the

---

Prosperidade) and its ritual and ecclesial trappings goes beyond the UCKG and Pentecostalism in general, affecting many denominations. But it has also been a dividing line. Some Pentecostal churches, together with a sector of historical Protestantism, have made it their main target in internal disputes in the Protestant world. André Corten suggests, correctly in our view, that the prosperity gospel is the way middle-class Pentecostals can construct their Evangelical identity (*Le pentecôtisme au Brésil: Émotion du pauvre et romantisme théologique,* Paris: Karthala, 1995).

[14] Freston, *Protestantismo*; A. P. Oro and P. Semán, 'Os pentecostalismos nos paises do Cone-Sul, Panorama e Estudos', *Religião e Sociedade,* vol. 18, no. 2, 1997, pp. 127-55.

spiritual entities of Afro-Brazilian religions; and complete deliverance (including economic) as the supreme goal. The first two are closer to popular sensitivities, while the last (with its emphasis on prosperity) seems to resonate above all with the middle classes. The differences in social structure between Brazil and Argentina have necessitated a rebalancing of these elements to the UCKG appeal. The lesser extent of Afro-Brazilian religion in Argentina[15] has not meant the suppression of the Afro-Brazilian nucleus, but its translation so as to function in terms of more general categories of deliverance. This consists both of deliverance from witch-craft and from situations associated with the development of psychologised figures of suffering. As an effect of this recomposition, and in contrast to Argentine neo-Pentecostal churches, the UCKG constructs a social image more closely connected to the prosperity gospel. These modifications allow the UCKG to be exported as a project for the lower-middle classes but with the chance of identification among the lower classes, besides offering a Pentecostal practice of greater intensity and drama than hitherto found in Argentina.

We shall now analyse four elements which combine to produce the meeting between this Brazilian church and the Argentine public: an institutional structure which allows it to create large and attractive congregations; the translation of a dynamic practice of exorcism; an advantageous mediation between 'legitimate' and 'illegitimate' religion; and the expression of material desires within the field of longings for spiritual peace.

Institutional structure: a distinct way of being the church

Wherever the Universal Church goes, it tends to reproduce certain specific characteristics that, combined with the local symbolic field, give it its uniqueness. We shall emphasise four traits in the Argentine context. First, as in Brazil the UCKG maintains a clear and rigorous distinction between members of the ecclesiastical apparatus and laypeople (reducible to a distinction between producers and consumers of religious goods)[16]

---

[15] In Argentina, there were presumably isolated and limited African religious practices, restricted to the population of African descent, until the end of the last century, when the size of this group fell abruptly. However, after 1960 Afro-Brazilian religions were (re)introduced from Brazil and Uruguay. Today, there are an estimated 1,000 *terreiros* (temples of Afro-Brazilian religions) in Argentina, which are frequented mostly by lower-middle and lower class people regardless of their ethnicity. Unlike in Brazil, where Afro-Brazilian religions enjoy social tolerance, in Argentina these religions are still stigmatised and their attenders are victims of prejudice and discrimination.

[16] This distinction is relative, as it may suggest a passive image of the members and contradict anthropological analyses which show the efficacy of mutual appropriation. But it is accurate when contrasted with what happens in other Pentecostal circles. Even making a creative and active appropriation of UCKG beliefs, its members have less chance of influence than in traditional Pentecostalism.

which contrasts with what happens in Argentine neo-Pentecostal churches where the frontier between hierarchy and laypeople is porous, movable and undefined. Secondly, the UCKG retains an ecclesiological model with few congregational moments beyond services and mass meetings. If this is already a marked trait in Brazil, it is even more so in Argentina where congregationalism is strong and is a substantial part of being Pentecostal.[17] The third trait is the retention of the weekly schedule of services with a different objective for each day, a novelty in Argentine Pentecostalism,[18] where church meetings are always devoted to general themes, with no more than specific moments within them (prosperity, deliverance, healing, family etc.), depending on the sequence of the service or on personal requests. The UCKG's model of a specific theme is parallel to its weak congregationalism. As a result, it promotes a way of being in the church which is less demanding than that of Argentine Pentecostals, and encourages conversions which would otherwise be too sacrificial. The fourth trait is in the field of doctrine and religious practice: the UCKG also exports without any change (and with important consequences) its emphasis on prosperity and the related theme of tithing as one of the focal points of its meetings.

On account of these traits, the Argentine Protestant field seems to be uniformly resistant to accepting the legitimacy of the UCKG. An example of this is the fact that the national pastors excluded UCKG churches from the Evangelical Census of the City of Buenos Aires, considering it to be doctrinally non-Protestant. Similarly, a national meeting of Pentecostal pastors decided to keep its distance from the UCKG, calling it 'iso-Pentecostal', i.e. a church which looks Pentecostal but is not. The UCKG is widely stigmatised in the Argentine Protestant world.

Exorcism: variations, problems and products of translation

On the other hand, there have been changes in the UCKG's public presence in Argentina which differentiate it from Brazil. For example, the Argentine UCKG has attenuated its frontal attack on other religions. In this, the UCKG tends to follow the Argentine Pentecostal churches, where expressions of contrast are controlled and even obliterated.

---

[17] For example, Pastor Giménez's Waves of Love and Peace consolidates its expansion by creating small churches in which members build ecclesial communities, promoting moments for pastoral counselling, Bible study and music in which the members have opportunities to meet several times a week outside the church service. It even co-opts small churches on the periphery which join the denominational network. Pastor Cabrera's Vision of the Future has not only mass services but also cell and family organisations in which Biblical education is given to attenders who may not be members of the church.

[18] In all UCKG churches, the services have a specific purpose each day, known as *correntes* (chains) or *reuniões* (meetings). Mondays are for the 'chain of prosperity', Tuesdays for 'healing', Wednesdays for 'the Holy Spirit', Thursdays for 'the family', Fridays for 'deliverance from demons', Saturdays for 'love' and Sundays for 'the Holy Spirit'.

The Argentine UCKG also shows variations in the practice of exorcism which is central to its identity and public image. Such variations (adaptations) serve as bridges across which the UCKG connects its own frame alignment with those of its public.[19] The bridges are necessary because the UCKG in Brazil is, as we have seen, strongly 'anti-Afro-Brazilian'. However, in Brazil Afro-Brazilian beliefs are part of a cognitive universe shared by diverse social and cultural groups,[20] so that everybody knows what an '*orixá*' or '*exu*' are. But in Argentina, Afro-Brazilian religions and their categories are much less widespread, more weakly articulated and less tolerated, which makes the UCKG's product less appealing.

For this reason, the most important bridges articulated by the UCKG have to do with the image of the devil. These bridges are intentionally or randomly concentrated around the translation of the Brazilian church's proposal for the Argentine public, and facilitate the productivity of its cultural principles.

Thus in the following three sections, we shall see that the UCKG changes and exports its doctrine of exorcism by means of adapting to local categories of suffering; translates its own categories of possession as a cause of sufferings; and, above all, generates possibilities for the more general principles of exorcism to take root at the local level.

Learning evil à la Argentina. The Brazilian pastors of UCKG churches in Argentina are aware of the difficulty of translating categories for demonic activity from the Brazilian context. This is because, as Semán and Moreira[21] show, for the church's public in Argentina belief in the devil is not widespread nor naturally intense, and because there are parallel doctrines for explaining evil, such as anguish, ambition, emptiness of the human soul and a whole series of categories of suffering which eliminate negative mystical causality even if they retain its positive counterpart as a cause of healing.

Today, UCKG pastors recognise that their Argentine public is not very disposed to believe in the devil. One Argentine member commented that he personally did not believe 'in the power of *macumba* or of witchcraft, but tried to console people who believed in these things'.[22]

Thus, the perception of this situation has led the UCKG pastors to adopt a strategy of downplaying their discourse on the demonic, but not of

---

[19] We use 'frame alignment' as it is used by Snow and colleagues in their studies of social movements (D. Snow *et al.*, 'Frame Alignment Processes, Micromobilisation and Movement Participation', *American Sociological Review*, vol. 51, no. 4, 1986, pp. 464-81).

[20] Gilberto Vehlo, *Projeto e Metamorfose: Antropologia das Sociedades Complexas*, Rio de Janeiro: Zahar, 1994, p. 14.

[21] *Op. cit.*

[22] Going further still: he had become unemployed and described the situation solely in economic terms, which implied a secularisation of the causes of evil.

abandoning it. They adapt it instrumentally according to their evaluation of the market, and relocate the components so as to produce (together with the other adaptations) a new meaning for deliverance.

Rehabilitation and invention of the devil (expressing and channelling repressed demand). The Argentine adaptations try to facilitate the incorporation of new codes of religious experience. As a whole, they give a meaning to deliverance from (resolution of) evils in a socio-cultural context in which the possible enemy is not mainly '*macumba*' or '*candomblé*' as in Brazil.

Teaching the devil à la Brazil. The first adaptation occurs in church services: the Afro⸱Brazilian names which make it easier to identify the devil, and the very logic of demonisation, are weak in the Argentine imaginary, so the services have to fill the gap. The main move in this direction involves transforming the services into classes. Semán and Moreira[23] have described how UCKG pastors transform exorcisms into moments of teaching about the devil and about Afro-Brazilian entities. The demons are presented and a question-and-answer dynamic is established with the public which makes it a teaching session. These authors also claim that the adaptations help towards the 'reinvention of the demonic' by recuperating and amplifying the weak or dormant figure of the devil in the Argentine imaginary. But we should note that this strategy is not always successful, due to the differences in Argentine religious culture. Many who learn about the devil in UCKG services distance themselves from this teaching and rework it as an element of proselytism. Semán and Moreira[24] cite the example of a woman who understood the teaching as 'a little bit of theatre'.

Synthesis and syntony: deliverance. This school of 'demonology' has unexpected effects. Part of the ritual present in Brazil has the effect in Argentina of stressing the UCKG's difference from Argentine neo-Pentecostals. In Brazil, Afro-Brazilian religiosity is not merely a system of verbal signs for constructing the demonic in the UCKG. The church's public lives these religious expressions in a corporal rather than linguistic code. Movements on the stage in the UCKG churches by those 'possessed' (small steps similar to those in the *terreiros*[25]) show that people 'incorporate' the demons being invoked and subsequently expelled by the pastors. These movements show that, at a deeper level than the verbal, there is a continuity with the bodily grammar on which Afro-Brazilian religion is based and reproduced.

---

[23] *Op. cit.*
[24] *Ibid.*
[25] A *terreiro* is the name given to the Afro-Brazilian place of worship.

When does something similar happen in Argentina? When the deliverance is based on a ritual sequence in which the pastors accompany demonic representations with music from horror movies. On this level, the UCKG's practice achieves something which the Argentine neo-Pentecostal churches find difficult: to involve the body as the basis of religious practice. But it is not an Afro-Brazilian bodily practice which is involved, since the latter has little space in Argentine society. It is rather a random syntony which refers to and expresses a different imaginary.

We give a brief example of how this takes place. One of the most frequent responses to incorporation and exorcism in the UCKG in Buenos Aires is a bodily reaction which at first seems disorganised: screams, insults and even people dribbling and shouting in rage. This bodily behaviour would seem incomprehensible without reference to the definition of being possessed which appears frequently in the interviews with the public. The fact of being captive to the devil is often referred to as a seduction by a 'powerful and sensual man', and the expulsion of the devil is often described in terms reminiscent of the film *The Exorcist*. This association, mentioned explicitly by informants, is the basis of this performance and serves to make it comprehensible. This is neither accidental nor inconsequential: it shows a tuning in to one of the ways the Argentine imaginary understands the devil, based on Catholic hagiography and the modern media, indeed one of the main images of the devil is that of the film rather than that of Lucifer with trident and tail.[26] This appeal brings to the fore a type of religious practice which was previously not put into effect.

This perhaps unplanned tuning in shows that the Argentine public is more receptive to this form of practice than traditional Pentecostal institutions suppose. In fact, pastors of Argentine churches have rejected the possibility of these practices because they imagined them to be distasteful to both the middle and lower classes.

Thus, these exorcisms which dramatise the specifically anti-Afro-Brazilian content of the UCKG offer something which part of the lower-middle and lower classes do not find in local Pentecostalism. One possibility of Argentine religious subjectivity is realised by a Brazilian church because Argentine pastors have opted not to do it and because Brazilians seem to master the art of this form of religion. If this is functional for the

---

[26] There are several reasons why this should be a privileged image. On the one hand, there is the popularity of the film *The Exorcist*, which makes it accessible to the mass public. On the other hand, there is the use which Pastor Annacondia (the most popular Evangelical figure in Argentina) has made of the same figure; he has used it since the beginning of his campaigns more than twenty years ago, being followed in this by several lesser figures in the Evangelical field. There is a third element for understanding the centrality of this image and other similar ones which make up a unique hagiography: the weakening of images proposed by the Catholics, many of which are made fun of by the Catholic faithful themselves and by Pentecostals.

Argentines, it is also functional for the UCKG, since it links it to an unmet demand and gives it its own niche in a terrain where it meets with closed spaces and suffers from a lack of legitimacy.

Making Argentines believe in the devil is not the only way the UCKG changes local religious subjectivity. It does it even more so when it makes urban lower-middle class people feel at peace by means of their bodies.

The Universal Church occupies an intermediate space between 'magic' and 'religion'[27]

A prevalent idea in Argentine society is that the religious field comprises institutions which are legitimate and unquestionable, alongside practices which are suspect or at least looked down upon. The latter are often referred to as 'magical'. Thus, for Argentine Pentecostals as well as for Catholic priests (much more for the former than the latter), the use of material mediations, being close to magical behaviour, is considered doubtful or even illegitimate.

Taking this distancing of religion from magic into account, we can see that the UCKG tries to occupy an intermediate space, or to use both forms of relating to the sacred. This strategy can be summed up as acting with 'magical' means, but in the name of the most legitimate and unquestionable belief in Argentine society: Christianity. The UCKG thus manages to accumulate the advantages of both, as no other Christian church in Argentina does. In other words, it presents itself as Christian, but carries on certain 'magical' acts which are censured or marginalised in all other churches and only accepted in the field of 'magic'.

This formula has been used with obvious success in UCKG rituals, unlike the situation in Catholic and Pentecostal contexts. Thus, the specific material mediations for a religious practice directed to satisfying immediate necessities are massively reproduced. The use of salt, roses, keys, oil, handkerchiefs and many other objects which vary over time is one of the most widespread practices in the UCKG and one of the most rejected by Argentine Pentecostals. Similarly with practices which Pentecostal churches and the Catholic hierarchy reject as superstitious (such as prayers for people who are made present at rituals through photographs, clothes or personal belongings), but which are common practice in the Universal Church. This is one of the key differences between the UCKG and the Argentine neo-Pentecostals, as confirmed by a pastor from one of the latter churches. Being of the opinion that it was necessary to have similar practices in order not to lose members to the 'Brazilians', and yet feeling inhibited by pressure from the Evangelical field, he said that his church should devise 'intermediate' proposals. The market loss shows what is attractive; and this pastor's difficulty in turning the situation around points to the unique position of the UCKG and the impossibility of Argentine Pentecostals occupying the same position.

The expansion of these practices is obviously not accidental. They are continuous with the 'magical' services usually consumed by the UCKG public and help to make their religious (in this case, 'magical') message acceptable. The existence of these facilitating channels is shown by recent research that, while not taking all possibilities into account, reliably reveals one type among others of UCKG attender. Moreira[28] detects the existence of a group of attenders who have been through a series of agencies which work with the urgent solution to specific problems, usually involving material mediations: clairvoyants, tarot readers, astrologers. In our research, we found that many people who had had a relationship to the UCKG did not try to keep a stable and strong link with it. They regarded their experience there as positive, and they had not left because of any negative experience. In other words, they used the UCKG as a service and not as the adoption of a new religious ideology. The type of requests possible in the UCKG seems to lead us to an analogous conclusion: what is impossible in Christian contexts regulated by priests or by Evangelical pastors happens in the UCKG. 'I request deliverance for my daughter-in-law who is resentful and a bad person', said a woman who did not hide her dislike for her son's wife. Although the objective was deliverance, the way of describing her daughter-in-law and of demanding her deliverance was anything but calm. While in Christian churches (classical Pentecostal and Catholic) this type of request is silenced, moderated or polished over by mediators who stress love of one's neighbour, the UCKG has no such restrictions.

Deliverance and prosperity: from being well to well-being

Changes in the UCKG's formula in Argentina complement the place and content acquired by the emphasis on feeling (being) well. The appeal to feel well is not new in Argentina or in the UCKG. But it is more stressed than in the original Brazilian form of this church, to the detriment of the anti-Afro-Brazilian exorcistic component.

The search for being well personally is connected to and resignified by the strong emphasis on prosperity as the utopian horizon and by the UCKG's position in the Argentine religious field. Thus, being well personally and enjoying material well-being are two interlinked and complementary objectives in UCKG discourse.

[27] We use this distinction without the ethnocentric bias which often accompanies the notion of magic. As Mauss and Hubert showed, the separation between magic and religion is very fluid because both are equally complex and intermingle. In other words, religions include 'magic' elements and magic includes appeals to supernatural divinities (M. Mauss, *Sociologie et Anthropologie*, Paris: PUF, 1950).

[28] Patricia Moreira, 'Inventando Tradições em Buenos Aires: considerações sobre a Igreja Universal do Reino de Deus', paper presented at VII Jornadas Sobre Alternativas Religiosas en Latinoamérica, Buenos Aires, 1997.

Even though prosperity preaching is not a novelty in Argentina, the UCKG clearly devotes more time to it than any other church. While Argentine churches devote a fifth or less of their services to preaching prosperity, in direct relation to tithing, the Universal Church devotes between a third and a half of its services to such questions. But the quantitative weight does not really highlight the uniqueness of the UCKG in the Argentine context. Its programme on Argentine television is an example of its cultural and religious position: smiling young people dressed in the formal or informal style of the middle classes are its privileged personages. Testimonies are also illustrative: the crisis of conversion always includes an economic section in which the person was about to lose everything, and the transformed life afterwards always includes an improvement in employment or in finances, or a new, high-powered job. All very different from testimonies in Argentine neo-Pentecostal churches where the stress is on modest job aspirations, a small savings account or purchase of household appliances.

We have said that well-being is connected with being well and that prosperity is presented as the final and almost complete outcome of the work of God among men. But this result is also a demand: no-one who suffers tribulations can be considered delivered. Thus, living in peace is an effect of deliverance, and living well is an effect of prosperity; but just as there is no peace without comfort, there is no definitive peace without prosperity. This is the privileged space for the UCKG to include the hedonism of its theology: well-being is both sign and effect of complete deliverance.

This is the movement by which the prosperity gospel comes to envelope the whole UCKG message. But obviously not all regular or occasional attenders attain this level. No matter. It is an emblem and a signpost which points to a horizon of desire. It is enough to have some people who get there, to make all the others identify with them on the level of expectations.[29]

The reception of the prosperity gospel shows how this discourse fits in with members' experience and becomes efficacious. As a discourse of positive confession, it fits in with the individualising tendencies of Argentine society. Members appropriate the prosperity discourse by means of an action in which they do their part and expect God to do his, based on expectations which prosperity teaching legitimates and where tithing is a witness to this personal pact. For example, to overcome

---

[29] One should also stress that the UCKG's signposts function so as to select its public: those who believe they cannot possibly reach this horizon, and those unconcerned with upward social mobility, will feel out of place in the church. This is not speculation: the public at the headquarters in Buenos Aires is economically better off than that of Argentine neo-Pentecostal churches in the same district, and clearly form a sub-type of the Evangelical field in general.

unemployment, an unemployed person starts out as a small-time vendor, certain of God's help for his firm.

This practice, almost of self-help, based on the idea and the trust that 'a child of God is deserving', links in with another element. Prosperity legitimates not only expectations but also desires related to material life in a broad sense, as expressed in these phrases of Bishop Edir Macedo, founder of the UCKG: 'the good things in life are there to be enjoyed', and 'sex is for having pleasure'. Thus, prosperity discourse explicitly functions as a licence to aspire to things not included in classical piety. In this sense hedonism, as a legitimation of enjoyment, is incorporated through the UCKG discourse into the daily life of many of its members.

In its process of transnationalisation the UCKG explores its own limits to change in order to adapt to Argentine sensibilities. It changes some of its referents without abandoning its own matrix, thus making itself appealing to part of the Argentine public. In this way the UCKG wins a place in Argentine society and shows itself to be different from other existing religious alternatives, as we have tried to demonstrate.

Since we are talking about an encounter, it is important to remember that characteristics of Argentine society influence the final content. P. Sanchis states that contemporary Brazilian religiosity is characterised by the co-existence of three temporalities: the pre-modern, which implies a 'fundamentally ritual-magical religious universe...dominated by obligations and ethically imperfect by our standards';[30] the modern, characterised by the ideal of the sovereign individual; and the postmodern, characterised by eclecticism, by the appropriation of elements from one's own and other symbolic universes. In Argentina, where social and cultural frontiers are more fluid, we can be said to find the conjunction and overlapping of the three temporalities in each social space and in each subject. We could even say that in that country there is a singular proliferation and mixture of diverse religious traditions (plus the effects of secularist ideologies and phenomena which allow us to speak of secularisation at certain levels of the social) brought about by the coexistence of holistic and individualistic languages, and the co-presence, interpenetration and conflict of traditions.

It is in reply to these characteristics that the UCKG's work in Argentina results in a sort of desecularising-modernising tendency, which is only paradoxical if the relationship between modernity and religion is thought of as mutually exclusive. But it is not paradoxical if we perceive the UCKG's ability to read multi-temporality in synchrony. In fact, the UCKG speaks of demons to those for whom this belief was losing its

---

[30] P. Sanchis, 'O campo religioso contemporâneo no Brasil' in Oro and Steil, *Globalização e Religião*, p. 104.

meaning, and at the same time speaks to them of an ideology of feeling well which includes psychologisms and the acquisition of identity through consumption. In this way the plurality of voices in the UCKG manages to connect with the plurality of temporalities inside each subject in Argentina. It manages both to restore value and centrality to religious traditions, and to create space for emotions which relate to forms of identity construction in modern ideologies. The UCKG thus crystallises a possibility in the new conditions of production of the religious field, and becomes one of the historic forces which counterbalance secularisation.

This uniqueness of the UCKG produces a specific relationship to its Argentine public, in which the devil is brought on to the religious agenda, consolidating new forms of religious performance. The Argentine members of the Universal Church learn that religion is deliverance and that deliverance is a movement of expelling demons. But in that country the demons are not identified, as in Brazil, with the entities of the Afro-Brazilian pantheon, but with disease perceived as a psychological tendency, a state of spirit etc. In this case the efficacy of deliverance happens without the need for the devil to manifest himself. It is in this sense of understanding and resolving evils, and of exporting and adapting exorcism (although without managing to spread its traditional concept of the demonic), that the secret of the UCKG's success lies.

We have tried to show here how a Brazilian neo-Pentecostal church divulged its discourse and religious product in Argentina and generated a unique synthesis which emphasises above all prosperity teaching and the intensification of exorcism as the route to 'feeling well'. We have detected the creation of a religious demand which had no previous institutional articulation in the Argentine context. It is in this perspective – of the creation of a new institutional space to meet the new needs and religious experiences of Argentine members – that we have attempted to interpret the transnationalisation of the UCKG to Argentina.

BIBLIOGRAPHY

Barros, Mônica do Nascimento, ' "A batalha do Armagedom". Uma análise do repertório mágico-religioso proposto pela Igreja Universal do Reino de Deus', MA diss., Universidade Federal de Minas Gerais, Belo Horizonte, 1995.

Birman, Patricia, 'Cultos de possessão e pentecostalismo no Brasil: passagens', *Religião e Sociedade*, vol. 17, nos 1-2, 1996, pp. 90-109.

——. 'Males e maleficios no Discurso Neopentecostal' in *O mal à Brasileira*, Rio de Janeiro: UERJ, 1997.

Boyer, Véronique, 'Possession et exorcisme dans une Église pentecôtiste au Brésil', *Cahiers des Sciences Humaines, ORSTOM*, 32 (2), 1996, pp. 243-64.

Corten, André, *Le pentecôtisme au Brésil. Émotion du pauvre et romantisme théologique*, Paris: Karthala, 1995.

Fernandes, Rubem Cesar, 'Governo das Almas' in *Nem anjos nem demônios*, Petrópolis: Editora Vozes, 1994, pp. 163-203.

Freston, Paul, *Protestantismo e política no Brasil. Da Constituinte ao Impeachment*, PhD diss., UNICAMP, Campinas, 1993.

Frigerio, Alejandro, 'Estudios Recientes sobre el Pentecostalismo en el Cono Sur: Problemas e Perspectivas' in Alejandro Frigerio (ed.), *El Pentecostalismo en la Argentina*, Buenos Aires: CEAL, 1994, pp. 10-28.

Mariano, Ricardo, 'Neopentecostalismo. Os pentecostais estão mudando', MA diss., FFLCH/USP, São Paulo, 1995.

Mariz, Cecília L., 'Etica e magia: uma analise do significado da libertação entre os pentecostais', paper presented at the *Congress of ANPOCS*, Caxambu, Brazil, October 1995.

——, 'O demônio e os pentecostais no Brasil' in *O mal à Brasileira*, Rio de Janeiro, ed. UERJ., 1997.

Mauss, Marcel, *Sociologie et Anthropologie*, Paris: PUF, 1950.

Moreira, Patricia, 'Inventando Tradições em Buenos Aires: considerações sobre a Igreja Universal do Reino de Deus', paper presented at VII Jornadas Sobre Alternativas Religiosas en Latinoamérica, Buenos Aires, 1997.

Oro, Ari Pedro, *Avanço pentecostal e reação católica*, Petrópolis: Editora Vozes, 1996.

—— and Pablo Semán, 'Os pentecostalismos nos paises do Cone-Sul, Panorama e Estudos', *Religião e Sociedade*, vol. 18, no. 2, 1997, pp. 127-55.

Parker, Christian, 'Globalização e religião: o caso chileno' in Ari Pedro Oro and Carlos Alberto Steil (eds), *Globalização e Religião*, Petrópolis: Editora Vozes, 1997, pp. 117-46.

Pierucci and Antonio Flávio, Reginaldo Prandi, *A realidade social das religiões no Brasil*, São Paulo: Hucitec, 1996.

Sanchis, Pierre, 'O repto pentecostal à cultura católico-brasileira' in *Nem anjos nem demônios*, Petrópolis: Editora Vozes, 1994, pp. 34-66.

——, 'O campo religioso contemporâneo no Brasil' in Ari Pedro Oro and Carlos Alberto Steil (eds), *Globalização e Religião*, Petrópolis: Editora Vozes, 1997, pp. 103-16.

Saracco, Norberto, 'Argentine Pentecostalism: Its History and Theology', PhD diss., University of Birmingham, 1989.

Semán, Pablo and Patricia Moreira, 'La Iglesia Universal del Reino de Dios en Buenos Aires y la recreación del diablo a través del realineamiento de marcos interpretativos', *Sociedad y Religión*, Buenos Aires, 1998, pp. 95-110.

Soneira, Jorge, *et al.*, *Sociología de la Religión*, Buenos Aires: Editorial Docencia, 1996.

Snow, David, *et al.*, 'Frame Alignment Processes, Micromobilization and Movement Participation', *American Sociological Review*, vol. 51, no. 4, 1986, pp. 464-81.

Vehlo, Gilberto, *Projeto e Metamorfose: Antropologia das Sociedades Complexas*, Rio de Janeiro: Zahar, 1994.

Vieille, Paul, 'Du transnational au politique-monde?', *Peuples Méditerranéens*, 35-36, April-Sept., 1986, pp. 309-38.

Wynarczyk, Hilario and Pablo Semán, 'Campo Evangélico y Pentecostalismo en la Argentina' in Alejandro Frigerio (ed.), *El Pentecostalismo en la Argentina*, Buenos Aires: CEAL, 1994, pp. 29-43.

THE TRANSNATIONALISATION
OF BRAZILIAN PENTECOSTALISM
THE UNIVERSAL CHURCH OF THE KINGDOM OF GOD

Paul Freston

The process by which the Universal Church of the Kingdom of God (UCKG or UC) has expanded to over fifty countries is an important example of a key religious change of the late twentieth century: the transformation of Pentecostalism into a global religion and the shift in its centre (of numerical growth and missionary initiative) to the Third World.[1]

The globalisation of Pentecostalism

The study of Pentecostalism helps overcome the parochialism of certain perspectives on religion in an era of globalisation. We must take into account what has actually happened to Christianity in recent decades: recession in Europe and stagnation in the US, countered by the expansion of Protestantism in Latin America and of many forms of Christianity in Africa and the Far East. But Beyer's *Religion and Globalization*,[2] for example, has nothing on this Christian (largely Pentecostal) growth in the Third World. Even globalisation theorists who discuss religion, such as Robertson[3] and Waters,[4] have nothing on it. The constitution of a global Pentecostalism[5] is often ignored by academia because it has occurred independently of religious initiatives from the developed West.

This global Pentecostalism is culturally polycentric.[6] The history of Christianity is of serial expansion, in contrast to Islam's progressive expansion.[7] Whereas the latter spreads from a constant heartland, Christianity suffers periodic shifts in its demographic and geographical centre.

---

[1] This chapter is based on fieldwork in Portugal, Britain and Brazil. A less up-to-date version in Portuguese is forthcoming (1999) in the journal *Lusotopie*.

[2] Peter Beyer, *Religion and Globalization*, London: Sage, 1994.

[3] Roland Robertson, *Globalization*, London: Sage, 1992.

[4] Malcolm Waters, *Globalization*, London: Routledge, 1995.

[5] The Pentecostal-charismatic wing accounted for 6 per cent of worldwide Christianity in 1970, and is currently estimated at 25 per cent (see Peter Brierley, *Changing Churches*, London: Christian Research, 1996).

[6] The struggle for a 'culturally polycentric Christianity' is regarded by Cox as the heart of the discord between Leonardo Boff and the Vatican (see Harvey Cox, *The Silencing of Leonardo Boff*, Oak Park, IL: Meyer-Stone, 1988).

[7] Andrew Walls, 'Christianity in the Non-Western World: A Study in the Serial Nature of Christian Expansion', *Studies in World Christianity*, vol. 1, no. 1, 1995, pp. 1-25.

Advances beyond its periphery are accompanied by decline in the old heartlands. The result is constant interaction with new cultures. In 1900, more than 80 per cent of professing Christians lived in Europe or North America; currently, about 60 per cent live in Africa, Asia, Latin America or the Pacific.[8]

According to Waters, a globalised world would have a single society and culture, probably not harmoniously integrated, and with high multicentricity.[9] Pentecostalism's foundation document, the Biblical narrative regarding the descent of the Holy Spirit on the day of Pentecost, in which each person in the cosmopolitan crowd heard 'the wonders of God in their own tongue', is the basis for its current polycentric globalisation. In fact, without much numerical impact, Pentecostalism set out from Los Angeles in 1906 and quickly reached the four corners of the earth through missionary and immigrant networks which intersected with the starting-points in American popular Protestantism. Born amongst the poor, blacks and women, on the underside of American society, Pentecostalism was exported at virtually no cost, often by non-Americans. It is this popular, counter-establishment Western Christianity which has become one of the most globalised religious phenomena. After considerable growth in recent decades, usually autonomously, in Latin America, Africa and East Asia, this Third World Pentecostalism now expands to other countries of the same continents and to the First World. In line with globalisation theories regarding the complexity of global cultural flows,[10] globalised Pentecostalism is characterised by 'a multisource diffusion of parallel developments'.[11] The British diaspora and Anglo-Saxon missions responsible for much worldwide expansion of Protestantism since the eighteenth century have now been overtaken by other diasporas (African, Caribbean, Latin-American, Chinese and Korean) and by other missions.

While many religions are becoming globalised, the scale of Pentecostalism is different. Pentecostal expansion often follows diasporas (Africans in Europe; Latinos in the US). Frequently, diaspora churches serve a broader clientele than at home, following categories imposed by the receiving society: Africans in general join Nigerian churches in England; Hispanics in general join Puerto Rican churches in the US.

There is also a missionary effort transcending diasporas. Little is known about the missionary movement of the new mass Third World

---

[8] Andrew Walls, 'The Western Discovery of Non-Western Christian Art' in Diana Wood (ed.), *The Church and the Arts*, Oxford: Blackwell, 1992, p. 571.

[9] Waters, *Globalization*, p. 3.

[10] Mike Featherstone, 'An Introduction' in Featherstone (ed.), *Global Culture*, London: Sage, 1990, p. 10.

[11] Irving Hexham and Karla Poewe, 'Charismatic Churches in South Africa: A Critique of Criticisms and Problems of Bias' in Karla Poewe (ed.), *Charismatic Christianity as a Global Culture*, Columbia, SC: University of South Carolina Press, 1994, p. 61.

Protestantism. While it can reflect tendencies in secular labour markets (cheap labour for Western-controlled missionary enterprises), it is mostly better studied as an autonomous Third World social movement. In 1993 the World Evangelical Fellowship estimated 40,000 Protestant missionaries from Third World countries, compared with 88,000 from the traditional missionary-sending centres. Soon the former may be the majority.

Latin America accounts for much of this. Pentecostal churches expand within Latin America and among US Hispanics. Brazilian missions, with a long tradition among the historical churches, are now mainly Pentecostal. A 1994 Protestant publication talked of 800 Brazilian missionaries abroad. In 1997 a newsmagazine spoke of 1,700.[12] The Assemblies of God, God is Love and the Christian Congregation are at the forefront. But the Brazilian church with the greatest foreign presence is the Universal Church of the Kingdom of God. We shall look at the UCKG's expansion in general, before concentrating on two case-studies: Portugal and England.

The global expansion of the UCKG

The Igreja Universal do Reino de Deus was founded in 1977 in a poor suburb of Rio de Janeiro by Edir Macedo, a former state lottery employee. I have examined the characteristics of this church elsewhere;[13] here, I mention only aspects relevant for understanding its global expansion.

Brazil has the second largest community of practising Protestants in the world, and the largest community of Pentecostals. So it is no surprise that the UCKG has expanded abroad; what surprises is the speed and extent of this expansion. The missionary vision is typical of many Brazilian churches, but the capacity to make this vision a reality has to do with a unique combination of elements. According to a survey in Rio,[14] the social composition of the UCKG is lower even than that of most Pentecostal churches. While 45% of the population earn under two minimum salaries, and 58% of Protestants, the UCKG rate is 63%. Only 21% of the population has four years or less of schooling, versus 39% of Protestants and 50% of UCKG members. Whites are 60% of the population, 49% of Protestants and only 40% in the UCKG. This grassroots base is linked with institutional power due to hierarchical organisation, political strength

---

[12] *Veja*, 23 April 1997.

[13] Paul Freston, 'Breve História do Pentecostalismo Brasileiro: 3. A Igreja Universal do Reino de Deus' in A. Antoniazzi *et al.*, *Nem Anjos Nem Demônios*, Petrópolis: Vozes, 1994, pp. 131-59; 'Pentecostalism in Brazil: A Brief History', *Religion*, no. 25, 1995, pp. 119-33; 'The Protestant Eruption into Modern Brazilian Politics', *Journal of Contemporary Religion*, vol. 11, no. 2 (May 1996), pp. 147-68; ' "Neo-Pentecostalism" in Brazil', *Archives de Sciences Sociales des Religions*, no. 105 (Jan.-Mar. 1999).

[14] ISER, *Novo Nascimento*, Rio de Janeiro, 1996, p. 10.

(seventeen members of Congress), financial wealth and media empire (daily newspaper, thirty radio stations and the third largest television network).

While seeing itself as heir to the Evangelical tradition, the UCKG also has links with traditional Brazilian religiosity. In the phrase of one leader, 'We do not follow a European or American Evangelical tradition; we start from the religious practice of the people'. As a result, in the opinion of the president of the Brazilian Evangelical Association, the UCKG is a new syncretic religion which mixes 'Evangelical teachings, precepts of the medieval Catholic Church and Afro-Amerindian elements'.[15] But it is also (thanks to constant methodological innovation facilitated by centralised control) a bricolage of practices from diverse sources, well adapted to times of globalisation.

One opinion poll found the UCKG had the lowest approval rating of the principal Brazilian institutions: only 17%, even lower than Congress.[16] Among Protestants, however, it is not so rejected. Another survey showed 32% of Pentecostals in São Paulo (versus 8% of the general population) saw positive aspects in the UCKG.[17] Even so, its image is worse than that of other denominations.[18] This negative image follows the UCKG abroad. However, the situation in each country has to be explained not by the church's image in Brazil but by the way this information is used by local protagonists with their own agendas.

The UCKG invests heavily in foreign expansion. In 1995, twelve of the twenty-two members of its World Episcopal Council were located abroad. Since it had 2,100 churches in Brazil and only 225 elsewhere, the bishops abroad looked after a much lower number of churches. Another indication is the care taken when starting work in new countries. A commission investigates the probabilities of success, studies relevant laws, devises the legal constitution of the church, evaluates the most appropriate discourse and the best locations for churches, besides carrying out rental or purchase of buildings.[19]

From data in UCKG publications and the secular media, I present a reconstruction of its worldwide expansion. Founded in 1977, the UCKG crossed Brazil's frontiers in 1985 when it opened in Paraguay.[20] Expansion was slow until 1990, reaching only the US, Argentina and Portugal.

---

[15] *Folha de São Paulo*, 7 Jan. 1996 and 10 Sept. 1995.

[16] *Jornal do Brasil*, 26 May 1996.

[17] *Folha de São Paulo*, 14 Jan. 1996.

[18] ISER, *Novo Nascimento*, p. 46.

[19] *Veja*, 19 April 1995 and 23 April 1997.

[20] The *Folha Universal* (the UCKG weekly newspaper in Brazil) of 21 Dec. 1997 affirms that the church started in the US in 1980. This may be a misprint, since Manuel Silva, 'A Brazilian Church Comes to New York', *Pneuma*, vol. 13, no. 2 (Fall 1991), pp. 161-5, seemingly referring to the same events, talks of 1986, and the TV Record documentary mentioned below suggests the church's first foreign undertaking was in Paraguay.

Perhaps unfruitful beginnings in the US, plus investment in the purchase of Brazil's TV Record network in 1989, limited foreign expansion in the 1980s. But in the 1990s the rhythm increased. By 1993, it is said to have reached various countries of Latin America (Colombia, Venezuela, Uruguay, Chile, Mexico, Puerto Rico, Honduras, Guatemala, Panama), Africa (South Africa, Angola, Mozambique, Botswana, Cape Verde, Guinea-Bissau) and Europe (France, Spain, Holland, Italy). By 1995, it is reported to have spread further: to the Dominican Republic, Nicaragua and El Salvador; Nigeria, Kenya, Malawi and Congo; England and Luxembourg; Japan and the Philippines.[21] Leaflets issued by the UCKG-England claim even quicker recent expansion: a late 1995 version talks of over forty countries; the mid-1997 version mentions over seventy countries. On the other hand, a TV Record documentary broadcast in October 1997 lists only forty-five countries, of which fourteen are in Latin America, thirteen in Africa, eleven in Europe, four in Asia and three in North America and the Anglophone Caribbean.[22] From subsequent church publications, it seems that by late 1998 the UCKG was present in at least fifty-two countries outside Brazil.[23]

In 1995 the number of churches abroad was estimated at 221, distributed as follows: Portugal fifty-two, Argentina twenty-two, US seventeen, South Africa seventeen, Mexico eleven, Paraguay nine Colombia seven, Mozambique seven, Philippines seven, Canada seven, other countries five or fewer. The continental totals were: Latin America seventy-five, Europe sixty-three, Africa fifty-two, North America twenty-four, Asia seven.[24] Later sources (especially the *Folha Universal*) suggest that by late 1998 there were at least 500 churches. The continental percentages may not have changed greatly.

Three cultural blocs account for over 90% of UCKG churches abroad: the Latin American bloc, including Hispanics in the US; the Portuguese-speaking bloc; and the African bloc. Some remaining countries may also fall into these categories. The Swiss churches were started by

---

[21] *Veja*, 19 April 1995; *Folha de São Paulo*, 17 April 1995.

[22] The countries were listed in the following order: Russia, Jamaica, Angola, Guinea-Bissau, Ivory Coast, Kenya, Malawi, Mozambique, Nigeria, South Africa, Tanzania, Uganda, Zambia, Zimbabwe, Cape Verde, India, Israel, Japan, Philippines, Dominican Republic, El Salvador, Guatemala, Honduras, Nicaragua, Puerto Rico, England, France, Germany, Holland, Italy, Luxemburg, Portugal, Spain, Switzerland, Canada, Mexico, the USA, Argentina, Bolivia, Chile, Colombia, Ecuador, Paraguay, Peru, Belgium. Several countries missing from this list are on lists published by the secular media, either by journalistic error or because the work there was discontinued, or even because the church forgot to include them in the documentary: Uruguay, Venezuela, Panama, Congo, Senegal, Botswana.

[23] In the *Folha Universal* from late 1997 to Nov. 1998 we see reference to new countries (Romania, Lesotho, Madagascar and Ethiopia), besides confirmation of Venezuela and Uruguay.

[24] *Veja*, 19 Apr. 1995.

Portuguese immigrants.[25] The French work began with Portuguese, and seems to have continued amongst blacks.[26] In Holland, it started amongst Portuguese-speaking immigrants, mainly from Cape Verde. The services in Dutch added subsequently seem to attract largely immigrants from Surinam.[27] The Japanese work seems to be amongst the Nippo-Brazilian immigrants. Thus, the Lusophone, Latin American and African worlds, with which the Brazilian homeland of the UCKG has cultural or linguistic links, provide the vast majority of the worldwide membership.[28] The non-Iberian white world, Asia and the politically inaccessible Middle East remain a challenge.

This does not mean the UCKG is incapable of the cultural adaptation (or, in Eastern Europe and Asia, the political negotiations) necessary for such challenges. In February 1997 the first church in Russia opened. In June it started daily services in Moscow's Progress Theatre.[29] Although the theatre rental was later rescinded by the city council, the church acquired its own headquarters and a daily radio programme. Faced with restrictive new laws for religious organisations, the UCKG joined with eight other churches to form the Russian Alliance of Pentecostal Evangelical Faith, which in March 1998 achieved full government recognition. Thus, the incipient UCKG could function on a par with Russian groups established since the early years of the century. In achieving the support of such groups the church's financial capacity and international presence were key: the UCKG took the president of the Alliance to observe its work in Portugal.[30] If it gets round restrictions on religious pluralism, the church may find greater space in Eastern Europe than in Asia or among the majority populations of the developed West. But the only other Eastern European country attempted thus far is Romania,[31] whose Latin-based language makes communication easier for Brazilian pastors.

The trajectory in the US confirms difficulties in crossing cultural frontiers. In 1986 an American pastor handed over a church in Manhattan to Edir Macedo and acted as his sponsor with the American authorities.[32] The following year, the UC began a cable TV programme. Today, it has over twenty churches, including a theatre in Los Angeles, a newspaper

---

[25] Programme on *TV Record*, 21 Aug. 1998.

[26] Programme on *TV Record*, 4 July 1998.

[27] In a programme on Holland (*Rede Família*, 15 Nov. 1998), the only white Dutch person to give a testimony was married to a woman from Cape Verde.

[28] Although outside these blocs, even Italy (Latin and Catholic heritage) and the Philippines (Catholicism and Spanish colonisation) are culturally close.

[29] *The Sower*, July 1997.

[30] *Folha Universal*, 10 May 1998.

[31] Programme on *TV Record*, 22 Aug. 1998.

[32] Silva, 'Brazilian Church'.

with a circulation of 100,000 and a television production studio.[33] But this story hides a basic change of strategy. Initially, services and programmes were in English. The church stagnated. A fascinating article, written in 1991 by a UCKG pastor, reflects the dilemma.

> Up to now, the [UCKG] is the reflection of a peculiar society... permeated by the belief and fear of the spirits and, consequently, exorcism is the most frequent practice.[...] We will have to see how [it] adapts to cultures in which people do not have the same fear of spirits.[...] Making converts in New York is not as easy as in Brazil. The people... think they do not need the help of anybody, much less someone from Brazil.[34]

The solution, however, was a change of public; this avoided the question of cultural adaptation. Television programmes and services switched to Spanish, and the Hispanic population then made growth possible.

According to recent UCKG statistics, its greatest success is in Portuguese-speaking Mozambique (thirty churches),[35] Colombia (forty-seven churches),[36] Argentina, South Africa and Portugal. In all these countries, stress has been laid on social work as a means of gaining the sympathy of the population and sometimes of overcoming political opposition to the church's presence.

South Africa may now rival Portugal as the strongest UC outside Brazil, and is said to cover the financial losses from all other UCKG churches in Africa. The first church opened there amongst Portuguese-speakers in 1992, but the transition to Soweto and to English was made by 1993.[37] In 1998, it filled Ellis Park rugby stadium for a ceremony which included 'dances and joyful songs of praise, mostly in African languages'.[38] By that time, it claimed 115 churches and 200 South African pastors, presumably all black.[39] South African pastors are also used as missionaries throughout Africa, as well as in Jamaica, England and the US. (The last-named country may be related to an attempt to break into the African-American world; in 1997 the UCKG claimed a church in Brooklyn catering for that community.)[40] However, Brazilian pastors also enjoy success. At the church in Pietermaritzburg, frequented by blacks and occasionally a few poor Afrikaners, services are in a mixture of English and Zulu, but

---

[33] *O Estado de São Paulo*, 18 Sept. 1995; *Folha de São Paulo*, 17 Sept. 1995; *IstoÉ*, 14 Dec. 1994.

[34] Silva, 'Brazilian Church'.

[35] *Folha Universal*, 18 Oct. 1998.

[36] *Folha Universal*, 13 Sept. 1998.

[37] *IstoÉ*, 14 Dec 1994; Ronaldo Didini in *Veja*, 23 Apr. 1997; *Folha Universal*, 14 Dec. 1997.

[38] *Folha Universal*, 11 Oct. 1998.

[39] At Ellis Park, thirty-five new pastors were consecrated. From the names, twenty-two of these were Brazilian or Portuguese and thirteen were black South Africans, but none were South African whites (*Folha Universal*, 11 Oct. 1997).

[40] *Folha Universal*, 21 Dec. 1997.

what impresses the blacks is the facility with which the white Brazilian pastors adapt culturally. 'These whites are blacks', they say, in a tribute to the UCKG's missionary methods which may presage success all over sub-Saharan Africa.

Success in South Africa may also be related to the moment of the country, in which newly-created expectations begin to be frustrated and new religious groups proliferate. The UCKG can appeal both to the disappointed as well as to those who need moral reinforcement to take advantage of the new opportunities.

Another success story is Argentina, where in 1997 the UC had forty-six churches.[41] But Latin America is not always receptive. In Chile, after six years' activities and despite having gained legal status, it was subjected in late 1997 to government pressures. Visas were denied to Brazilian pastors, on the basis of suspicions of irregular financing, a suspicion apparently communicated to Chilean authorities by elements within the Brazilian police. Despite lukewarm support from the Brazilian consulate, the UCKG's strength in the Brazilian congress ensured a satisfactory solution.[42] In Peru, it had to resort to using another name: the Comunidad Cristiana del Espíritu Santo.

This is not the first time the UC has faced a legal embargo, usually provoked by local opponents' use of the church's negative image in Brazil. Nor is it the first time it has got round the problem by using a different name. The tactic has been used in the North-East of Brazil, in Spain, in Italy and in Oporto. In Colombia and Mexico it is called Oración Fuerte al Espíritu Santo. Another tactic is to make agreements with already existing churches abroad (US, Japan) to make it bureaucratically easier to get started. As in Brazil, the UCKG abroad is characterised by creativity. We shall see examples in our two case studies from Europe.

The UCKG in Portugal: a Luso-Brazilian church?

The Universal Church began in Portugal in December 1989. By 1997, it claimed sixty-two churches: twenty-one in Greater Lisbon, ten in Greater Oporto, twelve in the South, thirteen in the Centre, a mere four in the very Catholic North and two in Madeira.[43] The following year, it was talking of eighty-five churches.[44] The official publication, *Tribuna Universal*, claimed a circulation of 50,000 in 1997. In 1995, the UCKG had programmes on twenty-three radio stations, six of which belonged to the church,[45] and a daily TV programme. There is great emphasis on social

[41] Programme on *TV Record*, 15 Aug. 1998.
[42] *Folha Universal*, 14 Dec. 1997 and 17 May 1998.
[43] *Tribuna Universal*, 10 Dec. 1997.
[44] Programme on *TV Record*, 6 June 1998.
[45] Five were in other names, due to legislation prohibiting groups from owning more than one station and 30% of another (*IstoÉ*, 14 Dec. 1994).

work: distribution of food and clothing, work with drug addicts, an old people's home and an orphanage. In this way, the church seeks the legitimacy denied it by important social sectors.

The UCKG's public is 'middle-aged women, maids, young people of all ethnic origins and retired people of both sexes'.[46] The *Tribuna Universal*[47] has an article about ageing which shows awareness of a possible clientele: 'An early exit from the job market is a relatively new phenomenon in Portugal, but may increase due to Portugal's entry into the European Community... The population between fifty and sixty-five is on unstable ground, since the trend is to reduce social rights.'

In a country where all Protestant churches (except Maná, a Pentecostal church of Portuguese origin) are small and stagnant, the attraction of the UCKG may have to do with the moment of entry into the EU and the abrupt development it has brought, on the one hand bringing opportunities for those who know how to take advantage of them, and on the other hand bringing anguish to those who feel left behind or whose traditional lifestyle is threatened. This creates an opening for the prosperity gospel which the UCKG preaches, as well as new social space for non-Catholic groups.

Although most UCKG leaders in Portugal are Brazilian, there is growing participation of Portuguese. But the church makes no effort to hide its origin. Critics in the media say it speaks 'the language of the Brazilian soap operas' so popular in Portugal.[48] The church itself proudly admits to what it calls a 'reverse "colonisation-evangelisation" '. Members assimilate the Brazilian way of speaking; in the prayers, 'everyone cries out to the Lord in "Brazilian".'[49] Pastors lead the way in this Brazilianisation; one of them, after leading a whole service in 'Brazilian', found it necessary to tell me he was in fact Portuguese to explain why he still longed to see what the UCKG was like in Brazil.

If the church in Portugal uses Brazilianisms it is because it knows they produce dividends. A church which plans its international expansion so well would not commit such an elementary error in Christian mission theory if it were prejudicial. Although there is anti-Brazilian feeling in sectors of Portuguese society, especially the middle class and sectors of the media and intelligentsia, the lower class is attracted to aspects of Brazilian culture. A partial Brazilianisation could be a form of resistance by those less favoured by European integration.

As in Brazil, the UCKG invests heavily in the media, taking 'advantage of what was left of an undignified national radio licencing process, [acquiring through intermediaries] radios with financial problems which

[46] *Público* (Lisbon), 2 Aug. 1995.
[47] 7 July 1996.
[48] *Público*, 27 Aug. 1995.
[49] *Plenitude*, Sept. 1997, p. 38.

needed an injection of capital'.[50] But television was more problematic. The church managed to get programmes on SIC and on the satellite channel Eutelsat (to reach emigrant Portuguese in Europe). But in 1995, it was legally prohibited from using Portuguese television.

At the same time as the saint-kicking episode in Brazil (in which a UCKG bishop, in a live TV programme, kicked an image of Our Lady of Aparecida, patron saint of Brazil, to show it could not answer prayers), similar problems occurred in Portugal. Similar in the sense of a resistance from important social sectors which showed the UC had too blatantly crossed the invisible frontiers that still mark the social and political space of Protestant groups in both countries. Kicking the patron saint on her national holiday, and attempting to buy the Coliseu theatre in Oporto, were overly daring steps for which the UCKG did not yet have the necessary support.

The Portuguese media had been calling for the authorities to react. '[The UC] has infiltrated our daily life, importing new expressions, strange rites... a truly multinational business...[whose growth] could go as far as political power. A route paved with much money and obscure twists, to which authorities and civil society reacted with apparent indifference until the Coliseu "affair".'[51]

The language is similar to that used by some Brazilian media: the comparison with the economic as a way of delegitimising the religious; the sinister phrases ('infiltrated', 'strange rites', 'obscure twists'); the encouragement of state intervention.

Some organs of the Brazilian press are no different. *O Globo,* which belongs to the media group most concerned about the media power of the UCKG, describes thus (November 1995) an incident in northern Portugal:

Teenagers destroyed a UCKG church.[...]After breaking everything, they painted on the floor words such as 'demon'.[...]Only the members were spared.[...]The 'bishop' João Luís threatens to hold a new service tomorrow morning in what is left of the building.[...]Everything happened after the evangelicals decided to use the York Cinema in a shopping mall.[...]The shopkeepers accused the sect's followers, without proof, of committing various thefts in the commercial area.

Probably the church's clientele looked more like the 'dangerous classes' than the usual clientele of the mall. The article attributes the cause of the disorders to a decision by the Evangelicals (the UCKG), and not to an orchestrated action by shopkeepers for economic reasons, and describes the bishop's decision to hold another service the next day in the ruins of the church, despite the physical risk, not as courageous but as a 'threat'.

Another Brazilian newspaper describes an incident in Portugal in language which creates greater identification with the UCKG: the church

---

[50] *Público*, 27 Aug. 1995.

[51] *Ibid.*

members 'heard xenophobic slogans which told Brazilians and the Universal Church to go back to Brazil'.[52] In late 1995, churches in three towns were attacked: Matosinhos, Venda Nova and Póvoa de Varzim. In reply, the UCKG circulated a note in English: *Inquisition in Portugal*. The message is clear: the Portugal which desires to be modern and European cannot allow such restrictions on freedom of religion.

Another UCKG initiative met with legal resistence: the founding of a political party. In Brazil, its participation in elections has been through a range of secular parties, so why create a party of its own in Portugal? Within the Protestant world, it would be a means for exercising hegemony. Outside, it would be a way of getting round exclusion in the party system and achieving (in the medium run) a certain bargaining power for conquering social and political space. In Brazil, the electoral system encourages parties to offer space for Protestant candidates, and allows these candidates to get elected on their own electoral strength. In Portugal, the pre-determined party lists prevent candidates from minority groups getting elected solely with the votes they bring to the slate. It would be necessary first to show the UCKG's electoral strength, and then bargain with some traditional party disposed to open a slot.

Creating the party was hard. The name would be Evangelical Party, an invitation to pan-Protestant electoral collaboration and a reply to the UC's exclusion from the Evangelical Alliance. Later, the name Social Christian Party was attempted. Registration was denied because the constitution does not permit religious parties. Soon afterwards, registration was achieved, with the name of Party of the People (Partido da Gente).

It was said the UC hoped to elect ten candidates to parliament in October 1995, with votes from all Protestants. But it is unlikely the hierarchy had such high hopes. Even to get a sizeable proportion of votes from UC members would be an achievement in a country with a solid party system. In fact, they received very few votes and elected no one. The UCKG's strong parliamentary presence in Brazil has yet to be replicated anywhere abroad.

The church has also faced battles within the Protestant community. At the time of the attacks on its buildings, the Portuguese Council of Christian Churches, consisting of historical denominations, repudiated the attacks but claimed to understand their motivation: 'We believe there is an expression of rage on the part of many who feel cheated'. However, the greatest clash has been with another representative entity, the Evangelical Alliance of Portugal (AEP).

In 1992 the UCKG applied to join the AEP, hoping for some of the respectability enjoyed by older Protestant sectors, and for allies in its battles. However, the report of an AEP commission, dated 1993, concludes that the UCKG's body of doctrines 'is very close to the doctrinal

[52] *Folha de São Paulo*, 13 Nov. 1995.

principles of the AEP, but its "guiding ideas"...as well as some of its practices, put it outside the traditional universe of the Portuguese evangelical churches'. There were said to be four main deficiencies. The UCKG has a 'rigid hierarchy with unipersonal discretionary powers'. Leaders are immune from evaluation, 'on the grounds they are "commanded" directly by God... in dreams, visions and through the Bible'. The UCKG uses 'magical-sacramental methods in the relationship between the "human" and the "divine", the "material" and the "spiritual"', such as red roses for health, yellow roses for prosperity, white roses for sentimental questions and photographs anointed with holy oils. Lastly, it does not emphasise 'fundamental doctrines of the Gospel, but its "guiding ideas", some of which are heretical'.

The list of heretical ideas includes the following: 'All evils...are of demonic origin'; 'healing is a right acquired through Christ'; 'pastors have the gift of healing...regardless of the faith of the sick person'; 'complete deliverance [from demonic oppression] is only possible through participation in the church; no-one is blessed at home'; 'baptism by immersion is an indispensable condition for all blessings'; 'through participation in Holy Communion...the participant enjoys the physical health Christ enjoyed'; 'all men are children of God...[disregards the problem of original sin]'; 'money is the lifeblood of the church'; 'tithing is fundamental for physical, spiritual and financial life'. Parts of this list are surprising, in light of UCKG practice elsewhere. It usually speaks against dreams and visions,[53] and is not known for a sacramentalist theology. Others seem to be phrases heard in sermons, and could be exegeted in a more orthodox way. Some criticisms could be applied to churches, or sectors of them, which belong to the AEP.

As for the 'magical-sacramental methods', the AEP here echoes Evangelical criticisms of the UCKG in Brazil. The UCKG does indeed break with the symbolic poverty of Brazilian Protestantism. But there do seem to be limits; although it makes ample use of symbols, there is no use of images in worship. Previous Pentecostalism had democratised the word through speaking in tongues and prophecies; the UCKG, however, breaks dependence on the word, making ample use of sight, touch and gesture. Soon after the AEP's refusal of the UCKG, an article by Bishop Macedo entitled 'Idolatry and Symbolism: the Difference' commented: 'Many Evangelical brothers have criticised us for our free distribution of roses, anointed handkerchiefs, consecrated oil etc.' But the Bible, he says, is full of symbols. Jesus also used physical elements such as clay to awaken faith, and the apostle Paul did miracles through his personal objects.[54]

[53] The second number of the UC magazine in England gives 'ten reasons why we shouldn't believe in dreams' (*The Sower*, May 1996).

[54] *Folha Universal*, 13 Mar. 1994.

It is possible the AEP's refusal of the UC had to do with wariness of the hegemonic force it would represent in the small and static Portuguese Evangelical world. The UC showed its displeasure by opening a rival entity, the Federation of Evangelical Churches of Portugal, literally right across the road from the headquarters of the AEP.

An AEP bulletin[55] throws light on the UC's possible concern with representative entities at the current stage of relations between Evangelicals and Portuguese society. It talks of conversations between the AEP and the government, intended to lead to official recognition of the Evangelical community through its representative organs, with the same rights enjoyed by the Catholic Church. It also talks of a commission with representatives of all confessions, including the Catholics, presided over by the president of the AEP, which is petitioning for the implementation of a law which grants religious groups daily access to public television.

Portugal, thus far, is the only country outside Brazil where the UCKG has achieved national visibility. It also seems to be the foreign country which supplies the most pastors. Perhaps the decision to open a church there in 1989 marked a new strategy after relatively fruitless effort in the US. Portugal would become the beach-head for international expansion, and not only amongst Lusophone communities, as we shall see in the case of England.

The UCKG in England: a black church?

England represents a very different religious field. In Portugal the UC is an unsettling force in a weak Protestantism in a traditionally Catholic country: a Protestantism dominated by churches of foreign origin and with little tradition of autochthonous churches. In England, on the other hand, the UC does not mean much in a traditionally Protestant but now secularised country, with a Protestant state church and a plethora of free churches. Although ethnic churches are growing, there is no tradition of success among the native white population by foreign churches, especially from outside the English-speaking world. What the two countries do have in common, besides membership in the EU, is the presence of immigrants from the former colonies.

The UCKG began in England in June 1995, with a small church in the London neighbourhood of Brixton. In October of that year, it bought the Rainbow Theatre in Finsbury Park for $4 million, having previously attempted to purchase the Brixton Academy for $6.4 million. Shortly afterwards, it opened a church in the second largest city, Birmingham. In March 1996, the 1,500 seats in the Rainbow were filled for the visit of Bishop Macedo. In the next month, publication of *The Sower* magazine began. By mid-1997, the English UC had its own bishop, Renato Cardoso, son-in-law of Macedo. In late 1998 the UC claimed four churches and three 'nuclei' (smaller centres with fewer services), and had the family as its main emphasis, in line with the Labour government's professed concern for the strengthening of family life.[56] The initial strategy had been to begin in grand style at the Brixton Academy, a famous concert hall. A secret bid had been leaked to the press, causing local opposition and intervention by the borough council. But the result was not wholly negative. The unknown UCKG was in the main newspapers. Although the media made some use of Brazilian anti-UCKG material, the tone was moderate, more of curiosity than concern. The Brixton Academy was not the English equivalent of the Coliseu in Portugal or the saint-kicking in Brazil, since the purchase was disallowed on cultural grounds. In England, with its liberal and Protestant tradition, there was no controversy about the very existence of the church, much less any destruction of buildings.

The Rainbow Theatre, which the UC acquired later, is in a mixed area: Indians, Pakistanis, Greeks, Irish, blacks and white English intermingle in the rather run-down streets. But the Brixton Academy shows the strategy with which the UC arrived. Brixton is the most famous black district of London. The small UC church functioning there is frequented almost exclusively by blacks, although the pastors in 1996 were Portuguese whites. Even at the Rainbow, 90% of the public is black. The UCKG in England has made the black community its main target and thus comes close to the category of 'Afro-Caribbean church' in the English religious world.

Talking about Peruvian Pentecostals in New Jersey, Vásquez says that Peruvian identity is dissolved in that of 'Hispanics' or 'Latinos' imposed by American society.[57] Similarly, immigrants (and their descendants) from Jamaica, Barbados, Nigeria or Ghana are redefined by British society as 'blacks'. At most, they are divided into 'West Indians' and 'Africans'.

In the religious field, many blacks are in churches classified as Afro-Caribbean. To understand the implications of this strategy for the UCKG, we need to know something of the English religious world.

Although the 'Celtic fringe' of Britain (Wales, Scotland and Northern Ireland) has higher figures, only 9% of the population of England frequent a church.[58] The theologically liberal churches are declining and the Evangelical ones growing. There is increasing Protestant fragmentation,

[56] *Folha Universal*, 23 Aug. 1998.

[57] Manuel Vásquez, 'Transnationalization and Religious Practices among Peruvian Christians in Paterson, NJ', paper presented at XX Congress of the Latin American Studies Association, 1997.

[58] Data on the British religious field are from Christopher Sinclair, 'Evangelical Belief in Contemporary England', *Archives de Sciences Sociales des Religions*, no. 82 (April-June 1993), pp. 169-81, Brierley, *Changing Churches*, and various editions of the *UK Christian Handbook*.

with many new charismatic groups. In Anglicanism, the Evangelical wing has grown (from 10% of the clergy and 15% of the laity in 1950, to 50% of the clergy and 35% of the laity in 1987). But Evangelicals in general are middle class, and much of their limited presence among the lower class is due to Pentecostals. The latter represent only 4% of British Protestantism, although they are the fastest growing segment in the 1990s.

In 1990 42% of British Pentecostals were in Afro-Caribbean churches. Caribbean immigration since the 1950s and African since the 1970s led to separate churches, often after frustrated attempts at integration into white churches. The Afro-Caribbean field is very polarised. On the whole, Caribbeans and Africans do not go to the same churches.

The 1990s are a moment of crisis for the black churches. On the one hand, their spiritual values are increasingly recognised as important for British Christianity. Together with the growing importance of evangelicalism comes the growing importance of blacks within Evangelicalism, symbolised in 1996 by the election of a black Pentecostal as head of the Evangelical Alliance. On the other hand, the churches are affected by the drama of 'naturalisation': the younger generation, born in the country, is impatient with old traditions and in search of its own identity. Another factor is that almost half the young people of Caribbean origin marry non-blacks. In this context, the UCKG (with its exotic origin, message of success and self-respect, attempt to integrate the poor of all colours, and its predominantly white leadership) can offer a halfway house between a traditional Afro-Caribbean and a white church.

While the UC deliberately started out amongst blacks, the church shows awareness of the dangers. The black community should be a beach-head, not a prison. The trap of becoming an Afro-Caribbean church haunts the UC's activities.

On the one hand, blacks are cultivated as the initial target and subsequent mainstay of the membership. The main Jamaican newspaper in London was used to announce the initial activities, at first with the testimony and photo of a black Brazilian, then, with a West Indian from London, and finally with four blacks from London (two West Indians and two Africans). The first issue of *The Sower* (April 1996) has the testimony of a black South African ('I tried doctors, witchdoctors, inyangas and sangomas'). The next issue declares: 'The devil has said in your mind "You can't do it! You are poor, you don't have knowledge, you are black, you have no rights to receive".' In July 1997 there is the testimony of a black couple from Birmingham: 'When on holiday in Jamaica, some friends introduced us to...'spiritualists'. But they really practised Obeah... 150 pounds for a blood bath [with the] blood of pigeons'. The testimony of a sterile Nigerian woman attacks the African 'spiritual' churches in London: 'There, my problems only became worse'. An advertisement for the Universal Classics shop stresses the availability of 'African designs'.

All this is reflected in the services: in Brixton, an almost totally black church; at the Rainbow, 90% black, perhaps two thirds Caribbean and one third West African. As in Brazil, the young man from the street can enter a UC service without feeling out of place, but one sees the influence of Caribbean ecclesiastical culture in the suits of the middle-aged men and the elegant hats of the women. At certain moments, especially the more joyful songs, the service suddenly looks typically Caribbean, except for the white Brazilian pastors. In the exorcisms, voodoo, obeah and West African divinities are mentioned. Occasionally, the possessed talk in African languages and are exhorted by the pastor, amidst applause, to 'speak a language I can understand; speak English'.

On the other hand, the UC seems aware of the danger of getting trapped in the 'black church' category, and tries to ensure the black community is a door into Britain and not its final destination. The first issue of *The Sower* has a testimony of a white Brazilian; the second issue, of an Indian from New York; a later issue, of an Indian from London ('my parents were strict Hindus'). Articles against Islam also show concern for the largest ethnic minority, the Asians. The evolving concern to move beyond the black community can be seen in publicity leaflets. One version has four testimonies: two of Africans, one of a West Indian and one of a white. A later version alters the proportions: one African, one West Indian and two whites.

An analysis of *The Sower* reveals other tactics for the English context. One is the attack on Islam: 'The symbols, traditions and rituals...come from a pre-Islamic Arabian pagan deity'; 'the true essence of Islam [is] a form of cultural imperialism'. In a Protestant context, another tactic more common than in Brazil is intra-Protestant polemic. The first issue says the magazine will warn against false teachings. The Evangelical church has turned into an 'improved Catholic church'. Just as 'Catholic' and 'Christian' are mutually exclusive in UC language in Brazil, so it seems are 'Anglican' and 'Christian' in England.[59] Leaders, movements and trends in the international evangelical world are attacked: Billy Graham 'teaches Catholics are just another Christian denomination'; the AD 2000 Movement 'preaches more than one gospel'; and the Toronto Blessing[60] is the target of several articles which attribute it to Satan. But anti-Catholic polemic continues, despite being attenuated in contemporary British evangelicalism: 'Evangelicals and Catholics together? Not the true evangelicals'; 'Roman Catholic Church charged with aiding in murders [during the Argentine military regime]'.

---

[59] *The Sower*, 4 Apr. 1996, pp. 2, 5, 6, 7; May 1996, p. 19.
[60] The Toronto Blessing, an ultra-charismatic phenomenon characterised by faintings and animal sounds, has influenced many British churches.

A publicity leaflet begins with a declaration of faith which places the UCKG within orthodox Christianity ('one God, eternally existing in three persons'), within Protestantism ('two ordinances – baptism in water and the Lord's Supper'; 'sanctification as a progressive work of grace'), within Evangelicalism ('the Scriptures in their original writings as fully inspired'; 'the substitutionary sacrifice' of Christ) and within Pentecostalism ('baptism of the Holy Spirit'; 'divine healing as an integral part of the gospel'). It affirms eschatology as the dynamo of the church ('the last chance to receive salvation' before the Second Coming – a greater emphasis now than in the early UC). As in Portugal, social work is stressed: 'faith without deeds is dead...orphanages, homes for the elderly, hunger relief campaigns, free medical assistance, blood donation, schools, reintegration of the homeless...'.

At a morning service in August 1997 at the Rainbow, Bishop Macedo himself led half the service. He conducted it in the usual UC oscillating rhythm, alternating loud music and fervent prayer with moments of calm and concentration. Following the usual emphasis for Sundays, and also Macedo's own recent stress on greater spiritual formation, he prayed: 'O Lord, more than healing or prosperity, give these people salvation'. The singing mixed traditional and recent English choruses with translations of Brazilian Evangelical songs. (In the afternoon service, a translation was sung of the famous UC song used after exorcisms: 'out, out, out'.)

On the same afternoon there was the annual Day of Decision service, with 1,500 people packing out the Rainbow. Surprisingly, Macedo did not appear; even in the morning, his appearance had been discreet and unannounced. In the afternoon service, the rhythm was very different, with exorcism predominating. The pastor called upon the evil in people's lives to appear: 'come out, manifest'. Initially, he invoked evil in general, later specifying voodoo, *oxóssi*, *candomblé* and other names which appeared to be West African religious entities. Africans were a majority amongst the exorcised.

The UC as a black church (in Britain) is in the tradition of the African Independent Churches.

'Many African Christians believe the [missionary] church is not interested in daily misfortunes, illness, encounter with evil and witchcraft.[...] The need is for a power beyond that of the spirits, diviners and sorcerers. The alleged syncretism in African Christianity is not so much a sign of a lack of Christian commitment as an expression of the fact that Christianity has not been made to respond fully to culturally-based religious aspirations. But in the independent churches, there is an open invitation to bring fears and anxieties about witches, sorcerers, bad luck, poverty and illness'[61].

[61] Allan Anderson, 'Pentecostal Pneumatology and African Power Concepts: Continuity or Change?', *Missionalia*, vol. 19, no. 1 (April 1990), pp. 67, 71f.

If the UC is based initially in the black community, the pastorate is based on Brazilian-Portuguese collaboration. Except for a few black English unpaid assistants, all the leadership is Luso-Brazilian. Portuguese, of course, can work anywhere in the European Union. In England, and much of Europe, the UCKG is a Luso-Brazilian church. It may already constitute the largest Protestant missionary effort ever to come out of Portugal.

Conclusion: global perspectives of the Universal Church

In the Introduction, we viewed Pentecostalism as a globalised and culturally polycentric faith. The combination is important. As Smith says, new traditions must connect with vernacular styles: 'It is one thing to be able to package imagery and diffuse it [but] quite another to ensure [the] power to move...populations...The meanings of even the most universal of imagery for a particular population derive as much from the historical experiences and social status of that group as from the intentions of purveyors.'[62]

A contemporary African theologian asks whether 'the modern Western world, in Christian recession but with increasing interest in the occult, [is so] impervious to the experiences of Christian transcendence recorded in the South?'.[63] Mass adoption of Christianity in Africa, he suggests, might have global relevance. The same might be asked of Brazilian Pentecostalism. Certainly, in ethnic, cultural and economic terms, Brazil is a bridge between Europe and Africa and its churches might have a bridging role for the Third World minorities at the heart of the developed West.

The UCKG is not only tuned in to global registers; it is also a most Brazilian religion. It appears to see itself as a Latin American Protestant reformation, that is, a Protestantism attuned to the religious traditions of the continent. In response to accusations of syncretism, it replies that one can be Evangelical and still use popular religious traditions as a starting point.

At the same time, the UCKG is in the tradition of Christian expansion in the European Dark Ages and in twentieth century Africa: of an encounter of the 'powers'. The UCKG is not free floating; as an Evangelical and Pentecostal church, it has to sustain this identity by plausibly justifying its actions for a sufficient number of Christians. Analysing the UC as a business can produce insights but is ultimately reductionist, because its whole economic empire is functional for its religious mission and cannot be explained in purely pragmatic terms. The problem it faces in many countries is that a certain image arrives together with the church itself. The negative image then predominates among elites before the UC can build a popular base and a political counter-force. In a country with long traditions of pluralism and religious freedom such as Britain, this is not serious. But it can be in countries like Portugal with a monolithic

---

[62] Anthony Smith, 'Towards a Global Culture?' in Featherstone, *Global Culture*, p. 179.
[63] Kwame Bediako, *Christianity in Africa*, Edinburgh University Press, 1995, p. 166.

religious tradition and recent democratisation. Even so, membership of the EU reinforces democratisation and should guarantee UC survival there. In Eastern Europe the UC could have a large field, but it faces difficulties not only from slow economic reform (given the UC ideology of self-employment as the route to success) but from lack of a pluralist tradition and from legal restrictions on religious freedom.

The UC uses Third World communities as an entry into the First World. Portugal is the exception, since the church there is basically amongst the native population, aided by linguistic and cultural affinity and perhaps by Portugal's still precarious 'Europeanness'. Thus far, the UC's international expansion has depended on some or all of the following factors: cultural affinities (Luso, Latin, African); religious pluralism and freedom; poor immigrants; and populations of Christian background (Latin-American, Caribbean, African, Portuguese, Russian). It is not yet clear whether the church will be successful among non-Christianised peoples, above all in Asia.[64]

In 1991 Manuel Silva said we should have to see 'how the [UC] adapts to new cultures in which people do not have the same fear of spirits...but, following Jacques Ellul's ideas, they may find that new demons are lurking in the big cities of the world and in other cultures'.[65] At that time, the UCKG replied by opting for the Hispanics and forgetting the Anglo-Americans. It has also not had success in the African American community, replete with churches and a developed awareness of cultural difference, and unlikely to welcome a church led by white Brazilians who would be classified as Hispanics. But in Britain it was easier to penetrate the black community, which is more recent, smaller, with fewer cultural resources, divided between West Indians and Africans and between immigrants and local born, and where the tradition of separate churches is new and still regretted by many. In addition, the UCKG leaders do not fit easily into any common ethnic category in British society.

The UC may be unique because, unlike other Third World Pentecostal groups, it has the political power and economic strength to guarantee some visibility even in the developed world. In current Protestantism, only South Korea could play a similar role. But Korea lacks the ethnic, cultural and linguistic links with other countries such as Brazil has with Europe, the Americas and Africa. In this respect, it is significant that the UCKG's presence in Asia is limited effectively to the Philippines and the Nippo-Brazilians in Japan. By the late 1990s, Asia was viewed by the church as its next great challenge;[66] it will certainly be the greatest test

[64] The UC opened a church in India in 1996, and claimed 200 members a year later. Its radio programme had been banned (*Folha Universal*, 20 July 1997).
[65] The reference to the French sociologist Ellul, author of *The New Demons* (1973), is noteworthy.
[66] *Folha Universal*, 21 Feb. 1999.

yet of the Universal Church's ability to live up to its name in contexts which are both non-Christian and have few cultural affinities with the Brazilian cauldron in which it emerged.

BIBLIOGRAPHY

Anderson, Allan, 'Pentecostal Pneumatology and African Power Concepts: Continuity or Change?', *Missionalia*, vol. 19, no. 1 (April 1990), pp. 65-74.

Bediako, Kwame, *Christianity in Africa*, Edinburgh University Press, 1995.

Beyer, Peter, *Religion and Globalization*, London: Sage, 1994.

Brierley, Peter, *Changing Churches*, London: Christian Research, 1996.

Cox, Harvey, *The Silencing of Leonardo Boff*, Oak Park, IL: Meyer-Stone, 1988.

Featherstone, Mike, 'An Introduction' in Mike Featherstone (ed.), *Global Culture*, London: Sage, 1990, pp. 1-13.

Freston, Paul, 'Breve História do Pentecostalismo Brasileiro: 3. A Igreja Universal do Reino de Deus' in A. Antoniazzi *et al.* (eds), *Nem Anjos Nem Demônios: Interpretações Sociológicas do Pentecostalismo*, Petrópolis: Vozes, 1994, pp. 131-59.

———, 'Pentecostalism in Brazil: A Brief History', *Religion*, no. 25, 1995, pp. 119-33.

———, 'The Protestant Eruption into Modern Brazilian Politics', *Journal of Contemporary Religion*, vol. 11, no. 2 (May 1996), pp. 147-68.

———, ' "Neo-Pentecostalism" in Brazil: Problems of Definition and the Struggle for Hegemony', *Archives de Sciences Sociales des Religions*, no. 105 (Jan.-Mar. 1999).

Hexham, Irving, and Karla Poewe, 'Charismatic Churches in South Africa: A Critique of Criticisms and Problems of Bias' in Karla Poewe (ed.), *Charismatic Christianity as a Global Culture*, Columbia, SC: University of South Carolina Press, 1994, pp. 50-69.

ISER (Instituto de Estudos da Religião), *Novo Nascimento: Os Evangélicos em Casa, na Igreja e na Política*, Rio de Janeiro, 1996.

Robertson, Roland, *Globalization*, London: Sage, 1992.

Silva, Manuel, 'A Brazilian Church Comes to New York', *Pneuma*, vol. 13, no. 2 (Fall 1991), pp. 161-5.

Sinclair, Christopher, 'Evangelical Belief in Contemporary England', *Archives de Sciences Sociales des Religions*, no. 82 (April-June 1993), pp. 169-81.

Smith, Anthony, 'Towards a Global Culture?' in Mike Featherstone (ed.), *Global Culture*, London: Sage, 1990, pp. 171-91.

Vásquez, Manuel, 'Transnationalization and Religious Practices among Peruvian Christians in Paterson. NJ', paper presented at the XX Congress of the Latin American Studies Association, 1997.

Walls, Andrew, 'The Western Discovery of Non-Western Christian Art' in Diana Wood (ed.), *The Church and the Arts*, Oxford: Blackwell, 1992, pp. 571-85.

———, 'Christianity in the Non-Western World: A Study in the Serial Nature of Christian expansion', *Studies in World Christianity*, vol. 1, no. 1, 1995, pp. 1-25.

Waters, Malcolm, *Globalization*, London: Routledge, 1995.

Part III. AFRICA

TIME AND TRANSCULTURAL TECHNOLOGIES OF THE SELF IN THE GHANAIAN PENTECOSTAL DIASPORA[1]

Rijk van Dijk

There is a growing body of literature which explores the encroaching forms of modernity in terms of time and temporality.[2] Modernity, in its forms of missionisation, colonisation and postcolonial state-formation in many parts of the African continent, presented and still presents itself as a rupture with a perceived past. It produces a before and after dichotomy that, through processes such as conversion to Christianity, creates a battleground between a 'superior' future and an 'inferior' past whereby superiority is proved in victory, inferiority in defeat.[3] Here, the process of conversion to Christianity should be interpreted as a conversion to modernity[4] in so far as it propounds a rupture with a personal and social past, rejecting former beliefs and spiritual practices. Modernity does not build on the past but encapsulates it for purposes of domestication and appeasement so that remembrance, mnemonics and forgetting are turned into a politics of nostalgia.

[1] The research on the Ghanaian Pentecostal Diaspora was funded by WOTRO through the programme on Globalization and the Construction of Communal Identities, to which the author is greatly indebted.

[2] Joseph K. Adjaye, 'Time in Africa and Its Diaspora: An Introduction', in J.K. Adjaye (ed.), *Time in the Black Experience*, London: Greenwood Press, 1994, pp. 1-17; Joseph E. Holloway, 'Time in the African Diaspora: The Gullah Experience' in Adjaye, *Time in the Black Experience*, pp. 199-213; Paul Antze and Michael Lambek, 'Introduction: Forecasting Memory' in P. Antze and M. Lambek (eds), *Tense Past: Cultural Essays in Trauma and Memory*, London: Routledge, 1996, pp. xi-xxxviii; Rijk van Dijk, 'Pentecostalism, Cultural Memory and the State: Contested Representations of Time in Postcolonial Malawi' in R.P. Werbner (ed.), *Memory and the Postcolony*, London: Zed Books, Postcolonial Identities Series, 1998, pp. 155-82; Birgit Meyer, '"Make a Complete Break with the Past": Memory and Postcolonial Modernity in Ghanaian Pentecostal Discourse' in Werbner, *Memory and the Postcolony*, pp. 182-209; Richard Werbner, 'Smoke from the Barrel of a Gun: Postwars of the Dead, Memory and Reinscription in Zimbabwe' in Werbner, *Memory and the Postcolony*, pp. 71-103.

[3] Zygmunt Bauman, *Postmodern Ethics*, Oxford: Blackwell, 1993, p. 226.

[4] Peter v.d. Veer, *Conversion to Modernities: the Globalization of Christianity*, London: Routledge, 1996.

A substantial body of knowledge has emerged in anthropology on the basis of Robertson's[5] and Turner's[6] writings on the politics of nostalgia, concerning the postcolonial state, groups within states and the constitution of the individual subject. Werbner[7] shows how the Zimbabwean state is wrestling with the issue of how to remember those who died in the liberation struggle in a way that corresponds with the creation of a national heroic identity. This crisis of memory is controlled by the Zimbabwean state, which in turn attempts to supervise the access of ethnic groups to state commemoration. Others emphasise projects of individuality that are fuelled by the nostalgic process of memory and forgetting as a counterforce to the encroachment of modernity in society.[8] On this last issue, the work of Antze and Lambek[9] analyses the intervention of morality and religion. Basing their approach on psychoanalytic theory, they claim that modernity turns past, memory and remembrance into a painful and threatening experience that still haunts the individual and cannot be forgotten, that dominates one's life and cannot be fully ruptured. Modernity demands that people be in control of their pasts but has little to offer by way of coming to terms with temporality. Hence religion and morality can be seen as creating the ritual practices and discourses that negotiate with 'tense pasts' within the context of modernity.

This claim is particularly relevant for the new forms of charismatic Pentecostalism that have swept over Sub-Saharan Africa and have taken root in countries such as Malawi,[10] Ghana[11] and neighbouring

[5] Roland Robertson, 'After Nostalgia? Wilful Nostalgia and the Phases of Globalization' in B.S. Turner (ed.), *Theories of Modernity and Postmodernity*, London: Sage, 1990, pp. 45-62; *Globalization: Social Theory and Global Culture, idem* (Section 10: Globalization London: Sage, 1992and the Nostalgic Paradigm).

[6] Brian S. Turner, *Orientalism, Postmodernism and Globalism*, London: Routledge, 1994, (Section 9: Nostalgia, Postmodernism and the Critique of Mass Culture).

[7] Werber, *Memory and the Postcolony*.

[8] Marilyn Strathern, 'Nostalgia and the New Genetics' in D. Battaglia (ed.), *Rhetorics of Self-Making*, Berkeley: Univ. of California Press, 1995, pp. 97-121; Deborah Battaglia, 'On Practical Nostalgia: Self-Prospecting among Urban Trobrianders' in *ibid.*, pp. 77-97.

[9] Antze and Lambek, *Tense Past*.

[10] Rijk van Dijk, 'Young Puritan Preachers in Post-Independence Malawi', *Africa*, vol. 62, no. 2 (1992), pp. 159-81; Rijk van Dijk, 'Fundamentalism and its Moral Geography in Malawi: The Representation of the Diasporic and the Diabolical', *Critique of Anthropology*, vol. 15, no. 2 (1995), pp. 171-91; van Dijk, 'Pentecostalism, Cultural Memory'.

[11] Paul Gifford, *New Dimensions in African Christianity*, Ibadan (AACC); Sefer Books, 1993; Paul Gifford, 'Ghana's Charismatic Churches', *Journal of Religion in Africa*, vol. 24, no. 3 (1994), pp. 241-65; Gerrie ter Haar, 'Standing up for Jesus: A Survey of New Developments in Christianity in Ghana', *Exchange*, vol. 23, no. 3 (1994), pp. 221-40; Rijk van Dijk, 'From Camp to Encompassment: Discourses of Transsubjectivity in the Ghanaian Pentecostal Diaspora', *Journal of Religion in Africa*, vol. 27, no. 2 (1997), pp. 135-60; Rijk van Dijk, 'The Pentecostal Gift: Ghanaian Charismatic Churches and the Moral Innocence of the Global Economy', Paper presented at the 13th Satterthwaite Colloquium on African Religion and Ritual, Univ. of Manchester, 19-22 Apr. 1997; Birgit

countries.[12] This particular form of Christianity is very much the product of transnational and transcultural modernity; its doctrines and its 'crusade' slogans demand a complete break with the past.[13] Each individual's past must be publicly denounced so as to attain full membership and subsequently there is continuous inspection of that break. This rupture is vital in order for the 'born again' believer to be considered a modern person in control of and destiny, and no longer restrained by the binding threads that have been 'concocted' to trap the individual within 'tradition'.

Therefore, Pentecostalism in modern African societies is both a debate within modernity as well as a discourse on modernity. It deals with the predicament of many living in the urban areas of a country like Ghana who experience on a daily basis modernity's imbalances and inequalities, its dark sides and unfulfilled promises. In cities like Accra, Pentecostalism constructs itself in a pivotal position between, on the one hand, a modern, enticing transnational and transcultural world, and on the other a local world where it confronts 'tradition' and 'past' with its politics of anti-nostalgia. It presents a corridor to the global world and has developed intimate relations with the 'new diaspora' of Ghanaian migrants to the West. As Pentecostalism appears to cut across national and cultural borders, it can best be studied within the context of an anthropology of transnationalism.[14] This approach investigates how identities are formed in situations where, as a result of diasporic flows, communities arise that neither seem to have a firm 'geographical' anchor nor the means to create the individual as a local, cultural subject.[15]

Meyer, ' "If you are a Devil you are a Witch and if you are a Witch you are a Devil": the Integration of "Pagan" Ideas into the Conceptual Universe of Ewe Christians in Southeastern Ghana', *Journal of Religion in Africa*, vol. 22, no. 2 (1992), pp. 98-132; Birgit Meyer, 'Translating the Devil: An African Appropriation of Pietist Protestantism; the Case of the Peki Ewe in Southeastern Ghana, 1847-1992', PhD diss., Univ. of Amsterdam, 1995; Meyer, 'Make a Complete Break'.

[12] Mathew A. Ojo, 'The Contextual Significance of the Charismatic Movements in Independent Nigeria' *Africa*, vol. 58, no. 2 (1988), pp. 175-92; Ruth Marshall, 'Power in the Name of Jesus', *Review of African Political Economy*, no. 52, 1991, pp. 21-38.

[13] Van Dijk, 'Pentecostalism, Cultural Memory'; Meyer, 'Make a Complete Break'.

[14] Arjun Appadurai, 'Global Ethnoscapes: Notes and Queries for a Transnational Anthropology' in Richard G. Fox (ed.), *Recapturing Anthropology: Working in the Present*, Santa Fe, NM: School of American Research Press, 1991, pp. 191-210; Nina Glick Schiller *et al.*, *Towards a Transnational Perspective on Migration: Race, Class, Ethnicity and Nationalism Reconsidered*, New York: New York Academy Series, 1992; Linda Basch *et al.*, *Nations Unbound: Transnational Projects, Postcolonial Predicaments and Deterritorialized*, Reading: Gordon & Breach, 1994; James Clifford, 'Diasporas', *Cultural Anthropology*, vol. 9, no. 3, 1994, pp. 302-38.

[15] Arjun Appadurai, 'The Production of Locality' in Richard Fardon (ed.), *Counterworks: Managing the Diversity of Knowledge*, London: Routledge, 1995, pp. 204-26; David Scott, 'That Event, This Memory: Notes on the Anthropology of African Diasporas in the New World', *Diaspora*, vol. 1, no. 3 (1991), pp. 261-84.

In this paper I will develop some of the insights that deal with the construction of individuality within modernity, and with the role that is played by transnational religion, in this case, Pentecostalism.[16] The debates on memory and nostalgia frequently examine the ways modernity promotes the transformation from dividuality to individuality,[17] from identity as shared by others to an identity that becomes 'free' from such constraints and relations. Pentecostalism appears to speak the language of liberating a person from a past where identity is locked in bonds relating to a certain social-cultural environment and to a web of local kinship relations. It is a part of modernity's relentless confrontation with a past that binds a person to the family, its ancestors and their curses. It proclaims 'progress' and 'prosperity' to be dependent on the outward rejection or at least the moral control of such relations. However, I will argue that one must adopt this position with caution, as the modes of the construction of subjectivity or, to invoke Foucault,[18] the technologies of the self, need to be explored within their cultural contexts. It would be a mistake to perceive and understand Pentecostalism exclusively on the basis of freeing the subject from the past by means of a singular and monolithic move towards individuality. In the urban areas of Ghana, Pentecostalism is not singular in its technology of the self; instead it seems to offer a plurality of *technologies* that varyingly stress dividuality and individuality as the ultimate aim of its religious/moral programme. I will begin by examining the urban forms of Pentecostalism in Ghana, then continue by locating them within a diasporic, transnational context; and finally conclude by discussing the constitution of the subject within these various modes. The conclusion includes observations about this paper's contribution to the study of time and temporality as applied to the role of religion in a globalising world.

Some dimensions of urban Pentecostalism in Ghana

As a general category, Pentecostalism has become the most popular form of Christianity in Ghana over the last twenty years. Between 1987 and 1992 the number of Pentecostal churches has grown by as much as 43%. Although there are many different forms of Pentecostalism, and not

[16] Susanne Rudolph and James Piscatori, *Transnational Religion and Fading States*, Boulder, CO: Westview Press, 1997.

[17] Douglas Kellner, 'Popular Culture and the Construction of Postmodern Identities' in Scott Lash and Jonathan Friedman (eds), *Modernity and Identity*. Oxford: Blackwell, 1992, pp. 141-77; Michael Lambek and Andrew Strathern (eds), *Bodies and Persons: Comparative Perspectives from Africa and Melanesia*, Cambridge University Press, 1998; Richard Werbner, 'Introduction' in R.P. Werbner and T. Ranger (eds), *Postcolonial Identities in Africa*, London: Zed Books, 1996, pp. 3-26; Antze and Lambek, *Tense Past*.

[18] Michel Foucault, 'Technologies of the Self' in Luther H. Martin (ed.), *Technologies of the Self. A Seminar with Michel Foucault*, London: Tavistock, 1988, pp. 114-31.

all of these are gaining popularity at the same rate, recent figures do show a marked increase in the spread of Pentecostalism throughout rural and urban Ghana. The Church of Pentecost is one of the oldest Pentecostal denominations. According to the National Church Survey, it has now become the largest single church with a steady adult membership of nearly 260,000 people belonging to just under 3,600 congregations (by comparison: the Presbyterian Church has a steady membership of about 180,000, divided across 1,900 assemblies). Pentecostalism in Ghana has also been 'institutionalised' through the founding of an umbrella organisation called the Ghana Pentecostal Council that now serves more than 120 Pentecostal churches. Many of these churches belong to what became known as the 'second Pentecostal wave' that has swept through Africa since the 1970s, and has led to the emergence, particularly in the urban areas, of a newer, charismatic type of Pentecostalism. These churches, such as Dr Mensa Otabil's International Central Gospel Church and Bishop Duncan Williams' Christian Action Faith Ministries, were founded in the late 1970s, and quickly attracted many members among a young and urban middle class seeking both success and prosperity in life.[19] This popular, second wave of Pentecostalism both followed and continued a process that can be described as the indigenisation of earlier mission-based Pentecostalism.[20] Missionary Pentecostalism was introduced to Ghana during the first three decades of this century and took root by the founding of churches such as the Assemblies of God and the Apostolic Church from England and the United States. Though it is sometimes viewed as belonging to the many so-called spirit-healing churches that emerged at roughly the same time,[21] differences in terms of ritual discourse and practices meant that eventually Pentecostalism took a different path from these other independent churches. In contrast to the new type of Pentecostalism, the spirit-healing churches are dwindling in number and their presence in urban areas has become negligible.

In their relations with various other forms of Christianity, the Pentecostal churches have engaged in a cultural dialectic on two fronts. First, they have challenged mainstream Christianity on the perception of evil, on the diabolisation of key elements of the cosmology and on the way to counteract witchcraft and evil spirits. Mainstream Christianity (Presbyterianism, Catholicism, Methodism and Anglicanism) has preferred to deny the existence of witchcraft (*bayi*) and has rejected the power of spirits (*adze*), amulets (*asuman*), and traditional healing practices as being mere superstition. It has absolutely refused to accommodate or

---

[19] Gifford, 'Ghana's Charismatic Churches'; Van Dijk, 'From Camp to Encompassment'; Van Dijk, 'The Pentecostal Gift'.

[20] Meyer, 'Translating the Devil'.

[21] Robert W. Wyllie, *Spiritism in Ghana: A Study of New Religious Movements*, AAR Studies in Religion, no. 21, Missoula: Scholars Press, 1980.

absorb any of the elements of African cosmology in order to save the pure faith from being contaminated by devilish and occult forces. The development of independent African Christianity and its diverse forms of spirit-healing churches can be interpreted as a process of coming to terms with the powers that mainstream Christianity denied and ignored, and as a way of providing individual members with healing and protection. While including Christian doctrines, churches such as the Nazarene Healing Church and the Musama Disco Christo Church provided healing through a range of objects and substances that clearly originated from ritual practices rooted in the veneration of *abosom* (family and ancestral spirits) and their worship through the shrine-priests (*okomfoo*). The use of herbs, candles, oils, baths, concoctions, magical rings and the like were very much a part of this world and were included in the spirit-healing churches' symbolical repertoires.

However, the Pentecostal churches engaged in a second dialectic with respect to these churches, as they could not accept practices that would signal the continuation of a cultural past that would make the church vulnerable to attacks from the Devil and his many demons. Ancestral spirits, witches and ritual practices that related to veneration and protection were consequently classified as demonic and were diabolised.[22] Healing and deliverance from such powers can only take place through the 'blood of Christ', the laying-on of hands and ecstatic prayer sessions in which the presence of the Holy Spirit is manifest through speaking in tongues (in Twi *kasa foforoo*). Objects and substances that relate to a cultural past are not allowed within its ritual practice and discourse. So while the mission-based Pentecostal churches started around 1950 to Africanise leadership and forms of worship, their own distinctive ways of dealing with evil forces in society grew in importance. This approach contradicted mainstream Christianity which denied the reality of these forces and opposed the spirit-healing churches' 'demonic' practices. It is important to note that while the Pentecostal churches grew in strength, the spirit-healing churches became weaker and less appealing and were less able to adjust to the changing fortunes of Ghanaian society as it entered a global system.

Although the older Pentecostal churches were clearly represented in Ghana's urban areas and could claim international links through their overseas branches, the new type of charismatic Pentecostal churches made internationalism their hallmark.[23] In Accra and Kumasi, churches were adding terms such as 'international', global' and 'world' to their names, thus promising a religiously inspired access to transnationalism.[24]

---

[22] Meyer, 'If you are a Devil'.

[23] Van Dijk, 'From Camp to Encompassment'; Gifford, 'Ghana's Charismatic Churches'.

[24] Examples include the well known International Central Gospel Church, the Global Revival Outreach Ministry, the Harvest Ministries International and the World Miracle

Furthermore, this new Pentecostalism appeared to be strongly inspired by the 'personalism' of American Fundamentalism and some of its charismatic leaders. A type of charismatic Pentecostalism has emerged that emphasises personalism in worship, leadership and organisation. Firmly located in the prosperity gospel, it propounds the notion of the individual's combined spiritual and socio-economic success. Leaders present themselves as people who emanate charismatic power, and who demonstrate acumen in business relationships.

Another salient feature from the mid-1980s onwards has been these churches' international self-presentation. The 'global claim' has become prominent. It shows that, unlike most spirit-healing churches, they can extend beyond Ghana and Ghanaian and West-African culture. Consequently, they have actively sought to enter other cultural contexts and have ascribed them a place in their ideology, organisation and subsequent religious experience. The claim is not simply that Ghana is 'too small a place for our message', but that entering other cultural contexts deepens, enriches and essentialises the religious experiences of Pentecostal communities. Operating from Accra or Kumasi, these churches began setting up branches outside Ghana, particularly in Western Europe and the US. Pentecostalism has connected with the 'new' African diaspora through its message for a mobile urban population eager to participate in a transnational movement.

Representing the diaspora

More than 12 per cent of the Ghanaian population is estimated to be presently living abroad[25] and the ambition of many young urbanites is to participate in intercontinental labour migration. Major communities of Ghanaians can be found in the US and the UK, in other Western European countries such as Germany and the Netherlands[26] and within the Western African region itself. These communities tend to maintain close links with Ghana and relatives living in Ghana, and this desire to establish a circulating movement of people is also an important part of the new Pentecostal churches. These churches have many connections with international Pentecostal circles that create an intensive exchange of people and materials both to and from Ghana. Conversely, some Pentecostal churches that have been founded in the Ghanaian diaspora ploughed their

---

Church. In some of these churches, their international approach is represented symbolically by placing flags near the pulpit from each country where branches have been established.

[25] Margaret Peil, 'Ghanaians Abroad', *African Affairs*, vol. 94, no. 326, 1995, pp. 345-67.

[26] Kwame Nimako, *Nieuwkomers in een 'gevestigde' samenleving: een analyse van de Ghanese gemeenschap in Zuidoost (Amsterdam)*, Gemeente Amsterdam, report to Stadsdeel Zuidoost, 1993; Gerrie Ter Haar, 'Strangers in the Promised Land: African Christians in Europe', *Exchange*, vol. 24, no. 1 (1995), pp. 1-33; Van Dijk, 'From Camp to Encompassment'.

way back to Ghana. In other words, alongside Ghanaian-based Pentecostal churches that have been set up among Ghanaian communities in Amsterdam, London or Hamburg, full-fledged diaspora Pentecostal churches originated with no formal links with Ghana. Pentecostalism has become a transnational phenomenon, which in its modern forms is reproduced in its local diversity through a highly accelerated circulation of goods, ideas and people. It has formed a moral and physical geography whose domain is one of transnational cultural inter-penetration and flow as created and recreated through travel and encounter.

There are approximately twenty-five Ghanaian Pentecostal churches in the Netherlands, with sizeable Ghanaian migrant communities found in Amsterdam, The Hague and Rotterdam.[27] They vary in membership from fifty to 600 adults and include both legal and illegal immigrants. In The Hague, which is the location of one half of my multi-sited research (the other being in Accra), six Pentecostal churches are currently operating in a community of (officially) 2,000 adults. Three of these churches have direct links with churches in Accra while the other three were founded in The Hague during the late 1980s. Styles of ritual practice, worship, the elements of personalism and international linkage echo what can be observed in Accra among these churches and therefore create a deep sense of transnational continuity, global unity and exchange, and direct accessibility for the Ghanaian immigrant.

However, there is a second domain of Pentecostal involvement in transnational relations that is quite distinct from these charismatic Pentecostal churches. While the charismatic Pentecostal churches have become important in the overseas communities, back home in Ghana what are known as 'prayer-camps'[28] have developed an influential relationship with the diaspora. Throughout Ghana, though usually at a close distance to urban areas, prayer camps are located where people can stay and have their personal problems attended to in a spiritual way. These prayer-camps are visited daily by hundreds of people. The largest prayer camp in the country is the one at Edumfa, near Cape Coast, and is led by the seventy-four-year-old Prophetess Grace Mensah. It received more than 75,000 visitors in 1996 of whom the majority stayed at the camp for seven days or more.

Guided by a charismatic leader, visitors come together on a daily basis for ecstatic prayers, spiritual healing sessions and periods of fasting. The problems that people present are numerous and range from unemployment to infertility, attacks from witchcraft, illness, misfortune and marital problems.[29] In addition, many younger people visit and stay at these camps

[27] Ter Haar, 'Strangers in the Promised Land'.

[28] Van Dijk, 'From Camp to Encompassment'.

[29] See also reports by Ghanaian authors: Francis Akwaboah, *Bewitched*, Ophwim, Kumasi: Christian Hope Ministry Press, 1994; Opoku Onyinah, *Overcoming Demons*, Accra: Pentecost Press, 1995.

in search of spiritual solutions to the problems they must overcome in order to participate in intercontinental migration. It is extremely difficult to obtain the visas, passports and work permits that are needed for emigrating to Western Europe and America, and therefore these young people feel that their desire for wealth and success is being frustrated. Many of these visitors share a widely held desire to travel to the West in order to escape from poverty. The blockage in participating in emigration is mainly perceived as a spiritual problem that is caused by evil spirits and witchcraft emanating from within the circle of the extended family. As will be subsequently discussed in greater detail, deliverance from these malign powers results in obtaining the much desired passport from a Western embassy. Praying and fasting for this objective at a prayer camp can be interpreted on the basis of the promise of transnational and transcultural location that these camps appear to hold and to proclaim. In many ways, they act as a window on the world. Although most of these camps have been incorporated into the larger and older denominational Pentecostal churches, such as the Church of Pentecost or the Christ Apostolic Church, nonetheless these camps and their leaders generally maintain their independent ways and channels of linking up with transnational connections. The leaders receive financial support from those followers who have managed to travel abroad.[30] In addition, followers in the West who become ill, or who suffer misfortune that is apparently caused by the spirit world and malevolent afflictions, can return to these camps for healing and deliverance.

Interestingly, charismatic Pentecostal churches have not been pursuing the approach of establishing or incorporating prayer camps; rather they are often quite critical of the way in which these camps function. Therefore, prayer camps have not been established in the diaspora and, as we will see in the next section, these diasporic charismatic churches have developed a different attitude towards deliverance. Although deliverance is the most important context for the constitution of persons as individual members of many of these churches in Ghana, these churches' 'technology of the self' is dominated by a different perspective in the diaspora.

Transnational technologies of the self

Deliverance has become the hallmark of many Pentecostal churches in Ghana's urban areas. Sermons often proclaim that people must be delivered from the powers of Satan which hold people trapped in bonds with demonic spirits and forces. These demonic forces are active within society at large and, more particularly, within the individual's immediate circle of family relationship. Deliverance (*ogyee*) should be preceded by 'breaking' (*obubu*): the spiritual breaking of the bonds that trap people in

---

[30] Van Dijk, 'From Camp to Encompassment'.

their past, in their upbringing within the family circle where the ancestors are venerated at family shrines through the practices of the shrine priests (*okomfoo*). Name-giving, outdooring (a ritual for new-borns), initiation, healing and all the other rituals performed at important events in an individual's life may signal the threads that bind that person to the family spirits which in turn, according to Pentecostal discourses, provoke danger and impurity.

Most churches include deliverance ministries that cater to 'breaking' with the past. 'Make a complete break with the past' is an often heard cry in the context of these ministries that serve within the churches' structure.[31] This break with the past operates on two levels: within individuals' personal lifestyles their engagement with present-day society may lead confirmed believers to become trapped in moral wrongdoing, consisting in the eyes of the Pentecostal leaders of a long list of evil practices, attitudes, and personal conduct. Specifically this includes drinking, stealing, other forms of criminality, greed and poverty, rudeness, envy and hatred. These are all re-defined in Pentecostal ideology as resulting from evil spirits or even as spirits manifesting themselves in these forms. Therefore, becoming Born Again is often portrayed as a battle between individuals and their immediate past. Even when they have rejected all these vices Born Agains are advised to remain alert as 'the Devil is shrewd' and may deceive a person in moments of weakness.

However, on a deeper level, the deliverance from one's ancestral past confronts the bondage of the *'longue durée'*. The past lives of parents, grandparents and great-grandparents are to be inspected for the sins that have been committed in the past. Any person alive today may be haunted by ancestral curses that create recurrent problems in terms of the bloodline in the present: families and individuals may experience problems with childbirth, and afflictions caused by ancestral spirits or other evil spirits that take the form of possession, madness and nightmares. Witchcraft is also seen as directly affecting blood-lines and kinship, emanating from within the circle of the family. According to Pentecostal ideology, these ancestral curses result from blood covenants that have been established in the past by devilish powers. To obtain control over dark forces, those forces that remain unseen but are very much part of the world of witchcraft and evil spirits, is regarded as involving a 'Devil's Contract' which means the sacrifice of a close relative, such as a son or a daughter, so as to make the covenant with the evil spirits or to be able to partake in the witches' affairs. In Pentecostal moral thinking, these blood covenants are the ancestral curses that are difficult to escape, ties and bonds that cannot be cut, that entrap and control, and cause all kinds of problems, afflictions, misfortune and evil in the present.

---

[31] Meyer, 'Make a Complete Break'.

For most Born Agains, it is not enough to follow the Pentecostal doctrine of stopping various forms of ancestral veneration such as the pouring of libations at name-giving ceremonies, at initiation ceremonies and at funerals. Even confirmed Born Again believers may still feel haunted by ancestral curses and may therefore encounter the problems, afflictions and misfortune that result from their past and from the web of social relations and commitments that tie a person to the family. As emphasised by deliverance rituals, the answer is a complete break with the past; that often means breaking with the blood tie that binds a person to an ancestral curse which is still operating from the past through the living relatives in the present. Therefore, a complete break with the past usually implies complete break with the family and this subsequently means rejecting those rituals such as initiation ceremonies and funerals that emphasise the connection with a family's bounded past.

Deliverance appears to emphasise a form of individuality whereby, on the level of both the immediate past and the *longue durée*, ties are being cut. There is a constant sealing off from those influences, circles and family ties that would make the individual prone to evil again. However, we will return to the issue of individuality later. Breaking and deliverance are therefore seen as key elements in the Pentecostal ritual structure. They occur in a variety of contexts and take different forms but are all geared towards the 'processing' of the person as a modern individual where modernity's connotation of ideology is that of being superior to inferior powers of tradition and the past.

Deliverance can take place during church services where people are invited to testify and are then touched by the Pentecostal leader so that the power of the Holy Spirit becomes manifestly present in each person's mind and body. People who step forward for 'anointing' will writhe on the ground, and sweat profusely as if battling with the forces that are to be driven out of the body. 'Breaking' is not easy; it can be agonising and exhausting, and results in people testifying to the rupture that they experienced on such occasions. Although shouts and cries are a common part of the 'breaking' of evil powers, supposed to take place under the loud exclamations of the name of Jesus, in some places people also shout out the main cause of the problem that is haunting them. In this way, deliverance takes the form of public penitence, turning into the open what once was hidden and from which the person longs to be freed.

In some ways the deliverance practices of the charismatic Pentecostal churches are based on and correspond to those of the prayer camps. Deliverance and breaking rituals offered to a large public almost on a daily basis are the prayer camps' *raison d'être*. In fact 'breakings' are the central activity of well-known, internationally operating prayer camps, such as the Bethel Prayer Ministries in Sunyani. A distinction is made between what are called 'local breakings' and 'international breakings'. Local breakings are regularly held at the camp and are geared towards demonstrating the power of deliverance on a national level. They are set in an atmosphere of excitement, and the media are invited to the camp to witness how 'breaking' restores health, happiness and fortune to those who step forward for healing and deliverance. The magazine *Bethel News* and some newspapers will regularly publish photographs of 'miracles': of how at these occasions the crippled threw away their crutches and the deaf regained their hearing. Generally, people come from throughout Ghana to participate in these local breakings.

However, international breakings are major events and always involve the leader/founder of the Bethel Prayer Ministries because he possesses the most effective and 'penetrating' charismatic powers. At international breakings, people from abroad are invited to come and attend. Through the camps' international linkages, special efforts are made to fly them in to Ghana. These breakings are publicised on an international level and are advertised in all the local media. Afterwards there are reports not only in the *Bethel News* but also on television and in international newspapers as well. As I demonstrated in an earlier article,[32] camp leaders have become both wealthy and influential personalities in Ghanaian society and this can cause problems and resentment within the church structure to which some of them are affiliated. The criticism by some of the Pentecostal leaders of the charismatic churches of this type of deliverance ritual however goes beyond such issues of money and power. Instead it concerns the 'techniques' of constituting the person as an individual, freed of the ancestral curses that seem to haunt him or her and for which deliverance was sought. These 'techniques' differ as do the discourses that produce them.

Techniques within the Pentecostal technology of the self

Meyer[33] rightly asserts the importance of questionnaires which people must fill out when they enter prayer camps in search of deliverance. These questionnaires usually cover an extremely detailed range of issues that the person is required to answer so as to be referred to the right person at the camp to deal with the problem. The general tone in which the questionnaires are cast is one in which the person is asked to scrutinise his or her past for any experience, any bit of information which may lead to a recollection and assessment of past life events. For instance, questions relate to initiation ceremonies the person has been through, to the family 'stools' where ancestors reside and shrine priests perform their rituals of ancestral veneration, to ritual baths a person may have taken, and to herbs, concoctions and incense that have been administered to the person for

[32] Van Dijk, 'From Camp to Encompassment'.
[33] Meyer, 'Make a Complete Break'.

purposes of healing and appeasement. The variety of questions is enormous and demonstrates the Pentecostal leaders' ability to penetrate the various strata of Ghanaian culture. Beyond that, they also show skill at evoking a remembrance of a personal past which subsequently is controlled, inspected and finally rejected by Pentecostalism. It is a remembrance that may have been partially forgotten, but with a power that still affects the present through the workings of the ancestors and must therefore be overcome.

The message, as Meyer states,[34] is that it is impossible to inscribe oneself fully in the present – by being born again – without being disrupted by an unremembered past. The remembrance of the past, as evoked by questionnaires, aims at counteracting this force so that the person can proceed in taking full control of his or her personal life. Therefore, some prayer camps, like the Healing Hope Prayer Camp at Ophwim near Kumasi (see the writings of its leader Akwaboah[35]) use 'counter'-baths to undo the power of ritual baths that may have been taken in the context of healing practices of some of the spirit-healing churches in the past. Hence, the person is being processed from the past so as to sever whatever still binds him or her to a life dominated by family blood-ties. As most of the records show, in which the names of all admitted to the camps are recorded, one of the main reasons for seeking healing and admission to the camp is to be 'protected' from the family (*banbo*). Prayer camp leaders would therefore claim that their 'breakings' and deliverance practices can liberate the person. Hence, prayer camps introduce the person to transnational and transcultural relations as an emergent stranger; as somebody detached from the bonds with the family, as protected from witchcraft and envy emanating from that circle of relatives and therefore unconstrained in the attempts to 'make it to the West', to 'get the papers' and to become prosperous. Real progress can only be made through controlling social commitments and relations that derive their force from the past. The prayer camps' discourse promotes a sense of strangerhood that starts at home and serves as a preparation and incubation to what they might expect when they travel to the West. Although support groups of the prayer camps have been formed in the West, in the process of travelling individuality is encountered. Aspiring migrants are entirely on their own and therefore require all the bodily empowerment and protection that the camp can offer.

However, leaders of charismatic Pentecostal churches in the diaspora react very differently to the individuality of the traveller who has left Ghana for the West. First of all, they accuse the prayer camps of lacking 'spiritual coverage'. By this accusation they mean that the camps' spiritual care for its visitors ends as soon the person walks out of the gate.

[34] *Ibid.*, p. 192.
[35] Akwaboah, *Bewitched.*

Spiritual care is terminated once the miracle has been performed or healing or protection have been provided. They feel that nobody at the camp is really interested in what happens to people afterwards: whether they indeed have been able to reach the West and how they achieved this. By contrast, the charismatic church leaders try to include new members in their own personalistic networks, to engage actively in face to face relations with them and to obtain a rather penetrating level of knowledge about their private lives. Thus if a member wishes to travel from Ghana to, for instance, the Netherlands, letters announcing his or her arrival will be sent from the church in Ghana to branches in places like The Hague or Amsterdam. Joining these churches is seen as entering a personalistic yet transnational circle where charismatic leaders maintain close and direct links. The 'spiritual coverage', so to speak, travels with people as they cross transnational and transcultural borders and there is therefore much less a sense of making somebody 'a stranger already at home'. Instead, in the diaspora, as soon as a person belongs to such a personalistic network, the local leader will feel responsible for that member. He may contact the local authorities on their behalf, may find them a place to stay and perhaps provide a circle of friends so that the side-effects of being a stranger in a host society are mitigated.

The second main difference between the prayer camp practices and those of the majority of the churches in the diaspora is that the latter usually place less emphasis on deliverance and remembrance. Large-scale public 'breakings' simply do not take place and the deliverance ceremonies of wider importance are only held when a well known charismatic leader happens to visit the Netherlands. Half of The Hague's charismatic churches are not even interested in deliverance and seem to concur with the critical views on this practice that are expressed in Ghana as well. Unlike the prayer camps, there is very little emphasis on filling out of questionnaires. This also means that these churches in the diaspora maintain a different position on remembering and rejecting a past as the royal road to individuality and individual progress. Although a person's past still remains a matter of some concern there is less ambivalence about the paradox which emphasises that what 'produced' the person in terms of previous experiences and family history (and which are invoked and remembered through ritual practice) are at the same time the things that should be rejected. Instead, for diaspora leaders the ambivalence seems to focus on individuality and the ways in which the person appears to be 'created' by the desire for immediate and future rewards, wealth and prosperity through living in the West. Individuality is time and again transformed into new dividuality where church-members are expected to define their identities in terms of what is shared by the leader. In The Hague, leaders are deeply involved with the personal lives of most of their members. Therefore, these churches only have a modest membership and a kind of 'division of labour' between leaders is maintained. People will identify themselves to one another metonymically by referring to the leader's name, saying 'I belong to Pastor D. or to Pastor S.', without mentioning the name of the church. Leaders are expected to be involved with personal problems and particularly with regard to what authorities may demand in the Dutch host society in terms of permits, passports and housing. Marriages, funerals and 'outdooring' (a ritual for new-born babies) are all areas where the leader's direct involvement and 'spiritual coverage' are required. Leaders refer to themselves as 'surrogate *abusua panyin*' which denotes the head of the family within the matrilineal extended family system of the Akan. In this sense, both in terms of discourse and practice the leaders and the churches are eager to construct a new dividuality, a context of identification where there are moments for binding one's identity to these social relations. The combination of social control extended by the churches, and their sheer success in dealing with personal problems in which they show great acumen, turn them into places where a new web replaces a former web of social relations that restricted a person to blood-lines and the power of the ancestors.

Any talk and public questioning of a person's past is taboo. For the majority of Ghanaian migrants in the Netherlands the past is a painful and sensitive terrain full of dangers regarding their present status in Dutch society. An obvious reason for this is that most migrants have had problems with obtaining residence permits at some point in time. In other words, they have experienced periods of illegality or have had to go to court to fight for a permit. Painful memories can also include periods of hardship that men and women have gone through so as to survive while illegal. Criminal trade and trafficking, prostitution and marriages of convenience may have been a part of the coping strategies that migrants have been forced to deploy during such intervals. This is reflected by a recent novel that contains autobiographical material about a Ghanaian woman who migrated to Germany but ended up working as a prostitute during her first years as an illegal alien.[36]

These churches preach the message that anybody is welcome, irrespective of their history, and that no one will be asked to reveal their past in writing, through questionnaires or any form of deliverance ritual. Leaders are expected not to involve themselves with dealing with the past but to concentrate on the present and immediate future circumstances. These churches also preach to the transnational travellers that real progress and prosperity cannot be attained by those who intend to remain locked in ultimate and extreme individuality (such as prostitution) within a host society where otherwise social relations are difficult to establish (the

---

[36] Amma Darko, *Beyond the Horizon* (novel), Oxford: Heinemann African Writers series, 1995.

language barrier is one of the obvious obstacles here). Dividuality is the key to success; a dividuality for which Pentecostal doctrines and religious practice have determined the perimeters and requirements. Therefore, this dividuality is based on a prolonged 'initiation' into the Pentecostal circle that focuses on extensive teaching and counselling. In addition, Bible schools, church classes, prayer circles, and all-night vigils are a common part of Pentecostal practice, but here they are considered vital to the personal relationship and shared identity that must be established between members and their leaders.

The attachment to the Pentecostal leader as a mode of interacting with the host Dutch society is just one side of the coin. As the foundation for identity construction, this attachment also cements the maintenance of social relations in Ghana. The leader represents the embodiment of a 'corridor' and is expected to develop and maintain relations with similar Pentecostal leaders and circles in Ghana. Leaders from the Netherlands frequently travel to Ghana and visit places such as Accra and Kumasi, where most of the immigrants in the Netherlands originally come from. Immigrants who then visit Ghana find it easy to access Pentecostal circles in these cities, as I myself have witnessed many times, and therefore have an environment at their disposal that can keep oppressive family relationships at bay. These visiting migrants, *burgers* or *bintoos* (from 'been to') as they are called, face the hardship in Ghana of being regarded the 'happy few' who have made it in life and are able to spend excessively. In other words, their attachment to the Pentecostal leader in the diaspora provides them with access to Pentecostalism in Ghana where blood-lines with their powers from the past are perceived as being fraught with danger, as relations that must be severed through deliverance so that the confirmed believer maintains his moral status and spiritual protection. Through the embodiment of the corridor, the spiritual coverage provided by the Pentecostal leaders in the diaspora refers back to the location where the desire for transnational travel actually originated.

This contribution has now turned full circle by starting in the context from which charismatic Pentecostalism arose to its advent and positioning in the diaspora and its return to what was left behind. I have tried to show that in this transnational but circular process, Pentecostalism cannot be viewed as a singular project of individuality that parallels expectations of encroaching modernity in African societies; instead different modalities seem to be present in the way that Pentecostalism has become a transnational and transcultural phenomenon. Although the emphasis is on deliverance in the Ghanaian context, which seems to suggest a singular move towards individuality, a severance of kinship ties, and a rejection of all those rituals (funerals, initiation, healing) that venerate the ancestors of the family, nonetheless other modalities do exist. There is criticism in Ghana of the 'emptiness' of deliverance, of the money-making that some leaders feel is behind such practices and of the personality cults that sometimes arise from these rituals. In the diaspora, the outward rejection of deliverance is largely based on the fact that an invocation of the past, the production of a remembrance of past experiences, is simply an area that is too sensitive to be disclosed. Instead a new form of dividuality is propagated in which the past is bracketed and is almost 'institutionally forgotten', to paraphrase a felicitous term coined by Douglas.[37]

Because of these painful experiences, some influential Pentecostal leaders in Ghana now openly discourage their younger members from participating in transnational migration. The desire to do so is publicly ridiculed, as I have witnessed myself, and in order to curb youthful pessimism concerning Ghana's limited opportunities for personal success, some of these churches are now operating their own scholarship and encouragement schemes. However, the success of these initiatives is doubtful as many young men still seek deliverance at one of the many prayer camps for the problems that they encounter in obtaining their 'papers'. Therefore the conclusion may be that as a discourse within modernity, Pentecostalism is engaging in a debate with itself, both at home and in the diaspora, as based on the different modalities it incorporates. Time, the conjectures of memory, remembrance, nostalgia and utopia in both settings appear to surface in these modalities in different ways. This has led me to conclude that a singular project of the transformation of dividuality into individuality, which modernity appears to prescribe, does not exist in Pentecostalism. Particularly in the diaspora, time and temporality may rather serve an opposite trajectory.

---

[37] Mary Douglas, 'Forgotten Knowledge', in M. Strathern (ed.), *Shifting Contexts. Transformations in Anthropological Knowledge,* London: Routledge, 1995, pp. 13-31.

BIBLIOGRAPHY

Adjaye, Joseph K., (ed.), *Time in the Black Experience,* London: Greenwood Press, 1994.

Akwaboah, Francis, *Bewitched,* London/Ophwim, Kumasi: Christian Hope Ministry Press, 1994.

Antze, Paul and Michael Lambek (eds), *Tense Past: Cultural Essays in Trauma and Memory,* London: Routledge, 1996.

Basch, Linda, *et al.*, *Nations Unbound: Transnational Projects, Postcolonial Predicaments and Deterritorialized Nation-States,* Reading: Gordon & Breach, 1994.

Battaglia, Deborah (ed.), *Rhetorics of Self-Making,* Berkeley, CA: Univ. of California Press, 1995.

Bauman, Zygmunt, *Postmodern Ethics,* Oxford: Blackwell, 1993.

Darko, Amma, *Beyond the Horizon* (novel), Oxford: Heinemann (African Writers Series), 1995.

Fardon, Richard, (ed.), *Counterworks. Managing the Diversity of Knowledge*, London: Routledge, 1995.

Fox, Richard (ed.), *Recapturing Anthropology: Working in the Present*, Santa Fe, NM: School of American Research Press, 1991.

Gifford, Paul, *New Dimensions in African Christianity*, Ibadan (AACC): Sefer Books, 1993.

——, 'Ghana's Charismatic Churches', *Journal of Religion in Africa*, vol. 24, no. 3 (1994), pp. 241-65.

Glick Schiller, Nina, *et al.*, *Towards a Transnational Perspective on Migration: Race, Class, Ethnicity and Nationalism Reconsidered*, New York: New York Academy Series, 1992.

Lash, Scott and Jonathan Friedman (eds), *Modernity and Identity*, Oxford: Blackwell, 1992.

Marshall, Ruth, 'Power in the Name of Jesus'. *Review of African Political Economy*, no. 52, 1991, pp. 21-38.

Martin, Luther H. (ed.), *Technologies of the Self. A Seminar with Michel Foucault*, London: Tavistock, 1988.

Meyer, Birgit, ' "If you are a Devil you are a Witch and if you are a Witch you are a Devil": the Integration of "Pagan" Ideas into the Conceptual Universe of Ewe Christians in Southeastern Ghana', *Journal of Religion in Africa*, vol. 22, no. 2 (1992), pp. 98-132.

——, *'Translating the Devil*; An African Appropriation of Pietist Protestantism; the Case of the Peki Ewe in Southeastern Ghana, 1847-1992', PhD diss., Univ. of Amsterdam, 1995.

Nimako, Kwame, *Nieuwkomers in een 'gevestigde' samenleving: een analyse van de Ghanese gemeenschap in Zuidoost (Amsterdam)*, Gemeente Amsterdam, report to Stadsdeel Zuidoost, 1993.

Ojo, Mathew A., 'The Contextual Significance of the Charismatic Movements in Independent Nigeria', *Africa*, vol. 58, no. 2 (1988), pp. 175-92.

Onyinah, Opoku, *Overcoming Demons*, Accra: Pentecost Press, 1995.

Peil, Margaret, 'Ghanaians Abroad', *African Affairs*, vol. 94, no. 326, 1995, pp. 345-67.

Robertson, Roland, *Globalization: Social Theory and Global Culture*, London: Sage, 1992.

Rudolph, Susanne and James Piscatori, *Transnational Religion and Fading States*, Boulder, CO: Westview Press, 1997.

Scott, David, 'That Event, This Memory: Notes on the Anthropology of African Diasporas in the New World', *Diaspora*, vol. 1, no. 3 (1991), pp. 261-84.

Strathern, Marilyn (ed.), *Shifting Contexts. Transformations in Anthropological Knowledge*, London: Routledge, 1995.

Ter Haar, Gerrie, 'Standing up for Jesus: A Survey of New Developments in Christianity in Ghana', *Exchange*, vol. 23, no. 3 (1994), pp. 221-40.

——, 'Strangers in the Promised Land: African Christians in Europe', *Exchange*, vol. 24, no. 1 (1995), pp. 1-33.

Turner, Brian S. (ed.), *Theories of Modernity and Postmodernity*, London: Sage, 1990.

——, *Orientalism, Postmodernism and Globalism*, London: Routledge, 1994.

van Dijk, Rijk, 'Young Puritan Preachers in Post-Independence Malawi', *Africa*, vol. 62, no. 2 (1992), pp. 159-81.

———, 'Fundamentalism and its Moral Geography in Malawi: The Representation of the Diasporic and the Diabolical', *Critique of Anthropology*, vol. 15, no. 2, 1995, pp. 171-91.

———, 'From Camp to Encompassment: Discourses of Transsubjectivity in the Ghanaian Pentecostal Diaspora', *Journal of Religion in Africa*, vol. 27, no. 2, 1997, pp. 135-60.

———, 'The Pentecostal Gift: Ghanaian Charismatic Churches and the Moral Innocence of the Global Economy'. Paper presented at the 13th Satterthwaite Colloquium on African Religion and Ritual, Univ. of Manchester, 19-22 Apr. 1997.

Veer, Peter v.d., *Conversion to Modernities: the Globalization of Christianity*, London: Routledge, 1996.

Werbner, Richard P. (ed.), *Memory and the Postcolony*, London: Zed Books, Postcolonial Identities Series, 1998.

Wyllie, Robert W., *Spiritism in Ghana: A Study of New Religious Movements*, AAR Studies in Religion, no. 21, Missoula: Scholars Press, 1980.

THE QUEST FOR MISSIONARIES

TRANSNATIONALISM AND TOWNSHIP
PENTECOSTALISM IN MALAWI

Harri Englund

Surprising observations may result when the ethnographer considers how Pentecostal Christians understand the transnational underpinnings of their religious life. For the Pentecostal Christians of Chinsapo township in Lilongwe, Malawi's capital, two notions appear to condense important aspects of this understanding: mutual dependence and spiritual maturity. Mutual dependence is a moral condition where the acts of 'assistance' (*chithandizo* in Chichewa) and 'care' (*chisamalo*) are crucial to defining persons as born-again Christians. Spiritual maturity is a closely related notion, understood as the extent to which persons acknowledge in practice their this-worldly dependence on one another.

While 'assistance' and 'care' ought to define the work of missionaries, Chinsapo's Pentecostal Christians by no means take their missionaries' spiritual maturity for granted. The poorest congregations contemplate sending their members as far afield as Finland to convert natives of that country who would then come to Malawi as the congregation's missionaries. Missionaries, in other words, are *made*; they do not simply appear to assist a congregation in its material and spiritual life. Far from posing a challenge to 'connect' local congregations to translocal institutions, transnationalism, from this perspective, makes those local congregations centres where diverse interests and stages of spiritual development are exposed. Accordingly, the congregation keeps the missionary under constant surveillance, and a failure to fulfil the congregation's expectations rapidly invites subversive discourse.

Despite their active engagement in making and assessing missionaries, Pentecostal Christians in Chinsapo township might be seen to succumb to a general dependence on external assistance. In Malawi during the 1990s, this dependence seemed to affect every level of society, from President Bakili Muluzi who informed Malawians of the appeals he made for more aid during his visits abroad, to poor villagers who burdened their relatives in towns with requests for assistance. For citizens in many postcolonial African countries, foreign debt, persistent poverty and the uncertain success of political pluralism also entail nostalgia for the early postcolonial and even colonial pasts. Writing about young secondary school students in Zambia, Anthony Simpson describes 'a moral discourse of failure'[1] where students express 'an ambivalence towards, and even a rejection of, their negritude'.[2] It is a failure, so striking in Zambia's continuing economic and political ills, which students attribute to innate racial qualities, best circumvented by formal education and, according to some, born-again Christianity.

Among Pentecostal Christians in Chinsapo township, the optimism and self-confidence that the 'second birth' fosters are no less effective as antidotes against the 'moral discourse of failure'. However, it is important to understand the specific moral arguments which underlie their apparent dependence on foreign missionaries. On the one hand, the 'missionary' is a term which applies to people of every complexion and nationality, even Malawian. For some congregations without foreign missionaries, the 'missionary' is the most frequent and generous benefactor, usually a prominent businessman living elsewhere than in the township. On the other hand, despite rejecting, like Pentecostal Christians in many other African settings, 'black people's medicine' (*mankhwala achikuda*) as the work of the devil, Chinsapo's Pentecostal congregations see little sense in launching unqualified assaults on 'tradition' or 'village culture' as such.[3] The village of origin continues to play an important role in the lives of most Pentecostal Christians in Chinsapo township, in both material and spiritual respects.

These observations pave the way for an appreciation of complexities in Chinsapo's Pentecostal Christians' quest for missionaries. Far from associating spiritual maturity with foreign missionaries' complexion and wealth, Pentecostal Christians undermine dependence by allowing ambivalence in their attitudes towards *both* 'blacks' (*akuda*) *and* 'whites' (*azungu*). The connotations of these notions are highly contextual and patently not racial. *Mzungu wokuda*, 'black white' or 'black European', is an African whose life-style is seen to revolve around the imitation of white people, facilitated by superior access to material wealth and imported consumer goods. Depending on the context, such a person may be generally condemned as an embodiment of immorality and selfishness; alternatively, the very association with wealth and prosperity invites expectations of assistance and care, regardless of whether the *mzungu* is black or white. Analysis must, therefore, situate widely used notions in the practice of everyday life, and this chapter draws upon a method that seems conducive to such a task: the extended-case study.[4] Its focus on the course

[1] A. Simpson, 'Memory and Becoming the Chosen Other: Fundamentalist Elite-Making in a Zambian Catholic Mission School' in R. Werbner (ed.), *Memory and the Postcolony: African Anthropology and the Critique of Power*, London: Zed Books, 1998, p. 209.

[2] *Ibid.*, p. 218.

[3] On such assaults among young born-again preachers in Blantyre, see R.A. van Dijk, 'Young Puritan Preachers in Post-Independence Malawi', *Africa*, vol. 62, 1992, pp. 159-81, and 'Fundamentalism and Its Moral Geography in Malawi: The Representation of the Diasporic and the Diabolical', *Critique of Anthropology*, vol. 15, 1995, pp. 171-91.

of events and relationships among particular persons is relatively silent on the theoretical assumptions as to how practice is to be understood. The approach in this chapter attempts to avoid the fallacy of much inter-actionist analysis which substitutes maximising individuals for persons embedded in social relationships.[5] Relationships both motivate and constrain persons.

The focus on the dynamic of personal relationships might seem in-compatible with the current academic discourse on transnationalism. After all, the key contribution of this discourse is to show how travelling and the electronic media expand the scope of social interaction so that part of one's social network is always *elsewhere* than oneself.[6] However, it is important not to confuse transnationalism with globalisation, be-cause their studies may require distinct methodologies.[7] Some studies of 'transmigrants', for example, have been inspired by the extended-case method in earlier studies of the Zambian Copperbelt towns.[8] This meth-odological continuity serves as a warning against confusing issues which need further elaboration with those that are obsolete in anthropological research practice. For some anthropologists, it has become a common-place to distance oneself from a 'locality-obsessed anthropological tradition'[9] while, at the same time, retaining an analytical interest in the notion of 'locality'.[10] Abstract distinctions abound between local, national, transnational and global agents and relations, all analytical devices still firmly rooted in spatial metaphors.[11] Against that, this chapter's focus on

[4] The classic examples of the method include M. Gluckman, 'Analysis of a Social Situa-tion in Modern Zululand', *Bantu Studies*, vol. 14, 1940, pp. 1-30 and 147-74; and V.W. Turner, *Schism and Continuity in an African Society: A Study of Ndembu Village Life*, Manchester: Manchester University Press, 1957. More generally on the method, see J. van Velsen, 'The Extended-Case Method and Situational Analysis' in A.L. Epstein (ed.), *The Craft of Social Anthropology*, London: Tavistock, 1967; and M. Burawoy, 'The Extended-Case Method', *Sociological Theory*, vol. 16, 1998, pp. 4-33.

[5] Cf. B. Kapferer, 'Introduction: Transactional Models Reconsidered' in B. Kapferer (ed.), *Transaction and Meaning: Directions in the Anthropology of Exchange and Symbolic Behaviour*, Philadelphia, PA: Institute for the Study of Human Issues, 1976.

[6] See e.g. A. Appadurai, *Modernity at Large: Cultural Dimensions of Globalization*, Min-nesota: University of Minnesota Press, 1996; and U. Hannerz, *Transnational Connections: Culture, People, Places*, London: Routledge, 1996.

[7] N. Glick Schiller, 'The Situation of Transnational Studies', *Identities*, vol. 4, 1997, pp. 155-66.

[8] L. Basch, N. Glick Schiller and C. Szanton-Blanc, *Nations Unbound: Transnational Projects, Postcolonial Predicaments, and Deterritorialized Nation-States*, Longhorne, PA: Gordon & Breach, 1994, pp. 30-1.

[9] W. van Binsbergen, 'Globalization and Virtuality: Analytical Problems Posed by the Contemporary Transformation of African Societies', *Development and Change*, vol. 29, 1998, p. 874.

[10] Following, above all, Appadurai, *Modernity at Large*.

[11] See e.g. D. Mato, 'On Global and Local Agents and the Social Making of Transnational Identities and Related Agendas in "Latin" America', *Identities*, vol. 4, 1997, pp. 170-2.

relationships allows an appreciation of multiple translocal currents in the practice of particular persons.

The difference between transnationalism and globalisation is, of course, between phenomena as much as between methodologies. In Malawi, for example, Pentecostalism hardly provides a truly global space for people's lives. The country's poor links to the electronic means of mass mediation contrast with the diverse uses of the electronic media among Pentecostal congregations in countries like Ghana and Nigeria.[12] In Malawi, the only nationwide radio station has long been under tight government control; Malawi Television was launched only in 1999 and even then for viewers living within an 80 km. radius from the commercial city of Blantyre; the ownership of even a simple transistor radio indicates relative affluence among the urban and rural poor alike. Video and audio tapes, magazines and pamphlets are accessible through some Pentecostal congregations, but they become scarce resources in the overall poverty of the Malawian mass media. As such, in transnationalism, blockages are as important to understand as flows[13] and the transnational networks which Pentecostalism appears to support[14] are not always enabling and empowering. They may also generate new social hierarchies or reinforce existing discrepancies in access to wealth and authority.[15] By highlighting specific relationships, this chapter is able to show how the empowering aspects of transnationalism sometimes foster social exclusion under the conditions of Malawi at the dawn of the twenty-first century.

Poverty and Pentecostalism in Chinsapo township

Throughout its colonial and postcolonial history, Malawi, land-locked and apparently without significant mineral resources, has never enjoyed the same level of prosperity as many of its regional neighbours in southern Africa with resources ranging from Zambia's copper boom to Botswana's diamonds, from beef production in Zimbabwe and Namibia to South Africa's industries. Malawi's poverty has always been relatively severe by regional standards, making it more like the war-ravaged Mozambique and Angola despite its own tranquillity. Early in the colonial period, Malawi became an important source of labour for mines in South Africa and Zambia.[16]

---

[12] R.I.J. Hackett, 'Charismatic/Pentecostal Appropriation of Media Technologies in Nigeria and Ghana', *Journal of Religion in Africa*, vol. 28, 1998, pp. 258-77; and R. Marshall-Fratani, 'Mediating the Global and the Local in Nigerian Pentecostalism', *Journal of Religion in Africa*, vol. 28, 1998, pp. 278-315.

[13] P. Geschiere and B. Meyer, 'Globalization and Identity: Dialectics of Flow and Closure', *Development and Change*, vol. 29, 1998, pp. 601-15.

[14] H. Cox, *Fire from Heaven: The Rise of Pentecostal Spirituality in the Twenty-First Century*, London: Cassell, 1996.

[15] Marshall-Fratani, 'Mediating the Global', p. 294.

[16] J. Crush, A. Jeeves and D. Yudelman, *South Africa's Labour Empire: A History of Black Migrancy to the Gold Mines*, Boulder, CO: Westview, 1991.

After independence in 1964, male labour migration continued on a large scale until the early 1970s when the Malawian government abruptly ended it.[17] This intervention released labour to plantations in Malawi, most of them owned by a small ruling elite and characterised by appalling labour conditions akin to slavery. When the government continued to favour a development strategy based on large-scale agriculture, smallholders, the vast majority of the country's population, had no incentives to grow maize, the staple in many parts of the country, as a cash crop. Lack of industrial development has also kept the pace of urbanisation modest, with over eighty per cent of the population classified as rural.

Like many other countries in sub-Saharan Africa, Malawi underwent a transition to political pluralism in the early 1990s.[18] Kamuzu Banda, styled as 'Life-President', lost the first multiparty elections for over thirty years in 1994, and Bakili Muluzi with his United Democratic Front (UDF) assumed power. The aftermath of the transition witnessed intensifying economic crisis especially among the poor. The value of the Malawi kwacha plummeted on several occasions, bringing unprecedented levels of inflation. The new government embraced neoliberalism with enthusiasm and, among other things, removed subsidies on agricultural inputs, cut government spending and encouraged private investment in health care and education. In a clear ideological battle against the regulation and oligarchy of the Banda era,[19] it also promoted small-scale entrepreneurship as a development strategy. With successive bad harvests and over-priced inputs, many smallholders saw little alternative other than to take the new government's exhortations of entrepreneurship seriously. It is not clear how much the current efforts to make ends meet have contributed to urbanisation. An informed guess, given the predicament of inflation and bad harvests, would suggest widespread cyclical migration between town and country rather than permanent urbanisation.

Chinsapo township, the setting of fieldwork in 1996-7, illustrates the impact of the post-transition crisis on Malawi's poor. The township's increasing popularity among poor migrants made the Lilongwe City Council change the city boundaries in the early 1990s so that the township became a part of the Lilongwe Urban administrative unit. Settling in old Chewa villages, for the City Council township residents are 'squatters' in an 'unplanned' area. Residents nonetheless have access to

[17] J. Kydd and R. Christiansen, 'Structural Change in Malawi since Independence: Consequences of a Development Strategy Based on Large-Scale Agriculture', *World Development*, vol. 10, 1982, pp. 355-75. W.C. Chirwa, 'The Malawi Government and the South African Labour Recruiters, 1974-1992', *Journal of Modern African Studies*, vol. 34, 1996, pp. 623-42.

[18] K.M. Phiri and K.R. Ross (eds), *Democratization in Malawi: A Stock-Taking*, Blantyre: Claim, 1998.

[19] G.Z. Mhone (ed.), *Malawi at Crossroads: The Postcolonial Political Economy*, Harare: Sapes, 1992.

accommodation through complex local housing and land markets, the terms of their contracts ranging from clearly exploitative arrangements to informal agreements of mutual help between relatives and colleagues. Housing has retained a rural character, with communal rather than individual water points; electricity only became widely available after 1996. Self-employed entrepreneurs, low-ranking civil servants, semi-skilled labourers, watchmen and domestic servants comprise the bulk of the township's population. Chinsapo's continuing growth is evident in its expansion, indicating perhaps both overcrowding in Lilongwe's old townships and many urban dwellers' diminishing ability to afford higher quality housing.

Chinsapo township has residents from all the districts of Malawi and even abroad. This mixture ensures a wide range of religious and healing practices, with the Catholic Church, the Presbyterian Church of Central Africa (CCAP), the Seventh Day Adventist Church and a mosque standing amidst a sea of other Christian denominations, independent churches and the practices of various 'traditional' healers (*asing'anga*). The Pentecostal scene itself is no less complex, although Chinsapo's 'Pentecostals' (*anthu achipente*) often view themselves as 'relatives in the Spirit' (*azibale a mu Uzimu*) who have little doctrinal reason to maintain strict boundaries of church membership. Such assertions of commonality are, however, as situational as are their negations. The extent to which ecstatic outbursts of glossolalia and physical confusion are tolerated is one example of differences between Pentecostal churches in Chinsapo township. While all the churches accept the practice of speaking in tongues as a 'gift' (*mphatso*) in the born-again condition, prolonged glossolalia, often accompanied by violent physical movements, is condemned in some churches as evidence of Satanic influence while in other churches it is encouraged as a means of deliverance. Moreover, while all the churches view the second birth as a process rather than as a sudden conversion, some churches require more Bible-study than others before baptism.

Further differences between Chinsapo's Pentecostal churches can be seen in the sheer appearance of their buildings. The prominent buildings of the Assemblies of God, the Apostolic Faith Mission and the Pentecostal Holiness Church contrast with the humbler houses and huts of several independent Pentecostal churches, tangible evidence for incommensurate access to external sources of assistance. The township is, however, a somewhat artificial unit for all Pentecostal Christians, because many important functions take place in the headquarters or among larger congregations elsewhere in the city. Some churches, such as the Universal Church of the Kingdom of God, Living Waters and River of Life, have no church buildings or active congregational life within the township, even though many members of these churches live in Chinsapo.

The township is, of course, an especially artificial unit for those congregations which have missionaries. The foreign missionaries with whom Chinsapo's Pentecostal Christians have contact are from America, Europe, Brazil and South Africa, but none of the foreign missionaries lives in the township. Their visits to the township are rare, prompted by special ceremonies such as the opening of a new church or the funeral of a prominent church member. More often it is, instead, township dwellers who travel to see their missionaries. For some pastors, many of whom could not afford electricity in their own houses during 1996-7, their missionaries' residences provided the facilities of fax machines and electronic mail to communicate with spiritual relatives in other countries.

A further distinction could be made between those churches which expand, through migrants themselves, from the countryside to the city and those town-based churches which are in the process of 'planting churches' (*kubzala mipingo*) in both urban and rural areas. The former are offshoots of old mission churches from the 1940s and are often dominated by migrants from the same villages or chiefdoms. The latter, on the other hand, encompass both new churches and sects coming from abroad and independent churches which migrants have established in town. This distinction, it should be stressed, is rather spurious and is not recognised by Chinsapo's Pentecostal Christians. First, the Assemblies of God, as is discussed below, is an example of a church which could fall into either category. It is well-established in certain rural areas after early missionary work but has also witnessed phenomenal growth from the 1980s onwards, particularly in towns. Second, the churches in the first category are by no means parochial ethnic congregations in town. No less than the churches in the second category, they urge their members to preach also outside church services, in markets and on street-corners, and welcome new members. Third, and perhaps most important, there are no striking differences in gospel among the various churches to which Chinsapo's Pentecostal Christians belong. Within the conventional distinction between prosperity and security gospels in Pentecostalism,[20] Chinsapo's Pentecostal Christians would seem to subscribe to the latter. Yet even here the distinction is somewhat blurred, especially if it is accepted that the notion of prosperity may be interpreted in different ways by township Christians and their middle-class counterparts in other congregations in the city.[21] In their prayers to God and their messages to pastors, Chinsapo's Pentecostal Christians long for secure employment and happy domestic life. 'Security' (*chitetezo*) is a recurrent notion, evoking the born-again condition as a refuge from witches who kill children and ruin successful

[20] See e.g. D.J. Maxwell, ' "Delivered from the Spirit of Poverty?'': Pentecostalism, Prosperity and Modernity Zimbabwe', *Journal of Religion in Africa*, vol. 28, 1998, pp. 350-73.
[21] Cf. Hackett, 'Charismatic/Pentecostal Appropriation of Media', p. 264.

business enterprises, tragedies all too familiar to the impoverished residents of Chinsapo township.

Missionaries and township Pentecostalism

Pentecostalism in Chinsapo township must be understood as a particular complex of meaning and practice, not as a form of Christianity disembedded from the historical context of township life. Far from representing some general truths about Pentecostalism, Chinsapo's Pentecostal Christians are persons in a specific existential predicament. Theirs is *township Pentecostalism* which imbues Christianity with the fears, horrors and frustrations of impoverishment. No spatial metaphor, or 'anthropological obsession with locality',[22] underlies this notion of township Pentecostalism. As was mentioned above, the social networks of Chinsapo's Pentecostal Christians span many localities, from their villages of origin to Chinsapo township itself, and from urban markets and work-places to congregations elsewhere in the city. 'Township Pentecostalism' is, in this perspective, more a socio-economic than a spatial notion. It is within its specific passions and aspirations that Pentecostal Christians' encounters with missionaries must be understood. Rather than being a phenomenon that provides new avenues to free oneself from township Pentecostalism, transnationalism, through disputes over and with foreign missionaries, is embedded in its particular relationships.

It is clear that a congregation's attachment to a transnational church can profoundly alter its position among Christian churches in the township. This is especially striking when two Pentecostal churches in Chinsapo are compared, churches whose early history in Malawi has been closely entwined: Assemblies of God (AOG) and Independent Assemblies of God (IAOG). According to teachers at the AOG's Bible College in Lilongwe, AOG was first established in northern Malawi in 1943 and, after more missionary work in different parts of the country, became a co-ordinated mission church in 1947. One of the Malawian pioneers in the church, known as Kalambule, had worked as a cook in Durban and become a born-again there. He returned to Malawi in the 1950s and was active in AOG, only to disagree with missionaries over polygamy. The latter had a pragmatic approach, emphasising Christians' ability to grow in their spiritual life and eventually discard improper practices. Kalambule could not accept such pragmatism, but it appears that his relation to missionaries had been tense all along. Missionaries had restricted him to preach only in his home district of Ntcheu, and when one missionary had publicly accused him of being a 'liar' (*wabodza*), he had announced his resignation from AOG and the establishment of a new church, IAOG. An American missionary, who had his own reasons to disagree with his

[22] Van Binsbergen, 'Mediating the Global', p. 874.

fellow missionaries, accompanied Kalambule and became the missionary for IAOG.

AOG remained well-established in some areas but did not compete on a large scale with older mission churches in Malawi. A new era dawned in 1982 when the Crossroads Cathedral in Oklahoma adopted the Malawian AOG as its main recipient of spiritual and material support. An ambitious programme of new churches and Bible schools began, and from the late 1980s onwards AOG has been at the forefront of the Pentecostal revival in the country. From 1989 to 1996 church membership increased by over 40%, 1996 alone witnessing an annual growth of 15%. The headquarters in Lilongwe's Area 15 comprise a huge church, an international Bible college and a 'campus' which competes in its spaciousness with most constituent colleges of the University of Malawi. In Chinsapo township AOG has by far the most imposing church building, complemented by a comfortable pastor's house and other premises where private primary and secondary schools offer students such unusual options as French. All the buildings are electrified, and the compound is encircled by a wire fence.

IAOG has derived no obvious benefit from the Pentecostal revival in Malawi. Kalambule died in 1990, and the American missionary, after over forty years in Malawi, was ailing by the 1990s and had returned to America by 1996-7. It was becoming clear to church members in Malawi that he was no longer available as their missionary. In 1995, a faction left IAOG and established the End Times Church, supported in Lilongwe by a new 'missionary', a Malawian businessman who had made a small fortune as a minibus operator. In Chinsapo, the contrast between AOG and IAOG could scarcely have been sharper. Whereas AOG attracted hundreds of well-dressed township dwellers from different parts of the country to its Sunday services, IAOG had difficulties to fill even half of its pews in a small, modest building and gathered, in the main, relatives and kin whose villages of origin were in the Ntcheu heartland of the church. Whereas AOG's well-lit church building was an exceptional sight at night in the township, a great worry among the members of IAOG was to raise enough funds to buy doors to their church. Without doors, children took the liberty to use it as a playground in the daytime, while drunkards relieved themselves there at night.

My participation in church services delighted this congregation more than perhaps any other in the township. Having already spent over two months with other Pentecostal congregations in Chinsapo, I had become familiar with the fact that the notion of a disinterested pursuit of anthropological knowledge made little sense to pastors and their congregations and that I was generally assumed to have personal thirst for the 'words of God' (*mawu a Mulungu*). No sooner had I begun to attend IAOG services than I was expected to take on some leadership role in the congregation.

During our conversations, the pastor and church elders always inquired which 'part' (*chigawo*) I would like to perform during the next service, whether, in short, I would like to preach or lead prayers and hymns. When I, referring to my ignorance of Pentecostalism, consistently declined such public roles, the requests abated.

However, my stories about the weak presence of Pentecostalism in my native Finland prompted the church elders to contemplate sending a small team there. The idea was to launch crusades in Finnish market places, at bus and railway stations and in other places where large numbers of people were present. Some of the Finns would then come to Malawi as the missionaries of IAOG. Trying to inject realism into this project, I described Finland's snowy winters in graphic detail. This made the church elders restrict their proposed crusade to two summer months. When I observed that my compatriots were unlikely to appreciate preaching in Chichewa, and that the church elders' English was somewhat halting, I was asked to be the interpreter during the crusade. Undeterred by climate and language, the church elders acknowledged the greatest difficulty in raising enough funds for the crusade. The congregation's bank account totalled 143 kwacha ($10). The church elders resolved to raise funds 'little by little' (*pang'ono pang'ono*), incurring debt (*ngongole*) if necessary.

The church elders were able to see humour, even absurdity, in some details of their proposed crusade to Finland. However, the basic idea captured their, and the rest of the congregation's, imagination for several weeks and appeared sound in its general outlines. It bespoke a mixture of zeal and despair, unflagging confidence in the gospel and profound disquiet over the appalling poverty of the church. The common history and the subsequent contrast in church growth between AOG and IAOG were not lost on the members of Chinsapo's IAOG. The contrast was made all the more striking by the fact that all the Pentecostal churches, including AOG, supported their pastors through tithes (*chakhumi*) and the occasional 'sacrifice' (*nsembe*) of food, clothes and money. Foreign missionaries insisted that they were in Malawi only to assist in planting churches and that every congregation had to support its own pastor. For the members of Chinsapo's IAOG, the differences in pastors' ability to devote themselves to their pastoral work could only be understood in the light of the initial access to external sponsorship. While AOG had a full-time pastor in Chinsapo, residing in the relative luxury of a large electrified house, the pastor of IAOG sold beans, groundnuts and vegetables on his bicycle in Lilongwe's residential areas in order to support his family of nine. They lived in two small houses whose poverty was indistinct from their neighbours' in the township.

As their confidence in their own spiritual maturity indicates, Chinsapo's Pentecostal congregations do not look up to missionaries as Christians more advanced than they themselves. Among some congregations, foreign missionaries arouse outright suspicion. One independent Pentecostal church appeared as welcoming as others on my first visit, but afterwards those whom I knew best in the congregation told me that the pastor had interrogated them on my true identity and interests. The pastor had warned them that a squad within the Catholic Church sent strangers to sow confusion (*chisokonezo*) among Pentecostal churches. These strangers behaved as if they were genuine born-again Christians but, in reality, they were serving the devil. The pastor's fear drew upon common suspicion towards Catholics, whom Pentecostal Christians generally condemn for 'worshipping idols' (*kupembedza mafano*), but he may also have had more personal reasons to dislike white people. More broadly, many Pentecostal congregations' reluctance to give strangers, even if wealthy foreigners, leadership roles derives from the understanding that even born-again Christians may remain under Satanic influence on 'some other side' (*mbali ina*) of their lives. According to this understanding, a person becomes a pastor after a long process by which church leaders and the congregation reach a positive judgement of his or her spiritual credentials.

Chinsapo's residents commonly make the observation that many white people leave much to desire as Christians. Watchmen and domestic servants are particularly conversant with the habits of white people, and their views are not always flattering. The failure of white people to go to church on Sundays, their liberal use of alcohol and the absence of the Bible in many expatriate households cause critical remarks. During a sermon in a major Pentecostal church in the township, which has white missionaries in Malawi, a pastor scandalised his congregation when he related a story about his encounter with a Canadian mathematics teacher during his secondary school years. The Canadian had urged his students to believe in geometry because its propositions could be proved. Religious beliefs, by contrast, could not be proved. God did not create people, the Canadian had proceeded to claim, but people created God. This claim sent the congregation gasping in outrage, followed by derisive laughter at the obvious idiocy of the Canadian's remark. The pastor used the story to illustrate how the worship of God, and not formal education, was the best guarantee against 'insolence' (*chipongwe*).

In their quest for missionaries, therefore, Chinsapo's Pentecostal Christians strive for mutual dependence as a *moral* relationship where all, foreign missionaries and local lay Christians alike, respect one another as subjects of God and relatives in the Spirit. Whites do not evoke postcolonial nostalgia, nor is their material wealth evidence of a lifestyle worth imitating. Rather, just as every member of the congregation shows respect towards God by being generous in tithing and sacrifice, so too the generosity of missionaries sustains their own Christian ethic. Conversely, *all* Christians, from newcomers in the church to pastors and missionaries, are mere human beings who stand in the perennial danger of 'falling' (*kugwa*) into sin. Taken together, these observations indicate the discursive resources which Chinsapo's Pentecostal Christians have at their disposal to monitor and subvert their missionaries. Foreign missionaries, the personifications of transnational connections, are enmeshed in the anxieties and aspirations of township Pentecostalism. The logic of their social relationships, and the moral arguments they entail, are best highlighted by an extended-case study.

'Children without a father': flows and blockages in township Pentecostalism

Pastors, congregations and their missionary. The key event of this case study is the excommunication of a pastor, the *dramatis personae* two Malawian pastors and one American missionary. However, the case becomes an *extended* study when the simple event and the small number of actors are merely standpoints to make underlying processes and relationships apparent in analysis. In order to safeguard privacy, all the actors have been given pseudonyms, and their Pentecostal church is known here simply as the Church. The key actors are Alaston Kamera, the excommunicated pastor in his mid-twenties, married with three children, a tenant in Chinsapo township and, before the crisis, the pastor of a congregation in his village of origin in Lilongwe District; Rodrick Chithunzi, in his early forties, married with five children, the pastor of the Church in Chinsapo and Conference Superintendent for central and northern Malawi; Bill Jenkins, an American missionary in his late forties who lives with his American wife and daughter in Area 43, a new affluent suburb in Lilongwe.

Alaston Kamera moved to the capital in 1987 and, after he had found rents too high in other townships, to Chinsapo in 1991. Like many other Pentecostal Christians, Kamera willingly dwells on his deplorable past, the time when he drank beer, smoke marijuana (*chamba*) and robbed people of their money and other valuables at night. Initiated into the Chewa secret society *gule wamkulu* (also known as *nyau*) in his village, he began to attend services in mainline churches in town. In 1992 his classificatory brother took him to the Church in Chinsapo, and Kamera soon became a born-again. With his banjo and singing talents, and as a successful exorcist of evil spirits (*ziwanda*), Kamera was bound to become a popular pastor. In 1993 he founded his own congregation in his village of origin, but although the congregation had some 290 members when he was excommunicated in 1997, its poverty never made it possible for Kamera to be a full-time pastor. Instead, he usually spent only Sundays with his congregation. He retained the business he already had before becoming a pastor, the sale of fresh milk in the more affluent suburbs of

Lilongwe. It involved waking up at 4 a.m. to collect milk from cold storage at Malawi Dairy Industries and, with cartons of milk on his bicycle rack, proceeding to suburbs on time for middle-class urban dwellers' breakfasts. The same routine also took place in late afternoons. Kamera made a daily profit of around 35 kwacha (just over $2), scarcely sufficient for buying food and clothes and paying rent, given the fact that he did not sell milk every day and that his wife did not have any business of her own.

It was Rodrick Chithunzi's forceful preaching that inspired Kamera to join the Church in 1992. Chithunzi is also a Chewa from a village in Lilongwe District and claims to have drunk beer and smoked cigarettes for 13 years after ending his secondary education. He changed (*kutembenuka*; 'to turn around') in 1985 when a friend introduced him to the Baptist Church. Chithunzi worked as an electrician until 1989 when a series of dreams revealed to him his future as a pastor in a Pentecostal church. In 1990, a voice told him the name of the Church in a dream, and Chithunzi found it in Kawale, one of the oldest high-density townships in Lilongwe. Now a born-again, he was sent to lead a small congregation in Chinsapo in 1990. First there were sixteen adults in the congregation, after six months fifty-seven, after a year ninety-two, and by 1996-7, over 300. Fierce and passionate as a preacher, Chithunzi was known to cause visions among his congregation. He also gained a reputation for being a successful healer, with both Pentecostal and non-Pentecostal patients flocking to his house to seek prayers. Within just five years, he moved from being a lay member to becoming Local Minister, then Ordained Minister, then General Treasurer for the Church in all Malawi and, in 1995, Conference Superintendent, the highest Church official in central and northern Malawi. The church building and his house in Chinsapo had grown accordingly. Listing his achievements, Chithunzi took particular pleasure in the fact that he had been responsible for planting twenty-six churches since 1991, of which twenty-three were still operating in 1996-7.

Such commitment to the Church, and his fluency in English, made Chithunzi the closest Malawian pastor to Bill Jenkins. Although he had been in Malawi since 1974, Jenkins could not preach nor keep up a conversation in Chichewa. Having long dreamed of a career as a professional player of American football, Jenkins became a born-again Christian when he was about to enter a college. In 1996-7, he was the Church's only foreign missionary in Malawi and also had southern Tanzania in his orbit. He kept regular contact with the Church in the US via fax and email from his residence. Every three years or so he made a visit to the US to report and to solicit new assistance. Jenkins was careful not to associate too closely with any particular congregation in Malawi and sometimes stayed at home on Sundays. A big man in an expensive dark suit, wearing a gold wrist-watch and a conspicuous ring, and driving a white pick-up car, he evoked awe among congregations when he did arrive to participate in services. Aware of embodying power and affluence, Jenkins never tired of reminding his pastors that, despite receiving his salary from the US, he was in Malawi only to support pastors to plant churches. It was the task of the congregation to maintain its pastor and the church building itself. During his conversations with me, Jenkins also emphasised the civic virtues which this approach inculcated into Malawians. Instead of hiring labour to build churches, the missionary provided congregations with materials only and thus encouraged 'self-help' and 'responsibility'. 'I think we are doing the right thing', Jenkins concluded.

Crisis and excommunication. During the rainy season of 1996-7, a thunderstorm partly destroyed Kamera's church in his village of origin. He estimated that the church needed a new iron roof and 1,000 new bricks. Jenkins, despite his principle of assisting only in the initial planting of churches, had once before provided funds for renovating Kamera's church. Faced with a new misfortune, Kamera wrote a letter to Chithunzi requesting money for the roof and bricks.[23] Chithunzi replied that it was not the practice of the missionary to assist churches beyond planting them. More correspondence ensued between Kamera and Chithunzi, even though they lived within a few minutes' walk from one another in Chinsapo. Kamera's missives were not diplomatic. His first response to Chithunzi observed in no uncertain terms that the policy of the Church was bad and that Jenkins ought to 'care for' (*kusamala*) local congregations after opening their churches because the congregations were poor. Kamera also added that he doubted whether Chithunzi wanted him to continue as a pastor.

When this dispute was emerging, Conference Secretary sent all pastors a circular letter inviting them to the Bible school of the Church and to some meetings in Blantyre, a southern Malawian city over 400 km. from Lilongwe. The invitation made clear that the Church could not provide transport for participants. Still combative from his first letter, Kamera instantly replied to Conference Secretary and Chithunzi that he did not have any money and that when he found money he bought food and clothes for his wife and children. Instead of sending a personal reply to Kamera, Chithunzi, as Conference Superintendent, wrote a circular letter to all pastors. He explained that according to the Constitution of the Church, no pastor receives a salary and after a church has been opened, it is the task of the congregation to maintain their church and to support their pastor. Conference Superintendent and the missionary, Chithunzi concluded, should not be approached with requests for money.

---

[23] Chithunzi later showed me his correspondence with Kamera. The latter did not retain copies of his letters.

Chithunzi did not have to wait long for another missive from Kamera. In an increasingly rambling and intemperate tone, Kamera declared that 'the laws of the Church were witchcraft' (*malamulo a mpingo ndi a ufiti*). Leaders (*atsogoleri*), he continued, urge others to pray for assistance from heaven (*ku mwamba*) while they themselves receive it from America, South Africa and other countries. He also asked whether a child can only be born and left on its own. Signing the letter on behalf of his congregation, Kamera ended with the words, 'Children without a father' (*ana opanda bambo*).

Dismayed, Chithunzi called Jenkins, Kamera and the other pastors in Lilongwe for a crisis meeting. It took place on a Saturday, lasted for eight hours and had the discussion of Kamera's behaviour as the only item on its agenda. Displaying Kamera's three letters as evidence, Chithunzi rebuked Kamera for 'despising' (*kunyoza*) Jenkins and asked the meeting to decide on appropriate disciplinary action. While some pastors preferred suspension to excommunication, no one could deny the gravity of the case. Kamera's accusation that witchcraft was enshrined in the Constitution was especially shocking. Much of the meeting was spent on discussing the extent to which congregations can expect assistance from the missionary, and Jenkins consistently maintained that Chithunzi's circular had said all that was essential in the matter. The discussion of principles, in effect, merely anticipated the inevitable decision to excommunicate Kamera. Jenkins' poor grasp of Chichewa and Kamera's equally poor understanding of English entailed that they had no common language for communication. Kamera simply listened with his head bowed to Chithunzi's translation of Jenkins' measured words. Jenkins said that he recalled Kamera as a good Christian and dedicated pastor and that he felt profound regret at being obliged to excommunicate him. Jenkins observed that any other action would have allowed problems to persist and to resurface in some other form later.

On the following Sunday, Chithunzi gave a visiting pastor from the northern Malawian city of Mzuzu the task of announcing Kamera's excommunication to the congregation in Chinsapo. The pastor stressed that Church members had to 'honour' (*kulemekeza*) their leaders at all times. He went on to give a sermon on proper Christian conduct, on the importance of showing Christianity in deed. Baptism and church membership, he said, did not make a person a true Christian, because even many drunkards and prostitutes had been baptised. Even though the sermon reiterated familiar Pentecostal convictions, it gained special significance coming immediately after the announcment of Kamera's excommunication. Very few in the congregation had been aware of Kamera's imminent castigation, and many exchanged expressions of surprise when the announcement was made. On a few Sundays thereafter, some from the congregation proceeded, with Bibles in their hands, to Kamera's house after the Sunday service to 'teach' (*kuphunzitsa*) him. Kamera, in turn, made sure that he was never available to receive these visitors. In fact, he was as defiant as ever. A friendly pastor's congregation near Chinsapo welcomed him to participate in the services of the Church. Kamera also held a meeting with the congregation in his village of origin. The congregation was angry because Church leaders had not consulted it about their decision to excommunicate Kamera.

At first, Chithunzi sent a member of his congregation in Chinsapo to conduct Sunday services in the village. Unknown to villagers, he failed to gather together as many of the congregation as Kamera had. Some began to pray in small groups in their houses rather than in the church. Chithunzi then sent Kamera's classificatory brother, the one who had introduced Kamera to the Church, although he had become rather inactive as a Christian. He was also unsuccessful in uniting the congregation and, moreover, failed to appear in the village every Sunday. Kamera himself had no intention of stopping preaching and continued to use the pastor's title (*mbusa*). The cousin of his wife was one of the founders of the independent Pentecostal church which he soon joined. Kamera's ambition was to open another church in his village of origin, convinced that he would thereby show Chithunzi and Jenkins that the congregation was prepared to leave the Church and follow him as their legitimate pastor. The missionary of the independent church was a Malawian: 'black' (*wokuda*), Kamera pointed out, approvingly.

After excommunication, Kamera seemed to lose all restraint in his criticism of Chithunzi and Jenkins. His remarks on the latter were especially revealing in their ambivalence towards both 'blackness' and 'whiteness' as concepts for contrasting moralities. On the one hand, in line with his letter where he accused Church leaders of receiving assistance from abroad while asking others to pray for it from heaven, Kamera abused Jenkins for neglecting the poor Christians of Malawi. According to Kamera, Jenkins could have obtained assistance for Kamera's congregation in no time through his telephone and fax. On other occasions, Kamera claimed that Jenkins had been so long in Malawi that he had become a black man himself, prone to 'cheat' (*kunamiza*) others in order to enrich himself. Kamera asserted that Jenkins had taken pictures of the most prominent church buildings in Lilongwe and sent them to the US, with a note saying that they were some of the churches he had planted in Malawi. Generalising about foreign missionaries in Malawi, Kamera also took pleasure in stories about their dubious strategies to solicit money from abroad. For example, claimed Kamera, a missionary went to an outdoor beer party and asked people to put their beer aside and raise their hands because he wanted to take a picture of them. After taking the picture, he bought them all beer as a sign of gratitude. The picture went abroad to show that there were many born-again Christians without church buildings in Malawi. The missionary would pocket the money thus solicited.

The dynamic of township Pentecostalism. A whole range of issues in understanding transnationalism and township Pentecostalism would be obscured if Kamera's excommunication were seen as a simple disciplinary action. Nor was it a consequence of rivalry in any other than a very superficial sense. At issue was, rather, an ongoing process by which the transnational flow of resources, connections and ideas came to be blocked by the dynamic of particular social relationships. The enabling aspects of transnationalism were embedded in, and in turn reinforced, local social hierarchies where, among others, the level of formal education, seniority and mentor-novice relations entailed significant differences in access to symbolic and material resources. However, close attention to the actual social fields of township Pentecostalism discloses that not all symbolic and material resources derive from transnational connections. The Pentecostal congregation in Kamera's village of origin associated itself more with its local pastor than with the missionary and other Church leaders. The latter's failure to provide assistance to 'children without a father' further alienated the congregation from the Church, making it possible for them to follow the excommunicated pastor to another Pentecostal church. Such localised bases of power, in turn, influence the activities of Church leaders, despite their privileged access to transnational connections. It is important, therefore, to appreciate the underlying process behind the conflict between Kamera, Chithunzi and Jenkins. A long sequence of events, and the development of Chithunzi's own aspirations, preceded the drama of excommunication.

While Kamera and Chithunzi each suspected that the devil was behind the other's conduct, both also acknowledged, during private conversations with me, their close co-operation when the Church began to grow in Chinsapo township. Kamera was among the earliest members in Chithunzi's congregation and regarded Chithunzi as his 'teacher' (*mphunzitsi*). From early on, he accompanied Chithunzi to preach in different parts of the city and in nearby villages. The two also went to funerals together. When Kamera began to establish the Church in his village of origin, both Chithunzi and Jenkins were impressed when they saw how dedicated the congregation was. Before a church building had been built, Kamera preached and conducted prayers for a large crowd under trees in the village. This also impressed another American missionary, Ted Wilson, who was based in Mozambique but often came to visit Church congregations in Lilongwe. It was Wilson's well-intended promises of support, and Chithunzi's role in mediating them, that first began to introduce a cleavage between Kamera and Chithunzi.

Like Jenkins, Wilson became Chithunzi's close friend. Wilson visited the US more often than Jenkins and developed the habit of bringing Chithunzi expensive gifts. Once he gave him a large knife; on another occasion, two suits. He also told Chithunzi that he would bring a suit to Kamera but urged Chithunzi not to tell him in case Wilson's wife would disapprove of this plan. Chithunzi told Kamera, however, adding that they were not supposed to tell anyone. After Wilson's next trip to the US the suit was delivered to Kamera, and Wilson soon told Chithunzi of more plans to support Kamera. Impressed with Kamera's congregation, Wilson promised a new iron roof and cement for the church building but again asked Chithunzi to keep this promise confidential. Chithunzi, in turn, once more informed Kamera about the prospect of assistance and said that they were not supposed to spread the news. The friendship between Chithunzi and Kamera went sour when Wilson did not return from the US. After sixteen years of marriage, his wife left him, and Wilson, now a divorcee, was not permitted to continue as a missionary. Kamera now thought that Chithunzi had grabbed a part of Wilson's gifts and had therefore urged Kamera to remain quiet. No longer inhibited, Kamera freely publicised his view of Chithunzi's greed.

This conflict emerged six months before the acrimonious correspondence between Kamera and Chithunzi. When the correspondence took place, Chithunzi had filled the first year of his three-year term as Conference Superintendent. He made no secret of his desire to be re-elected, and critical pastors, such as Kamera, were a definite disadvantage. No one thought that Kamera would pose a challenge to Chithunzi in the election; he was too young and inexperienced in the Church hierarchy to stand as a candidate. Because all Church members were entitled to vote, Kamera and other critical pastors could command a substantial proportion of the votes through their congregations.

Embroiled in conflict and controversy, Chithunzi had his own plans to make his prominence more visible in the Church. He anticipated Jenkins' fund-raising visit to the US later in 1997, keen to exploit his good relationship with the missionary. Chithunzi was convinced that his church, which was often crowded during Sunday services, needed a new wing to almost double its size, and he saw in Jenkins' forthcoming journey an opportune moment to solicit funding for it. On the one hand, if he lost the next election, he confided in me and a few in his congregation, the new Conference Superintendent would hardly support his plans. On the other, he urged his congregation to make enough bricks before Jenkins' journey so that the missionary could be encouraged to ask for money for an iron roof in the US. Even before the journey, Chithunzi announced during a Sunday service, a large number of bricks would solicit money from Jenkins to buy firewood for baking them.

For all his care to enunciate the Constitution of the Church to other pastors, Chithunzi thus appeared able to circumvent the rule that the missionary only assisted pastors in planting churches. At issue was, however, less the deliberate abuse of a position in the Church hierarchy than a corollary of a moral bond. The relationship between Chithunzi and Jenkins had its own dynamic of obligations and privileges, a dynamic which compelled Chithunzi's congregation to make its contribution of bricks before requesting money from the missionary. The fact that Chithunzi's reading of the Constitution could prevent similar relationships between other pastors and the missionary gives tangible evidence for blockages in the flows of transnational connections. Yet as this extended case-study shows, a blind pursuit of wealth and power was not the underlying principle by which rivalries and conflicts emerged. Persons were obliged to make the moral condition of mutual dependence apparent in their practice.

This perspective on mutual dependence as a moral condition yields two broad conclusions on transnationalism and township Pentecostalism in Malawi. First, to recall the problem of dependence from the beginning of this chapter, there is no hint of a sense of personal or collective failure in township Christians' quest for missionaries. Missionaries are not expected to release township Christians from some fundamentally evil condition but to engage with their poverty as subjects who share the same moral codes. Spiritual maturity on both sides is, in effect, a precondition for morally tenable material assistance. As has been seen, affluent Finns needed to be converted in order to make their wealth morally acceptable. Chithunzi and Kamera, in turn, suspected one another of Satanic influence when a dispute over material assistance arose.

Second, by being active in eliciting and assessing their foreign missionaries' work, Chinsapo's Pentecostal Christians also provide insight into personhood in their specific form of Pentecostalism. Rather than promoting individualisation, the theology of all Pentecostalism emphasises a new life in Christ, the acceptance of the Holy Spirit in person whereby the Pentecostal subject is, in Ruth Marshall-Fratani's words, 'consecrated to a higher power'.[24] Chinsapo's Pentecostal Christians see the 'second birth' as a gradual process where the validity of personal experiences, such as dreams and glossolalia, as signs of divine guidance must be publicly ascertained in the person's everyday conduct. The idea of a process also entails a notion of 'growth' (*kukula*), and pastors, in particular, owe their personal growth as born-again Christians to a mentor-novice relation where a more established pastor, together with a missionary, assists in planting one's church. Even more, this chapter has shown how the antithesis to individualism is not necessarily communalism. The morality of mutual dependence has entailed as much conflict as communalism.

---

[24] Marshall-Fratani, 'Mediating the Global', p. 286.

The focus of this chapter on particular relationships has been attuned to the study of a setting where, in the absence of the electronic media, transnationalism rather than globalisation provides a perspective into Pentecostalism. On special occasions, such as during the preparations for the Ernest Angley Miracle Crusade in 1997, video films of born-again Christianity elsewhere in the world are shown in the city. Some pastors are also able to accompany their missionaries to neighbouring countries in order to celebrate the opening of new churches there. These events, and the magazines and pamphlets which Pentecostal Christians in townships occasionally see, undoubtedly contribute to a sense of belonging to a widespread movement. However, most Christians in Chinsapo are too poor and too unfamiliar with English to detach themselves from their immediate relationships in the township and in the country. Nor do they harbour any obvious desire to do so; the stuff of their Pentecostal lives is in their personal relationships. As this chapter has shown, these relationships are the loci through which translocal currents flow and are blocked, from a township dweller's power base in his village of origin to a foreign missionary's problems with subversive local pastors in his church. When anthropologists contemplate 'the need for further conceptual development'[25] in the study of transnationalism and globalisation, they will do well to keep their abstractions in close dialogue with ethnography. Even in the study of transnationalism, there is no gainsaying the value of intensive fieldwork. It is through the intimate knowledge of particular relationships that the dynamic of flows and blockages can best be apprehended.

[25] Van Binsbergen, 'Globalization and Virtuality', p. 873

BIBLIOGRAPHY

Appadurai, A., *Modernity at Large: Cultural Dimensions of Globalization*, Minneapolis: University of Minnesota Press, 1996.

Basch, L., N. Glick Schiller and C. Szanton-Blanc, *Nations Unbound: Transnational Projects, Postcolonial Predicaments, and Deterritorialized Nation-States*, Longhorne, PA: Gordon & Breach, 1994.

Burawoy, M., 'The Extended-Case Method', *Sociological Theory*, vol. 16, 1998.

Chirwa, W.C., 'The Malawi Government and the South African Labour Recruiters, 1974-1992', *Journal of Modern African Studies*, vol. 34, 1996, pp. 623-42.

Cox, H., *Fire from Heaven: The Rise of Pentecostal Spirituality in the Twenty-First Century*, London: Cassell, 1996.

Crush, J., A. Jeeves, and D. Yudelman, *South Africa's Labour Empire: A History of Black Migrancy to the Gold Mines*, Boulder, CO: Westview, 1991.

Geschiere, P. and B. Meyer, 'Globalization and Identity: Dialectics of Flow and Closure', *Development and Change*, vol. 29, 1998, pp. 601-15.

Glick Schiller, N., 'The Situation of Transnational Studies', *Identities*, vol. 4, 1997.

Gluckman, M., 'Analysis of a Social Situation in Modern Zululand', *Bantu Studies*, vol. 14, 1940.

Hackett, R.J., 'Charismatic/Pentecostal Appropriation of Media Technologies in Nigeria and Ghana', *Journal of Religion in Africa*, vol. 28, 1998, pp. 258-77.

Hannerz, U., *Transnational Connections: Culture, People, Places*, London: Routledge, 1996.

Kydd, J. and R. Christiansen, 'Structural Change in Malawi since Independence: Consequences of a Development Strategy Based on Large-Scale Agriculture', *World Development*, vol. 10, 1982, pp. 355-75.

Kapferer, B., 'Introduction: Transactional Models Reconsidered' in B. Kapferer (ed.), *Transaction and Meaning: Directions in the Anthropology of Exchange and Symbolic Behaviour*, Philadelphia, PA: Institute for the Study of Human Issues, 1976.

Marshall-Fratani, R., 'Mediating the Global and the Local in Nigerian Pentecostalism', *Journal of Religion in Africa*, vol. 28, 1998, pp. 278-315.

Mato, D., 'On Global and Local Agents and the Social Making of Transnational Identities and Related Agendas in "Latin" America', *Identities*, vol. 4, 1997, pp. 170-72.

Maxwell, David, ' "Delivered from the Spirit of Poverty?": Pentecostalism, Prosperity and Modernity in Zimbabwe', *Journal of Religion in Africa*, vol. 28, 1998, pp. 350-73.

Mhone, G.Z. (ed.), *Malawi at Crossroads: The Postcolonial Political Economy*, Harare: Sapes, 1992.

Phiri, K.M. and K.R. Ross (eds), *Democratization in Malawi: A Stock-Taking*, Blantyre: Claim, 1998.

Simpson, A., 'Memory and Becoming the Chosen Other: Fundamentalist Elite-Making in a Zambian Catholic Mission School' in R. Werbner (ed.), *Memory and the Postcolony: African Anthropology and the Critique of Power*, London: Zed Books, 1998.

Turner, V.W., *Schism and Continuity in an African Society: A Study of Ndembu Village Life*, Manchester: Manchester University Press, 1957.

Van Binsbergen, W., 'Globalization and Virtuality: Analytical Problems Posed by the Contemporary Transformation of African Societies', *Development and Change*, vol. 29, 1998, p. 874.

Van Dijk, R.A., 'Young Puritan Preachers in Post-Independence Malawi', *Africa*, vol. 62, 1992, pp. 159-81.

——, 'Fundamentalism and Its Moral Geography in Malawi: The Representation of the Diasporic and the Diabolical', *Critique of Anthropology*, vol. 15, 1995, pp. 171-91.

Van Velsen, J., 'The Extended-Case Method and Situational Analysis' in A.L. Epstein (ed.), *The Craft of Social Anthropology*, London: Tavistock, 1967.

TRANSNATIONALISATION AND LOCAL TRANSFORMATIONS

THE EXAMPLE OF THE CHURCH OF ASSEMBLIES OF GOD OF BURKINA FASO

Pierre-Joseph Laurent

One of the most notable features of Burkina Faso[1] since the mid-1980s has been the rapid growth of the Church of the Assemblies of God. In its cities today, little offence is taken at the clamour of prayer groups meeting in the evening in private homes, at the forceful praises emanating from churches on Sunday mornings when the faithful pay homage to their almighty God, or at the cries of the exorcised 'sick' ringing through the neighbourhoods. Even in the most isolated villages of the Mossi country, the traveller cannot avoid encountering the ubiquitous blue placards hung on the eaves of large adobe buildings with sloped tin roofs, marking one of the Pentecostal community's places of worship.[2]

Today the Assemblies of God count nearly 400,000 baptised members out of a population of 10.4 million, 1,800 pastors and 1,750 places of worship.[3] The various confessions of the country are divided into traditional religions (25.9%), Islam (52.4%), Roman Catholic Christianity (15%), and Protestant Evangelical Christianity (4.5%), of which the Assemblies of God comprise more than ninety percent.[4] This church was established in Burkina Faso in 1921 and in December 1996 celebrated its sixty-fifth anniversary. The dazzling success experienced today by the Pentecostals in Ouagadougou (there were only 125,000 on the occasion of their 50th anniversary in 1972) only dates from the mid-1980s. This expansion has occurred in parallel with the rapid urbanisation of Ouagadougou, the return of immigrants due to the collapse of the plantation economy in Ivory Coast and xenophobia towards the Mossi reigning

---

[1] This country was known as Upper Volta from its independence in 1960 till 1984.

[2] The terms 'Pentecostal', 'Protestant', 'Americans', 'the Church', and the 'Work' are used here interchangeably to designate the Church of the Assemblies of God in Burkina Faso. The term 'Pentecostal' is practically never used by members of Assemblies in Burkina Faso to designate their church or their religious identity. The terms 'Protestant' and 'American' are those most commonly used by members. This situation is related perhaps to the almost total domination by the Assemblies of the Protestant field.

[3] From information gathered in 1996, according to the present president of the Assemblies of God of Burkina Faso, Pastor Pawentaoré; see also 'Faites connaissance avec les Assemblées de Dieu', *Éclair*, no.8, Dec. 1996 (Ouagadougou), p. 5.

[4] Based on an extrapolation of the figures of B. de Luze, 'La situation actuelle des différentes églises', *Afrique contemporaine*, vol. 159, no. 3, 1991, p.24. and on the census of 1996.

there, the numerous cases of 'madness' observed within the returning migrant population, the appearance of new, incurable diseases, the weakening of the state's ability to intervene and, according to the statements of the authorities of the Assembly of God, the Sankarist revolution from 1983 to 1987.

It would be wrong to consider the Church of the Assemblies of God as 'a new religious movement'. It has a long history, which cannot be reduced to its recent explosion in the cities: its role in the rural areas and the membership of peasants must be seen in the context of its evolution. In order to untangle the influence of the singular history of individuals from key aspects of the evolution of the Church of the Assemblies of God of Burkina Faso, I have chosen to follow a chronological presentation. Initially, I shall approach the Assemblies of God as a transnational church which produces the image of a certain form of modernity. Subsequently I will examine the advance of global phenomena profoundly transforming local societies, wherein the Assemblies of God represents for many the rediscovery of a homogeneous group marked by closely-knit social relations.

The Assemblies of God of Burkina Faso

The Church of the Assemblies of God of Burkina Faso has played an important role in the expansion of the movement on the African continent; thus one frequently encounters Mossi pastors responsible for missions in neighbouring countries. At the same time, its influence on sister churches throughout Africa is renowned. Since the turn of the century, many missions have been implanted on the continent by the mother church based in Springfield, USA. It is interesting to note that American pastors found among the Mossi an especially solid bedrock on which to lay the cornerstone of 'the Work'. As of 1914, Pastor H. Wright, missionary in Sierra Leone, projected organising a trip into the Moogo (Mossi country). Yet the missionaries had to await the end of World War I to put their plan into action. Pastor W. Taylor undertook an initial prospective visit to Ouagadougou early in 1920.

According to Pastor Daniel Compaoré, retired president of the Assemblies of God of Burkina Faso from 1967 to 1979, the extreme poverty of the central plateau incited Mossi pastors to participate more fervently than most in reinforcing the Assemblies of God, to the point that they themselves rapidly assumed the destinies of the church, without further recourse to missionaries.[5] Following pastor Taylor's reconnoitring trip, the American mission – composed of two couples, Mr and Mrs Wright (already residing in Sierra Leone, they joined the group later) and

[5] The Africanisation of the authorities of the Assemblies of God of Burkina Faso dates from 1955. Cf. 'Faites connaissance avec les Assemblées de Dieu', p. 4

Mr and Mrs Leeper, as well as two young women, Misses M. Peoples and J. Farnsworth – landed at the port of Dakar in 1921. The voyage was particularly hazardous and perilous, as they all were in those days. After a long trip, the missionaries reached Ouahigouhia, the seat of the powerful Mossi chiefdom of Yatenga.[6] They continued on their way, traversing Yako, and finally, in late 1921, reaching Ouagadougou and the residence of Moogo Naaba (king of the Mossi). Once in Ouagadougou, the American pastors soon clashed with the Catholic missions already installed in the city,[7] who counselled the Moogo Naaba to expel the Protestants from Ouagadougou. The king sent them to one of his ministers, Konga Naaba, in order to find them a location out of harm's way. This area remains occupied till today by the central headquarters of the Assemblies of God.

The first converts were for the most part Mossi peasants, from among whom ten pastors were ordained on 30 November 1934. They then took up their posts on the Mossi plateau. From this point on, the American missionaries chose the Mossi empire as their principal site of implantation and evangelisation. The historical singularity of the Church of the Assemblies of God of Burkina Faso accounts for the numerical importance of Mossi in this Church, as well as their decisive cultural influence. Therefore it is not by chance that, even today, the Assemblies of God recruit principally from among the Mossi. Most of the pastors belong to this ethnic group, even when they have their ministry elsewhere.

The act of recognition of the 'Assemblies of God of Upper Volta' was promulgated in 1955.[8] Territorially, the Assemblies of God of Burkina Faso is divided into seven regions. Each region is directed by a board elected by the pastors of the region. The Church of the Assemblies of God is based on an institutional structure which, in certain hierarchical aspects, resembles the political organisation of the Mossi kingdoms.

[6] See M. Izard, *Le Yatenga précolonial. Un ancien royaume du Burkina*, Paris: Karthala, 1985.

[7] To understand this it is worth remembering that shortly before the French took Ouagadougou (1886), the intense activity expended by the Germans and French in the direction of the Mossi country and the north of Ivory Coast irritated the English already settled in the Gold Coast (Ghana). They feared being dispossessed of their 'hinterland' which made up the Moogo. In response, London quickly sent an agent to Mossi country to sign treaties of trade and friendship, forbidding the signatories any relations with the Germans or French. In fact, this move was above all to limit the French encroachment into a hinterland the English considered as theirs. Catholicism accompanied the colonial conquest lasting from 1896 to 1904. The White Fathers inaugurated their first missionary establishment at Koupéla in 1900. In 1901 the Our Lady of the Immaculate Conception Mission settled in the capital of Moogo (Empire of the Mossi). For more information, see R. Otayek, 'L'Eglise catholique Burkina Faso', in F. Constantin and F. and C. Coulon (eds), *Religion et transition démocratique en Afrique*, Paris: Karthala, 1997, pp. 221-58.

[8] Document dating from 7 September 1955, with the number 2705/APAS.

Thus, just like the chiefs of the Mossi villages (*Tenga naaba*), the pastor leads his community.[9] On an intermediate level of organisation, they gather monthly within a regional organisation, directed by a pastor-in-charge; this echoes the Mossi structure of intermediary kingdoms (chiefs of dependent kingdoms, more familiarly called canton chiefs: *ko'mbe'mba*). Finally, on the national level, in Ouagadougou, seat of the Moogo Naaba, an elected board presides over the destinies of the church.

This efficient and hierarchical structure allows the circulation of information and resources in both directions. Thus, today development activities (small dams, swamp draining, credit to buy agricultural material) initiated by Burkinabe NGOs (FEME, ODE) linked to the Assemblies of God,[10] rely on the institutional structure of the church for the putting in place of these projects, and on village representatives, organised into a well-ordered community, for their implementation on the ground. [11]

Conversion to an imported modernity

Especially in the rural areas, the Protestants, or 'the Americans', as they are called in Burkina Faso, have been perceived since the 1920s as embodying the image of a certain modernity. From the start, the Assemblies of God have embodied transnationalisation: in their perception of participating in a version of modernity, adherents feel they belong to an elected people, one which, along the road to social mobility, identifies itself with the exterior signs of social and economic success (internationalised clothing such as the coat and tie, consumption of imported food like coffee, bread). This observation requires an examination of the way these globalising effects brought in by these Protestant groups find expression within the singularity of Mossi society.

In the village, the Assemblies of God offer the faithful a space of liberty, within which they courageously try to undertake new initiatives. The impetus behind such initiatives may have arisen as a result of migr-

[9] In an earlier study I suggested a comparison between the function of the pastor and the Mossi chiefs. P.J. Laurent, 'Prosélytisme religieux, intensification agricole et organisation paysanne: Le rôle des "Assemblées de Dieu" dans l'émergence de la Fédération Wend-Yam in Burkina Faso' in J.-P. Jacob and P. Lavigne-Delville, *Les associations paysannes. Organisation et dynamiques*, Paris: APAD/IUED/Karthala, 1994, p. 176.

[10] D. Diallo and R. Otayek, *Dynamisme protestant, développement participatif et démocratie locale. Le cas de l'Office de Développement des Eglises evangéliques*, Ouagadougou: ORSTOM, p. 15 (forthcoming), J.G. Yaro, 'De l'évangelisation au developpement local: spécificité des ONG d'inspiration protestante au Burkina Faso', Colloque International ONG et développement: du Nord au Sud (Afrique, Amérique Latine, Asie), Bordeaux-Talence: Communication Tome 1, CNRS/ORSTOM/ Regards, 1996, pp. 277 – 93.

[11] See P.-J. Laurent, *Une association de développement en pays Mossi. Le don comme ruse*, Paris: Karthala, 1998.

ation experiences or contacts with development co-operatives or simply suggested by the rapid transformation of their environment. These new ideas constitute, or more exactly have constituted for some time, one of central factors behind the internal coherence existing among the urban elite of the Assemblies of God, the peasant-pastors and their faithful: the directing elite conceives the modernising project of the Work and the rural communities carry it out. In this sense, for the period prior to 1985, a description of church practices in the rural areas can be taken as representative of the Assemblies of God as a whole.

The attraction, for certain villagers, of the communities of the Assemblies of God in the rural areas, and in particular its pastors, lies in their projection of an image of relative economic success, as I have argued elsewhere.[12] To put it briefly, the dynamism of the peasant-pastors, and more generally, the rural Protestant communities, comes from their capacity to deal with change. The young pastors return to their villages after their training as poor as they left, but rich in potential. This is the case of pastor W. Zoungrana, who established himself in the village of Sadaba during the 1980s, after four years of Bible study. That fact that he remained a peasant gives all the more weight to the social and economic initiatives he has undertaken, and his faith and religious training are seen as a launching pad toward other activities.

Whereas some resign themselves through fear or anguish to the many changes in lifestyles sweeping through the Mossi plateau, the pastors, armed with their Bible study and training as church leaders, have assimilated other ways of being in the village, promoting for example the introduction of the rudiments of a modern rural economy. The 'prosperity gospel' (which I will discuss in the context of Mossi society below) coupled with a new economic *savoir faire*, allows for the conception of a new spatio-temporal horizon[13] which constitutes an essential basis of proselytism in the rural areas during the period preceding the mid-1980s.

Pastor W. Zoungrana is a typical example of a rural pastor:

'In December 1979, I finally found a village to settle in as pastor. Some time after my arrival, I created a group. The same year, I dug three wells. Then I began cultivating vegetables. I planted a lot, but that year animals devastated my garden. [...] The next year, in 1981, I cultivated an even bigger garden. I obtained good land near the well. This time I did very well. I grew cabbages and onions. I was able to buy a cart and donkey. The next year, I continued cultivating and was able to buy four oxen.'[14]

---

[12] See P.-J. Laurent, 'Prosélytisme religieux'.

[13] See P.-J. Laurent, 'Les conversions aux Assemblées de Dieu du Burkina Faso. Entre l'assemblée du développement et le réseau de grande socialité', *Journal des Africanistes*, no.47, 1998.

[14] These purchases can necessitate years of work for a Mossi family. For that matter, most of them never manage to amass enough money to pay for this materiel. A new

The pastor, despite the fact that he remains above all a villager and peasant, nonetheless embodies the image of a certain modernity: in his adherence to the restrictions and rules governing Pentecostal life,[15] and through the social recognition that his knowledge acquired at Bible school attracts. He draws people to him desirous of this modern aura, an attraction which is rendered possible because of his proximity to the 'grassroots'.

Members of the Assembly of God in the village form a minority group, creating a refuge in which they may express their desire, certainly still weakly affirmed, to distance themselves from the socio-economic rules of kinship, without, for all that, really wanting or being able to separate themselves from them. In the village, this process is nothing less than 'doing development': a project inconceivable without the conversion process, which legitimates the transgression which the invention of individual trajectories implies, and can be used against the defence mechanisms of village communalism. In other words, the community of the faithful may be understood as a group which enables a distancing from certain village relationships, considered too constraining or onerous.

Change, development, or even individual control over modes of accumulation necessitates keeping the process of kinship redistribution at bay, here rendered imaginable by conversion to the Assemblies of God. Conversion leads to effective protection against the constraining forces of village communalism, protection acquired by belief in the 'power' of God. Jesus is a 'large rock' behind which adepts with individualist ambitions may hide themselves. The Pentecostal peasant, tempted by 'getting ahead on his own', still remains uneasy about the rancour or jealousy which, according to him, is bound to surface among neighbours, parents or friends, confronted with the dwindling possibilities of mutual aid or help in times of need. In other words, in a context favouring both non-secularisation and weak economic development, the promotion of individual trajectories leads to a 'witchcraft crisis', where the deviant, having attempted to distance himself and rely on the protection conversion confers, is pressured to return to the kinship group.[16]

---

donkey and cart represents the sum of 180,000 CFA francs, which is a very large sum on the Mossi plateau. Some villagers only make 8,000 CFA a year from the sale of fruit from their tenant farming (groundnuts, cowpeas, *voandzou*).

[15] The principle things forbidden are monogamy, consuming alcohol and tobacco, going to the cinema, dancing in public places.

[16] See J.-P. Dozon, *La cause des prophètes: Politique et religion en Afrique contemporaine*, Paris: Seuil, 1995, p. 95. See also F.C. Fisiy and P. Geschiere, 'Sorcellerie et accumulation, variations régionales' in P. Geschiere and P. Konings (eds), *Itinéraires d'accumulation au Cameroun*, Paris: Karthala, 1993, pp. 99-129.

The 'spatio-temporal' change that the establishment of a individualistic socio-economic project represents carries with it new questions and anxieties.[17] Thus the withdrawal from kinship obligations and activities which this implies motivates adherence to Pentecostalism. P. W. Zoungrana puts it this way:

I'm Protestant. I've chosen the Assemblies of God as 'a principal religion' [sic]. Whenever I encounter problems, I pray to God and he accepts my prayer. During the period when I had problems starting the Wend-Yam federation,[18] I spoke to God. People consulted and paid witch-doctors to kill me. They sacrificed everything to their fetishes: dogs, goats, beef, everything except humans. When these things happened, I asked everyone to try to protect himself. Me, I have my God.

Economic success, or more precisely, the desire to accumulate for oneself, or to get married by mutual consent without the intervention of relations,[19] results in profound upheaval for the village as a social group.

These changes inscribe themselves in a new relationship to communal village life and the universe of mutual dependence which characterises it, and testify to the influence of transnational religion on Mossi society. Those behind these changes would be unable to realise them without conversion to protect their transgression. The protective power of conversion is made evident at the very arrival of a pastor in the village; one of the first things he does is conduct an *auto-da-fé*. New in the village, impatient to show others the efficacy of his all powerful God, he literally challenges the witches and witch-doctors to a duel to prove God's power and demonstrate the new horizons he opens to converts.

The conversion of a witch-doctor has great symbolic importance. Public destruction by fire of his charms and fetishes used to manipulate nature and the social environment amounts to a declaration of allegiance to an omnipotent God, through the eradication of any intermediary between the Most High and mankind. The process of conversion occurs as the outcome of a combat from which the pastor or preacher – often called the 'soldier' of God – emerges victorious: the new adepts 'give themselves' to God with more fervour than to the strongest of witch doctors.

---

[17] In this sense I am close to Robin Horton who, in treating as 'microcosm' the (concrete) divinities linked to fertility, and as 'macrocosm' the belief in a supreme God, sees in this shift between immanence and transcendence a belief system intended to explain, predict and control spatio-temporal events. Hence, all major changes in socio-cultural life can bring on a reorientation of the articulation between the two poles of belief. R. Horton, 'African Conversion', *Africa*, vol. 41, no.2, 1971, pp. 85-108.

[18] The Wend-Yam federation: a peasant organisation working for the social and economic development of Oubritenga province.

[19] See P.-J. Laurent, 'Dynamiques matrimoniales chez les Mossi du Burkina Faso, pratiques de l'Eglise des Assemblées de Dieu, des ainés, des cadets de l'Etat', in G. de Villars (ed.), *Phénomènes informels et dynamiques culturelles en Afrique*, Paris: Institut Africain/L'Harmattan, no. 19-20, 1996, pp. 166-83.

The traditional mode of Mossi thinking remains however in all the fullness of its functions and ultimately justifies the conversion. The ensemble of traditional beliefs (Islam included – if not especially) turns out to be most alive, although diabolised by a semantic amalgam in which ancestors, spirits, fetishes, charms, jujus and other 'Great Gods' are all henceforth assimilated to the work of the Devil. They incarnate the enemy that needs to be fought in order to formalise 'liberty' (for example, choosing a marriage partner or accumulating wealth). Proselytism, the importance accorded to testimony and, by extension, conversion, refers to a relationship of force.

In this sense, the Assemblies of God embodies a 'development assembly', a metaphor which refers to the idea of a transnational modernity conveyed by this church, and assumes a particular form in relation to the Mossi universe. It remains now to examine the modalities of this local appropriation, in particular the process of distancing from the logic of redistribution that characterises kinship relations. In other words, is it possible to isolate the extent to which converts interiorise the aspects of Pentecostal doctrine which express membership in terms of a conversion to modernity? According to M.-C. and E. Ortigues, 'religious traditions [in Africa] conceive physical and moral evil under the form of persecution; not simply disease but also liability are always explained by the intervention of a force external to the subject.'[20] Still following Ortigues, 'aggressiveness repressed by the law of communal solidarity reappears in the form of ideas of persecution.'[21] Hence, on the contrary, the interiorisation of the Christian notion of guilt – in the sense of becoming responsible before God for one's acts – not only involves the transformation of the conception of evil in terms of persecution, but also becomes an indicator of these transformations.

The following story was related to me by Sambo Kaboré (the old man with the cart in the story) and by Bargo Towindé, a 'believing healer'[22], both of whom are from the village of Loumbila, 25 km east of Ouagadougou. My interlocutors wanted me to understand the idea that conversion leads the faithful believer to become responsible before God (rather than men). In a more general sense, this account bears on the conception of evil, and on a process of learning the sentiment of Christian guilt.[23] Yet

---

[20] M.-C. and E. Ortigues, *Oedipe africain*, Paris: L'Harmattan, 1984, pp. 281-2.

[21] *Ibid.*, p. 269.

[22] The 'believer-healer' may be defined as one of the faithful having received the gift of healing from the Holy Spirit, to which is often added the gifts of discernment, speaking in tongues (glossolalia), interpretation and prophecy. He is generally distinguished by his ardour in proselytising. Even though members of the Assemblies of God sometimes call him prophet, it seems to me more appropriate to call him 'believer-healer', in Mooré, the language of the Mossi, *wend nor ressa* (God's interpreter) or *wend nam tem twand da* (he who does God's work).

[23] And in this sense, in the particular context described by this account, A. Zempléni is

this account also reveals a complex of various elements, the analysis of which demonstrates that the categories of persecution and guilt are above all analytical constructions and not all-encompassing ideas, even if, as I will try to show, they express a dynamic of real change. In other words, in the case below Pentecostal membership refers less to a conversion in the etymological and radical sense of *convertere* (turning oneself towards), but rather to an adaptation to changes in lifestyle. It is more a question of distancing from village communalism than of its negation.

Old Sambo Kaboré was born around 1923. He was a weaver, and through this activity he became relatively wealthy. He had left his native village many years before in order to start a trading business, firstly with Ghana - importing kola nuts – and then he began selling wood in Ouagadougou. His success, it was said, provoked misunderstanding among his brothers and jealousy towards him. One day he discovered a 'gri-gri' buried at his door. He was afraid, not only for his safety, but because of what he was thinking: he wanted to kill anyone who resented him (for having become rich), which meant his own family. From that moment on, he saw 'fetishism' as constituting a dead end. In response to the transformation of his spatio-temporal horizon, through his long distance trade, which contrasted with the closed village space, he was to choose another form of protection, that of an almighty God and his pardon. Around this time, a youth told him about the Assemblies of God. He converted, as he explained it to me, in order to find peace. His younger brother resented him a lot, but he decided to offer him gifts and find him a wife. What distanced him from a traditional conception of social relations was not the offering of gifts, but rather the failure to respond to aggression.

The following episode, recounted by Bargo Towindé (a 'believer-healer' in Loumbila) relates Sambo Kaboré's path to final conversion:

I know an old man who attends the Loumbila Church. He's rich. One day, he had to return to his native village to attend the funeral of a family member. He arrived and moved in with his family. There, the elders of the village, who had assembled together, wanted to give him a test; I mean, to do something bad to him. They wanted to attack him with their fetishes and kill him to get his money.

Here we observe the confrontation between an individual and members of his native village whom he had left in order to begin trading. (He

---

correct when he argues that; "prophetism brings a transitional response to this general movement of individualisation [...] By substituting the ideology of demonic responsibility for the ancient schema of persecution, he (the prophet) sanctions for some (those who confess) and denies for others (their families) the decline of a socio-psychological mechanism which, in any case, has already turned against the individual. By establishing an intersubjective structure (still) characterised by the external, enunciated division of the individual into a subject who speaks and his evil, projected double, he speaks about and – through the place that this structure always reserves for the vicissitudes of persecution – he manages the process of interiorization of guilt.' A. Zempleni, 'De la persécution à la culpabilité', in C. Piault (ed.), *Prophétisme et thérapeutique*, Paris: Hetman, 1975, pp. 215-16.

subsequently tried to distance himself psychologically; in the pastor's words, at this point he had only converted 'by mouth'.) In other words, he had put certain distance between himself and the redistribution processes which put into play, like a sword of Damocles, jealousy, witch-craft or the fear of being bewitched. In this fashion he removed himself more generally speaking from notions of mutual dependence and con-ceptions of evil based on persecution, elements which are, among others, constitutive of village communal life. The story continues with the attack of a demon, which takes the form during his exorcism of an evil spirit sent by the village chief to kill him. Here, evil in the form of persecution is still present.

However, the rest of the story reveals the old man moving towards a greater interiorisation of the rules of Protestantism, and, at the same time, towards a (relative) change in his consciousness of evil. Sambo Kaboré then undergoes a sort of second conversion, this time 'of the heart', where after he commits a sin – that of not paying his tithe – it is God that tests him. The faithful counsel him to make good his accounts, for 'God alone reads men's hearts'.

The old man had gone back to the village accompanied by one of his sons. The local chief who was supposed to greet them was out to get them. He refused to let the son enter. The frightened child cried out. The old visitor was afraid, he realised that they wanted to kill him. The demon took advantage of his fear and entered into him!

The old man was possessed by the demon. He returned to Loumbila, but couldn't sleep anymore. He got up at night. He saw evil visions. He came and asked me to pray for him. When I started to pray, I saw that he was possessed. Then I set up a rendezvous with him at the Church. I gathered the faithful and together we chased out the demon in the name of Jesus. We prayed and demanded that he get out in the name of the authority of Jesus. Once he finally decided to leave the old man's body, the demon told me he was the spirit of Tenga Naaba (the village chief) and that it was he who had sent him. 'I came to destroy the old man', he said. He then left, saying that he was going back to where he had come from.

Without anticipating the rest of the story, I will simply note that the de-mon is a spirit who refers to the village chief and thus to the traditional universe of the ancestors (the group).[24] Custom is neither contested, questioned, nor destroyed. It henceforth incarnates the evil from which it is important to protect oneself through the search for an adequate form of spiritual power.

The old man felt well again. Satisfied, he attended prayer sessions. Yet, on one visit to the Church, he asked to be prayed for. At that moment, God revealed himself among us and told him to pay attention to his business, otherwise would have problems. Since I [Bargo Towindé] was not there at that session, I was unable to know about the danger he was going to run into.

[24] According to Ortigues *Oedipe Africain*, 'The foundation of common morals is the Custom of ancestors, the law of dead Fathers'.

We then instructed the old man. We did some calculations and told him that because he was not faithful in paying his tithe he was going to have problems. He then admitted that, in fact, he had not been paying his tithe regularly. We then counselled him to pay it correctly from then on.

This passage stresses the idea of fidelity and thus of the confidence one should have in one's relationship with God. The old man, aware of his fault, admitted his sin. Yet it is not really a God of love and pardon we have here: the old man had sinned and would be punished.

Ten days later, the inevitable problem arrived. In fact, the old man loved money. He has a donkey and cart and uses it to do a charcoal business with the capital city. In any case, he makes a lot of money with it. One day, when he'd left for Ouagadougou with a full cartload, he saw a big 'eighteen-wheeler' truck coming towards him. At that instant, a car tried to pass the truck. The car, driven by a white man, hit the back of the cart. The old man was walking along, holding tightly onto his donkey when he was thrown across the road. The donkey, who nearly crushed him, never got up again. The white man was killed and the cart demolished.

Everybody was killed, but the old man was unharmed. God's revelation came to pass, but since we had prayed to intercede for him, the action of God was real, but the disaster was mitigated. Since God had told him to pay attention to his activities, the problem had to happen. We men cannot really know God's plan.

In April 1998, the old man declared that he keeps a strict account of his income. The Church has replaced his family, he explained; the faithful are his brothers and sisters. He has become a deacon and adviser to the pastor. From time to time he sells an ox to support the community's actions. It would be interesting to analyse further the circulation of the tithe, in order to understand the nature of the redistribution at work: is it a question of its concentration in the pastor's hands in the guise of compensation for spiritual services rendered and/or a redistribution mechanism which, in the final analysis, is similar to the kinship processes ? Did the old man not begin to pay his tithe under pressure from the faithful and thus from a group?

Here conversion expresses a capacity for adaptation – the hope of a certain economic success which manifests itself, as in the case above, through the accumulation of personal wealth – in reaction to transformations in living conditions. For the village as a social group, these changes represent major upheavals and Pentecostal membership the most sociological way of distancing oneself from village communalism and the constraints it now seems to entail; the ideal or perhaps the utopia which underlies this religious trajectory can be summed up by the idea of maintaining good relations with one's entourage in case of need, while no longer being answerable to it.

These complex processes synthesise the particular forms which globalisation takes within these Mossi Protestant groups, conveyed here by the guiding image of conversion to a transnationalised belief. In concluding this part of the discussion, I would like to stress the idea that the Assemblies of God, while acting as a carrier for many transformations and thus being able to provide concrete sites where these changes can be experimented with, still leads to a phenomenon of *métissage*, or creolisation, in which the local appropriation of global forms results in distancing from a village communalism rather than its destruction or denial. Through these churches, one witnesses not the destruction of social bonds of kinship but their transformation. Thus the idea of an African modernity in which the Assemblies of God participates concerns the maintenance of the bonds of community, despite the processes of globalisation (uniformity, standardisation, speculation) which the churches embody, processes which may ultimately destroy such bonds. Here, it is a question of a paradoxical connection, favoured by conversion to the Assemblies of God, between the 'we' of the community (that of E. Durkheim's segmentary societies) and the 'I' of modernity. In other words, this transnational church nature appears to lead to the development of new groups or new 'tribes' with reinvented forms of sociality. I shall turn now to this question.

The Assemblies of God as a multi-functional community of great sociality

In cities or semi-urban zones and progressively in villages, the services of the Assemblies of God are inflamed by the invocation of the Holy Spirit. Intense emotion, described in the cases of churches in Brazil, Peru, the United States and Korea, is making its appearance here. Replacing sober ceremonies in which healing rituals occupied a marginal place at the end of services, with the pastor praying while distractedly laying his hands on the faithful at their request, prayers of deliverance from demons, animated by 'believer-healers', are flourishing and competing with the Sunday service and its pastor. The faithful, informed in dreams by God, discover that they have been given gifts.[25]

After some spectacular event, usually a miracle, which reveals the gift to his entourage, the healer seeks the support of prayer groups. As his reputation consolidates itself, he may sometimes feel the desire to distance himself from the Church and its pastors, in order to exercise his gift more freely. Emmanuel Sawagodo is a thirty-year-old Mossi; every Thursday he leads the deliverance prayer in a church in a poor neighbourhood of eastern Ouagadougou:

I was 23 years old and I was working on my older brother's plantation in Ivory Coast. I 'didn't know the papers' and I was the catechist's assistant [...] I had a

---

[25] The doctrine of the Assemblies of God distinguishes the following gifts: revelation (notably the gift of discernment of spirits), gifts of powers (faith healing, working miracles), gifts of inspiration (prophecy, speaking in tongues and the gift of interpretation).

revelation to do the Lord's work. Mark 16:18: [sic] 'Jesus said to lay your hands on the sick and they will be healed'. I had this at heart, but nothing like that was going on among the Catholics. In August 1990, a voice told me to arise and go be converted by the pastor Elie Sawagodo [...] The pastor told me that I was already filled with the Holy Spirit. I prayed all day long. I began to speak in tongues [...] God told me to leave the cocoa field and go and preach the Good News and pray for the sick [...]

As I prophesied, people saw I had the gift of healing. A voice told me: 'Lay your hands on them and I shall heal them'. When I laid my hands on them, children vomited poison. When they breathed, smoke came out of their nostrils. God told me: 'As of today I give you authority over the sick'.

Today, Emmanuel Sawagodo is back in Burkina Faso and exercises his gifts in the neighbourhood mentioned above. Every Wednesday, in front of sometimes as many as a hundred people, he leads the 'prayer of deliverance' from demons: dressed in a coat and tie, sometimes on the edge of exhaustion, he exorcises for hours at a time. On other days, the 'sick' file into his place. With his assistants, he prays to obtain their healing. God, as the Holy Spirit, reveals himself to Emmanuel through 'speaking in tongues' (glossolalia), which he immediately interprets and uses to give his diagnosis. In the name of the 'fire of God', he orders demon(s) to leave his patients. Following a deliverance session, a believer testified in front of the assembly:

I was converted and gave my life to Jesus a long time ago. But then I back-slid and returned to the 'world' again. Seven years ago, I broke with the Lord. After that I was possessed by a spirit of fear and a spirit of weakness. Even if God spoke to me, I didn't have the strength to do his will. Now, that He's begun to come back, I feel I'm finding the solution to my problem. I no longer feel possessed by a spirit of fear. Before, I would not have been able to stand up and speak to the assembly like I am now, to tell you what God has revealed to me. Now I can and I thank the Lord.

In the poorer neighbourhoods, and at times in the villages, the Pentecostal churches, or more precisely, the prayer groups – which are not necessarily situated in churches nor led by a pastor – are proving to be spaces of great sociality. These groups, run by the 'healer-believers', are able, through miraculous manifestations of the Holy Spirit, to resolve immediately, without charge, and for everyone, the problems of solitude (by reinventing family ties), disease, suffering, unemployment and adversity.

Emmanuel Sawagodo :

It is now time that we call upon the flame of the Eternal. Impure spirits will leave, demons will flee, sicknesses will go. God cannot go back on his word, he will accomplish His Works. We are going to call upon him now; let those who sing, sing with force. The Lord has revealed to me the way the battle will take place (...). The Lord has prepared everything. The flame will descend here and if the flame descends, the demons will flee. Diseases will go because the Lord has prepared the way.

This phenomenon is recent and represents a popular evolution not controlled for the moment by the governing pastors of the Assemblies of God. On this level, it seems useful to recall that the coherence of the Assemblies of God rests on its modernising image, promised by both the directing elite of the church and by the pastors settled in the rural areas. Yet another path, with its roots in the poorer sections of the population, sometimes rural but especially in urban areas, is emerging.

The Pentecostals experienced great success, this time among the poorer and especially urban population, during the revolutionary Sankarist regime (1983-7) and following the still more drastic restrictions imposed by the state on the population after the signing of the structural adjustment programme in 1992. This period has also been one of increased urbanisation and the rapid demographic growth of Ouagadougou. These transformations have given the Assemblies of God a second wind, and the Church now resembles in certain aspects – notably through the miraculous manifestation of the Spirit, solving problems of disease, unemployment and suffering in the here and now – its sister Pentecostal Churches in Liberia,[26] South Korea, Brazil,[27] Chile, Guatemala and Peru.[28]

Confronted with unprecedented problems of a socio-economic and political nature arising in the wake of the growth of the city and processes of globalisation which thrive on the destruction of particular or local explanations of the world, the Assemblies of God affirm themselves, more than ever before, as a refuge and place where group bonds may be recomposed.

Everything takes place as if parts of the population in the cities or the countryside were testing the limits of a type of development which leads to the unravelling of their organisational fabric. Far from manifesting themselves exclusively in urban areas, these changes traverse the Moogo (Mossi country), thus showing that in certain aspects, the global is clearly evident at the local level. The following extracts were gathered from Oubritenga villagers in January 1998:

People don't help one another anymore. There's no more love. Today, money, development and jealousy have become very important. So if you don't have the means, don't expect people to come to your home for a *sosoaga* [a self-help association for farmers].[29]

---

[26] See R. Marshall, 'Power in the Name of Jesus: Social Transformation and Pentecostalism in Western Nigeria "Revisited"', T. Ranger and O. Vaughan (eds), *Legitimacy and the State in Twentieth Century Africa,* Basingstoke: Macmillan, 1993, pp. 213-46.

[27] See A. Corten, *Le pentecôtisme au Brésil. Émotion du pauvre et romantisme théologique,* Paris: Karthala, 1995.

[28] See D. Stoll, *Is Latin America Turning Protestant?,* Berkeley and Los Angeles: University of California Press, 1990.

[29] The speaker signifies here that the monetarisation of this practice leads today, more than before, to a sort of proto-salarisation of agricultural work.

What does custom govern today ? Custom is nothing more than fetishes! It's fear and jealousy that drive everybody to look for protection.

There are no more fathers or mothers in the families: today it's the cinema that educates the children [...] The child only recognises the relative who has the most money, meaning the one who feeds him. If his father or mother don't have any money, he will ignore them. In that case, he'll leave the family to wander around and do bad things.

The destruction of the old forms of mutual aid and the difficulties of survival seem to act together, not to produce a transition from a traditional society towards modernity, but rather to reinforce the sentiment of a crisis of meaning. This crisis relates to the failure of certain references used in the past to construct identity, which delimit the relationship to space, the earth or to the ancestors, a process which only exacerbates the precariousness of daily life. This situation implies a rupture with the experience of previous generations. Existing conceptions of community, as well as of giving, trust, assistance, mutual dependence and otherness, are transformed by the contractualisation of exchange relations, and thus modify the mechanisms producing the bonds of kinship.

The social fabric is torn apart, while particularism, exclusion and intolerance increase. This leads to the segmentation of society, characterised by the development of new networks of different varieties, or groups based on elective affinity, to which the communities of the Assemblies of God now correspond. Confronted with the void occasioned by the destruction of traditional communities, sections of the population are tempted by offers which promise security: populist and fundamentalist movements, sects and ethnic nationalisms.

For many, confronted with a gamut of demographic, environmental, political, social, economic and cultural transformations, membership in the Assemblies of God represents an effective means of survival. The Assemblies of God develops into a complex of networks, networks which have become central to the religious wave sweeping the country today, and which involve a real transformation of the country's supernatural geography. Emmanuel Compaoré, 'believer-healer':

Twenty-four people expected to be healed. Today, their bonds are surely broken. Jesus has broken these bonds. We're going to praise God, because he's an almighty God [...] We've seen twenty-four people delivered from demons. They can now testify. Among the singers, there's one who suffered from stomach aches; during the deliverance, the hand of the Eternal saved him. Glory be to God.

The Pentecostals organise themselves into multi-functional communities of great sociality. The faithful are confronting an unprecedented crisis of meaning which is resumed in the idea of the obsolescence of the traditional explanation of the world and of a form of modernity whose material advantages are slow in coming. These communities assure their members a strong and coherent identity, a site for the elaboration of survival strategies anchored in multiple economic logics and new social practices and, above all, with an offer of healing in the here and now, meaning an effective interpretation of illness or misfortune, or, to put it another way, a reassuring interpretation of the world. Far from producing the prototype of a form of individualism, the adepts of this transnationalised religion are engaged in processes of the recomposition of social ties in response to the effects of globalisation on Mossi society. E. Sawadogo preaches:

God has revealed to me that there's someone with bilharzia here, and the voice told me to pray for this person. The voice told me that while we pray, there are people with bilharzia here; it hasn't yet taken place but the Lord wants to heal them. [A woman gets up. Sawadogo goes on]. We're going to pray for you and next week you'll witness. Don't take any more pills. Jesus is telling you to stop.

For the Mossi, membership in the 'Americans' church' does not really amount to the adoption of new knowledge and rejection of the old. It is rather a question of seeking new forms of equilibrium between individual projects and group obligations or membership in networks. If the influence of globalisation is making itself felt, to the benefit of this transnational religion, it leads to a powerful process of creolisation. On one hand, the desire for protection from others whose potential victim one still imagines oneself to be, albeit in a different way than in the past which encourages conversion to an all-powerful God, goes hand in hand with the desire to distance oneself from the kinship group in order to achieve personal financial success, a position which is legitimated by the doctrine of prosperity. On the other hand, conversion combines both individual strategies and membership within a collectivity, which results in a complex process of reinventing social ties. In response to the breakdown of the old forms of material and symbolic life, the community of believers develops as a network of chosen belonging marked by its sociality.

In this study, we are in the presence of individualisation 'African style', which combines the processes of individuation and the recomposition of communal solidarities.[30] Here conversion addresses principally the question of social ties, in terms of both partial emancipation from them and their reaffirmation in a context of psychological, social, economic, demographic, ecological and cultural change in which the idea of a 'disenchantment of the world' has no meaning.

These two central images transmitted by the communities of the Assemblies of God in Burkina Faso are grounded in the singular histories of individuals, but also in the current situation in the country. With a concern for clarity, I have discussed these various processses according to a chronological principle. Thus the conversion of peasants, as well as a

---

[30] Cf. on this A. Marie (ed.), *L'Afrique des individus*, Paris: Karthala, 1997.

certain urban elite, to a form of 'modernity' expressed in the image of a powerful God and the doctrine of prosperity precedes conversion motivated by the desire for immediate solutions to questions raised by the new upheavals in society.

The initial coherence of the Assemblies of God of Burkina Faso comes from its modernising image, as described above, disseminated both by the ruling elite of the Church and by the pastors and their communities in the rural areas. However, another direction is emerging, with its roots in the poorer sections of the population, sometimes rural, but especially within urban areas, based essentially around the figure of the believer-healer.

The Church of the Assemblies of God responds, in the early part of its current expansion, to a desire for change, a desire which expresses itself, for example, in terms of accumulation of personal wealth, or the personal choice of marriage partners. In the context we are dealing with, these changes represent upheavals so important that their protagonists will not take the risk without the support conferred by conversion to a powerful God, a power superior to the laws of the group they intend to transgress. This practice is the most sociological way of distancing oneself from one's entourage and thus reducing the constraints it presently seems to embody. Nevertheless, through this type of conversion one witnesses not so much the destruction of a traditional mode of thought as the process of invention or negotiation of another form of intersubjectivity. The uncertainty fostered by economic expansion seems to favour the diversification of strategies promising socio-economic security and at the same time the creolisation of the supernatural, opening new registers between immanence and transcendence, in response to demands for internal adaptation in a society confronted with change.

Following this initial period, from the mid-1980s onwards another tendency within Pentecostal communities has joined the first and in certain cases has transformed the processes described above, while at the same time, in other instances, it has produced a synergy between these two types. In the wave of conversions rolling in since the mid-1980s, everything happens as if parts of the urban population in particular, but also those in the rural areas, are testing the limits of a type of development which leads to the unravelling of their organisational fabric. In this context, the many groups organised by and around the Assemblies of God have become social networks which represent for many an effective means of survival.

BIBLIOGRAPHY

Constantin, François and Christian Coulon (eds), *Religion et transition démocratique en Afrique*, Paris: Karthala, 1997.

Corten, André, *Le pentecôtisme au Brésil. Émotion du pauvre et romantisme théologique*, Paris: Karthala, 1995.

de Luze, Bertrand, 'La situation actuelle des différentes églises', *Afrique contemporaine*, vol.159, no.3, 1991, pp. 27-32.

de Villers, Gauthier, *Phénomènes informels et dynamiques culturelles en Afrique*, Paris: Institut Africain-L'Harmattan, no.19-20, 1996.

Diallo, D. and René Otayek, *Dynamisme protestant, développement participatif et démocratie locale. Le cas de l'Office de Développement des Eglises evangéliques*, Ouagadougou: ORSTOM (forthcoming).

Dozon, Jean-Pierre, *La cause des prophètes. Politique et religion en Afrique contemporaine*, Paris: Seuil, 1995.

Geschiere, Peter and Piet Konings (eds), *Itinéraires d'accumulation au Cameroun*, Paris: Karthala, 1993.

Horton, Robin, 'African Conversion', *Africa*, vol.41, no. 2, 1971, pp. 85-108.

Izard, Michel, *Le Yatenga précolonial. Un ancien royaume du Burkina*, Paris: Karthala, 1985.

Jacob, Jean-Pierre and Philippe Lavigne-Delville, *Les associations paysannes, organisation et dynamiques*, Paris: APAD/IUED/Karthala, 1994.

Laurent, Pierre-Joseph, *Une association de développement en pays Mossi. Le don comme ruse*, Paris: Karthala, 1998.

Laurent, Pierre-Joseph, 'Les conversions aux Assemblées de Dieu du Burkina Faso: entre l'assemblée du développement et le réseau de grande socialité', *Journal des Africanistes*, no. 47, 1998, pp. 67-97.

Marie, Alain (ed.) *L'Afrique des individus*, Paris: Karthala, 1997.

Marshall, Ruth, 'Power in the Name of Jesus: Social Transformation and Pentecostalism in Western Nigeria "Revisited"' in Terence Ranger, and Olufemi Vaughan, (eds), *Legitimacy and the State in Twentieth Century Africa*, Basingstoke: Macmillan Press, 1993.

Ortigues, Marie-Cécile and Edmond, *Oedipe africain*, Paris: L'Harmattan, 1984.

Piault, Christian (ed.), *Prophétisme et thérapeutique*, Paris: Hetman, 1975.

Stoll, David, *Is Latin America Turning Protestant?*, Berkeley and Los Angeles: University of California Press, 1990.

Yaro, J.G., 'De l'évangélisation au développement local. Spécificité des ONG d'inspiration protestante au Burkina Faso', *Colloque International ONG et développement : Du Nord au Sud (Afrique, Amérique Latine, Asie)*, Bordeaux-Talence: Communication Tome 1, CNRS/ORSTOM/ Regards, 1996, pp. 277-93.

THE EXPANSION OF PENTECOSTALISM IN BENIN: INDIVIDUAL RATIONALES AND TRANSNATIONAL DYNAMICS

Cédric Mayrargue

The Beninese religious field, long dominated by 'traditional' religions, with the Vodun (voodoo) faith at the forefront, has seen a gradual diversification over the course of this century. Muslim, then Christian (Catholic and Methodist) communities have grown throughout the country. Prophetic and Afro-Christian churches have also emerged, the most important of which is the Celestial Church of Christ, which first appeared in the Porto-Novo region in 1947. The expansion of Pentecostalism must therefore be situated from the outset in this heterogeneous religious environment. Despite the fact that it has not so far been the subject of any specific study,[1] this phenomenon constitutes one of the strongest contemporary religious dynamics in the country.[2] Although the emergence of churches claiming to be Pentecostal can be dated back to the 1960s, it was the 1980s in particular that witnessed real growth in the number of movements and places of worship. Since the early 1990s, this trend has gathered considerable speed, and the Pentecostal movements, both native and imported, have met with unprecedented success, especially in urban areas.

The originality of Pentecostalism as a Christian religious expression stems from the importance accorded to the Holy Spirit and from the emotion felt by the converted. Direct, personal contact with the Holy Spirit – the outpouring of the Spirit – is at the heart of the Pentecostal experience. For some, this experience manifests itself in speaking in tongues or miraculous healings. Like all important religious changes, the growth of Pentecostalism is also linked to specific historical dynamics and to the changes that affect the societies in which they occur. In this light, the aim of this chapter is to recount and analyse this phenomenon in Benin. To study the reasons for the success of Pentecostalism requires a consideration of the context – religious, socio-economic and political – in which it develops, of the individual characteristics of its composite structures – the churches, the missions – and of the practices of those who are converted to it.

---

[1] The interest of both Beninese and foreign researchers has long been, and still is, limited to the Vodun faith. This has resulted in the masking of important dynamics and changes.

[2] See A. de Surgy, 'La multiplicité des Eglises au sud de l'Afrique occidentale', *Afrique contemporaine*, no. 177, 1996, pp. 30-40.

I propose the hypothesis that the success of Pentecostalism may be explained by the balance between a religious demand, linked to problems that are heightened under the present circumstances in Benin and to needs that are barely – if at all – satisfied, and a supply which, replete with virtues reinforcing its power, appears to be particularly efficient. But Pentecostalism does not merely provide destabilised individuals with answers and solutions; it also provides meaning and creates the dynamics of identity. Carried forward by individual rationales and transnational flows, it is popularising the rebuilding of identity at work in Beninese society.

I will begin by presenting this Pentecostal expansion, emphasising the context in which it has occurred and highlighting its main characteristics. Next, I will analyse this phenomenon as the meeting of individual paths and the proselytism of a religious circle. I will reflect upon the motivations, factors and rationales which guide these individuals, emphasising their search for solutions to problems or for the satisfying of needs, and then study the symbolic register used by these religious movements in their evangelistic work. Finally, I will focus on the construction of identity related to the growth of Pentecostalism, linking the dynamics of individualisation to those of the transnational field.

The growth of Pentecostalism in Benin

Two problems make it particularly difficult to quantify the Pentecostal phenomenon in Benin. The first is a matter of definition: which churches and which movements fit into this category? Should we rely on the denominations chosen by the organisations and stick solely to those which claim the Pentecostal appellation, thereby running the risk of excluding some others? I prefer to focus here on a religious circle that has permeable frontiers, grouping together movements with a certain number of characteristics in common.

The second difficulty lies in the evaluation of the current extent of Pentecostalism. Religious movements have to declare their existence and obtain authorisation from the Beninese Ministry of the Interior, Security and Territorial Administration. However, many of them do not carry out this formality, or wait several years before doing so. The waiting period between the request for authorisation and its granting by the ministry should also be taken into account. Nevertheless, on the basis of the official registers, the work carried out by other researchers[3] and my own observations, I estimate at between 100 and 200 the number of religious structures, mainly Christian, that have emerged over the last ten years. As for the number of people these movements comprise, the 1992 census

---

[3] Particularly the census of religious movements, carried out by J.-C. Barbier, a sociologist from ORSTOM assigned to Benin.

indicated that there were 6.0 percent of 'other' Christians in the country (in other words, people defined as neither Catholic nor Methodist Protestant). If the weight of Celestial Christianity and the Afro-Christian churches is taken into account, these figures give little indication as to the number of Pentecostals. One observer, himself a minister and head of a missionary organisation, estimated in 1996 that Evangelical churches comprised 300,000, while pointing out that this estimate 'should be treated with the utmost caution'.[4] We can therefore estimate that between 100,000 and 200,000 people are members of Pentecostal organisations.

Pentecostalism thus remains a minority phenomenon in the Beninese religious field, even within Christianity, which is still dominated by the historical weight and the social influence of the Catholic Church. But its visibility and its current expansion make it one of the country's major contemporary religious dynamics. Before moving on to a review of the main characteristics of the spread of this new religious expression, we will briefly present the context in which it has occurred.

A context favourable to the growth of Pentecostal movements

The religious context. The Beninese religious field is characterised by its plurality and its flexibility. There is no longer a genuinely dominant religious pole and the large categories, particularly Christians and followers of the 'traditional' religions, have been tending to even out, according to data from the 1992 census.[5] The traditional faiths seem to have lost ground to the new religions, but neo-traditional forms and new Vodun faiths have met with a certain amount of success, while Islam is strengthening its position in the north and the east of the country and the Catholic Church, which has a good territorial network, is in a dominant position in the south. The inhabitants of the two largest towns (Cotonou and Porto-Novo), where one finds the people most affected by Pentecostalism, are mainly Christian or Muslim. The expansion of Pentecostalism has thus occurred in a splintered, constantly changing environment. However, two other characteristics appear to be important. First, the fact that for more than a century Beninese society has been shaped by the Catholic and Methodist expressions of Christianity,[6] then subsequently by inde-

---

[4] M. Alopko, 'L'histoire des églises et missions évangéliques au Bénin' in J.R. Krabill (ed.), *Nos racines racontées. Récits historiques sur l'Eglise en Afrique de l'Ouest*, Abidjan: Presses bibliques africaines, 1996, p. 92.

[5] Aside from the 6% of other Christians, there were 35% of followers of traditional religions, 25.9% of Catholics, 20.6% of Moslems, 3.5% of Methodist Protestants, 1.9% of followers of other religions and 6.4% of people without a religion (*Second General Census of the Population and Housing*, Feb. 1992).

[6] The first attempts to introduce Christianity to the territory which is now called Benin go back to 1661. Evangelisation, however, did not really begin until the second half of the nineteenth century, spreading from the coastal regions by means of Methodist missionaries (as from 1843), then Catholic ones (in 1864).

pendent forms which have always developed alongside important social changes. Dissident churches, breaking away from the Christian missions, emerged at the end of the last century in Nigeria and a little later in Benin (the Boda-Owa, founded in Porto-Novo in 1901). Similarly, the Aladura churches which developed in the Yoruba region rapidly crossed the border; for example, the Sacred Order of Cherubim and Seraphim shortly after its birth in 1925. Pentecostalism thus made its appearance in a strongly Christianised environment (63% of the inhabitants of Cotonou declared themselves Catholic in 1992). Secondly, the impregnation of Beninese society by the Vodun faiths must be emphasised, particularly in the southern and central regions, with other 'traditional' faiths existing in the rest of the country. This historical, but also current weight of Vodun explains the permanent recourse to religion in times of trouble and material problems.

The political and administrative context. 1990 saw a turning-point in Benin, with the liberalisation of political life. Following the social movements and the multi-sector mobilisation that had come to a head during the previous year, and faced with his inability to respond to the people's demands, the head of state, M. Kérékou, who had been in power since the coup d'état of October 1972, called a National Conference. This conference took place in February 1990 and, following the proclamation of its sovereignty, led to a transition period during which a new constitution was adopted and elections organised. N. Soglo, the transition-period prime minister, was elected president of the republic in March 1991, and large-scale reforms were set in motion.[7] Religious freedom was once again proclaimed and protected. This context thus appears to have been favourable to the flourishing of churches, which were now able to grow without hindrance. Many religious organisations, which had not carried out or been able to carry out the administrative formalities, registered at the ministry. This liberal political and administrative setting favoured the arrival of foreign churches which could now start up their activities on Beninese soil without fear of repression.

A situation of crisis and uncertainty. The economic crisis was particularly hard-felt in Benin. The social effects of the structural adjustment programmes sharpened the daily problems of the population, who attempted to find survival solutions in informal or illegal activities. The urban classes were the first to be hit by the new forms of pauperisation. Elsewhere, the political ups and downs and the limited scale of the changes instigated by the new authorities led to a feeling of disappointment. Added to the economic standstill, social malaise, growing insecurity,

---

[7] See R. Banégas, 'La démocratie "à pas de caméléon". Transition et consolidation démocratique au Bénin', PhD diss., Institut d'Etudes Politiques de Paris, 1998.

and disorientation in the face of rapid social change was political disillusionment; all these factors contributed to increasing anomie and unease. This was fertile ground for the development of new religious forms, which were able to give meaning to these changes and domesticate them or, conversely, offer an alternative.

The context in which Pentecostal expansion is situated is therefore marked by a particular religious environment and a new political liberalisation. It is above all characterised by the uncertainty and unease of the people most affected both by social change and daily problems. Rather than see a sort of determinism, we should link a social phenomenon such as Pentecostal growth to the context in which it is situated, so as to gain a better grasp of its main characteristics.

The characteristics of Pentecostal expansion

Pentecostalism appeared relatively recently in Benin. The Assemblies of God were present in the north of Benin from missions established in Upper Volta after the Second World War,[8] but their influence was for a long time restricted to this region. The Pentecostal Church, at the time still called the Apostolic Church of Ghana, established itself near the Togo border in the 1950s and reached Cotonou in 1965, without meeting much success for many years. The 1980s saw the arrival of many movements, such as the Evangelical Faith Mission, the Church of God of Prophecy and the Deeper Life Bible Church. Since the beginning of the 1990s, there has been a real expansion in the Pentecostal sphere, manifested in several forms: the continual arrival of new structures from Nigeria and Ghana (the Redeemed Christian Church of God, the Church of Christ, Action Faith); the creation of local churches (the Ministry of Hope, the Holy Spirit Bible Church); and the growing success of churches that had been established much earlier. The Pentecostal Church in Benin now has more than 170 congregations, spread over virtually the whole country. This expansion of the Pentecostal circle has also influenced the other Christian movements. Charismatic Renewal has developed within the Catholic Church since the end of the 1970s and has expanded spectacularly during the past few years. The weekly gatherings in the St. Michel or Bon Pasteur parishes of Cotonou bring together hundreds of people. The Methodist Church is also confronted with the growth of Pentecostalism and as yet has found no answer, causing discontent among certain young ministers. However, Benin was affected later than most African countries by the Pentecostal wave, which first spread in English-speaking countries.

[8] They obtained authorisation from the colonial authorities in 1947 and were soon joined by the SIM (Sudan Interior Mission, which has since become the International Mission Society). In 1949 a 'territory-sharing' process took place between the Assemblies of God (north-west), the SIM (north-east) and the Methodist mission (south and centre).

Pentecostalism is indeed an exogenous phenomenon in Benin. Of course, indigenous structures are being developed today within this sphere, but they sometimes remain dependent on transnational networks. There are, however, small local churches that are completely independent. Two origins can thus be distinguished, and two ways in which the Pentecostal movements emerged: the transnational and the indigenous. The first churches arrived in Benin from English-speaking African starting-points such as Nigeria or Ghana.[9] These were either movements of American or, more rarely, European origins, established first in English-speaking countries before moving on to their French-speaking neighbours, or native churches founded in these African countries, which then moved into Benin with expansionist strategies in mind. This movement was facilitated by geographical proximity and by the presence of the same ethnic group across the borders. This is the case for the Deeper Life Bible Church,[10] whose Nigerian founder, W. F. Kumuyi, is Yoruba. The highly permeable nature of the Benin-Nigeria border which lies across Yoruba country made these exchanges easier and, in 1986, the Church sent a Yoruba missionary to Cotonou. The Foursquare Church followed more or less the same route. This American movement has been established in Nigeria for a long time and first attempted to set up in a Beninese village near the border in 1969. A congregation opened in Porto-Novo in 1981, then another in Cotonou in 1986. Ghana has also been the starting-point for many Pentecostal organisations. The example of the Pentecostal Church has already been mentioned: following its inception in Ghana, it spread to Togo, then to Benin. Even today the majority of its congregations are based in Mono, the region bordering Togo. More recently, other Ghanaian churches such as Action Faith or the Stream of Life Ministries have opened places of worship in Cotonou.

These movements regularly organise crusades or evangelisation campaigns, with foreign 'speakers' from Nigeria or Ghana, but also 'great men of God' from Europe or North America. The indigenous Pentecostal churches sometimes call upon these outside resources. Although the birth of these organisations is presented as being the result of a vision or a call, it is often linked to a split inside existing churches, resulting from rivalries or personal competition. The problem of dependence on a head-quarters situated outside the country is often one of the reasons behind the split. The emergence of indigenous Pentecostalism has led to the appearance of independent churches which often remain modest in size.

[9] For a study of Pentecostal movements in Nigeria, see R. Marshall, 'Pentecostalism in Southern Nigeria: an Overview' in P. Gifford (ed.), *New Dimensions in African Christianity*, Ibadan: Sefer, 1993, pp. 8-39. As for Ghana, see G. ter Haar, 'Standing up for Jesus: A Survey of New Developments in Christianity in Ghana', *Exchange*, vol. 23, no. 3, 1994, pp. 221-40.

[10] M. A. Ojo, 'Deeper Life Bible Church of Nigeria' in P. Gifford (ed.), *New Dimension*, pp. 161-85.

The present expansion of Pentecostalism is concentrated in urban areas. The rural areas and even the small towns have remained untouched or have been affected only very recently. This concentration in urban areas contrasts with the older movements present since the 1940s or 1950s, such as the Assemblies of God or the Pentecostal Church, which were strongly implanted in rural areas or small towns from their inception. The city is not only the place where the socioeconomic crisis is most strongly felt, but it is also the primary site of social change, opening out to the world and trends towards individualisation. Cotonou alone attracts virtually all the new Pentecostal forms. A week does not go by without crusades, evangelisation campaigns, training seminars and other events. Banners decorate the crossroads, church signs appear along the roadsides. Certain movements which have no place of worship rent public or private venues. Rallies, conferences, prayer meetings, night vigils and services are held in a variety of sites: a former cinema (Ciné Vog), arts or sports centres (le Hall des arts et de la culture, le Palais des Sports) and conference rooms (le Centre de promotion de l'artisanat, or, for the wealthiest, le Centre international de conférence). Open-air sites are also used, such as the former Place Lénine. This dynamism can be measured not merely by this increasing visibility and all these special events, which have become routine in Cotonou, but also by the race to set up churches, district by district. The Pentecostal Church in Benin, which by the end of the 1980s had only two congregations in the economic capital, had 17 in Cotonou and the surrounding area in 1998.

The extreme heterogeneity of the Pentecostal sphere must be emphasised. Foreign movements mingle with indigenous structures, churches and missions; some organisations comprise dozens of parishes in several regions of the country while others are small, with no fixed meeting-place at all. In total, several dozen types of structures belong to the Pentecostal sphere. Movements start up and schism is rife, making the Pentecostalism field in Benin particularly unstable and unsettled. There are of course links among these various forms. From time to time churches get together to organise the coming of internationally-renowned preachers such as Reinhard Bonnke, Carlo Brugnoli or Jim Smith. Movements claiming to be non-confessional organise interdenominational events, open to all the organisations in the born-again circle. The International Evangelisation and Spiritual Awakening Mission organises the Pan-African Conference of Giants of the Faith every two years in Cotonou. Youth on Mission took advantage of the arrival of a hospital ship from its central organisation headquarters between December 1997 and April 1998 to organise an 'open-day' Christian festival and increase the number of evangelisation sessions. On a more formal level, there are two structures which unite a certain number of Christian churches: the Council of Protestant and Evangelical Churches of Benin (CEPEB) and the Federation of Evangelical

Churches and Missions of Benin (FEMEB). But many structures, particularly the smaller ones, do not participate in these groups and go as far as refusing any contact with other churches, including other Pentecostals. This is the attitude of the Wisdom of God in Christ Ministries, which cultivates its individuality by turning in on itself. Other small movements which often have only one congregation have no relations with the big denominations. In addition, the question of introducing Pentecostal elements is sometimes broached in the Christian churches that have typically remained prudent on the subject, a question which often divides church leaders. Ministers sometimes complain that their superiors or the lay directors of the Evangelical churches they work for are too reticent with regard to the outpouring of the Spirit and divine healing.

The 'born-again' movements, which speak of a rebirth in Christ and which impose a radical conversion on the faithful by means of a 'genuinely' biblical baptism, have made increasing progress. Their public is urban, mainly female, but socially diverse. Although the majority of the faithful is made up of people from modest backgrounds, there are more and more civil servants and managers. This great diversity is related to the origin and type of the church. The churches with foreign origins, particularly American, are particularly attractive to the middle classes, and their implantation in urban areas brings them into contact with a socially diversified population. Their theology is at times very well-elaborated and they often preach the 'gospel of prosperity'. Indigenous movements touch a more working-class population, are often present in suburban areas and can set up more easily in the rural milieu.

Among the newly converted there are many former Catholics, most of whom have passed through many different denominations before arriving at Pentecostalism. Certain Pentecostal movements count former Muslims among their ranks, often shopkeepers attracted by the gospel of prosperity. This theology links economic success and enrichment to conversion to Christianity, and addresses above all shopkeepers and businesspeople. The mixed nature of the ethnic composition of Cotonou (even though the Fon are preponderant) favours plurality in churches. However, the origin of the church and the identity of its founder heavily influence recruitment procedures, as the case of the Yoruba churches demonstrates.

Pentecostalism therefore appears to be one of the most active religious expressions in Benin. I will now turn to the analysis of its success, focusing successively on the steps taken by individuals, then the strategies of the movements. It is the convergence of these two rationales which lies behind this success.

The itineraries and motivations of the converted

Before developing explanations for the success of Pentecostalism, we must start by looking at the converted and tracing the paths which they have taken. I will base this analysis on what individuals themselves say and the reasons they put forward to explain their religious orientation. In a certain sense, it is a matter of giving individual initiative its proper place, rather than reducing everything to the strategies and the proselytism of the movements in question. I argue that the choice of Pentecostalism appears, at a given moment, to be the last religious resort for people who often have a long history in this field.

Religion as a resort. Faced with difficult situations and new problems, many inhabitants turn to religious practices in the hope of finding solutions, remedies and assistance. Turning towards religion in times of trouble is a sensible and rational reaction, especially in a traditional religious environment where, for example, the divine is consulted to give meaning to problems and to provide solutions. Solutions to material problems are thus sought in the spiritual field. Moreover, other means which could provide assistance are increasingly uncertain. In a context of social disintegration, individuals can expect little - in terms of mutual help, security and redistribution - from the family or the state, to take two very different institutions as examples. The attraction of religion therefore does not lie so much in the content of its discourse or in its beliefs, but rather in its efficacy. The success of Pentecostalism can thus be analysed not only as a response to the emergence of new problems, but also as a result of the loss of efficacy of other religious options and of the failure of all other attempts to find assistance. Indeed, many converts have rich religious pasts with an accumulation of religious experiences. When believers do not receive the expected satisfaction, or are faced with disappointment or apparently insoluble new problems, they may take a chance and change their religious community. For new believers, Pentecostalism, with its novelty and aura of success, appears to be the last stage and the (provisional?) end of their religious journey.

If we accept that those who convert to Pentecostalism are mainly in search of a solution to their problems and satisfaction of their needs, we must examine them and distinguish between old and new problems.

Health and the search for protection. Health and fertility difficulties are the foremost problems leading people to seek solutions in the religious sphere. A non-medical explanation is given for these disorders and a human or supernatural origin is attributed to them. As well as the belief in such origins to these problems, the cost of modern medical care, aggravated by the effects of socio-economic crisis, the real (or imagined) limits of 'traditional' medicine and the failure or suspicion of magico-religious practices all contribute to this turn towards Pentecostalism.

More generally, the search for protection, or 'armour', in the face of attacks by enemies or witches is commonly mentioned. In an environment where almost all events have a mystic cause such problems are seen by people as being caused by the action of malevolent individuals with supernatural powers, and thus the search for power is seen as the best way of protecting oneself from attack. The Afro-Christian churches and prophetic movements have grown by playing the role of the anti-witch, or the witch-finder. The Catholic Church, long reluctant to recognise this reality, no longer hesitates in developing the practice of exorcism. The Pentecostal movements are particularly at ease with this sort of approach; the recognition of the reality of evil supernatural powers and the provision of 'supernatural weapons' to do battle with them are central to Pentecostal doctrine and practice, not only in Benin, but throughout the world.

Success, wealth and new needs: If assistance is expected from religion to resolve medical problems and to provide powerful protection, the desire for wealth and success is becoming an essential element in the demand for religion. More than any other religious movement, Pentecostalism plays explicitly on this other dimension and even contributes to creating these needs. It is thus hardly surprising that its expansion should coincide with the increased affirmation of this sort of desire. From the peddlar to the market trader to the big businessman, all wish to see their activities prosper. To achieve this they rely on divine benediction as a means of accessing enrichment and success. The theme of the gospel of prosperity is echoed particularly in the urban business population.[11]

The crisis and the new day to day difficulties it is causing, along with the acceleration of social change which increases the feeling of uncertainty, also create new needs and new desires. The economic crisis, further accentuated by the effects of structural adjustment programmes and the consequences of the devaluing of the CFA franc, has thrown into question certain statuses and benefits taken for granted (the end of systematic recruitment of graduates by the civil service from 1986, a reduction in the number of civil servants). More importantly, it has blocked the process of social mobility and called into question the traditional forms of solidarity and self-help (because of the drop in the standard of living), thus leading to the pauperisation of urban populations. In a parallel development, the opening out to the world market, via Nigeria in many fields, and the distribution of new products into the Beninese market,

---

[11] In March 1998 the World Mission Agency used posters to appeal to the inhabitants of Cotonou to 'discover the secrets of financial peace' within the framework of a 'Breakthrough Seminar' on the theme of 'Breaking Financial Hardship'.

have created desires which are increasingly difficult to satisfy. New needs have thus appeared in this period of political uncertainty, socio-economic crisis and general unease. Although the economic situation has improved in terms of the demands of international financial institutions (positive growth rate, reduction of inflation), the population has benefited little. Likewise, the enthusiasm in the wake of the fall of the Kérékou regime has been replaced by disappointment with the new leadership, which has been unable to respond to raised hopes. The population no longer expects much from the state, except perhaps those who have private access to it.

This context of uncertainty and of the search for well-being and social success is of central importance. Individuals, plunged into a situation of crisis and insecurity, feel the need to be reassured. Having accumulated religious experiences without the results hoped for, or at least without durable solutions, they continue their search. It is in this context of destabilisation and uncertainty that Pentecostalism appear. With the solutions it claims to provide, its modes of expression and expansion and its dynamism, it is well adapted to this current context, insofar as it provides concrete solutions while making visible major social changes. I will now examine why Pentecostalism has met with such success, perhaps more than any other religious form, and how it presents itself to some as the most convincing solution. In order to do so, I will turn my attention from the believers to the Pentecostal organisations.

The symbolic register of Pentecostalism: novelty, modernity, rupture, efficacy

I have argued that the success of Pentecostalism is closely linked to the religious, social and political situation at the historical moment when it entered Beninese society from the outside, and have indicated the importance of socio-economic difficulties, increasing poverty in the urban environment, loss of bearings, a shared feeling of unease, and the emergence of new needs. But in order to understand how it spread throughout Benin in the 1980s and grew even more rapidly during the present decade, the strategies of the actors involved and the global dynamics of this religious movement must also be considered. In both the North-American based missions and churches and the local organisations, Pentecostalism arrived in most cases from neighbouring Anglophone countries, thus reflecting the expansionist rationale of a religious movement with universalist pretensions. The lack of co-ordination and the atomisation of these organisations, along with a certain rivalry among them, have meant that this expansion is somewhat disordered. Religious entrepreneurs, the 'importers' and founders of churches, also have their own rationales and interests to defend. All try to make their own churches more visible, thus hoping to reach more believers. Each movement has its own dynamic (some keep precise accounts of the number of people converted or baptised), which contributes to the dynamics of the Pentecostal expansion as a whole.

The warm welcome given to this form of religious expression can be explained by the features which are emphasised and the registers employed by Pentecostal actors in their operations to win over the Beninese population. It is also the consequence of an active effort in symbolic elaboration. I will analyse successively four elements of this symbolic repertory which have been particularly emphasised: novelty, modernity, rupture and efficiency.

Novelty. Arriving in a rich and varied religious field, Pentecostalism first appeared to be an innovation, in terms of both the activities and the organisation of the movements. As far as the forms of evangelism are concerned, these churches highlight campaigns and crusades which aim to reach as wide an audience as possible. They are often held in the open air, the space being organised around a dais, with loudspeakers to enable the message to be heard beyond the immediate audience. Indoor venues are sometimes hired: banners are hung on the walls of the buildings and in different strategic places in the city to publicise the event. Advertisements are broadcast on radio and television. Events organised by Pentecostal organisations may also take on other forms: seminars, conference camps, miracle nights, major prophetic gatherings. Much importance is given to music and sometimes short plays are staged. All of these are new forms of evangelism, where believers leave the church and carry the message out into the streets. The Good News is spread throughout various districts of the city door-to-door; many brochures and leaflets are distributed. The permanent activities of the churches or interdenominational movements of Pentecostalism are also innovative in nature: prayer evenings and nights, intercession and healing sessions, Bible study. The structure of these organisations differs from those established earlier; although the position of the minister, who is often the founder, is central and respect for the hierarchy is a golden rule, lay members can reach positions of responsibility such as leading prayers, or can have their charismatic gifts (such as healing or prophecy) recognised.

Modernity. Not only is Pentecostalism new in the Beninese religious space, it also seeks to be modern. Symbols of modernity, which are often reduced to its technological expressions, are employed. An example of this is the use of modern musical instruments: electric guitars, drum kits, synthesisers. This is a far cry from the 'traditional' instruments based on percussion which are used in Vodun ceremonies and even from the 'modern' borrowings of certain prophetic faiths with their bands. The rhythms are resolutely innovative.

Video has made an appearance with the filming of special ceremonies and evangelism campaigns. Screens are sometimes set up so that people can watch the event which is underway or recordings of past 'miracles' performed by the preacher present. At the end of the meeting, cassettes are put on sale for those who want to relive the intensity of the event.

The English language is increasingly used in Pentecostal events. Some Nigerian or Ghanaian movements which target the immigrants from these countries naturally use this language. But even when other churches call on preachers, they are often English-speaking. The texts of the posters on the walls of Cotonou are often written in English with a very approximate French translation, despite French being the official language of the country. When speakers come from Europe or North America, they also speak in English. English seems to have greater evocative power than French, even though it is not understood by all those who are listening to these messages. The word 'amen' is increasingly pronounced in English fashion and expressions such as 'Praise the Lord' are frequently heard.

Last but not least, clothing is also used as an indicator of the intention to display modernity. Ministers and preachers wear suits and ties, sometimes in bright colours. Rare are those who wear traditional dress, even when such dress does not have any religious connotations. Wearing a suit and tie can be a way of expressing the rejection of traditional religious cultures and symbolising, in contrast, membership in a much wider, more modern community. At the same time, the three-piece suit is also one of the signs of social success. Finally, it clearly sets the minister apart from his Catholic or Methodist counterparts, thus highlighting through his clothing the break with tradition that he represents.

Rupture and externality. Pentecostalism develops in opposition to all the existing forms of religion. It refuses all compromise and all discussion with other religions and denominations. It rejects both the 'pagans' (Vodun or Muslim followers) and the 'false Christians' (particularly Catholics), refuses all ecumenism and claims to hold the only, Bibilical truth, and represents itself as the sole path to salvation. It implies a total break with the convert's former beliefs, expressed as a total conversion, a second birth committing the whole individual. This break can be expressed through the destruction of fetishes and *grigris*, which are sometimes burned, and can be completed through baptism by immersion. A central element of this symbolic system is testimony. Former witches come to testify about what they did and members tell of their life in the occult. The language of rupture is thus twofold: the break with former beliefs and practices and the break with the life led until that moment, with the two breaks linked as one. Religious conversion must also be accompanied by a change in behaviour in social life. The fact that Pentecostalism is a religious movement which came from outside the country can only strengthen this impression of a radical change. This is just as clearly expressed, however, in the indigenous churches. The imported or exogenous dimension of Pentecostalism, with all that it represents in terms of prestige and modernity, only increases its power and attraction, just like the aura that surrounds the imported products which can now be found in Beninese markets. But its success is mostly due to its claims to efficacy.

Efficacy. While this is first and foremost part of the symbolic field, at the same time it involves a belief in its effectiveness on the part of the converted. In fact, it represents a promise, if the titles of certain Pentecostal events are anything to go by: Pastor Adetola of the Ephrata mission (based in Abidjan) regularly organises evenings in Cotonou which are called 'miracle nights'; 'Three Days of Wonder' were organised by the Christ Ascension Church in May 1998; the Christian Pentecostal Mission proposed victory nights on the theme of 'Power Jam '97'; while the 'All Christians Interdenominational Camp Conference' organised in July 1997 by the Divine Grace Gospel Ministries promised 'Victory and Glory' to those who attended.

Tales of miracles accomplished by ministers in the past and public accounts given by the beneficiaries of miracles – those who have been healed, have managed to give birth or have been freed – also play an essential role. The word – that of the preacher, of ministers, of the miraculously cured and also of devoted believers – is also central to this discursive construction of efficacy. But the curious are also convinced by what they see. The outpouring of the Spirit descends on certain participants, who begin speaking in tongues. Above all, the ceremonies are often concluded by sessions of miracle healing in which the splendour and power of the preacher are supposed to be expressed. By emphasising miracles, divine healing and the palpable intervention of the Holy Spirit, and by making immoderate use of testimonies and accounts, Pentecostalism displays its power and its efficacy. For those faced with serious problems and who have had recourse to religion without success, it appears as the much sought-after solution, with the support of all this ample proof.

It is this visible demonstration of its claim to efficacy, its methods of projection (crusades, music, etc.) and its careful presentation which holds the key to Pentecostal expansion in a Beninese society in search of an identity. With its varied structures (churches, missions, interdenominational movements), Pentecostalism is thus growing by playing on a certain number of registers and by highlighting its ability to provide solutions to problems and to satisfy needs. It attracts because it provides a destabilised population with simple, concrete answers and demonstrates its immediate, material efficacy. By placing the individual in relation with a global movement, by mixing individual and transnational rationales, it plays an integral role in the rebuilding of identity.

Identity-building in Pentecostalism: individual rationales and transnational dynamics

Increasing individualisation in the urban milieu and opening out to the world both facilitate the independence and diversification of religious choices, thus creating favourable conditions for the expansion of Pentecostalism. Indeed, its development seems to respond to individual rationales and to be part of a context of opening outwards. Identity-building develops around these two powerful dynamics, individualisation and globalisation. The question of identity is approached here in a dynamic perspective. When we speak of identity-building, we mean a process of interaction between the individual actors and a given milieu, leading to the formation of features, signs and sentiments that are specific to the group. This formation of identity in terms of an association with a Pentecostal community does not exclude other identities.[12] It is added to the identities that the individual recognises and can mobilise to suit the circumstances. By bringing personal answers to everyone, by highlighting the aspect of community, by deploying its transnational character, is Pentecostalism the creator of new identities?

The individual rationale. The Pentecostal approach in Benin is first and foremost an individual, rather than a family or group approach. It is part of the individualisation process, whereby individuals emerge as autonomous actors, freeing themselves from the ties of community.[13] In these churches one comes across wives without their husbands, husbands without their wives and children without their parents. We have seen that the causes (problems, illness, need) that lead citizens to these movements are personal. Acquaintances – neighbours, colleagues - rather than members of the family, are the ones who tell people about the movements and who invite them to crusades and evangelism campaigns. The inhabitants of Cotonou sometimes have little in the way of family in the city. The 'traditional' links thus tend to loosen more easily, facilitating the process of autonomy of individuals, including their choice of religious membership.

If the step towards Pentecostal movements is taken without the family, it can also be taken against the family. This choice can be a means of emancipating oneself, by opposing the family with regard to its religious practices: traditionalist, Catholic or even Muslim. Sometimes the problems which condition the search for religious solutions are directly imputed to relatives and the family environment. This is the case with accusations of witchcraft that are made to explain illness or bad

---

[12] J.-F. Bayart reminds us that 'none of these "identities" exhausts the panoply of identities that an individual has'. J.-F. Bayart, *L'illusion identitaire*, Paris: Fayard, 1996, p. 99.

[13] See A. Marie (ed.), *L'Afrique des individus*, Paris: Karthala, 1997.

luck: the origin of the wrong is never far away and often lies with the family or somebody close.

Pentecostal membership, however, can coincide with ethnic identity. This is the – quite specific – case of certain Nigerian churches which mainly turn to immigrants from the neighbouring eastern part of Benin (as in the case of the Christ Ascension Church for the Igbos of Cotonou, mainly made up of shopkeepers). It is also the case of churches that are open to all but which recruit relatively homogeneously in ethnic terms. But in these examples as well, the step taken by the follower remains an individual one.

Pentecostalism and access to the universal. Becoming a 'brother in Christ' means leaving an environment (the family, the village, the ethnic group) which appears closed and overbearing; it means gaining access to a form of modernity and being part of a global culture. The faithful can follow international meetings and listen to preachers from other countries in the sub-region or, even better, from North America and Europe. They can take part in seminars in which believers from neighbouring countries participate. The more enterprising among them become part of transnational networks and travel to conventions in Nigeria, Ghana or Togo. This claim to the universal is also to be found among the indigenous Pentecostal movements, as demonstrated by their choice of names. There is the International Mission, the World Mission or the Universal Church, even though these organisations are only to be found in Benin and only count a few congregations. It must, however, be noted that foreign origin can be the source of problems within these movements. The conflicts which have often broken out in the Pentecostal Church in Benin originate, aside from matters of personal rivalry, from accusations made against the dominant influence of the central Ghanaian Pentecostal Church. This movement has been reproached for sending part of the funds collected by its Beninese branch directly to headquarters in Accra. The authoritarian manner with which it appoints and moves ministers in Benin has also been criticised by some people who have left the church. These splits have brought about the birth of other organisations such as the Pentecostal Church of Faith, the Pentecostal Church of the Awakening or even, recently, the Awakening of the Pentecostal Church in Benin.

A new community. As is also the case with other religious movements, Pentecostal practice enables people to go beyond the frontiers of groups such as the family, the region or the ethnic group, and to be part of a new community.[14] Recruitment by this new community goes beyond the

---

[14] A. Marie reminds us that the religious arena is 'one of the social spaces in which individuals can find a base in their quest for relative independence and for critical distance

usual cleavages that are part of society. According to the converted, a great warmth emanates within the Pentecostal movements. The faithful are asked to live this religious experience to the full and to participate in the many regular activities (services, prayer evenings, Bible study, specific meetings for individual groups) as well as the special ones (crusades, seminars with guest speakers, retreats). In general, all the movements organise events – aside from those on Sundays – on Wednesdays and Fridays. The more active among the faithful can join music groups, choirs, evangelism teams or parish committees. Specific groups are held for children, young people or women. In the Pentecostal Church in Benin, those most committed to evangelism activities join the Witnesses of Christ movement. Solidarity networks are formed within these movements, particularly when one of the faithful falls ill and is visited at home by other members. However, this type of assistance and self-help can be a screen for quite strict practices of control. It is not rare, in reduced groups or small congregations, that the names of absentees are noted and the individuals in question then visited to inquire about the reasons for their absence. In the same way, the financial contributions of the faithful to the life of the church can be monitored carefully; some movements keep genuine accounts.

Through the many activities, the friendly integration of newcomers, the interest shown to the faithful and even the forms of control, the converted develop a sense of belonging to a community. They mix with people who sometimes have very different social, ethnic and regional origins, but who have often come for identical reasons. Aside from their religious activities, their everyday behaviour must also distinguish them from other people, whether through respect for certain rules (no alcohol or cigarettes) or through controlling their sexuality and rejecting adultery. This community-building is strengthened by their opposition to the rest of society in general and the 'forces of evil' or 'enemies' in particular. With this integration process, the converted gradually forge a new identity for themselves. They become brother or sister in Christ. Apart from the church they belong to, they can participate in the activities of many inter-denominational movements and in manifestations jointly organised by several Christian structures. This identity-building process is thus not limited merely to the level of communities of reduced size; it has a much broader dimension, linked to the world-wide stature of the Pentecostal phenomenon. The converted are not only members of a church, but are also part of the 'real' Christian people and thus belong to a more important community. The rebuilding of identity takes place through the creation of a new group, but also by opening outwards.

---

with regard to their communities and their original habits'. A. Marie, 'Avatars de la dette communautaire. Crise des solidarités, sorcellerie et procès d'individualisation (itinéraires abidjanais)' in A. Marie (ed.), *L'Afrique des individus*, p. 305.

A transnational identity? The Pentecostal option, as well as resolving problems and satisfying needs, leads to participation in a new community, often of reduced size. This community is nonetheless part of a vaster whole which goes beyond the borders of countries. The identity of the converted is not rebuilt by the community dimension alone, but also by this transnational aspect.

One of the characteristics of Pentecostalism resides in its transnational dimension, which owes itself to its origin (virtually simultaneous birth in several places), its nature (the absence of a centre) and its growth (through many channels). This is particularly true for Benin, as the atomisation of structures and proliferation of emerging branches attests. The question can be asked as to what the transnational dimension brings to the identity-building at work in Pentecostalism. The converted, it must be reiterated, are first and foremost searching for material and personal solutions. Pentecostalism is a stage which may be temporary in their often complex religious development. The faithful are welcomed, assisted and trained. More than membership of a particular church, they are seeking to belong to the general world of Christians. Together with the other born-again and baptised brothers and sisters in Christ, they constitute a people which knows no geographical or ethnic frontiers and which does not define itself in territorial terms. The rivalries and frictions, sometimes very virulent, that exist among the churches and ministers or between competing movements seem to have little effect on the faithful, who mix without difficulty at common events and occasionally even change from one movement to another.

The faithful feel they belong to something that is both vast (the 'real' Christian people) and distinct from others. They are not alone, they are carried by a movement, a wave that reaches virtually every country in the world and which creates a religious space without limits. Pentecostalism also contributes to the de-legitimisation of national and state borders by using their permeability. The feeling of belonging to a nation, the Beninese identity, is now in competition with a religious identity in the making, one which escapes the logic of states and borders and is being built outside the national field.

By responding to needs, material or otherwise, the expansion of Pentecostalism contributes to the spreading of standards and values that are of exogenous origin, particularly regarding questions of wealth or personal success. The spreading of the gospel of prosperity is taking place on the transnational register, spurred on by North American movements (the Full Gospel Businessmen's Fellowship International) and leading to an ideology of enrichment which may end up creating new lifestyles.

This new solidarity and construction of identity growing within Pentecostalism remain dependent on many other dynamics, especially when the flexibility of religious membership is kept in mind. Through the success it has encountered and the social changes it has popularised, the expansion of Pentecostalism in Benin nonetheless reminds us that the religious field remains one of the main vehicles of change in Africa and that the restructuring of Beninese society today comes in many forms, from individualisation to perm〜ability to transnational flows.

BIBLIOGRAPHY

Banégas, Richard, 'La démocratie "à pas de caméléon". Transition et consolidation démocratique au Bénin', PhD thesis, Institut d'Etudes Politiques de Paris, 1998.

Bayart, Jean-François, *L'illusion identitaire*, Paris: Fayard, 1996.

de Surgy, Albert, 'La multiplicité des Eglises au sud de l'Afrique occidentale', *Afrique contemporaine*, no. 177, 1996, pp.30-40.

Gifford, Paul (ed.), *New Dimensions in African Christianity*, Ibadan: Sefer, 1993.

Krabill, James R. (ed.), *Nos racines racontées. Récits historiques sur l'Eglise en Afrique de l'Ouest*, Abidjan: Presses Bibliques Africaines, 1996.

Marie, Alain (ed.), *L'Afrique des individus*, Paris: Karthala, 1997.

Ter Haar, Gerrie, 'Standing up for Jesus: A Survey of New Developments in Christianity in Ghana', *Exchange*, vol.23, no.3, 1994, pp. 221-40.

THE NEW PENTECOSTAL NETWORKS
OF BRAZZAVILLE

Elisabeth Dorier-Apprill

The emergence and multiplication of new and independent charismatic churches under Pentecostal influence, which refer to themselves as 're-vival churches', is a very recent phenomenon in Brazzaville, whereas it has been widespread for a long time in Southern and Eastern Africa, and in Congo-Kinshasa.[1] This peculiarity is linked to the policy of religious restriction pursued until the 1980s by single-party military communist governments, which established almost complete control over religious life with an 'anti-sect' law recognising only seven churches between 1978 and 1991.

The new freedom of worship, proclaimed in Congo in 1991 with the National Conference and the process of political democratisation, has favoured the dazzling expansion of a renewed religious offer, which the recent civil wars (1993-4 and 1997-8) do not seem to have restrained. On the contrary, several dozen independent churches under Pentecostal influence hold a particularly notable place in this new context due to their youthfulness (most of them are less than ten years old) and their rapid success.

Not that these independent churches prevail in quantitative terms: the influence of the great historical Christian churches, on the contrary, has tended to increase, while a renewal and diversification of messianisms, Kongo prophetisms and neo-traditional movements[2] can be observed. Yet the 'revival' churches distinguish themselves by their rapid success with social or cultural categories which are relatively privileged and open to modernity. The causes of this success are numerous. We shall focus here on those which relate to the universalist and transnational aspirations of certain social categories traumatised by the violence of current political crises.

During the seven years since the National Conference, which marked the end of a quarter of a century of communist rule and which liberalised religious life, Congolese society has undergone an abrupt transformation linked to the collapse of the rent-based economy and its state characterised by a logic of redistribution, civil wars, crime and flight to the towns.

[1] On West Africa, see de Surgy, 'La multiplicité des Eglises au sud de l'Afrique occidentale', *Afrique Contemporaine*, no.177, 1995, pp. 30-44.

[2] Notably Ngunzism, a current of typically Kongo Afro-Christian prophetism, close to Kimbanguism. See E. Dorier-Apprill and A. Kouvouama, 'Pluralisme religieux et société urbaine à Brazzaville', *Afrique Contemporaine*, no. 2, 1998, pp. 58-76.

In 1993-4, in the summer of 1997 and in late 1998, three bloody 'civil wars' ravaged the capital, sharpening latent ethno-regional tensions to the profit of political party leaders. In 1993-4 the first war brought the army and the presidential militias into conflict with the opposition supported by its own militias. This war divided Brazzaville in two, causing 2,000 deaths and the displacement of more than 100,000 people as a result of inter-ethnic violence. In 1997 the much more serious conflict between the government and former President Denis Sassou Nguesso involved not only militias but also factions of a divided army. After having caused thousands of deaths and a mass exodus of Brazzaville residents, the conflict ended in the seizure of power by the Northern General Sassou Nguesso.[3] Since 1997, part of the population continues to be held hostage between defeated militias redeployed in organised crime and victorious militias incorporated into the army and the police, where they perpetuate arbitrary and violent practices. In late 1998 fighting between the army and Southern militias resumed south of the capital. The heavy bombing of the southern districts of the city and the acts of violence and looting by the army brought about a new stream of tens of thousands of refugees.

By basing their strategy of seizure and maintenance of power on the manipulation of ethno-regional or intergenerational cleavages – heavily arming the youth and knowingly instigating three civil wars between militias – the competing political parties led to the country closing in upon itself. These days, Brazzaville is no more than an isolated secondary capital, an airline terminal, connected to the ocean by a single railway which is unreliable because of banditry.

The loss of the monopoly on violence is but the most brutal symptom of a profound disintegration of the postcolonial state, both as a political construct and as a social aggregation producing collective identity. Religious movements crystallise the diversity of local reactions to this situation of failure, disorder and loss of referents.[4] Certain syncretic and neo-traditional churches disquietingly legitimise the tendency towards ethnic cleavages, territorialisation and cultural isolation through a valorisation of reconstructed 'ancestral traditions' and the sacralisation of places and territories of the country.[5]

The churches in the Pentecostal field, on the other hand, with their connections to movements of international evangelisation, offer their followers a pan-African and global opening-up founded on Biblical val-

---

[3] E. Dorier-Apprill, Jacquier-Dubourdieu and Abel Kouvouama, 'Le religieux, vecteur de nouveaux modèles de comportement économique? Le changement des paradigmes de la solidarité, du travail et de la richesse dans le discours des Eglises évangéliques (Congo-Madagascar)', Workshop 'Ménages et crises', ORSTOM, Marseilles, 24-26 Mar. 1997.

[4] See A. Mbembé, *Afriques indociles. Christianisme et pouvoir d'État en société postcoloniale*, Paris: Karthala, 1988.

[5] Notably the *Boulamananga* Churches, which refer to Kongo prophetism. See Dorier-Apprill and Kouvouama, 'Pluralisme religieux'.

ues which are radically universalist and trans-territorial and which break openly with ancestral traditions. In addition, the majority of revival churches surveyed in Brazzaville display egalitarian and decentralised modes of operation[6] and are structured through highly flexible networks which seek to branch out through the whole country by transcending ethno-regional cleavages. This is an important point which can explain the appeal of these churches in the Congolese geopolitical context.

During the two-year period of calm which followed the first war we carried out a survey[7] of religious movements existing in Brazzaville. In addition to the forty parishes of the large institutionalised churches (Catholic, Protestant, Salvationist, Kimbanguist), we were able to locate 250 new places of worship belonging to small and medium-sized independent churches of various kinds (neo-traditional, prophetic, Evangelical, Pentecostal, etc.). Among the churches which appeared between 1987 and 1997, we counted at least eighty new denominations known as 'revival' denominations, under Pentecostal and fundamentalist influence. This 'revival' scene tends to atomise into multiple autonomous denominations of highly unequal size (some are mere small groups), not counting the prayer groups.

The census, based on counting the established places of worship, presented several methodological problems connected to the highly changing character of the denominations. Today, behind the visible anarchy of proliferation, local networks[8] are forming, which give Pentecostalism a growing influence in the social field of Brazzaville. It is those links which held our attention, as they reveal religious actors' strategic mode of insertion into a complex and disrupted urban social structure.[9] In order to reconstitute the origins, filiations, segmentations and connections into federations and networks, we interrogated the main actors (founders, pastors, evangelists) and compared these interviews with one another as well as with the few written sources which we were able to collect.

The genesis of 'spiritual revival' in Congo

In Congo, the use of the term 'revival' in preference to the term 'Pentecostal' is tied to local religious history and notably to the existence of a

---

[6] For a comparative analysis of churches institutions, see J.-P. Willaime, *La précarité protestante*, Paris: Labor et Fides, 1992.

[7] Field data (census, questionnaires, interviews) collected street by street, in six out of seven *arrondissements* of the city, between Dec. 1995 and Apr. 1997 by E. Dorier-Apprill and A. Kouvouama (research assistants: Basile Osséré and Jacob Massengo). We had carried out a first census already in 1987, in one section of the city.

[8] The official designations 'federations' and 'communities' hardly correspond to their highly flexible modes of operation, characterised by lack of constraint and hierarchy.

[9] See Y. Grafmeyer and I. Joseph (eds), *L'École de Chicago*, Paris: Champ Urbain, 1979; U. Hannerz, *Explorer la ville*, Paris: Minuit, 1980; and D. Parrochia, *Philosophie des réseaux*, Paris: PUF, 1993.

strong charismatic sensibility within the great Christian churches which were authorised before 1991. Historically, the Evangelical Church of Congo (Église Évangélique du Congo – EEC) was the first to experience such a movement, described as 'spiritual revival', in 1947. At the time, the EEC was led to recognise the charismatic gifts of healing, intercession, visions and speaking in tongues which testify to the presence of the Holy Spirit, and even institutionalise them during celebrations dedicated to the healing of the sick.[10] The new field of independent churches, also known as 'revival' churches, whose founders sometimes (but not always) hail from the EEC, distinguishes itself from the latter by a radicalisation of Pentecostal referents: increased valorisation of the emotion tied to the intimate contact between the Christian and the divine Spirit, increased valorisation of a personal reading of the Scriptures and the total recognition of the principle of 'universal priesthood'. Although healing (physical or psychological) does not hold a central place in actual services,[11] it is considered nonetheless to be the tangible sign of the active presence of the Spirit in the community, a presence itself tied to the fervour of the congregation. When we interrogated one of the pastors of the young Federation of Revival Assemblies on what separates his Church from the EEC, he declared:

'What separates us? In fact, not much...we also recognise manifestations which are a bit disturbing, manifestations said to be of the Spirit. [...] They did not accept that we pray with our hands raised; in fact, we were too exuberant in our way of doing things. [...] Besides, we have a lot more hymns and songs; and then we introduced in our practice, let's say, certain liberties with prayer, in the exercise of worship. [...] Then I think the fundamental point is that generally among us, what is called revival churches, nobody has a, let's say, theological kind of training; no one has gone through an Institute or a Faculty of Theology; so this frustrates them a little, the leaders [of the Evangelical Church].'

In Brazzaville, another local factor also explains the rejection of the name Pentecostal: the concern to avoid comparison with a local commercial sect which took, in the 1970s, the controversial name of Assembly of Pentecost (see *infra*). Certain revival churches, concerned about their independence, also reject in this way any idea of subordination to the French or American Assemblies of God whose missionaries regularly carry out rounds in Brazzaville. Nonetheless, in their outlook and in their mode of operation, these young churches, known as revival churches, evidently belong to the broader Pentecostal movement which has been developing for some decades in Africa.

---

[10] E. Dorier-Apprill 'Christianisme et thérapeutique à Brazzaville', *Politique Africaine*, no. 55, Oct.1994, pp. 20-31.

[11] In general, prayer sessions are dedicated specially to addressing misfortune.

History of the structuring of the Pentecostal field

The expansion of independent churches on the Pentecostal scene in Brazzaville is linked to the conjunction of two religious dynamics, one internal, the other external. The introduction of Pentecostalism in Congo dates back to the early 1970s, with the settlement in Brazzaville and Pointe Noire of missionaries sent by the French Assemblies of God.

At the same time, an internal dynamic was set up around the charismatic and controversial personality of Demba Esaïe, also known as Papa Esaïe, and his 'Assembly of Pentecost'. This sect, situated in Brazzaville at the junction between the downtown area and Poto-Poto, and whose activities are essentially founded on the healing (which one must pay for) of the sick, merits an important place in the history of the revival, since it is from this sect that most current revival churches stem. Indeed, when the missionaries of the Assemblies of God came to survey Brazzaville in the early 1970s, this was the only existing church with a 'Pentecostal-sounding' name; hence it was in this church and its founder Demba Esaïe that the missionaries placed their hopes of developing Assemblies of God in Congo. This is where the majority of pastors of current revival churches, who were then seeking new forms of religious spirituality, converged and met.[12] Because of its mercenary drift, the acts of violence committed against the sick, and the cult of personality practiced by Papa Esaïe, 'The Assembly of Pentecost' very rapidly lost the support of Western missionaries.

Followed by young adherents, these missionaries organised Bible classes and trained a new generation of young Pentecostal religious leaders, more 'orthodox' in their praying and healing practices. Yet after 1977 and the 'anti-sect' law, the missionaries of the Assemblies of God were all expelled from Congo.[13] The first pastors trained by the missionaries then created underground prayer groups, which later became the first revival churches in Brazzaville. During the period of religious prohibition, these prayer communities continued to gather in hiding.[14] After the coming to power of Colonel Sassou Nguesso, the relaxing of the pressure on churches allowed them to gradually gain greater visibility.

During the liberalisation which preceded the National Conference, the Congolese Labour Party tolerated progressively more religious pluralism, but on the condition that 'sects' (according to the terminology then in use) gather together in associations. From this injunction stems one

---

[12] This is the case with CAPEC founders and several FAR pastors. See *infra*.

[13] In 1977 the assassination of President Marien Ngouabi gave the '*ultras*' the opportunity to challenge the Christian churches accused of complicity, and to radicalise the anticlerical position of the government.

[14] While the other 'sects' and independent churches were banned, the Assembly of Pentecost, close to the government, was not harassed and continued to look after the dignitaries of the regime!

of the present characteristics of the religious field in Brazzaville. It is strongly structured into strategic federations and networks which enable the churches to defend their interests against the public authorities. From 1985 onwards, this evolution permitted new rounds of missionaries sent by the Action Missionnaire des Assemblées de Dieu en France (Missionary Action of French Assemblies of God). These missionaries prompted the organisation of several small Pentecostal groups within the Communauté des Assemblées du Plein Evangile au Congo (Community of Full Gospel Assemblies in Congo - CAPEC). Various independent churches gradually joined CAPEC, merging into three 'ministries'.[15] The CAPEC president today is the correspondent in Congo for the Missionary Action of French Assemblies of God.

Yet as this organisational process was undertaken directly under the care of the Assemblies of God, several revival churches with a more fundamentalist sensibility and with claims to independence were founded as early as the 1980s, among them the Church of God. From the 1991 National Conference, which legalised their existence, independent revival churches were to multiply dramatically in Congo, gaining their autonomy through successive branching off from this common double root. These churches have contributed to broadening and 'popularising' Pentecostal religious sensibility beyond the direct control of the Assemblies of God.

In spite of the 'multiplication of the Pentecostal offer' and the inevitable rivalries resulting from this competition, an undeniable complicity has led revival churches to seek to operate in networks, exchanging information and invitations, and from time to time organising services together. Beyond religious culture proper and the friendly pressures exerted by visiting Western missionaries, this complicity rests on the relations of proximity and mutual acquaintance between the different actors involved in the expansion of these churches. Several pastor-founders[16] are intellectuals who met in the course of their studies or university careers and share a common history and common cultural values, even beyond the religious field. Subsequently, their religious itineraries crossed, very often in the church of Papa Esaïe, or through association with the first Pentecostal missionaries visiting in Brazzaville. The majority of churches were born through segmentation, following conflicts or divergence of 'visions' (some churches emphasise praise; others centre more on Bible studies). In any event, pre-existing social ties from school, university, student militancy etc. undeniably facilitated the organisation of the Pentecostal field in Brazzaville into networks.[17]

[15] *Vie Nouvelle* (New life), *Sauver pour Servir* (Saving to serve) and *Semence de Vie* (Seed of life), each with its own leaders.

[16] Notably those of the Federation of Revival Assemblies. See *infra*.

[17] D. Hervieu-Léger, 'La transmission religieuse en modernité, éléments pour la construction d'un objet de recherche', *Social Compass*, vol. 44, no. 1, 1997, pp. 131-43.

Networks with differentiated profiles

Today, several categories of Pentecostal churches in Brazzaville can be distinguished according to their origins and those of their leaders:[18] CAPEC churches, structured under the care of the Missionary Action of Assemblies of God; dynamic fundamentalist churches led by educated and socially well-integrated elites; a multitude of small groups founded by very young people, notably young immigrants from Kinshasa; and finally a small number of churches with foreign origins, established through expansion from Congo-Kinshasa and more recently from Brazil.[19]

Beyond doctrinal divergences, the composition of the three main local networks of 'revival' churches turns out to reveal above all the different aspirations, social tensions and generational cleavages which traverse Congolese society. Three leader profiles can be distinguished according to the length of their practice, their age, their dogmatic position and their ties with 'Foreign'. These three examples are not exhaustive, for they only cover a part of the religious groups present in Brazzaville.[20]

The Community of Full Gospel Assemblies in Congo (CAPEC) is marked by a longer history and gathers previously independent churches together under the form of three 'ministries'. Recruitment is wide (10,000 faithful and 178 parishes are claimed in the country), and the 25 parishes of Brazzaville cover all the popular neighbourhoods. Their churches (simple tin 'sheds') and material resources remain modest. Their leaders, who are all socially and economically disadvantaged men in their sixties, hold a 'social elder' status tied to long religious journeys which include neo-traditional experiences prior to joining the Pentecostal movement. The cohesion of CAPEC seems artificial and fragile, for some of its members defend a free and highly syncretic conception of Pentecostalism which gives priority to emotion in praise and intercession in prayers, the Bible constituting at times no more than a very remote reference. Divergences among the three 'ministries' associated with these differences and power struggles continue to worsen, in spite of several reconciliation attempts.

On the other hand, the Communauté des Églises de Réveil (Community of Revival Churches - CER) is a more informal group, composed of a few dozen small independent churches (which are sometimes merely small groups). Their common denominator is that they were founded and are now led and attended by young people (all are less than thirty years old), for the most part 'unemployed graduates', often immigrants from

[18] Systematic survey of the leaders of revival churches. The last civil wars prevented us from doing the same with their members.

[19] Chronologically, the local dynamic preceded these exogenous implantations. There were, in 1997, only two very modest Brazilian settlements.

[20] The churches founded through expansion from Kinshasa are excluded from this discussion, for they do not belong to any of these federations.

Congo-Kinshasa. Their dogma is rather vague: Biblical texts are often interpreted literally and worship practices are dominated by healing prayers. The generational tie is strong and a source of pride; the leaders of these small churches often meet and invite each other to reunions and common services: 'For all of us, it is through the CER that we came to know each other, that I was invited to preach in other churches'. 'God is calling out to young people. Society also has a growing number of young people. And these young people carry the burden of revival... Each one believes that he has received something from the Lord and wishes to reveal it.'[21]

Their discourse is often very hard towards the elders, as the following declaration, made by one of the young leaders of the CER during a re-union preparing for an evangelisation campaign, testifies:

'There is a kind of contempt from those who arrived before us and who feel they are better: "The young, what can they do? What can they place at the disposition of the Church?" [...] It is the parable of the new wine and the old wineskins; the Lord does a major work; it is like Moses and the ancient ones who turned round for a long time in the desert: and we are a generation of Joshuas, men who want to cross the Jordan. We are living in different times, times in which each one has his own Bible, in which each one receives the Holy Spirit. [...] It is like the ebb and flow; and we see through the ebb and flow the waste which the elders left behind.'

These young religious actors, all concerned with emancipating themselves from their position as 'social minors', assert their rejection of modes of social control based on the extended family and the law of primogeniture. They also assign an essential - even central - place to the 'theology of prosperity' and spend a lot of energy attempting to organise joint events and to create international ties which generally begin by exchanges with Kinshasa. This generational question is evidently crucial in a city without employment like Brazzaville,[22] where the young, who have been educated massively in the course of the last ten years, no longer have any prospect of finding paid employment except in the army, the police or the militias.

The most dynamic network is the Fédération des assemblées de réveil (Federation of Revival Assemblies - FAR), which gathers 45 young independent churches whose audience is growing and whose faithful number from a few hundred to a few thousand.[23] These churches are also informally tied to various African and global Pentecostal networks, as

---

[21] Remarks made by CER pastors, preparatory meeting for a faith convention, Aug. 1996.

[22] There is no industrial activity in Brazzaville, except for the production of beer and soft drinks.

[23] Some of them are implanted only in Brazzaville. The oldest ones, such as the Church of God or the Confédération Chrétienne Évangélique (Evangelical Christian Confederation - CCE), implanted throughout the country and in Pointe Noire, claim several thousand members.

well as to parallel networks (such as the Full Gospel), without being affiliated. Each church remains autonomous. The founders-pastors of the 45 churches of the FAR are all academics or businessmen in their forties. Although they attach great significance to the effusion of the Spirit during services, they also defend an enlightened Biblical fundamentalism, considering Bible reading to be essential.

We are interested here in the ethical discourse of these religious functionaries of the FAR. They express a double claim of rupture, in their distancing from all neo-traditional representations and practices (magic, cult of the dead, sumptuary funerals, customary marriage, polygamy) - which are systematically vilified as 'Satanic' - and in their rejection of 'dialectical materialism', which occupied the political and cultural field for several years, and claimed to channel the religious within the only established churches.[24]

An ethic based on consented acculturation

In the eyes of these pastors, only a burning and 'purified' Christian faith, sustained by membership in a 'strong' and uncompromising Christian church, is capable of making one impervious to family pressures and above all to the supernatural powers at work in the excesses of mortuary rites, considered to be the main hindrance to the development of Congo. The Bible, and only the Bible, is capable of neutralising these forces.

'The Bible says, let the dead bury the dead. [...] You go to the villages, there is more invested for the dead. [...] The most beautiful houses are the cemeteries, the graves; these are permanent. I saw graves with living rooms. [...] This is the work of Satan; it is the complicity of the Devil; it is the system which ruins the living, and this stifles the economy a great deal. The man who loses his uncle, in the tradition, he must first build the grave. [...] There is pressure, there is constraint on one who does not part with the power of God. [...] We [the "true" Revival Christians], will turn away from this system. [...] Free to decide [...] mourning is not worth it. [...]This is why I believe there is no development without Revival, and these things often escape decision-makers from abroad.'[25]

Among the leaders of this Church network, one also observes a concern with making an individualistic ethic emerge. This is supported by a vigorous discourse on the transformation of family models, a discourse which aims to promote the conjugal tie (founded on religious marriage) and the nuclear family ('family unit'). All engage more or less in the same discourse, conservative in some respects (advocating, for instance, the removal of women from public affairs), modern in others, calling into question the constraining practices of customary marriage (with dowry), polygamy, or even mutual aid obligations within the extended family, as so many 'paganisms' inspired by 'Satan', as so many hindrances to individual enterprise and beyond to the development of the country.

'Here in Congo, families are elastic; you see, my maternal family, there are more than 1,000 people in it; but you see, me, I don't know these people anymore. [...] I am completely removed from their system; I really prayed for all that, even when they do their vigil, their thing, I can't go, and they can't tell me you, you didn't come. To be that strong, you really have to pray; you have to fight'.[26]

The intensification of poverty and the breakdown of public institutions increases, at first, the resort to lineage solidarity. All urban residents who still earn a stable income feel one day the financial burden of this assistance and see domestic savings swallowed up under family pressure. In the context of the current crisis, these demands are increasingly perceived as unbearable intrusions in the domestic economy.[27] The ethical valorisation of the conjugal tie and of the parent-child tie can contribute, by condemning as 'parasitism' the 'excesses' of demands for help within the lineage setting, to building - upon Evangelical bases - a new paradigm of 'well-ordered' solidarity, at once more restricted (compatible with the needs and even the prosperity of the nuclear family) and occasionally extended (outside the lineage, towards 'brothers and sisters in Christ').

'The history of nations shows that Christian communities lead an exemplary family life because of their piety and decency; this is completely different in the pagan communities engaged in a crazy race for pleasures.'[28] What is astonishing is less the actual content of discourse, and its culturalist dimension, which evokes both that of Western missionaries and certain discourses of the late 1950s about 'obstacles to development' and 'dualism', than its being taken up again, half a century later, by urbanised elites trained in revolutionary thought.[29] These elites consider today that only Biblical fundamentalism is capable of transforming the economic and social system through a break with local traditions and an opening up to Western ethical and economic values.

At the same time, the discourse of these 'revival' movements insistently reasserts the value of individual initiative in the production of wealth, founding on the letter of the Bible the necessity of work and the entrepre-

---

[26] *Ibid.*

[27] Dorier-Apprill *et al.*, *Vivre à Brazzaville*, In Brazzaville, in the late 1980s, more than half of all households lived on public service income. Although, since 1996, the salaries of civil servants have been paid regularly again, the arrears accumulated since 1991 add up to more than fifteen unpaid months.

[28] Ecumenical journal *La Religion*, Brazzaville, no. 4, Feb./Mar. 1996.

[29] These positions also echo the point of view of the Missionary Action of the French Assemblies of God, diffused through brochures and a website, points of view which stigmatise harshly 'the obscurantist and archaic practices such as the hold of witchcraft, fetishism, the cult of ancestors with the fear of spirits, as well as the proliferation of syncretic movements which combine elements of Christianity with traditional religions'.

neurial spirit: in this spirit, the creation of businesses is no longer a last resort imposed by the crisis, but a true 'behavioural ethic' founded on an ethic of belief! The pastors and founders of churches of the Federation of Revival Assemblies sometimes take the initiative in suggesting themselves a 'neo-Weberian' frame of analysis for their ethical project by referring very explicitly to the Anglo-Saxon model: 'All that God talks about is becoming rich, this is what he says to Abraham: "get rich!" But how can one become rich by remaining like this?...When you read the Bible from A to Z, it is nothing but the idea of construction... Besides, Anglo-Saxon countries, which are Protestant, have put the emphasis on work.'[30]

The revival pastors' will to convince – themselves and others - that the Bible has the power to transform 'African mentalities' is evident. Listening to some of them and their smooth argumentation, one sometimes has the impression of reading, word for word, *The Protestant Ethic and the Spirit of Capitalism*! It must be noted that all are generally well-read, and the impact of the multiple magazines, brochures, and works intended for proselytism distributed by the networks of European or North American correspondents needs to be taken into account. This point is also taken up by the Missionary Action of the Assemblies of God: the backwardness of the African economy is judged severely, attributed to the 'fratricidal wars ... poor administration by some leaders...negative aspects of colonialism and Marxism, ever growing external debt because of the importation of manufactured products, often rudimentary agriculture.'[31]

Led by educated and Westernised, modern elites who display a common aspiration for an opening up to global modernity, the churches of the FAR also recruit massively among social or cultural categories that are somewhat privileged and open to the modernity of their discourse and modes of operation. They are either effective elites, young 'potential' elites (who perceive themselves as such) or frustrated (in particular 'young unemployed graduates') elites.

The distribution of the principal churches of the Federation of Revival Assemblies in the urban space of Brazzaville reveals their differentiated recruitment. During our 1995-6 survey, we observed a significant concentration of FAR bases close to housing developments built or funded by the state and destined for the middle and upper classes, near administrative zones and the airport (OCH, Plateau des 15 Ans, north of Moukondo), and along the paved roads and shopping streets which extend the downtown area to the north.

In these neighbourhoods, conversely, we found hardly any small prophetic or neo-traditional churches, nor any CAPEC church settlement,

---

[30] Interview with V. D., scientist and member of the revival Church Philadelphie and of the Full Gospel.

[31] Action Missionnaire des Assemblées de Dieu de France, 1998.

for that matter. By late 1996, several great Brazzaville Pentecostal churches still had no presence in the popular neighbourhoods of the periphery (except CAPEC and the Church of God, which led systematic evangelisation campaigns in these neigbourhoods), others contented themselves with modest outposts, whereas, conversely, prophetic and neo-traditional churches were multiplying. The mid-1997 war inevitably brought about recompositions. During the hostilities, revival churches, on account of their implantation in these strategic neighbourhoods where most of the fighting took place, were directly affected by material destruction. Yet the dynamic of implantation and the organisation into networks of 'revival' churches is unfailing: their universalist values and their will for a pan-African and global opening up only gained in influence as a result.

Transnational networks

While asserting their autonomy, all the revival churches accounted for in Brazzaville are interconnected at the local, national and regional (Central Africa) level. They all valorise, with their faithful, their belonging to ramified transnational networks, an affiliation which responds, as it were, to the universalism of the Biblical message, expressed, for example in visits by foreign preachers, or foreign mail read in a loud voice at the end of services. Evidently the enormous media resources brought into play by Western preachers (mobilisation of the Brazzaville stadium or the Parliament buildings, satellite transmission, distribution of video cassettes) also aim to impress and to induce not only spiritual enthusiasm, but also adhesion to a conquering and ascending - if not transcending - model of modernity founded on mobility and on the growth of international exchanges.[32]

In Brazzaville, the churches in the Pentecostal field show an exceptional ability to integrate the young urban elites that are leading them into these international (especially Anglo-Saxon) networks. This is achieved through invitational exchanges between pastors, preaching tours, Bible classes in English (simultaneously translated into French, but not into the vernacular language), travel, congresses or other world 'faith conventions' - such as those held periodically in Seoul and attended by representatives of various Brazzaville churches - or regional ones such as the 'Convention of Giants of the Faith' organised in Cotonou in September 1996 and amply advertised in Brazzaville in the previous weeks. Services of these 'giants' are generally broadcast in the form of video cassettes.[33] Within this Pentecostal scene, one must consider trans-confessional and international movements linked to the business world which seek

---

[32] E. Dorier-Apprill, 'Les enjeux socio-politiques du foisonnement religienx à Brazzaville', *Politique africaine*, no. 64, Dec. 1996.

[33] J. Gutwirth, 'Religion télévisée et business audio-visuel', *Archives de sciences sociales des religions*, 83, July-Sept., 1993, pp. 67-89.

to reach African urban elites. These include the International Christian Chamber of Commerce[34] (ICCC) and, especially, Full Gospel Businessmen's Fellowship International[35] which presents itself as an 'interconfessional world gathering of charismatic laymen' aiming to 'bring believers to open up to the power of the Holy Spirit without leaving their churches' through oral testimonies expressed in meetings organised most often in large hotels, to which each member invites personal or work contacts. In Brazzaville meetings were held, before the 1997 war, in the Mbamou Palace (*Sofitel local*). Besides its spiritual dimension, the Full Gospel valorises professional investment and constitutes a truly active world network which enables its members to travel and to make contacts of all kinds through the religious connection. The International Christian Chamber of Commerce, founded by the Swedish industrialist Gunnar Olson, has a more concrete vocation. On a global scale and linked to other Evangelical networks, it is composed of individual members and firms, and can be joined in return for a sizeable yearly membership fee (to be paid in dollars exclusively). It is not a question of evangelising, but rather of making the professional practice of members more dynamic by introducing in it a Christian ethic. In its luxurious publications (made of glossy paper and copiously illustrated), the ICCC valorises the entrepreneurial spirit and virtuously achieved prosperity. It settled (laboriously) in Brazzaville in 1990, with recruitment difficulties linked to the civil war episodes as well as to the weakness of the local entrepreneurial and commercial classes.

Simultaneous membership in several religious and professional networks enables leaders of churches within the Pentecostal field to centralise information, to locate decision centres, to master increasingly complex mediation systems at the local, national and international levels, and to gain unique experience *vis-à-vis* the foreign and the resources it provides. In Brazzaville, developing the transversality of one's religious and professional networks becomes a necessity for anyone who wishes to become an entrepreneur in spite of the decay of local institutions and the material ruin of a city devastated by civil war. Thus the regional representative of the Union pour l'étude de la population africaine (Union for African Population Studies-UEPA), a pan-African organisation which is based in Dakar and which hands out small grants for scientific research, is a member of the Full Gospel and of an important local revival church. Similarly, the founder-pastor of the active Pentecostal church Néhémie[36] is also an academic, an agronomist, the former director of the Rural Development Institute of Congo and a member of the Full

[34] In Brazzaville, this implantation is still modest.

[35] The Full Gospel Businessmen's Fellowship International publishes the journal *Voix*, which distributes 1 million copies in twenty-two languages.

[36] Revival Church founded in 1991.

Gospel Fellowship.[37] The Néhémie Church, which is at the centre of a very intense spiritual and social life (services or prayer meetings several times a day, Sunday school, choirs etc.), has promoted various economic projects with a local development focus, providing work to unemployed youth, reforestation (in the Pool), food assistance to villages. Some of these projects were financed by the World Food Programme thanks to the kind support of its representative in Brazzaville – who is also a member of the Full Gospel.

Revival churches thus contribute to establishing new solidarities of all kinds with neighbouring Democratic Congo and with Anglophone countries considered to be the leaders of the continent (South Africa, Nigeria), as much as with Western (notably Anglo-Saxon) countries. At the junction between the local and the global, these new churches have thus encroached on a monopoly until then reserved for the state apparatus: the relationship to the foreign,[38] as a supplier of legitimacy. Thanks to this relationship, these new churches have acquired a social and cultural power of influence through the formation of new elites, who are inserted into mediating networks integrating regional, national and international levels, networks often linked to active NGOs.

In addition to their fundamentalist discourse and their promotion of emancipatory values in relation to local traditions, revival churches effectively contribute to diffusing new paradigms concerning the way to conceive social cohesion in urban space, in particular, a mode of operation through networks of free individuals or contractual associations, a mode which is opposed to the holistic and communitarian model. By network we mean a system of horizontal relationships developing through connections established among individuals and groups who are characterised by a diversity of origins and situations and who institute reciprocal exchanges. Networks are characterised by the autonomy of each member and by the non-structural character of hierarchy. The profusion of Pentecostal churches does not originate this creation of networks, but constitutes one of the spaces in which a new relational culture can flourish and become formalised.[39]

---

[37] The Full Gospel consists of a world network of businessmen - the term is used in the broad sense of fellowship with an active professional life - who share their 'testimonies of faith in the power of the Holy Spirit' and their prayers in convivial meetings generally held in public places (large hotels). The goal is to promote evangelisation. In concrete terms, the relationships thus established constitute, as this example shows, a world-scale influence network, highly developed also in North America and in Europe.

[38] L. Dubourdieu, 'Représentation de l'esclavage et conversion: un aspect du mouvement de réveil à Madagascar', *Cahiers de Sciences Humaines: ORSTOM*, vol. 32 no. 3, 1996, pp. 597-610.

[39] J.-F. Bayart, 'La Cité culturelle en Afrique Noire', *Religion et modernité politique en Afrique Noire*, Paris: Karthala, 1993, pp. 299-310.

Yet if the recent proliferation of Pentecostalism in Brazzaville finds part of its explanation in a general process of transnationalisation, it would be highly reductive to interpret it strictly as the epiphenomenon of a global dynamic. Indeed, the history of the development of Pentecostalism in Brazzaville has shown the importance of the missionary activities of the Assemblies of God, as well as that of legal obligations, political opportunities and local dynamics. In the particular context of Congo (political and economic deadlock, diplomatic isolation, disintegration of the state and the political field), and in a religious field which has been historically restricted by the influence of the great historical Christian churches and by entrenched Kongo messianic movements, what are the prospects? The new Pentecostal field can appear as the only space for an opening up to a 'world order' - to escape national disorder, a 'space of the possible' in which the necessary social, cultural and generational recompositions may be realised.

BIBLIOGRAPHY

Action Missionnaire des Assemblées de Dieu de France, *Quel avenir pour l'économie africaine?*, 1998, published on internet site, *http://www.ag.org*.

Bayart, Jean-François, 'La cité cultuelle en Afrique Noire' in *Religion et modernité politique en Afrique Noire*, Paris: Karthala, 1993, pp.299-310.

De Surgy, Albert, 'La Muliplicité des Églises au sud de l'Afrique occidentale', *Afrique Contemporaine*, no. 177, 1995, pp. 30-44.

Dorier-Apprill, Elisabeth, 'Christianisme et thérapeutique à Brazzaville', *Politique Africaine*, no. 55, Oct.1994, pp. 20-31.

――, 'Les enjeux socio-politiques du foisonnement religieux à Brazzaville', *Politique africaine*, no. 64, Dec. 1996.

―― and Abel Kouvouama, 'Pluralisme religieux et société urbaine à Brazzaville', *Afrique Contemporaine*, no. 2, 1998, pp. 58-76.

――, Lucile Jacquier-Dubourdieu and Abel Kouvouama, 'Le religieux, vecteur de nouveaux modèles de comportement économique? Le changement des paradigmes de la solidarité, du travail et de la richesse dans le discours des Eglises évangéliques (Congo-Madagascar)', workshop 'Ménages et crises', ORSTOM, Marseilles, 24-26 March 1997.

――, Abel Kouvouama and Christophe Apprill, *Vivre à Brazzaville. Modernité et crise au quotidien*, Paris: Karthala, 1998.

Gifford, Paul, 'Prosperity : A New and Foreign Element in African Christianity', *Religion*, 20, Oct. 1990, pp. 373-88.

Grafmeyer, Yves and Isaac Joseph (eds), *L'École de Chicago*, Paris: Ed. du Champ Urbain, 1979.

Gutwirth, Jacques, 'Religion télévisée et business audio-visuel', *Archives de sciences sociales des religions,* 83, July-Sept. 1993, pp. 67-89.

Hannerz Ulf, *Explorer la ville*, Paris: Minuit, 1980.

Hervieu-Léger, Danielle, 'La transmission religieuse en modernité, Éléments pour la construction d'un objet de recherche', *Social Compass*, vol. 44, no. 1, 1997, pp. 131-43.

Elisabeth Dorier-Apprill

Jacquier-Dubourdieu, Lucile, 'Représentation de l'esclavage et conversion: un aspect du mouvement de réveil à Madagascar", *Cahiers de sciences Humaines: ORSTOM*, vol. 32, no. 3, 1996, pp. 597-610.

——, 'La conversion, voie du politique ou de l'identité?', *Social Compass*, vol. 43, no. 2, pp. 223-42, June 1996.

Mbembé, Achille, *Afriques indociles, christianisme et pouvoir d'État en société postcoloniale*, Paris: Karthala, 1988.

——, 'Christian Fundamentalism and Development in Africa', *Review of African Political Economy*, 52, Nov. 1991, pp. 9-20.

Parrochia Daniel, *Philosophie des réseaux*, Paris: PUF, 1993.

Willaime, Jean-Paul, *La précarité protestante*, Paris: Labor et Fides, 1992.

INDEX